TWILIGHT OF EMPIRE

ALSO BY GREG KING AND PENNY WILSON

Lusitania: Triumph, Tragedy, and the End of the Edwardian Age

The Resurrection of the Romanovs: Anastasia, Anna Anderson and the World's Greatest Royal Mystery

The Fate of the Romanovs

ALSO BY GREG KING

The Assassination of the Archduke: Sarajevo 1914 and the Romance that Changed the World (with Sue Woolmans)

Wallis: The Uncommon Life of the Duchess of Windsor

Twilight of Splendor: The Court of Queen Victoria During Her Diamond Jubilee Year

The Court of the Last Tsar: Pomp, Power, and Pageantry in the Reign of Nicholas II

Mad King: A Biography of Ludwig II of Bavaria

The Murder of Rasputin: The Truth About Prince Felix Youssoupov and the Mad Monk Who Helped Bring Down the Romanovs

Last Empress: Life and Times of Alexandra Feodorovna, Tsarina of Russia

TWILIGHT OF EMPIRE

THE TRAGEDY AT MAYERLING AND THE END OF THE HABSBURGS

Greg King and Penny Wilson

ST. MARTIN'S PRESS NEW YORK

 Printed in the United States of America. For information, address
St. Martin's Press, 175 Fifth Avenue, New York, N.Y. 10010.

www.stmartins.com

The Library of Congress Cataloging-in-Publication Data is available upon request

ISBN 978-1-250-08302-9 (hardcover)
ISBN 978-1-250-08303-6 (ebook)

First Edition: November 2017

10 9 8 7 6 5 4 3 2 1

To Sue Woolmans

ACKNOWLEDGMENTS

Even after more than a century, the subject of Mayerling remains controversial. In researching and writing this book, we have tried to remain as close as possible to the few known facts while exploring divergent ideas offering alternative explanations. Despite the rather obvious hurdles involved in tackling an historical affair and two mysterious deaths clouded by decades of controversy, we believe that we've been able to reach some new conclusions offering a starkly different take on the liaison between Crown Prince Rudolf and Mary Vetsera.

In retelling the Mayerling story, we have arranged this book into four distinct sections. In part 1, covering events up to January 28, 1889, we set the scene for the tragedy. In part 2 we attempt to give a straightforward account of the tragedy and immediate aftermath, keeping the narrative clean of warring claims and intrusive analysis. Part 3 of the book focuses on the various conspiracy theories that have surrounded the story for more than a hundred years. Part 4 of the book looks back at what has come before, setting in context events in earlier chapters, analyzing psychological motivations, and revisiting controversies with fresh explanations. In the process we reveal what we think actually happened at that snowbound lodge in the early-morning hours of January 30, 1889. Although no one can know with certainty what took place in Rudolf's bedroom, we believe our reconstruction to be correct, in accord with the facts, supported by psychological analysis, and bolstered by previously overlooked forensic evidence. What emerges is sometimes surprising, even shocking. In a sense Rudolf and Mary were both victims: He, psychologically damaged and likely suffering from serious mental illness; she, used and abused by those around her. Both were caught up in a dangerous and deadly waltz while many of the supporting players—including Baroness Helene Vetsera and Marie Larisch—played sordid, even grim, roles in the tragedy. Mayerling is ultimately a tale of exalted but damaged personalities enacting a terrible folie à deux set against the glittering backdrop of imperial Vienna, and amid mental instability, blackmail, venereal disease, rumors of incest, and political treason. Beyond the sugary romanticism often attached to the story is one even more dramatic than the persistent legend that has enveloped the tragedy for more than a hundred years.

In telling that story we have been fortunate to have the support of many professional colleagues, family, and friends, without whom the task would have been impossible. Several descendants of those most closely involved in the tragedy and its aftermath have shared information and insights, including HRH Dom Duarte Pio, Duke of Braganza; HSH Princess Sophie of Hohenberg; and Paul A. Slatin, who generously shared with us the unpublished *Abschrift* written by his grandfather, Court Commissioner Dr. Heinrich Slatin, about his experiences at Mayerling.

Penny Wilson would like to thank her family for their support: her parents, Edward and Mary O'Hanlon, of Tucson, Arizona; Peter and Lynne O'Hanlon of Providenciales, Turks and Caicos Islands; James and Tricia Manara of Phoenix, Arizona; Jon Phillips of Tucson, Arizona; Peggy, Eric, and Ryan Cartwright of Riverside, California; Barbara Wilson of Riverside, California; and Mary Kelsey and Dominic of Winchester, California. And above all, time and time again, thanks to Tom Wilson for everything he does.

As always, Greg King thanks his father, Roger King, for his continued support and encouragement.

For always keeping the doors open when she was unavailable, Penny Wilson thanks her employees and coworkers at City Gym in Riverside, California: Matthew Crouch, Nicole Flaherty, Gio Gonzalez, Haley Hyland-McIntyre, Ian Melgar, Olivia Mercado, Basil Trenham, Chris Wilkins, Alvin Wright, and Teddy Yelland. Thanks also to longtime friends and gym rats Gino Gonzalez, Eugene Mejia, Clayton Nicodemus, Kristy Orona, Gabby Perez, Jennifer Rider, Jisel Wilson-Schell, and Lupita Wilson. Finally she expresses many thanks to the member of City Gym, particularly Don Lowrey, Chris Schaper, and Donna Zeeb.

Greg King would like to thank Janet Ashton, Paulette Blum, Diane Eakin, Jeannine Evans, Professor Joseph Fuhrmann, Brien Horan, Cecelia Manning, Susanne Meslans, Scott Michaels, Brad Swenson, and Debra Tate for their years of continued support, advice, and friendship.

Penny Wilson thanks Eric and Lisa Hocutt and Austin Hocutt for being the ideal traveling companions on the Big Island of Hawaii, and longtime friend Christopher Kinsman, just for living across the road, brewing beer, and being brilliant. She also thanks—as ever since her first book back in 2003—the good folks at PS Facebook. Too numerous to mention (and because she could not endure the shame of forgetting any names), these are the finest chance-met internet friends anyone ever had, intelligent, kind, supportive, clannish, and unfailingly witty, who make it possible for her to get through the day. Simon Donoghue deserves thanks for simply being the best, and Penny Wilson looks forward to meeting him in person this year for deep philosophical conversation and shenanigans. And she thanks the one-and-only Oscar Shearer for many years of friendship.

We wish to thank our agent, Dorie Simmonds, for her encouragement and advice throughout the research and writing process. Charles Spicer, our editor at St. Martin's Press, enthusiastically supported this book from the very beginning and helped make it a reality. And April Osborn, associate editor at St. Martin's, has always been unfailingly gracious in shepherding the work to its completion.

For offering advice on various aspects of the story and providing valuable information, we would like to thank Janet Ashton; Arturo Beéche of eurohistory.com; Coryne Hall; Orla Hickey, Group Public Relations Executive at Claridge's Hotel in London; Marlene Eilers Koenig; Professor Ilana Miller; Karen Roth; and Katrina Warne.

The friendly and helpful staffs at the Haus-, Hof- und Staatsarchiv and the Österreichische Nationalbibliothek in Vienna have eased the research for this book. We owe a special debt of gratitude to Joan Blacker, Interlibrary Loan Coordinator at the Everett Public Library in Everett, Washington, who worked miracles on our behalf and managed to obtain the most obscure publications related to the Mayerling tragedy for our benefit. She has our unwavering thanks.

Denise C. Clarke and Alfred Luckerbauer sacrificed their time and a sunny Easter day to travel to Mayerling and Heiligenkreuz, helping us bring the story up to date from the time of our previous visits. They also took magnificent photographs for us, although sadly only a few can be included in this book. Oscar Shearer patiently cleaned up and prepared many of our other photographs. Simon Donoghue read through the ever-changing manuscript and offered critical and sage advice on presentation and possible motivations. And Mark Andersen has been unbelievably generous in sharing a wealth of rare and invaluable books, exhibition catalogs, and other materials that have helped us flesh out the story in greater detail.

Assessing and understanding psychological motivations became essential in reexamining the story. We owe an immense debt to Dr. Stefanie Platt, Greg King's second cousin and the former director of Clinical & Forensic Services at the Institute on Violence, Abuse and Trauma/Family Violence & Sexual Assault Institute of San Diego, California, who reviewed the personalities and evidence in the Mayerling tale. Without actual clinical interviews, it was impossible for Dr. Platt to offer definitive diagnoses of people long dead, but her advice and insight guided us in making educated guesses and positing plausible behavioral explanations for our main characters. While the hypotheses presented here belong only to us, this book would surely have been less compelling without Dr. Platt's generosity.

Finally we are happy to extend our eternal gratitude to royal author and historian Sue Woolmans. No one has been more enthusiastic about this book, and no one has done more to help us complete it. From reading and rereading different versions of the manuscript and sharing her own research to providing us with dozens of rare books and obscure materials, she has been tireless in her efforts. We thank her for her selfless dedication and are proud to call her our friend.

DRAMATIS PERSONAE

THE HABSBURGS AND THEIR ROYAL RELATIVES

Franz Josef I, Emperor of Austria-Hungary (*Kaiser von Österreich-Ungarn*), born August 18, 1830, died November 21, 1916; reigned 1848–1916; Rudolf's father.

Elisabeth, Empress of Austria-Hungary, "Sisi" (*Kaiserin von Österreich-Ungarn*), born December 24, 1837, as Duchess Elisabeth in Bavaria, married Emperor Franz Josef I April 24, 1854, assassinated September 10, 1898, in Geneva; Rudolf's mother.

Rudolf, Crown Prince and Archduke of Austria-Hungary (*Kronprinz und Erzherzog von Österreich-Ungarn*), heir to the throne (*Thronfolger*), born August 21, 1858, married Princess Stephanie of Belgium May 10, 1881, died January 30, 1889, at Mayerling.

Stephanie, Crown Princess and Archduchess of Austria-Hungary, born May 21, 1864, as Princess Stephanie of Belgium, married (1) Crown Prince Rudolf, May 10, 1881; married (2) March 22, 1900, Hungarian Count Elemér Lónyay de Nagy-Lónyay és Vásárosnamény, March 22, 1900, died August 23, 1945; Rudolf's wife.

Elisabeth, Archduchess of Austria-Hungary, "Erszi," born September 2, 1883, married Prince Otto Weriand von Windisch-Grätz 1902, died March 16, 1963; Rudolf's daughter.

Gisela, Archduchess of Austria-Hungary, born July 12, 1856, married Prince Leopold of Bavaria 1873, died July 27, 1932; Rudolf's sister.

Marie Valerie, Archduchess of Austria-Hungary, born April 22, 1868, married Archduke Franz Salvator 1890, died September 6, 1924; Rudolf's sister.

Sophie, Archduchess of Austria-Hungary, born as Princess Sophie of Bavaria 1805, married Archduke Franz Karl, died 1872; Rudolf's paternal grandmother.

Karl I, Emperor of Austria-Hungary, born 1887, married Princess Zita of Bourbon-Parma 1911, reigned 1916–1918, died 1922; Rudolf's second cousin once removed.

Zita, Empress of Austria, born Princess of Bourbon-Parma 1892, died 1989.

Albrecht, Archduke of Austria-Hungary, Duke of Teschen, born 1817, died 1895; Inspector General of the Imperial and Royal Armed Forces; Rudolf's great-uncle.

Ferdinand IV, Grand Duke of Tuscany, born 1835, died 1908; reigned 1859–1860.

Johann Salvator, Archduke, born 1852, youngest son of Grand Duke Ferdinand II of Tuscany, renounced titles and assumed name Johann Orth 1889, disappeared at sea 1891; Rudolf's distant cousin.

Leopold Salvator, Archduke, born 1868, eldest son of Grand Duke Ferdinand IV of Tuscany, renounced titles 1902 and assumed name Leopold Wölfing, died 1935; Rudolf's distant cousin.

Louise, Archduchess, born 1870, daughter of Grand Duke Ferdinand IV of Tuscany, married Prince Frederick Augustus of Saxony 1891 (later Crown Prince of Saxony), divorced 1903, died 1947; Rudolf's distant cousin.

Miguel, Duke of Braganza, born 1853, died 1927; widower of Rudolf's first cousin Princess Elisabeth of Thurn und Taxis, had liaison with Mary Vetsera.

Philipp, Prince of Saxe-Coburg and Gotha, born 1844, married Princess Louise of Belgium 1875, divorced 1906, died 1921; Rudolf's brother-in-law.

Louise, Princess of Saxe-Coburg and Gotha, born Princess Louise of Belgium 1858, married Prince Philipp of Saxe-Coburg and Gotha 1875, divorced 1906, died 1924; Rudolf's sister-in-law.

Marie, Countess von Larisch, born Countess Marie von Wallersee 1858, married Count Georg von Larisch 1877, died 1940; Rudolf's cousin.

VETSERAS AND BALTAZZIS

Albin, Baron von Vetsera (Freiherr von Vetsera), born February 28, 1825, married Helene Baltazzi April 2, 1864, died in Cairo November 14, 1887; received Imperial Order of Leopold and named to hereditary knighthood in the empire March 24, 1867; received Imperial Order of Saint Stephen of Hungary October 2, 1869; named hereditary baron of the empire January 30, 1870; Mary's father.

Helene von Vetsera, born May 25, 1847, in Marseilles, daughter of banker Theodor Baltazzi and his second wife, Eliza Sarrell; married Albin Vetsera April 2, 1864; died February 1, 1925; Mary's mother.

Ladislaus von Vetsera, born 1865, died December 8, 1881, in Ringtheater fire; Mary's brother.

Johanna von Vetsera, "Hanna," born May 25, 1868, in Constantinople, died February 28, 1901; Mary's sister.

Marie Alexandrine von Vetsera, ("Mary"), born March 19, 1871, died January 30, 1889 at Mayerling.

Franz von Vetsera, "Feri," born November 29, 1872, died in battle at Kolki, Russia, October 22, 1915; Mary's brother.

Baltazzi, Elizabeth, born 1842, married Albert Llewellyn Nugent, 3rd Baron Nugent, 1862, died 1899; Mary's aunt.

Baltazzi, Marie Virginie, born 1848, married Otto, Count Stockau, 1875, died 1927; Mary's aunt.

Baltazzi, Alexander, born 1850, died 1914; Mary's uncle.

Baltazzi, Hector, born 1851, died 1916; Mary's uncle.

Baltazzi, Aristide, born 1853, died 1914; Mary's uncle.

Baltazzi, Eveline, born 1854, married Georg, Count Stockau 1872, died 1901; Mary's aunt.

Baltazzi, Heinrich, born 1858, died 1929; Mary's uncle.

COURTIERS

Auchenthaler, Dr. Franz, Court Physician to His Majesty (*Leib-und Hofarzt Seiner Majestät*), born 1840, died 1913.

Bombelles, Vice Admiral Count Karl von, Lord High Chamberlain of Rudolf's court (*Obersthofmeister*), born 1832, died 1889.

Bratfisch, Josef, born 1847, died 1892; Rudolf's preferred fiacre driver.

Ferenczy, Ida von, born 1839, died 1928; reader to Empress Elisabeth.

Fritsche, Lieutenant Viktor von, born 1857, died 1945, secretary to the Crown Prince's Secretariat (*Sekretär dem Sekretariat des Kronprinz*).

Gondrecourt, Major General Count Leopold, born 1816, died 1888; Rudolf's military governor, replaced by Latour von Thurmberg.

Latour von Thurmberg, Colonel Josef, born 1820, died 1903; Rudolf's governor.

Loschek, Johann, born 1845, died 1932; hall porter (*Saaltürhüter*) and occasional valet (*Kammerdiener*) to Rudolf.

Slatin, Dr. Heinrich, born 1855, died 1929, court secretary (*Hofsekretär*) in the Lord Marshal's Office, led seven-member court commission to investigate Rudolf's death at Mayerling.

Widerhofer, Dr. Hermann, born 1832, died 1901; Court Physician (*Hofarzt*) and Personal Physician to the Crown Prince (*Leibarzt des Kronprinzen*).

INTERESTED PARTIES

Caspar, Marie, "Mitzi," born 1864, died 1907; Rudolf's mistress.

Hoyos-Sprintzenstein (Hoyos), Count Josef, "Josl," born 1839, died 1899; Rudolf's hunting companion, present at Mayerling.

Jahoda, Agnes, Mary Vetsera's maid.

Schratt, Katharina, born 1853, died 1940; actress at the Burgtheater, Franz Josef's mistress.

Szeps, Moritz, born 1835, died 1902; editor of *Neues Wiener Tagblatt* and *Wiener Tagblatt,* Rudolf's friend and confidant.

Tobias, Hermine, born 1865, died 1929; Mary Vetsera's piano teacher and friend.

DRAMATIS PERSONAE

OFFICIALS

Károlyi, Count István, "Pista," born 1845, died 1907; member of the Hungarian parliament and proponent of Hungarian independence.

Krauss, Baron Franz von, born 1840, died 1919; Vienna's chief of police (*Polizeipräsident*) in 1889.

Szögyény-Marich, Ladislaus von, born 1840, died 1916; departmental head of the Ministry of the Royal Household and of Foreign Affairs for Hungary, Rudolf's executor.

Taaffe, Count Eduard von, born 1833, died 1895; Austrian prime minister (*Österreichs Ministerpräsident*).

Tisza, Kálmán von, born 1830, died 1902; Hungarian prime minister and leader of the Liberal Party.

PART I

PROLOGUE

JANUARY 27, 1889

That Sunday evening an opalescent veil of darkness cloaked Vienna. Puffy pink-gray clouds spilled snow over the broad Ringstrasse, capping the red-tiled roofs of its remaining medieval houses and its formidable array of baroque, neo-Renaissance, and neoclassical facades with delicate white hoods. Gas flames flickered in wrought-iron streetlights, creating ghostly halos in the frigid air as horses panted and puffed along avenues lined with rows of linden and lime trees stripped bare by winter. Shimmering beneath its mantle of shifting powder, suspended in the amber of a January night, Vienna seemed every inch the cosmopolitan center of a great and proud empire.

Europe's royal families were at the apogee of their power and prestige as 1889 began. From the Pacific Ocean lapping at the edges of Siberia to the Mediterranean, from frigid Scandinavian fjords to the Atlantic waters edging Ireland, tsars, kings, sultans, emperors, grand dukes, and princes ruled countries large and small, bound together by dynastic marriages and shared privilege. Some still clung to absolutist notions of autocratic power, but even those whose hands had been forced by the march of time to recognize constitutions and easily swayed parliaments often secretly harbored a belief in the divine right of kings.

And so it was here in Vienna, imperial capital of the proud

Habsburg dynasty. It was a place of studied artificiality, of theatrical illusion: rococo palaces, sugary pastries, coffee topped with copious dollops of whipped cream, and dashing officers squiring white-gloved ladies in an endless whirl of Strauss waltzes. Palaces and parade grounds, cathedrals and cobbled squares all whispered evocatively of a glorious past; columned facades shielded rococo ballrooms where the prisms of Bohemian crystal chandeliers refracted crimson, white, and gold in mirrors that might once have greeted Mozart or Beethoven.

The Danube Basin and the surrounding Vienna Woods lent the city an almost provincial feel despite its cosmopolitan exterior. Until the 1850s rampart-topped walls and picturesque gateways arose from grassed-over moats, wrapping the narrow, cobbled streets in a protective embrace. Then the new Ringstrasse had swept the medieval aside in imitation of Second Empire Paris, creating magisterial squares, broad gardens, and appropriately grand avenues for Habsburg ceremonials. Here, too, aristocratic Vienna—and would-be aspirants—drove in crested carriages and promenaded each afternoon, proudly displaying the latest Parisian and Viennese fashions, a "gay, well dressed, talkative mass of people rushing both ways," recorded a visiting Julia Dent Grant, granddaughter of the former American president, "getting tangled up and untangling themselves."[1]

Vienna had always carried a whiff of the exotic, standing as it did between East and West. Twice soldiers had successfully repelled the invading Turks; when the sultan's army fled in 1683, they left behind bags of what soon became one of Vienna's enduring symbols: coffee. Now, on this January evening, the city's coffeehouses were—as always—surging with gossip, news, and philosophical talk. Sitting beneath wispy clouds of blue smoke curling from cigarettes, a few of the intellectuals absorbed newspapers and journals from Budapest, Paris, London, Berlin—even from New York—that offered tantalizing talk of growing nationalism and spurred debate.[2] The Habsburgs, it was true, ruled with a parliament, but theirs was a conservative, often reactionary rule, and an undercurrent of avant-garde ideas simmered just beneath Vienna's outwardly genteel surface. True radicalism was a rarity, however. Unlike St. Petersburg, where bomb-wielding nihilists potentially lurked behind every potted palm, Vienna's would-be revolutionaries channeled their frustration into artistic, intellectual, and cultural radiance as the city saw the rise of composer Gustav Mahler, architect Otto Wagner, artist Gustav Klimt, and Sigmund Freud.

Much of Vienna, or so it often seemed to observers, lived in a protective cocoon of leisurely, cheerful gaiety. It was better to ignore unpleasant reality than to fight: Most Viennese, recorded the British diplomat Lord Frederic Hamilton, seemed "quite content to drift lazily down the stream of life, with as much enjoyment and as little trouble as possible."[3] Amiability was favored over raw ambition; comfort and charm were more useful in daily life than ostentatious display and haughty manners. "The people of Vienna seem to any serious observer to be reveling in an everlasting state of intoxication," Austrian politician Franz Schuselka aptly wrote. "Eat, drink and be merry are the three cardinal virtues and pleasures of the Viennese. It is always Sunday, always Carnival time for them. There is music everywhere. The innumerable inns are full of roisterers night and day. Everywhere there are droves of fops and fashionable dolls. Everywhere, in daily life, in art and in literature, there prevails that delicate and witty jesting. For the Viennese the only point of anything, of the most important event in the world, is that they can make a joke about it."[4]

Ostensibly there was less gaiety that January 1889 than usual. The emperor's father-in-law had recently died, and royal mourning meant that the usual round of court balls and dinners had been canceled, although private entertainments continued. And so it was this January 27. The day had come and gone, but nightfall saw a burst of activity at Vienna's Hofburg, the rambling imperial palace whose disparate wings and jumbled facades had metastasized over the centuries around innumerable cobbled courts. Restless horses clopped hooves against uneven pavements as liveried grooms harnessed them to carriages painted black on top and bottle green on the underside, with gold-rimmed wheels to distinguish the occupants as members of the ruling house.[5] Soon enough the line of carriages was in motion, a contingent of bodyguards in gold, silver, and green liveries galloping alongside beneath the swirling snow.[6]

Though it was a Sunday, a few lights still burned in the neo-Gothic Rathaus, or City Hall, with its lofty tower; lighted the Renaissance-style Burgtheater; shone against the massive marble columns and ornate neoclassical pediments of the Reichsrat, the Austrian Imperial Council; and shimmered across the Opera House's Renaissance loggia—none of the buildings more than thirty years old but wrapped in a variety of historical patinas meant to convey the permanence of the Habsburg empire. Most of the capital, though, was quiet as the line of imperial carriages rumbled toward the Italianate facade of 3 Metternichgasse. Behind windows flooded with light, the ballroom of the Imperial German Embassy pulsed with a colorfully clad, vibrant crowd of privileged guests moving in and out of the banked flowers and forest of potted palms. Court mourning had been set aside, at least in this extraterritorial bit of Germany, to celebrate the thirtieth birthday of Kaiser Wilhelm II, who had come to the throne when his father, Friedrich III, succumbed to cancer the previous June. Much to Austria's annoyance, Prussia had become the dominant force in Europe. However, Vienna's military alliance with Berlin demanded that the ruling Habsburgs demonstrate some modicum of honor for the event, even though most despised both their Germanic rival and the brash young kaiser.

The German ambassador, Prince Reuss, scion of a family that confusingly named all male members Heinrich and numbered them accordingly, waited to receive his guests. The ambassador was Heinrich VII. For this soiree he'd filled his ballroom with an impressive array of Austria's insular aristocracy. Most lived in isolated splendor, intermarrying for generations to prevent the introduction of unwelcome outsiders into their closed circle. A mere two hundred families—Auerspergs, Liechtensteins, Metternichs, Schwarzenbergs, Esterházys, and the like—occupied the highest level of society.[7] Their intense charm, oppressively mannered courtesies, and taste for polished living carried—like Vienna itself—more than a whiff of studied theatricality. "No one," wrote Julia Grant, "asked them to be intense or intellectual or ambitious, and they never were."[8] It was a common complaint. "Viennese society is pervaded by a great moral indolence and a want of energy and initiative," recorded Walburga, Lady Paget, wife of the British ambassador, Sir Augustus Paget. "Politics, religion, literature, art, and sciences are hardly ever alluded to in general talk."[9]

On this particular night the aristocratic elite and members of the diplomatic corps ringed the edges of the ballroom—a sea of brocade and velvet gowns, sparkling diamonds, and handsome uniforms in a kaleidoscope of reds, greens, and blues bedecked with sable- or fox-trimmed dolman jackets and gold braid. A space was left at the center of the room; a flutter of fans and the rustle of silk floated over the crowd. The ambassadors of Great Britain, Spain, Italy, Bavaria, Russia, France, and Turkey waited expectantly, sipping Champagne with the Austrian prime minister, Eduard von Taaffe; Cardinal Prince Cölestin Ganglbauer, the archbishop of Vienna; and the papal nuncio, Monsignor Luigi Galimberti.[10]

In one corner Prince Reuss exchanged pleasantries with Princess Louise of Coburg, while her husband, Prince Philipp, circled the room.[11] The Coburgs occupied a position of prominence at court. In 1881 Louise's sister Stephanie had married Crown Prince Rudolf of Austria-Hungary and come to live in Vienna. Rudolf immediately took to his new brother-in-law. The two became constant hunting companions and, it was said, partners in less admirable pursuits as well. Opinion in Vienna, though, always tended to indulge the self-indulgent, and a charming veneer excused much.

A little after ten a signal alerted Prince Reuss that his guests of honor had arrived; excusing himself to Princess Louise, he left the corner to welcome the star attractions. The future of the empire and the glory of the Habsburgs rested on the slim shoulders of Crown Prince Rudolf, now uncomfortably attired in the dark broadcloth dress uniform of Prussia's 2nd Brandenburg Uhlan Regiment to honor the kaiser. Rudolf was thirty, though he looked far older. His brownish-red hair was distressingly thin, his drooping mustache oddly pointed, and his features creased with worry; dark rings circled pale, restless eyes. His expression, recalled his wife, seemed to hint at "a process of internal dissolution."[12]

At her husband's side, Crown Princess Stephanie appeared statuesque, pretty if not beautiful, with a pert nose, an exquisite complexion, and a tangle of frizzed golden hair topped by a diamond tiara. She was, her sister Louise remembered, "beautifully gowned" in a gray silk dress.[13] Stephanie appeared to relish the attention, but she often seemed ill at ease—and not without reason: Too proud, much of Vienna thought, too stiff, and damned as so unsympathetic that she had driven her husband from their marital bed. Aware that her critics were always ready to pounce, Stephanie struck one observer as "timid to excess," with a strained smile and an overwhelming desire, once the official greetings ended, "to try to get into a corner, away from everyone."[14]

Fifteen minutes later the orchestra struck up the Austrian national anthem, "God Save Our Emperor," as Franz Josef I entered the room, attired in the uniform of a Prussian field marshal. At fifty-eight the emperor of Austria and apostolic king of Hungary carried himself as erect as any soldier. Franz Josef had been on the throne since the age of eighteen; few people could remember any other ruler. Tufts of close-cropped gray hair sprouted from his increasingly bald head; bushy mutton-chop whiskers and a mustache cloaked the unsightly traces of an infamous Habsburg jutting lower lip. He gave the appearance of a contented, benevolent, but "altogether magnetic" figure, fully conscious of his own imperial dignity but far too polite to wield it in public.[15] Rudolf, it is said, bowed deeply to his father and kissed his hand as he entered the ballroom.[16]

He entered alone—without his enigmatic wife—but then, as

everyone had come to expect, Franz Josef was often alone. Beautiful, aloof, and mysterious, Empress Elisabeth had never succeeded in winning the affections of her husband's Austrian subjects. Her obvious sympathy for all things Hungarian caused resentment, and she had done much damage by repeatedly running off to Madeira or Corfu claiming poor health, or obsessively riding with the most fashionable hunts in England and Ireland. Her appearances at court diminished with the passing years; even without her father's recent death, few would have expected to see her at the German reception that evening.

Stephanie was exchanging pleasantries when Rudolf suddenly spotted her sister Louise. Leaving his wife, he crossed the ballroom as if possessed. "She is there!" he quietly hissed to his sister-in-law. Louise knew exactly whom he meant.[17] Indeed, many were now openly staring at the slight young girl in the light-blue gown trimmed in yellow who had just entered the ballroom, and whose appearance "aroused universal admiration and attention."[18] A lover's-knot diamond brooch glittered on her décolletage, shimmering with every breath; a diamond crescent adorned the "artistically arranged coils" of her dark-brown hair; and a sapphire bracelet—a gift from the crown prince—wrapped her wrist.[19] "Superb and glowing," recalled Louise of Coburg, seventeen-year-old Baroness Mary Vetsera looked every inch "the seductress," certain "of the power of her full and triumphant beauty."[20]

Reaction in the ballroom was immediate: Everyone knew that Mary Vetsera was Crown Prince Rudolf's latest mistress—the Viennese court thrived on gossip—though no one had likely imagined she would be brazen enough to so publicly flaunt the relationship as her dark eyes followed her lover around the room. A few prominent ladies glared at her with disapproval; others seemed to relish the uncomfortable scene unfolding before their eyes.[21] Mary boldly walked up to Count Josef Hoyos, one of Rudolf's favorite companions and frequent hunting partners, and transfixed him with her "dazzling beauty. Her eyes seemed larger than they were, and sparkled mysteriously." Her efforts at conversation were inconsequential, mostly about Rudolf's hunting and his lodge at Mayerling, but, Hoyos recalled, "her whole personality seemed to blaze."[22]

Rudolf watched in disbelief as his mistress stared at him across the room; a few hours earlier, Mary had coldly confided to a friend that she hoped Crown Princess Stephanie would notice her that evening and be jealous.[23] The young baroness had no problem in attracting attention, though her lover was less than enamored of the spectacle. "Oh, if somebody would only deliver me from her!" Rudolf cried to Louise. He was, Louise thought, in a "state of nervous exhaustion." She tried to draw him out by commenting on Mary's obvious beauty, but Rudolf seemed uninterested. Finally he turned from his sister-in-law, muttering, "I simply cannot tear myself away from her."[24]

The emperor left after an hour, but Rudolf and Stephanie remained, both watching as Mary Vetsera eased her way across the gleaming parquet floor until she stood at the center of the ballroom, delighted that all eyes seemed focused on her. Finally Rudolf went up to her, and they exchanged a few words; onlookers thought that the lovers seemed unusually serious as they spoke.[25] The crown prince, thought Walburga Paget, looked "dejected" and "sad," and could barely fight "back his tears."[26] His unease only increased when he rejoined Stephanie and continued to greet the guests, aware that all eyes were watching him. Flanked by her mother, Baroness Helene Vetsera, and by her sister, Hanna, Mary moved down the reception line, inching ever closer to the crown princess. Finally they came face-to-face, a horrified Stephanie at her husband's side as he coldly nodded at his mistress. The atmosphere in the ballroom was electric.[27]

Rudolf was too steeped in etiquette to snub his mistress openly, and he again exchanged a few words with the young lady, who smiled broadly back at him. Then Mary defiantly stared at Stephanie. According to a police report, she stood straight and unbending before the crown princess; seeing what was happening, Helene grabbed her daughter's arm and quickly jerked her to the floor in a clumsy curtsy.[28] No one in the ballroom knew that they had just witnessed one of the final scenes in a high royal drama destined to shock the world: In eighty hours Rudolf and his mistress would be dead.

CHAPTER ONE

Forty years on the throne: Even as he marked the occasion in December 1888, Franz Josef must have worried about the future. He had held his disparate empire together; *Viribus Unitis*—With United Strength—went the formula he used to describe his rule. That unity was illusory, its complaisant peace constantly threatened by growing nationalism among Franz Josef's Hungarian, Bohemian, and Slav subjects. How much longer could the old order live on?

Living up to—and preserving—Habsburg tradition ruled Franz Josef's life. Habsburgs had reigned as Europe's preeminent Catholic dynasty since the thirteenth century. Military conquest wasn't really their forte: Instead their influence spread across the continent through propitious marriages—"Let others make war. You, Happy Austria, Marry!"—went the popular saying.[1] At the height of their power Habsburgs and Habsburg relations served as Holy Roman Emperors and occupied the thrones of Austria, Hungary, Bohemia, Spain, Naples, Milan, France, and the Netherlands. They could boast great rulers—Emperor Charles V and Empress Maria Theresa—as well as some of history's most pathetic figures, including Maria Theresa's unfortunate daughter Marie Antoinette. But one by one most of these kingdoms, provinces, and territories had severed ties with Vienna. The fall of the Holy Roman Empire in 1806 left the Habsburgs as emperors of Austria and kings of Hungary,

Lombardy, and Venice, a motley collection of lands artificially united beneath the yellow-and-black imperial banner and held together by the most fragile of political threads.[2]

Franz Josef didn't have a Machiavellian bone in his body, but his resolute mother, Archduchess Sophie, proved that she was made of sterner stuff. One of the daughters of King Maximilian I Josef of neighboring Bavaria, Sophie had arrived in Austria as the bride of Archduke Franz Karl, heir to the unfortunate epileptic and imbecilic Ferdinand I.[3] Armed with a belief in her intellectual superiority, Sophie soon dominated her agreeable, unambitious husband. In 1848, when revolution swept across Europe, drove the kings of France and Bavaria from their thrones, and violent demonstrations in Vienna and Budapest forced Ferdinand's abdication, it was Sophie who most clearly recognized the danger. Thinking that her weak-willed husband couldn't stomach suppressing the rebels, she persuaded Franz Karl to sign away his rights in favor of their eighteen-year-old son Franz Josef.

Sophie passed up her only chance to be empress, but she was merely exchanging one form of power for another. "The only man" at the imperial court, officials called her, as she quickly dominated her son and became his indispensable adviser in all things.[4] Believing that his mother's foresight had saved the throne, Franz Josef blindly followed her dictates—to disastrous effect. A bigoted reactionary, Sophie urged her son to fight growing Hungarian nationalism by subverting the kingdom's constitution and supporting ethnic minorities to rebel against the dominant Magyars. The parliament in Budapest replied by refusing to recognize Franz Josef as king and in April 1849 named Lajos Kossuth as head of a new Hungarian republic. With his empire on the brink of civil war, Franz Josef relied on Russian soldiers sent by Tsar Nicholas I to ruthlessly crush the revolt.[5] When the rebellion was subdued, Franz Josef treated Hungary like a conquered country: In the first five years of his reign the young emperor ordered thousands executed, in keeping with his dictum that "Those who disobey, be they prince or clergy, must relentlessly be pursued and punished."[6] In February 1853 a Hungarian tailor named János Libényi attacked Franz Josef while the emperor was taking his regular afternoon promenade. Libényi's aim was bad, and the emperor escaped without serious injury. But Franz Josef used the incident to send a clear message to Magyar nationalists: Libényi was publicly hanged as a traitor in Vienna.[7]

Urged on by his mother, Franz Josef inaugurated his second decade on the throne with an ill-advised war in Austria's Italian provinces. One by one Lombardy, Naples, Tuscany, Modena, Sicily, and Parma were all lost as a humiliated emperor slunk back to Vienna in disgrace. Protesters mobbed the streets, demanding that Franz Josef abdicate in favor of his younger brother Maximilian; Franz Josef managed to save his throne only by granting his subjects a new constitution in 1861. Still, he retained enormous power: He could write and impose laws when parliament was not in session, could dissolve the body at will, and could fire officials without cause. Even with the constitution, Franz Josef never abandoned his conviction that God had placed him on his throne and charged him with the onerous duty of maintaining order.[8]

The peace won was temporary. The emperor's attempts to promote himself as head of the thirty-nine-state German Confederation brought him into conflict with Chancellor Otto von Bismarck, who insisted on Prussian supremacy. The Seven Weeks' War of 1866 pitted Vienna against Berlin. Hungary openly rebelled, siding with Prussia, and Austria suffered a humiliating defeat at Königgrätz; sensing weakness, Venice—the last Italian province still under Habsburg rule—broke away from Vienna. Hungary, too, took advantage of the chaos after the Seven Weeks' War to force Vienna's hand. Franz Josef barely managed to keep his remaining possessions together by signing the Ausgleich in 1867, a compromise between Austria and Hungary that granted the Magyars considerable autonomy and created the Austro-Hungarian Empire, known as the Dual Monarchy.

More bad news came from Mexico, where Franz Josef's brother

Maximilian and his wife, Charlotte, had unwisely assumed a French-backed throne to rule the new empire in 1864. The misadventure lasted a mere three years before French emperor Napoleon III withdrew his support. Mexican rebels overthrew their emperor: On June 19, 1867, they stood Maximilian against a wall in Querétaro and executed him by firing squad. The tragedy left Charlotte unhinged. Declared insane, she spent the rest of her life locked away in a Belgian castle, a tinsel crown atop her head as she held court for the phantoms of her past.[9]

Humiliating military defeats, loss of territory, repression followed by forced concessions, and personal tragedies—these became the hallmarks of Franz Josef's reign. "The Emperor of Austria, Apostolic King of Hungary, of Bohemia, of Dalmatia, Croatia, Slavonia, Galicia, Lodomeria, and Illyria; King of Jerusalem; Archduke of Austria; Grand Duke of Tuscany and Cracow; Duke of Lorraine, of Salzburg, Styria, Carinthia, Carniola, and Bukovina; Grand Prince of Transylvania . . . ," went only half of his string of titles.[10] His was a curious empire encompassing some forty-five million Austrian Germans, Magyars, Czechs, Rumanians, Moravians, Poles, and, after 1878, the South Slavs—Slovenians, Croats, and Serbs—and Muslims in the occupied Balkan provinces of Bosnia and Herzegovina. A Babel of languages, ethnic identities, warring nationalist sentiments, and conflicting faiths, the Habsburg Empire faltered on out of habit, bound together only by the monarch in Vienna, even as Great Britain, imperial Germany, and even backward Russia modernized and grew in industrial, economic, and military strength.

"You see in me," Franz Josef once told American president Theodore Roosevelt, "the last monarch of the old school."[11] The dashingly handsome young man who had come to the throne at eighteen was now fifty-eight, the "chosen guardian of the fame and reputation of his House," as one of his aides-de-camp, *Flügeladjutant* Lieutenant General Baron Albert von Margutti, explained.[12] Franz Josef used "ceremonial politeness" to create "a sense of distance between himself and others."[13] He was agreeable but remote, ever conscious of his rank. The emperor, Margutti recalled, even thought "that for him to shake hands was an altogether exceptional mark of esteem, and that he must not be too free with it."[14]

Although everyone agreed that the emperor was charming and polite, the polished veneer concealed the soul of an autocrat. "Everything about him," recalled a courtier, "including his memory, had to be unchallenged, unchallengeable."[15] Franz Josef prided himself on his self-control, and only rarely did he stray from his usual soft, conversational tones. But while he occasionally gave voice to his frustrations, the emperor made no such allowances for others. "Unseemly expressions," "gesticulations," or even impulsive laughter were deemed a "discourtesy to his Imperial dignity."[16] Slights against Habsburg dignity—real or perceived—in fact consumed much of Franz Josef's attention. He once greeted a proposal that guards should no longer present arms to baby Habsburgs in their carriages as an insult to the imperial house.[17] An officer who dared appear before him with a medal out of place, a button undone, or a sash askew set Franz Josef "quivering with rage."[18] There is a story that perfectly encapsulates this obsession with outward propriety: One night, in the midst of a severe cold, Franz Josef awoke with a cough so violent that he could not catch his breath. Alerted to the dire emergency, the physician in attendance rushed to the emperor's bed; although gasping for air, Franz Josef still managed to berate the poor man for not having changed into the customary frock coat demanded by court etiquette.[19]

Franz Josef lived in self-imposed isolation. Aside from shooting he had no real interests, dismissing most art, music, and literature as wastes of time.[20] "Our Emperor," his only son scathingly wrote, "has not one friend; his character and temperament do not permit it. He stands isolated on his pinnacle. With his servants he discusses the official business of each, but he anxiously avoids any other subject, hence he knows very little about the thoughts and feelings of the people, of the ideas and opinions of the nation. . . . He believes we are now in one of the happiest epochs of Austria's history; this is what he is told officially."[21] Officials played their part in this intellectual isolation, assuring Franz Josef that his people were happy. Withholding contradictory information, they even printed special editions of the daily newspapers, editions that carefully eliminated hints of unrest or potentially troublesome developments.[22]

In contrast to Vienna's burgeoning intellectual reputation, the emperor prided himself on the simplicity of his views. "For him," asserted one courtier, "only primitive concepts exist. Beautiful, ugly, dead, living, healthy, young, old, clever, stupid—these are all separate notions to him and he is unable to form a bridge leading from one to the other. . . . His ideas know no nuances."[23] This black-and-white approach dominated. To Franz Josef "the people" fell into one of two categories: a loyal but nameless citizenry whose faces blurred one into another as they cheered imperial rule, or the equally intangible crowd of rebels and revolutionaries he had fought in 1848, in Hungary, in Italy, and now in the fragile empire. Antiquated conceptions of duty drove Franz Josef relentlessly onward as he confronted one disaster after another, providing a rigidly ordered refuge from a hostile modern world.

Filling his days with routine paperwork helped Franz Josef escape his unhappy marriage. In his first years on the throne the handsome young emperor had freely bestowed his sexual favors on a specially selected succession of "hygienic" young aristocratic women, forming a kind of Viennese harem.[24] But soon enough his mother insisted that he marry—and Sophie had just the right candidate, someone who was not only a good Catholic but whom she could also easily control: Princess Helene, one of the ten children born to Sophie's sister Ludovika and her husband, Max, who carried the junior title Duke *in* Bavaria to distinguish him from the more regal Dukes *of* Bavaria. This was dipping a bit too perilously into an already thin gene pool: Not only was Helene—called "Nené" in the family—Franz Josef's first cousin, but her aunt Karolina Augusta had married Emperor Franz I of Austria. Aunt Sophie, of course, had married Archduke Franz Karl—and in doing so had become her own sister's daughter-in-law. The Bavarian Wittelsbachs boasted more than their fair share of eccentrics, and frequently incestuous marriages—including twenty-one previous unions with the Habsburgs—had resulted in fragile temperaments and mental instability.

Sophie and Ludovika, though, gave little thought to such concerns, and brought their children together at the alpine resort of Bad Ischl in the summer of 1853. Here their careful plans dissipated as soon as Franz Josef saw Helene's fifteen-year-old sister, Elisabeth. Called "Sisi" within the family, the young girl was stunningly beautiful, with light brown eyes and long chestnut hair. Brought up in relative simplicity at her father's little Gothic revival castle of Possenhofen on the shore of Lake Starnberg outside Munich—a place where cows wandered through the rose garden and the furniture was threadbare—she seemed an ebullient, refreshing change from the sophisticated young ladies in Franz Josef's orbit. Accustomed to a son who always gave way to her wishes, Sophie was horrified when Franz Josef announced that he wanted to marry Elisabeth: The young girl was too immature, too uneducated, too emotional, and too high-strung, she asserted, to become empress of Austria. But the more Sophie argued, the more Franz Josef insisted.[25] When he finally proposed to his startled cousin, Elisabeth accepted, but, in a hint of things to come, soon collapsed in tears, sobbing, "If only he were not an emperor!"[26]

When, on the evening of April 24, 1854, Franz Josef led his bride to the altar of Vienna's Augustinerkirche, Elisabeth was terrified and briefly fled the reception that followed in tears.[27] She dreaded her wedding night and tried to hide herself behind a bank of pillows: Franz Josef humored her insecurities for two nights, but on the third he took possession of his wife.[28] Passionate about everything but sex, Elisabeth felt humiliated that everyone knew of her deflowering; indeed, her mother-in-law, Archduchess Sophie, apparently made a point of openly questioning her son about the details.[29]

Sophie quickly became Elisabeth's bête noire. The two proud

women, fighting for Franz Josef's attention and jostling for emotional dominance, soon came to resent each other. Sophie, said one of the empress's ladies-in-waiting, tried to "come between the two married people, always forcing a decision between mother and wife, and it is only by God's grace that an open break did not occur. She wanted to break the influence of the Empress over the Emperor."[30] Accustomed to the freedom of her former life at Possenhofen, the new empress felt trapped in a gilded cage. The Habsburgs lived and died by the infamous Spanish etiquette of their court, a sixteenth-century remnant from their Iberian rule. Accustomed to being deferred to, the punctilious Sophie insisted that her daughter-in-law learn, respect, and obey every archaic rite without question. When Elisabeth resisted, Sophie chastised: "Your Majesty," she once snapped, "evidently thinks you are still in the Bavarian mountains."[31]

Elisabeth rebelled at attempts to instruct her in her duties and court ceremony, earning her lectures on removing her gloves at dinner, on riding too much, and on her overt shyness. Sophie filled her daughter-in-law's household with a contingent of aristocrat ladies whose principal duties were to spy on Elisabeth and spread word of her mistakes in Viennese society.[32] The more Sophie insisted, the deeper Elisabeth dug in her heels, sulking, treating her duties with contempt, and refusing to make even minor concessions to her "nasty" mother-in-law.[33] And Franz Josef was caught in the uncomfortable middle, as wife and mother each besieged him with complaints about the other.[34]

However reluctant she was, Elisabeth fulfilled her principal duty by providing her husband with four children, though the imperial nursery soon became yet another battleground in her war with Archduchess Sophie. As soon as they were born, the children were whisked from their mother's arms to a nursery where Sophie reigned supreme. Elisabeth was allowed no say in their upbringing and, as a consequence, developed little maternal instinct. Instead she vainly viewed her children as a "curse," saying, "When they come, they drive away beauty."[35]

Franz Josef refused to intervene, though he graciously indulged his wife's selfish caprices. More and more the unhappy Elisabeth avoided her duties; she rarely appeared at court, preferring to seclude herself with her animals, her poetry, and her small circle of intimates. If she felt unwell, if her hair wasn't looking its best, if inspired to compose—Elisabeth often used any excuse to abruptly cancel appearances at balls, dinners, and receptions, oblivious to the hurt feelings or damage to her prestige.[36] Desperately in love with his beautiful wife, Franz Josef deluged "my dearest angel Sisi" with effusively romantic letters, assuring her of his devotion while pleading that she not go riding so often, and asking that she "show herself in the city" to avoid alienating his subjects.[37] But his pleas went unheeded as the empress sank into gloomy depression. The idea that she might be tainted with hereditary madness both fascinated and repelled Elisabeth. Once, when Franz Josef asked what she would most like for her birthday, Elisabeth declared in all seriousness that he should give her "a fully equipped lunatic asylum," so that she could study the patients in depth.[38] One of her more disagreeable eccentricities involved a young African boy called Rustimo. Given to her by the shah of Persia, the boy was coddled and fawned over, dressed up in elaborate costumes, and treated as a prized toy, "a joke," as the historian Brigitte Hamann noted, used merely to provoke outrage—until such time as Rustimo protested and the empress ruthlessly sent him away "like a monkey whose manners were not up to scratch."[39]

Unable to share her husband's passionate sexuality, Elisabeth withdrew, and Sophie—ever watchful for opportunities to influence her son—urged Franz Josef to seek romantic comfort elsewhere, and he soon strayed from his marital vows.[40] Unlike in his youth, the women Franz Josef now consorted with were neither carefully selected nor "hygienic." It is unclear exactly what happened, but it seems likely that Franz Josef contracted gonorrhea and infected his wife with the disease at the end of 1859. Elisabeth's joints swelled, she broke out in a rash, and she was in great distress: Secret consultations with a series of physicians reportedly confirmed venereal disease.[41]

Elisabeth was still young and prided herself on her beauty, yet her husband had looked elsewhere. From this point onward she made a conscious decision to live according to her own terms, terms that only rarely made concessions to her responsibilities as empress or role as a wife and mother; perhaps out of guilt Franz Josef indulged her as she all but abandoned her duties.[42] She began a peripatetic existence, fleeing Vienna for Madeira, where she spent the winter of 1860, officially seeking a cure for anemia. Extended stays in Corfu and Malta followed: Nearly two years passed before Elisabeth returned to Vienna, but she never remained long, seeking consolation and distraction in composing morbid poetry and wandering across Europe, from fashionable resorts to the fields of England, where she rode to hounds with a fervor approaching mania.

The empress also developed a mania for all things Hungarian, a passion likely driven by her mother-in-law's antipathy for that country. Viennese tongues clucked over her circle of Magyar confidants, especially her friendship with the dashing Count Gyula Andrássy. She took up the Magyar cause in the wake of the Seven Weeks' War, pushing her husband to sign the new compromise with Hungary that created the Dual Monarchy.[43] To celebrate the couple's crowning in Budapest in 1867, Hungary presented Franz Josef and Elisabeth with a country residence, the baroque palace of Gödöllö, where the empress increasingly spent her time when in her husband's empire. Franz Josef's concessions temporarily won Elisabeth back: In 1868 she gave birth—in Budapest—to her last and favorite child, a girl named Marie Valerie.

"I have been so persecuted, misjudged, and slandered, so hurt and wounded in the great world," Elisabeth once declared.[44] Depressed, she gave herself over to a quest for eternal youth. After 1870 she refused to sit for photographic portraits, wanting people to remember her only as young and beautiful. Vain about her exceptionally long hair, she refused to have it cut even though its weight gave her constant headaches. After its weekly washing, her maid had to brush it and count the number of hairs Elisabeth had lost.[45] The empress slept with slabs of raw veal tied around her face to guard against wrinkles; bathed in olive oil; and refused to use a pillow for fear it would crease her face.[46] Each morning she was weighed: If she had gained even an ounce, Elisabeth subsisted on a diet of clear soup, milk, wine, juice squeezed from a cut of beef, and raw eggs. Exercising for hours on gymnastic equipment she installed in her rooms, Elisabeth soon developed anorexia.[47]

By 1888, and after thirty-four years of marriage, both Franz Josef and Elisabeth had grown cynical. "Marriage," Elisabeth declared, "is a nonsensical institution. One is sold as a child of fifteen and takes an oath one does not understand but can never undo."[48] Her reader Ida von Ferenczy thought that Elisabeth respected Franz Josef, "but I doubt she loved him."[49] Devoted as he was, even the emperor once candidly spoke of the "bitter experience" of his marriage.[50] He continued to pour out his heart in letters to his wife, but Elisabeth often replied coldly, finding excuses to avoid both her husband and Vienna; if he didn't like her "habits," she once wrote threateningly, she could "be pensioned off" and replaced with a more sympathetic consort.[51]

Franz Josef took it all in stride. "I must simply make the best of it and continue to bear patiently the lonely existence to which I have long been accustomed," he wrote sadly to his wife.[52] He buried himself in his work, following a routine that itself gave comfort to his ordered mind. The emperor arose shortly after four each morning, was dressed by his valet, and by six was inevitably in his study, where a seductive portrait of Empress Elisabeth by Franz Xaver Winterhalter offered a ghostly reminder of his absent wife. Audiences and reports filled his days, interrupted only by an afternoon walk. Simple in his tastes, Franz Josef regularly dined on boiled beef and pork knuckles washed down with beer. Except for those evenings when he had to preside over court functions or attend the theater, the emperor was usually asleep by nine.[53]

Perhaps the kindest thing Elisabeth ever did for Franz Josef was to provide her husband with a mistress, the actress Katharina Schratt. After 1860 Franz Josef had indulged in any number of affairs and is said to have fathered several illegitimate children, but his relationship with Schratt proved to be something entirely different.[54] He first took notice of the pretty young actress during a performance at Vienna's Burgtheater in 1884.[55] Sensing the attraction, Elisabeth asked Schratt to tea, delicately explaining that she wanted to travel but that someone must care for her husband in her absence. Schratt agreed, and Elisabeth soon left Vienna with a clearer conscience.[56]

For the next three decades Schratt became the closest thing Franz Josef ever had to a true confidante. Although rewarded with lavish gifts, she asked for nothing, providing the emperor with emotional comfort and a refuge from his troubled reign. A few historians, quoting cautious letters written between the pair in 1888, have insisted that the emperor and the actress were never lovers.[57] Yet Schratt faithfully reported her menstrual periods to the emperor, who was, after all, only in his fifties when the relationship began.[58] As the biographer Joan Haslip wrote of the friendship, "One is inclined to doubt whether it was always so platonic."[59]

Now this man of dull habits and autocratic temperament marked forty years on the throne. With the losses of his Italian provinces, military defeat by Prussia, and political blackmail by Hungary, Franz Josef had little cause for celebration. Elisabeth was absent—as indeed she so often was—when the anniversary came, and the scandals and disappointments weighed heavily on the emperor's shoulders. Yet his country was at peace, and a chorus of voices assured him that his subjects were content. Perhaps Franz Josef believed that better days lay ahead; any such illusions were about to be shattered in a way that shook the monarchy to its very core and brought unforeseen tragedy into the very heart of the imperial family.

CHAPTER TWO

First there had been a girl, named Sophie after her grandmother on her birth in 1855; then Empress Elisabeth gave birth to another daughter, Gisela, the following year. Sophie died of complications from measles at the age of two, and Gisela couldn't inherit the throne ahead of any living male Habsburg.[1] But on August 21, 1858, a 101-gun salute announced that the empress had finally given birth to a son at Schloss Laxenburg, some fifteen miles outside Vienna.[2] "Magnificently built and very strong," Franz Josef declared, though he thought his new son was a very ugly baby.[3] But he finally had an heir, and from the first Franz Josef heaped expectation on his shoulders. Along with the string of titles—Crown Prince of Austria and of Hungary, *Thronfolger* (heir to the throne), Archduke and Prince of Austria, Hungary, and Bohemia—came a string of names: Rudolf Franz Karl Josef of Habsburg-Lorraine, evoking the glorious accomplishments of Count Rudolf of Habsburg, who had founded the dynasty in the twelfth century.

Rudolf, like his sisters before him, was taken from his mother's arms to a nursery where Archduchess Sophie enforced the court's onerous Spanish etiquette: The new mother couldn't nurse her son, contact was limited, and always under Sophie's censorious gaze. Sophie, not Elisabeth, chose Rudolf's nurse, the widowed Baroness Karolina von Welden, to provide him with maternal attention.

"Wowo," as Rudolf called his nurse, became one of the few stable influences in his young life.[4]

In Great Britain, Queen Victoria idealized her private family life to win popular support; such a concept was alien to the Habsburgs. They had no desire to humanize themselves, to live as examples of familial unity to appeal to the masses. The emperor's devotion to duty and the empress's desire to wander Europe in the wake of her domestic disappointments left Rudolf emotionally adrift. It wasn't often that he saw both of his parents, and even when he did, it was only for a rigidly controlled sixty minutes before Baroness Welden returned him to the nursery.[5]

Franz Josef treated his young son like a military cadet, someone to be trained and shaped by discipline so that he would "show a good deal of courage, manliness, and industry." When a scared four-year-old Rudolf shied away from a group of boisterous soldiers, Franz Josef wrote to his son that it was "a disgrace."[6] Shy by nature and uneasy showing any emotion, the emperor was friendly but reserved with his son. Franz Josef could not forget that he was emperor, and exalted conceptions of his role demanded that he always act as sovereign first and father second. Informalities leading to unwelcome intimacies were discouraged: Indeed, Rudolf's youngest sister, Marie Valerie, characterized the relationship between father and son as "self-conscious."[7] There was something so distant in Franz Josef's manner that even Rudolf's tutor once begged the emperor to consider the crown prince's "sensitive heart" when speaking to him, and to treat him "not sternly, but kindly."[8]

Empress Elisabeth was an inconsistent, erratic presence in her son's life, and she often let animosities sour their infrequent time together: As soon as Archduchess Sophie entered a room, Elisabeth fled, leaving Rudolf a bewildered and upset pawn in their personal power struggles.[9] Rudolf adored his mother: She was a magical, beautiful figure who flitted in and out of his life. He worshipped an abstract ideal, desperate for her love and affection, but Elisabeth was unable to take much interest in him. In 1863 Elisabeth refused to cut short her holiday in Bavaria on learning that Rudolf had typhoid, and so it was Sophie who nursed him through the disease.[10] Constantly traveling, Elisabeth filled letters to her son with lines like, "Do not forget your Mama," or "Think of your Mama often," but her behavior undermined any sense of emotional security: She often let days pass before answering Rudolf's letters, saying that she had been too busy traveling, riding, or even attending the theater to answer him.[11] Even when she did reply, Elisabeth made it clear she was only going through the motions: "I have just written good little Gisela a long letter," she reported to her three-year-old son, "and so there's nothing left to tell you."[12] After years of such treatment, Rudolf complained that his mother "no longer cares for anything" other than her own interests.[13]

The kind of happy domestic family life depicted in popular Victorian lithographs and sentimental postcards eluded the Habsburg heir. His father was too unimaginative and distant, while his mother, caring more about her own diversions, ignored her only son. This left Rudolf anxious and high-strung: even as a young boy he suffered from poor health. Temperamentally he was his mother's son: charming and agreeable one minute, withdrawn and depressed the next. Wild tantrums when denied something he wanted were common. Rudolf was also manipulative: Disliking confrontation, he was inevitably agreeable only to avoid emotional scenes. Early on, he learned to use his ill health and claims of headaches to escape unwelcome situations and evade unpleasant obligations.[14]

At six Rudolf was forcibly torn from his beloved "Wowo" and his sister Gisela to begin his formal education, destroying any vestige of stability.[15] Like the nursery, the schoolroom became a battleground in the ongoing war between Empress Elisabeth and Archduchess Sophie. Sophie rebuffed the empress's attempts to push for a liberal education, declaring, "How can Elisabeth, badly brought up as she is, and with no idea of how to behave, be expected to bring up the heir to a great empire?"[16] On his mother's advice Franz Josef appointed Major General Count Leopold Gondrecourt as his son's governor, charged with toughening up the "nervous" crown prince.[17]

A professional soldier, Gondrecourt brought with him a reputation for exaggerated piety, harsh language, and needless cruelty.[18] Following the emperor's charge, Gondrecourt delighted in employing methods both emotionally and physically abusive. At night he crept into the young boy's room and fired off pistols to wake a terrified Rudolf from his sleep.[19] At six every morning, in rain and snow and by the light of a lantern, he made Rudolf do military drill in the courtyard.[20] Then there was the day Gondrecourt took his young charge to the zoo. He locked Rudolf in a cage and shouted that a wild boar was coming to kill him as the boy screamed in terror.[21]

This brutal regimen took a toll on six-year-old Rudolf: He suffered from terrible nightmares and frequently wet his bed.[22] In May 1865 a traumatized Rudolf collapsed: The imperial court said it was diphtheria, but it is likely that the young boy had suffered a nervous breakdown.[23] Even the self-absorbed empress finally recognized the danger, insisting that Gondrecourt be fired. When Franz Josef refused to go against his mother's choice, Elisabeth gave him an ultimatum: "I cannot stand to see such things going on," she wrote. "It must either be Gondrecourt or myself. . . . It is my wish that I alone should have full and unlimited power in all matters concerning the children, the choice of those who surround them and their place of residence, and complete control of their upbringing. In short, I must alone decide everything concerning them until their majorities."[24]

Faced with this threat, Franz Josef relented. Having won her battle, Elisabeth retreated back into her own self-centered life—"she was incapable of sustaining interest in Rudolf very long," as one of her biographers noted.[25] The emperor replaced Gondrecourt with Elisabeth's choice, the liberal Colonel Josef Latour von Thurmberg. Like Gondrecourt, the forty-five-year-old Latour von Thurmberg was a career army officer; he'd even lost a finger battling Italian soldiers in 1849. But unlike his predecessor, Latour von Thurmberg was gentle, cultured, and had an innate sympathy for his young charge, whom he likened to a "whipped dog" on assuming his post.[26] He became Rudolf's confidant, the closest thing he had to a trusted friend.

Rudolf, Franz Josef insisted, "must not become a free thinker, but he should become thoroughly acquainted with the conditions and requirements of modern times."[27] Given Latour von Thurmberg's liberal reputation, the worry was real. "I could not approve of the entire tendency of these studies to introduce the Crown Prince to all branches of knowledge and public life," wrote one of the emperor's adjutants, "to name professors and tutors of the most liberal conviction and to allow him, according to the unfortunate, existing court regulations, to complete his studies." He feared that "the youthful, easily excited mind of the Crown Prince, the immaturity of his concepts, and his extravagant though undeniable high intelligence" would lead Rudolf to absorb "ideas and tendencies not corresponding to the future monarchy's conservative character."[28]

Expectations buried Rudolf: As future emperor, he must become the most knowledgeable, most adept, most learned prince the Habsurgs had ever produced. Just as Queen Victoria and Prince Albert attempted to turn their son Albert Edward, the Prince of Wales, into an "ideal man," so too did Franz Josef burden his son with unreasonable goals. And in both cases, unrelenting pressure and expectation crushed spirits, leaving the boys anxious, nervous, and ultimately rebellious against the ideas thrust upon them.

Latour von Thurmberg selected men of respectable achievement and liberal inclination to tutor the crown prince. The problem wasn't quality but rather quantity: Nearly fifty different instructors pushed a disparate array of subjects at a superficial, head-turning pace. From seven in the morning to eight at night, instructors drilled Rudolf in Austrian, Hungarian, Bohemian, and European history; world history; grammar; literature; geography; arithmetic; politics; economics; jurisprudence; natural science; military history and strategy; and lessons in Latin, French, Magyar, Czech, Polish, English, and Croatian.

On top of this was instruction in gymnastics, swimming, riding, fencing, and dancing, along with music and art.[29] The latter two subjects left Rudolf cold. He was his father's son when it came to the arts, disliking operatic and orchestral music, shunning literature, and finding no escape in paintings.[30]

Having endured a similar educational regime, Franz Josef saw no reason to alter the heavy burdens heaped upon his son. But Rudolf wasn't the compliant, unemotional and unintellectual pupil his father had been. The speed of lessons and rapid shifts in focus left Rudolf, as Latour von Thurmberg complained, incapable "of thinking methodically."[31] Another tutor wrote that Rudolf was "inclined merely to skim the surface of the subject at hand"; coupled with his "lack of concentration in observing and thinking and also his want of precision following a lecture and rendering it verbally," the young student never developed the ability to critically analyze and assess information.[32]

Then there was religion. Lessons in Catholic catechism reinforced guilt and the necessity for perpetual penance that preyed on Rudolf's anxious mind. At ten he burst into uncontrollable, guilty sobs when asked to make his first confession, which Latour von Thurmberg thought unnerving and quite out of proportion to any boyish transgression. But this apparent piety soon turned to cynicism. As a boy Rudolf rushed through his prayers as an unwelcome chore; by fifteen he was questioning Catholicism itself.[33] "The Clergy," Rudolf wrote in an essay on the Middle Ages, "always hand in glove with the proud aristocracy, used their influence over the people and did not permit the development of any free ideas; the church chose ways dangerous for itself, for eventually the people would realize how they were treated and recognize the sacrilege of those indulgences and other means which the clergy had used to enrich themselves."[34] Rudolf declared that he had "no sympathy whatever for the influence of the Church on the State," and detested "all tendencies toward Church influence. I would much rather send my children to a school whose master is a Jew than to one whose headmaster is a clergyman." A strong Catholic Church, he believed, always resulted in "evil consequences."[35] And, to his mother's second cousin King Ludwig II of Bavaria, Rudolf declared, "I consider the Christian faith, in the narrow forms demanded by our Church, quite unacceptable for any educated man who has reached a stage of mental development that allows him to rise above common life and logically think and ask questions."[36] It is not surprising that the adult Rudolf was an unapologetic, though private, atheist.

Rudolf's words reflect something of his inquisitive nature, but he struggled to understand his tendency to anxiety and depression. A notebook entry made at the age of fifteen reveals his troubled state of mind:

> Thoughts of all kinds race through my head; it seems confused, all day long my brain boils and toils the whole day long; one goes out, another comes in, and each possess me, each tells me something different, sometimes serene and happy, sometimes black as a raven, full of fury; they fight and from the struggle truth slowly develops. I always wonder: how will it end? Are we spirits, or are we animals? Animals, that is what we are. Have we descended from apes or has man always existed as a species of his own? Often I ask myself: are you already a madman, or will you become one? I realize I shall know all I want to know, but one thing is certain: one must always strive, always endeavor, to achieve more and always more, not titles and dignities nor riches—leave that to the venal races who trace their ancestors to the birth of Christ. No, I want knowledge.[37]

Latour von Thurmberg never showed such writings to the emperor, who undoubtedly would have been astonished by his son's musings. Ostensibly Rudolf was flamboyantly liberal. Also at fifteen he had written:

> During the French Revolution the King, the nobility and the clergy were punished for their own iniquities and for those of their forebears. The punishment was rough and bloody, but it was a necessary and salutary catastrophe. The government has changed and is a step nearer to the Republic. Monarchy has lost its old power and clings to the trust and love of the people. . . . Monarchy stands as a mighty ruin, which may remain from today till tomorrow but which will finally disappear altogether. It has stood for centuries and as long as the people could be led blindly all was well. Now the end has come. All men are free, and in the next conflict the ruins will come tumbling down.[38]

And a few years later he asserted: "Our age requires new points of view. Everywhere, especially in Austria, there is reaction, which is the first step toward a downfall. Those who preach reaction are the most dangerous enemies."[39]

Some of these views stemmed from Rudolf's sincere conviction, but there was also an element of rebellion against his father's archaic court and rigid conservatism. He remained his father's son when it came to his privileged position. Change was necessary, but for Rudolf this meant change enacted within the existing monarchical framework: The same young man who spouted liberal ideologies shared Franz Josef's belief that God had selected the Habsburgs to rule.[40] The liberal Rudolf, Latour von Thurmberg complained, "began to think that he was omnipotence personified."[41]

Rudolf's political views were also inconsistent. Initially favorable to the Czechs, he came to resent Bohemian nationalism as a threat to Vienna's power.[42] He also harbored ambivalent feelings about Austria's role in the Balkans: At times he suggested that the South Slavs under Habsburg rule should be given their own semiautonomous state in an effort to counteract any Russian influence or potential expansion. At others he seemed to think that Austrian involvement in the Balkans would lead only to political and military trouble.[43]

Rudolf inherited his mother's love of Hungary, once writing that he felt "irresistibly drawn toward the dark forests" and thrilled at its sunsets, where "the leaden darkness was separated from the light of the departing day by a belt of orange broken only by a few bright, isolated stars, while the low-lying woods and swamps wrapped in blue vapors and feathery mists assumed ghostly indefinite shapes."[44] He'd learned the country's history and language from the Benedictine priest Jácinth János von Rónay, a surprising choice given that Rónay had taken part in the 1848 rebellion against Austrian rule and Franz Josef had actually signed a death warrant against him as a "traitor."[45] Rónay eventually abandoned such troubling separatist views, though he supported more Magyar autonomy and the creation of a third nation in the empire, comprising Bohemia and Moravia.[46] This left Rudolf torn between liberal dreams of an independent nation and a personal conviction that the Habsburgs must always wear the Crown of Saint Stephen.

Latour von Thurmberg's work came to an end in 1877. He deemed his student "a puzzle." On the one hand, he said, "I've never met a more talented man." But, he complained, Rudolf lacked character.[47] On July 24, a month short of his nineteenth birthday, the crown prince was declared to be of age. With his inquisitive mind Rudolf would undoubtedly have benefited from being allowed to continue his studies at a university, but this was contrary to Habsburg etiquette, and he remained something of an intellectual dilettante, unable to evaluate conflicting information and subject to rash judgments on political issues.

On reaching his majority, Rudolf became entitled to an annual stipend from the government's civil list of 45,000 gulden (approximately $287,550 in 2017).[48] This was a considerable amount of money: A university professor typically earned some 2,000 gulden a year ($12,780 in 2017). Yet his wandering mother regularly spent three times her son's annual allowance on one of her frequent

European holidays.[49] Franz Josef also typically gave archdukes palaces in Vienna when they reached their majorities; he refused to do so with his son, handing over a bachelor apartment in the Hofburg's Schweizerhof wing and forcing Rudolf to share his roof, as if reinforcing his subservient position.

The emperor also appointed a group of officers as his son's new household, naming Vice Admiral Count Karl von Bombelles, whose father, Heinrich, had once procured Franz Josef's mistresses, as the crown prince's *Obersthofmeister*, or lord high chamberlain of Rudolf's court.[50] The choice proved disastrous for the impressionable Rudolf. Described as "unscrupulous, with the mentality of a lackey" and a "hard-living man of the world," Bombelles followed his father's example by introducing Rudolf to the pleasures of women and alcohol. He had, complained a courtier, "a masterly capacity for flinging open to the Prince all the doors of worldly distraction," acting "the role of Mephistopheles to perfection" as he shepherded Rudolf "into all possible and impossible adventures."[51]

At the beginning of 1878 Rudolf traveled to Great Britain, where he hoped to reunite with his mother, who was there to ride to hounds. But the empress, who prided herself on being a brilliant equestrienne, caused problems. Rudolf was an indifferent rider at the best of times; worried that he would disgrace himself, Elisabeth warned her son that he wasn't good enough to emulate her pursuit.[52] "I shall certainly take care to avoid riding to the hounds," Rudolf sarcastically replied. "Our public does not regard it as heroic to break one's neck, and my popularity means too much to me to throw it away on such things."[53] The situation was so tense that, although they traveled aboard the same train, Elisabeth avoided being alone with Rudolf.[54]

Rudolf generally acquitted himself well, however, and pleased Queen Victoria by being "most easy to get on with," though she worried that he "looks a little over-grown and not very robust."[55] But his subsequent visit to Ireland went badly: No seat had been provided for him at a ball in his honor at Dublin Castle, and neither the viceroy nor the lord mayor of Dublin would cede his chair. After the lord mayor cut in front of the crown prince on the way to dinner, Rudolf had had enough, and despite apologies abruptly left the next day.[56] His foul mood eventually erupted against his mother. There was much gossip about Elisabeth's relationship with her favorite riding companion, Captain George "Bay" Middleton, and Rudolf let it slip that he thought his mother was infatuated with her handsome English friend and making a fool of herself. Elisabeth was furious; "filled with bitterness," she insisted that she would never again trust her son.[57]

The usual course of action for a Habsburg archduke—service in the army—awaited Rudolf on his return to Austria. Franz Josef appointed him a colonel in the 36th Imperial and Royal Infantry Regiment stationed in Prague, though not before he had replaced liberal officers with reliably conservative voices.[58] The commanding officer, Major Friedrich Hotze, praised Rudolf as "quite extraordinary," noting his "warm heart and a noble character developed beyond his years." Yet Hotze couldn't ignore his "impetuous and impulsive" nature, warning that without clearly defined goals the crown prince could veer into an aimless, idle life.[59]

"I belong to the Army, body and soul," Rudolf once insisted.[60] But Latour von Thurmberg, the man who knew him best, thought that the crown prince "lacked almost everything" necessary to be a good soldier. Unlike his martinet father, who obsessed over the smallest of military details, Rudolf was undisciplined and careless about appearances.[61] A fellow officer once complained that Rudolf seemed "tired, bored, and absent-minded" during drill: He ignored the regimental report and "gazed vacantly into space," more concerned that his boots were splashed with mud. In the midst of the review he summoned a groom, who rushed over with a cloth and carefully wiped his boots. When this was over Rudolf continued to "stare into space, without taking the least notice of what was going on around him."[62]

By the time he was twenty Rudolf had grown into an elegantly attractive though not particularly handsome young man of medium height; a wispy mustache and side-whiskers echoed his slightly curly, reddish-brown hair.[63] Light-hazel eyes constantly shifted according to Rudolf's moods; after their meeting in 1878, Russian aristocrat Princess Catherine Radziwill recalled "a certain mournful expression" in them, along with a wistful, almost sad smile.[64] But there was an air of delicacy about him, reflected in his slight frame and often wan complexion.[65] Rudolf spoke with the accent peculiar to aristocratic Vienna, a distinct mixture of musical notes and guttural intonations; he often skipped "from one subject to another" in disjointed fashion.[66] He had inherited his mother's charm, yet his polite and courteous manners, thought Princess Radziwill, "were rather cold and not exempt from a shade of disdain."[67]

Intelligent, well read, interested in science, and a talented writer, Rudolf impressed many. "He is clever," recorded Empress Elisabeth's lady-in-waiting Countess Marie Festetics, "but after all, he is young still and has had no guidance."[68] A former tutor, decrying the "Mephistophelean expression" on Rudolf's face, warned: "Do not allow the introspective speculations I detect in your eyes to embitter your existence."[69] Rudolf's mercurial moods were famous—"one moment gentle and shy," recalled a cousin, "and the next blazing forth at some fanciful iniquity like a savage Oriental despot."[70]

Franz Josef appreciated his son's intellect but did not share it: He took Rudolf's curious, often abstract ideas and liberal opinions as wayward rebellion. Never able to bridge the emotional gulf separating them, father and son maintained an outwardly pleasant détente that cloaked insecurities and mutual distrust. To the end Rudolf craved his father's approval, but Franz Josef could never bring himself to confide in his heir or entrust him with any real responsibilities.

Empress Elisabeth once deemed her son "a bad-minded boy" and a "very dangerous enemy," warning that he would turn on anyone "if he ever gets the chance."[71] Rudolf had essentially grown up alone, tended by nannies and tutors but with no real sense of family intimacy. Until the age of six he was closest to his sister Gisela, but education separated them; after Gisela married Prince Leopold of Bavaria in 1873 he rarely saw her. A ten-year age difference meant that Rudolf had little in common with his youngest sister, Marie Valerie: indeed, although they shared the same roof, Marie Valerie admitted that she often went months without seeing her brother.[72] Not that Rudolf would have confided in her: Marie Valerie was their mother's pet, her favorite child and constant companion, upon whom she showered all the attention and affection she had denied her son. "It is you alone that I love," she once confided to her youngest daughter."[73] Resenting this obvious favoritism, Rudolf often treated Marie Valerie coldly. For her part, Marie Valerie complained that her brother was so formal and aware of his own position as crown prince that he even kept his own family at arm's length and never offered confidences.[74] Considering himself far superior to the Wittelsbachs, Rudolf caused great offense by insisting that his mother's Bavarian relatives treat him as crown prince.[75]

Twenty years of life had left Rudolf a young man of immense contradictions. Heir to unprecedented privilege, he had suffered through a childhood that left him psychologically damaged and emotionally abandoned. Family life offered no comfort: The distant father, the absent mother, and the strained formality of the Austrian court only enhanced feelings of isolation and alienation. A haphazardly enacted education had awakened sparks of imagination within his keenly intelligent mind, yet it had left him without the skills needed to analyze and reason through contradictory information. Liberal inclinations clashed with autocratic conceptions of his own position, resulting in wildly conflicting ideas for the future. And yet this was the emotionally fragile young man on whose thin shoulders rested the fate of his father's uneasy empire.

CHAPTER THREE

"Love," wrote Rudolf at fifteen, "is certainly one of the most beautiful things in the life of all living things."[1] A year earlier Latour von Thurmberg had escorted him to a fish hatchery, where doctors explained the facts of life.[2] Abstraction gave way to reality when, according to rumor, Franz Josef tasked an adjutant with procuring a healthy, discreet young woman to shepherd his son through his first sexual encounter.[3]

A perfect storm quickly surrounded Rudolf. "What temptations assail such a young man!" worried one of his mother's ladies-in-waiting.[4] Youth, wealth, and rank, he soon discovered, had their privileges. "Female hearts positively dropped into the lap of the Crown Prince," noted a counselor at the German Embassy in Vienna. Many young ladies considered "surrender to the young, elegant and charming Prince" as nothing short of "a patriotic duty."[5]

Rudolf, said a cousin, "was mad about women," and saw no reason to deny himself.[6] The Prince of Wales had recorded of the nineteen-year-old who visited London in early 1878, "For a young man of his age, it is surprising how much Rudolf knows about sexual matters. There is nothing I could teach him."[7] Rudolf wasn't discreet about his interests, and he made few distinctions between the married and the unmarried; his romantic overtures to Archduchess Maria Theresa, the third wife of his uncle Archduke Karl

Ludwig, strained an already bad relationship.[8] Not that Rudolf's taste remained consistent for long: After using his position to charm numerous women to bed, he usually grew bored and soon moved on to a new liaison.[9]

A courtier recalled that Rudolf had "very little regard for women, outside their appointed role in the order of things"—in other words as submissive wives and mothers. His approach was cynical. Women, Rudolf declared, were "eternal victims of self-delusion," willing to abandon any principles in pursuit of romance.[10] A streak of misogyny infused his perception: "How tedious some women can be!" he once complained. "Women bore me to death when they are not laughing or singing. As a matter of fact, are they good for anything else?"[11]

These affairs were physical, not emotional, and Rudolf viewed them through a curiously bureaucratic lens. The names of his sexual partners were entered in a ledger, with red ink used to denote those women Rudolf had deflowered, and black deployed for other conquests. He developed a system every bit as rigid and snobbish as the court's Spanish etiquette to reward his partners. Those belonging to princely families recognized as being of equal rank for the purposes of marriage received a silver box engraved with a copy of Rudolf's signature and coat of arms; noble ladies admitted to court but not of equal rank were given boxes stamped with his name and coat of arms, while those who lacked entrée received boxes engraved with his name and archducal crown.[12] Dispatch of a silver box inevitably marked the beginning of the liaison's end, usually accompanied by a warm though unmistakably final note: Rudolf asked one woman, whose virginity he had taken to remember him as the person who "introduced you into the mysteries of love."[13] His "propensity for easing persons from the memory" was true of his sexual conquests: "As soon as they had been presented with their cigarette boxes and been duly entered in his register," wrote one relative, "the matter was closed for him, for there was little these women could give him. His sexual indulgence was curiosity rather than the urge to satisfy a physical appetite, and curiosity in this sphere was soon satisfied as there was little that was novel in it."[14]

Some of these liaisons, however, were more serious than others. In 1880, the crown prince supposedly secretly married his distant Habsburg cousin Maria Antonia, daughter of Grand Duke Ferdinand IV of Tuscany, when she became pregnant. As she was dying of consumption, it is said, the emperor had the marriage annulled; Maria Antonia died in 1883, after allegedly giving birth to Rudolf's son in 1881.[15] An affair with the Viennese actress Johanna Buska is also said to have led to the birth of an illegitimate son in 1881.[16] Rudolf apparently didn't trouble himself over such developments: Indeed, his grandson Prince Franz Josef von Windisch-Grätz once claimed that his grandfather had more than thirty illegitimate children.[17] Mothers were bribed into silence, their children soon forgotten.

Even the wives of Rudolf's best friends were considered fair game. In the late 1870s, it was whispered, he began a liaison with Princess Louise, wife of his friend and frequent hunting companion Prince Philipp of Coburg.[18] A member of the Austrian branch of the German aristocratic house of Saxe-Coburg and Gotha, the prince was once unflatteringly described as "an unattractive, squat, myopic, coarse-natured creature."[19] A heavily built bearded man, Philipp shared Rudolf's love of sensual pleasures and supposedly catered to his insatiable tastes. Coburg always "kept tongues wagging" in Vienna, said one lady, with his "reputation of intriguing" and boasts about being in the know in "all sorts of interesting secrets, diplomatic as well as personal."[20]

In 1875 the thirty-one-year-old Coburg married his seventeen-year-old first cousin once removed Princess Louise, the eldest daughter of King Leopold II of Belgium. Horrified by her husband's amorous overtures on their wedding night, Louise had fled the palace in her nightgown and hidden in a greenhouse before her mother, Queen Marie Henriette, lectured her on her marital duties and sent her back to Philipp's arms.[21] Louise eventually bore her husband two children and gradually carved out a life for herself in Vienna, using her husband's money to make herself a leader of the fashionable set. Coburg was blatant about his own extramarital affairs, and Louise followed his example, though with more discretion than her husband.[22]

With a succession of liaisons meeting Rudolf's amorous needs, he long resisted the idea of marriage. "I am not cut out to be a husband," he once told Latour von Thurmberg, "and don't propose being one so long as I can help it."[23] But by 1880 Franz Josef insisted: There was already too much talk about his son's reputation in Vienna. According to the Habsburg Family Statute of 1839, Rudolf had to marry a Catholic of equal rank, which reduced the field of potential brides to the royal houses of Bavaria, Spain, Saxony, Portugal, or Belgium, or to one of the empire's princely families recognized as *ebenbürtig* (equal for purposes of marriage).[24] Franz Josef first suggested Princess Mathilda of Saxony; certain that she would grow obese, Rudolf rejected her. The emperor then proposed the Infanta Eulalia of Spain, whose lack of obvious physical charms left Rudolf cold.[25]

It was Princess Louise of Coburg who offered a solution. "I have a sister who is like me," she told Rudolf.[26] Belgium was a mixed bag: The monarchy had been established only in 1831, an offshoot of the German house of Saxe-Coburg and Gotha, and offered little dynastic luster. But there were important ties: King Leopold II was Queen Victoria's first cousin; his consort, Queen Marie Henriette, had been an Austrian archduchess before her marriage; and Franz Josef's brother Maximilian had wed Princess Charlotte of Belgium—though given her insanity the latter was scarcely a recommendation. But Franz Josef charged Count Bohuslav Chotek, the Austrian minister in Brussels and father of the ill-fated Sophie—the future consort of Rudolf's equally ill-fated cousin and successor, Archduke Franz Ferdinand—with undertaking negotiations.[27] With his father insisting, and having exhausted most of the other possibilities, Rudolf reluctantly traveled to Belgium in the spring of 1880.

Like Rudolf, Princess Stephanie of Belgium, born in May 1864, had endured an unhappy childhood. King Leopold II had no interest in his daughters and treated his wife with contempt, flaunting his numerous affairs at court.[28] After the death of his only son, Leopold openly resented his daughters; Stephanie later wrote of his "indifference, injustice, and unfaithfulness," which seared her youth.[29] Aside from his affairs, Leopold's only concern was amassing a vast fortune by exploiting his Congo Free State through brutal repression. Franz Josef himself openly disliked the king, calling him "a thoroughly bad man."[30]

Stephanie was just fifteen when Rudolf arrived in Brussels at the beginning of March 1880. Slightly taller than Rudolf, with small eyes and an unremarkable face, she prided herself on her golden hair and fine complexion; one of Franz Josef's adjutants said that she "always had a friendly smile or a few kind words for everyone."[31] Raised with exalted conceptions of her role as a princess, Stephanie could be just as proud and unbending as her future husband, but she also shared his ability to charm. Nor was she the intellectual nonentity often depicted in critical memoirs: Stephanie was well read, artistic, and had a quick mind. These were her good points, but, like Rudolf, she was also obstinate and suspicious. And she did not share the crown prince's anticlerical leanings: When it came to religion, Stephanie was an unimaginative, rigid Catholic.[32]

King Leopold called Stephanie into his study. "The Crown Prince of Austria is here to ask for your hand in marriage," he announced. "Your mother and I are very much in favor of this marriage. It is our desire that you should become the future Empress of Austria and Queen of Hungary."[33] Stunned at this news, Stephanie was pushed into a room to meet her visitor. "The Crown Prince," she wrote, "could not be called handsome, but I found his appearance by no means displeasing." Yet she detected "something unfrank and hard about his gaze. He could not bear to be looked at directly in the face. About his wide mouth, which was half-hidden by a small mustache, there was a queer expression which was difficult to read."[34] Rudolf dutifully asked Stephanie to become his bride within days of meeting her, and, as dutiful as he, she consented. Even if Rudolf did not quite fit her image of a prince charming, the fairy tale he promised seemed enticing: "A new world presented itself alluringly to my imagination," Stephanie recalled. "A splendid world, one in which I should have an exalted mission."[35]

The engagement nearly evaporated when Queen Marie Henriette walked in on Rudolf in the arms of the actress Anna Pick, his latest mistress, whom he had brought to Brussels to keep him company while he wooed Stephanie.[36] But dynastic ambition overcame any moral qualms, and the engagement was duly announced. With his father forcing his hand, Rudolf adopted an uncharacteristically optimistic tone: To Latour von Thurmberg he described Stephanie as "pretty, good, clever, very well bred," someone who would "become a faithful daughter and subject of the Emperor and a good Austrian."[37] A few days later, declaring that he was "intoxicated with happiness and contentment," he deemed his fiancée "a real angel, a good and faithful being who loves me, a very intelligent and tactful companion for life who will stand successfully and sympathetically by my side in all my difficult undertakings."[38]

Franz Josef was relieved, but not so Empress Elisabeth. "Nothing good can come out of Belgium," she complained, adding, "Hasn't Charlotte been experience enough for us?"[39] Arriving in Brussels to offer her halfhearted congratulations, Elisabeth did nothing to conceal her contempt for Leopold II and his consort. The empress also mocked her son's fiancée and openly criticized her clothing as "the height of tastelessness"; the slights were so obvious that even Rudolf complained of his mother's cold behavior.[40] Rather than offer Rudolf comfort and guidance, Elisabeth, as one of her biographers noted, "failed him, as she had so often failed him in the crucial stages of his life."[41]

Stephanie prepared for her future duties, but the wedding had to be postponed for a year when it was learned that the fifteen-year-old had not yet begun to menstruate.[42] Leopold II further complicated matters by refusing to provide his daughter with any dowry larger than the 100,000 gulden (approximately $639,000 in 2017) his sister, Charlotte, had received more than twenty years earlier; an insulted Franz Josef gave Stephanie an additional sum and agreed to grant her an annual allowance from his own funds.[43] "He's nothing but a money-grubbing tradesman," the emperor declared of the Belgian king, "and I can't stand people like that."[44]

Rudolf wed Stephanie at Vienna's Augustinerkirche on May 10, 1881, exchanging rings that had belonged to their common ancestor Empress Maria Theresa, as artillery salvos rattled the windows. King Leopold and his wife, Stephanie recalled, "beamed with gratification," while Empress Elisabeth—who denounced the bride as "a clumsy oaf"—openly sobbed.[45] When they left for their honeymoon at Laxenburg, Rudolf was silent and Stephanie nervous, "alone with a man I hardly knew." She found the rooms at Laxenburg cold and dark, with no flowers or any sign of celebration. Then came the wedding night, when Rudolf took possession of his bride: "What torments!" Stephanie recalled. "What horror! I had not the ghost of an idea what lay before me, but had been led to the altar as an ignorant child. My illusions, my youthful dreams, were shattered."[46]

These initial disappointments faded with the passing weeks. Even Stephanie later admitted it was untrue that her marriage "had been unhappy from the outset. It did not fulfill my girlish ideals; there had been a lack of affectionate spiritual companionship; there had been nothing more than a sort of enforced association without cordiality. Still, though disappointed in many respects, I had done my best to understand the Crown Prince's nature."[47] Rudolf's sister Marie Valerie even thought that Stephanie's "love for her husband comes close to adoration."[48] They soon took up residence in Prague when he was stationed with the army, though Stephanie complained that Rudolf's duties consumed most of his time: When separated—at least in these first years—he sent his wife warm, effusive letters: Stephanie was his "Dearest Angel," while he signed himself, "Coco."[49] To Latour von Thurmberg he wrote: "I am very much in love with her and she is the only one who could induce me to do many things."[50] But Stephanie was soon dismayed to find that Rudolf's outward piety was all a show: "He had no true fear of God," she wrote. "He lacked a sense of duty and responsibility, so that later when life came to make its claim on him he lacked the power of religious faith and moral restraint."[51]

On September 2, 1883, Stephanie went into labor at Laxenburg. Everyone hoped for a son; indeed, Rudolf confidently filled his letters to Stephanie with talk of the boy they would name Václav.[52] When she gave birth to a girl, Stephanie broke into tears; Rudolf reassured her, but all his talk of "Václav" left Stephanie convinced that he was disappointed.[53] The baby, named after Saint Elisabeth of Hungary as well as her paternal grandmother, was known within the family as Erszi, a diminutive form of the Hungarian Erzsébet (Elisabeth). "Mother and child are very well," Rudolf wrote to a friend. "Stephanie looks blooming as usual, as if nothing has happened. The little one is a stunner of seven pounds, perfectly well and strongly developed, with many hairs on her head, very much alive: she shouts terribly and drinks a great deal without the slightest difficulty."[54]

This brief idyll ended in December 1883, when Franz Josef appointed Rudolf commanding officer of the 25th Infantry Division in Vienna and the couple reluctantly returned to the imperial capital. The move marked the beginning of Rudolf's downward spiral. In Prague he had reigned unchallenged as the dynasty's sole representative; in Vienna, where his father commanded all attention, Rudolf would be reminded daily of his subordinate position and lack of political influence .[55]

The emperor reinforced this sense of impotence by refusing to give Rudolf and Stephanie their own palace in Vienna, forcing them to live beneath his roof in a suite spread along the Hofburg's Schweizerhof Wing. Stephanie found these rooms "gloomy and inhospitable," decorated and furnished in "bad taste." Much to her horror there was no indoor plumbing: She bathed standing in a portable rubber tub, rinsed with water from wooden buckets, and used chamber pots were carried through corridors "under the eyes and noses of any who might happen to be there." Unwilling to endure these traditions, Stephanie had two bathrooms installed at her own expense. There was no electricity or even gas: Rooms were lighted with "horrible paraffin lamps, which stank all the time" and smoked until they inevitably broke. Kitchen odors constantly filled the rooms, and the food itself was unappetizing; when Stephanie dared hire a French chef to prepare meals, the imperial court deemed it an insult to Austrian cuisine.[56]

Stephanie lacked the ability to hide her disillusion; Empress Elisabeth, who had spent her first years in Vienna complaining about her mother-in-law, now repeated the pattern with Rudolf's wife. "She did not make the slightest attempt to help or advise" her daughter-in-law, noted one historian, who added: "Whereas Archduchess Sophie interfered too much, Elisabeth erred on the side of interfering too little. Her cold, impersonal manner invited no confidences." Treating Stephanie with disdain, she openly derided her as "narrow-minded, superficial, and a bigot."[57] The imperial court followed Elisabeth's lead. Stephanie's critics became legion: She was "devoid of all feminine qualities," with "neither charm nor sex appeal," a relative hyperbolically commented, "ugly, domineering, tactless and unintelligent," with "the perfect instinct for doing the wrong thing."[58] People mocked her clothing and her appearance: She was awkward, in contrast to Vienna's genial society; her eyes were too small, too closely set, and her smile was too condescending.[59]

The political impotence, the alienation, and the snobbish criticism—they all took a toll on Rudolf and Stephanie's marriage. Perhaps they were too dissimilar in character and temperament to withstand the pressures bearing down on them. Rudolf toyed with philosophical and political discussions; Stephanie liked fashion and enjoyed her role as future empress. But disintegration took time: Even Stephanie admitted that they had shared happy moments and memories, despite what she termed "a lack of affectionate spiritual companionship." She tried in her own way "to adapt myself to him, to interest myself in his plans, his activities, his tastes, that thereby I might make our life together more congenial."[60]

Rudolf increasingly retreated to a world, Latour von Thurmberg recalled, dominated by "flattering parasites," and "lost his moral balance" by hurling himself into "an unceasing round of pleasure."[61] By 1885 he was spending two-thirds of the year hunting with his faithful horde of retrievers and setters and a coterie of trusted confidants like his brother-in-law Prince Philipp of Coburg.[62] Knowing that Rudolf liked nothing better than whiling away the night at some tavern, surrounded by workers singing the sentimental tunes that appealed to him, Stephanie once decided to join him. She was appalled at the places of "dubious reputation" where her husband seemed to be a regular fixture. Stephanie found sitting in the smoke-filled room, breathing in the persistent odor of garlic, watching as men played with greasy cards while girls danced on tables to zither music until dawn, scarcely proper behavior for the next emperor and his consort: The entire experience repelled her. "I simply could not understand what pleasure the Crown Prince could find in these places," she later wrote.[63]

Fidelity in royal unions is often rare, and Rudolf soon strayed with great regularity. Not content with his usual conquests, Rudolf's insatiable nature carried him—and Prince Philipp—to the establishment of Frau Johanna Wolf, Vienna's most successful and notorious madam, who kept a contingent of beautiful young girls scattered across Europe's capitals.[64] Rudolf could always count on Frau Wolf to provide amorous company to share his bed.[65] In 1885 she introduced Rudolf to her latest addition, twenty-one-year-old Mitzi Caspar. Pretty though not beautiful, with a dark complexion and uncomplicated charm, Mitzi soon became Rudolf's favorite mistress. Although she remained "one of the city's best known and expensive prostitutes," Rudolf spent 60,000 gulden ($383,400 in 2017) buying her a house at 10 Heumülgasse and showered her with money and jewels.[66]

In the hothouse atmosphere of imperial Vienna, word of Rudolf's escapades inevitably reached Stephanie; her sister Louise was only one of many ladies at court who eagerly repeated the crown prince's latest indiscretions into his wife's ear.[67] The gossip was so prevalent that it spread across Europe. Rudolf, Queen Victoria confided to a granddaughter, "led a very bad life," which left "poor Stephanie . . . not happy" and made it impossible for her to have "any respect or love" for her husband."[68] One night, returning to the Hofburg from the opera, Stephanie spotted her husband's carriage waiting outside the house of a certain countess whose favors Rudolf was then enjoying. The crown princess had her own carriage stopped, climbed into her husband's, and ordered his driver to return her to the palace, leaving her abandoned vehicle in the street as a silent but visible rebuke. It did not take long for the incident to pass from tongue to tongue; Franz Josef was furious, not with his son, but with his daughter-in-law, and he summoned Stephanie to an angry meeting where he denounced her for causing a public spectacle.[69]

The imperial court heaped scorn on Stephanie. The neglected wife was denounced as unable to hold her husband's attention and affection. "It is impossible to warm to her," Archduchess Marie Valerie wrote in her diary, adding, "How can Rudolf love this cold and arrogant woman?"[70] Rather than cast a critical eye on her son's behavior, Empress Elisabeth derided her hated daughter-in-law as a "bumpkin," mocking her "long, fake tresses," denouncing her as "jealous" and "impossible," and adding that she was someone "I never want to set eyes on."[71] For Stephanie it was an embarrassing repetition of her father's flaunted infidelities: Just as Leopold II had humiliated her mother with his endless succession of mistresses, so too was her own husband now victimizing and insulting her, making her the object of ridicule in Vienna.

Finding no sympathy at court, Stephanie went to a Jesuit cleric. If only he would intervene and speak to Rudolf of his duties, she was sure that her husband would abandon his frivolous way of life; in what must have been a particularly embarrassing admission, she even asked the priest if he could persuade Rudolf to sleep with her again, so that she could provide him a son. The poor man duly met the crown prince and laid out Stephanie's plea, but Rudolf was furious at this unwelcome interference.[72] Accusing Stephanie of spying on him, Rudolf left their shared rooms and retreated to his old bachelor apartments in the Hofburg, spending his days in an exotic Turkish salon he created, complete with tigerskins, a tented ceiling, and hookahs set on ornately carved tables.[73] Stephanie was forbidden entrance: When she once dared disobey, Rudolf shouted and screamed until she fled in humiliation.[74] He read all of Stephanie's private letters before allowing them to be mailed, and ordered that when he was away she was to see no one other than her ladies-in-waiting.[75] Increasingly the time Rudolf and Stephanie did spend together was marked by loud arguments, accompanied, it has been said, with hurled china and vases that servants discreetly swept up afterward.[76]

Then, at the beginning of February 1886, Rudolf suddenly fell ill. The emperor later had his son's medical files destroyed, and multiple pages in the imperial Apothekarie's prescription books were removed or doctored.[77] Still, enough concrete clues remain to decipher what happened. The public was told that Rudolf was suffering from severe rheumatism and a bladder infection.[78] In fact, on February 16 the imperial physician Dr. Franz Auchenthaler, diagnosed venereal disease.[79]

It was later claimed that Rudolf was suffering from syphilis.[80] His autopsy report is lost, but an excerpt leaked to the press hinted at some unnamed abnormality in Rudolf's brain.[81] In 1921, Baron Albert von Margutti, who served as Franz Josef's adjutant, reported that one of the post-mortem physicians had discovered "advanced paralysis" of the brain, resulting from syphilitic infection. Margutti claimed confirmation from the court physician Dr. Josef Kerzl, who in turn said that he learned it from the imperial physician Dr. Hermann Widerhofer, who helped conduct the autopsy.[82] In addition

Rudolf received occasional prescriptions for mercury chloride after 1886, which was then the only treatment for syphilis.[83] Yet the time line makes this diagnosis questionable: "Advanced paralysis" was then common medical shorthand for the effects of the final, tertiary stage of syphilis, which, if the disease was left untreated, took a number of years from initial infection to destruction in the brain.

Another prescription Rudolf received presumably solves the mystery. At first Auchenthaler treated Rudolf with zinc sulfate and morphine for the pain; then, on February 16, the doctor added oil of Copaiba balsam. This had no effect on syphilis, but it was the most common treatment for a particularly virulent strain of gonorrhea.[84] Typical symptoms included painful urination, bladder infections, unsightly discharges, and lesions on the penis and scrotum. Joint pain and inflammation of the eyes were also frequent symptoms—and Rudolf began to suffer from these complaints.[85]

Given the multitude of Rudolf's sexual encounters with a variety of dubious women, including Frau Wolf's prostitutes, it would not have been surprising that he contracted gonorrhea. It was common among the Austrian military: One source estimated that somewhere between 10 and 20 percent of the emperor's soldiers were infected with venereal disease.[86] Revelation of the disease fell on an already fragile mind. Gonorrhea was treatable but permanent: Painful symptoms would recur at varying intervals and without warning. Diagnosis was not only shameful but also often unintentionally fatal, as many suffering from venereal disease chose to kill themselves rather than suffer moral opprobrium and the unknown terrors of the future.[87]

Even worse, Rudolf infected his wife.[88] Stephanie was on the Adriatic island of Lacroma when she suddenly fell ill with "intolerable pains."[89] "I myself did not suspect the cause of my complaint," she later said, thinking at first it was a bad case of peritonitis. "Everything was hushed up upon orders from above, and the doctors were sworn to secrecy." Two gynecologists came to examine her: She thus learned that "the Crown Prince was responsible for my complaint."[90] The gonorrhea caused pelvic inflammation and destroyed her Fallopian tubes—and any chance that Stephanie would again give birth.[91]

Horror at being infected by her husband with a painful and incurable disease that prevented any additional children shattered whatever sentimental feelings still bound Stephanie to Rudolf. She had endured her husband's flaunted affairs, but now his careless action had destroyed Stephanie's raison d'être at court: to provide a male heir to the Habsburg throne. The diagnosis of gonorrhea left her powerless, undermining her position and condemning her to a shadowy existence.[92]

Starting in 1886 Rudolf relieved the painful symptoms of gonorrhea with an ever-increasing and dangerous mixture of drugs, including morphine, opium, and cocaine—all prescribed by imperial physicians.[93] Even today this causes unease in Austria, and a few authors have claimed that the prescriptions recorded in the admittedly doctored court pharmacy books were too infrequent to have sustained addiction.[94] But Rudolf had no difficulty persuading physicians to prescribe medicines to assuage his pain, nor, with his questionable circle of friends, would he have had any trouble obtaining such drugs on his own. On top of this ever-expanding pharmacopoeia, Rudolf added copious amounts of Cognac and Champagne, which increasingly left him in a mental haze.[95]

It didn't take long for the effects of this regimen to take their toll. By the summer of 1886 Rudolf was lethargic and apathetic, with dark circles rimming his eyes. "He suffered more and more from nervous unrest and from violent temper, culminating in what was tantamount to complete mental decay," Stephanie wrote; he stayed out all night, and when he returned home he was inevitably "in a most disagreeable frame of mind."[96] That July, Duke Karl Theodor in Bavaria, Rudolf's uncle, wrote that the crown prince now seemed a "sinister person."[97]

Rudolf was oblivious to the devastation he had wrought through his careless actions; although he could not deny that his marriage was strained, he continued to humor Stephanie with intimate, even sensual letters suggesting that he longed for a reconciliation and asking about her menstrual periods.[98] "I think we could sleep together this one night," he wrote to her of an upcoming reunion, adding, "It would be very nice to cuddle up in bed again."[99] But Stephanie's trust had been destroyed: "It was plain to me," she recalled, "that the Crown Prince had completely withdrawn from me, and moved into a different world." Married life, Stephanie declared, "had become impossible," and she retaliated by taking her own lover.[100] She first met Count Artur Potocki, a handsome, thirty-eight-year-old widower, in the summer of 1887, and soon began an affair with him. Unlike her husband, though, Stephanie was discreet: She used her sister Louise as a go-between to arrange meetings with "Hamlet," as she referred to Potocki.[101] Rudolf was apparently too self-absorbed to notice his wife's infidelity, while Stephanie now considered her marriage a union that existed in name only.

People began to notice how nervous the crown prince seemed, how carelessly he enacted his official duties.[102] Rudolf disappeared for hours, avoiding his father's ever-watchful detectives by climbing out a window in his Hofburg bachelor apartments, scurrying along a rooftop terrace, and descending a narrow staircase to escape through a small iron door in the old Augustiner Bastion. There he could climb into an inconspicuous fiacre driven by Josef Bratfisch, who became his ally in these escapades. Born in 1847, Bratfisch worked as a driver for a Viennese cab company; known as "the Little Dumpling" owing to his short, squat figure, he had enjoyed some fame as a singer of the sentimental songs Rudolf found so appealing.[103]

Bratfisch faithfully delivered Rudolf to Vienna's seediest nightspots, where the crown prince passed his time drinking and openly consorting with prostitutes.[104] But the potent cocktail of drugs and alcohol took a humiliating physical toll. Now the man who had prided himself on his sexual conquests was often impotent; according to Mitzi Caspar he had to be drunk to get an erection.[105] This only added to the sense of failure and frustration that increasingly dominated Rudolf's life.

On March 3, 1887, Rudolf composed a will—his second. His first, written ten years earlier, had warned of political oppression but still contained hints of his joys in life, ending, "A last, farewell kiss to all the beautiful women in Vienna whom I have loved so dearly."[106] His second will was bereft of personal thoughts as he gave directions for dividing up his estate. Recognizing that his marriage was all but over, he tellingly snubbed his wife, asking that his father be appointed legal guardian for their only daughter.[107]

CHAPTER FOUR

In the spring of 1887 a young lady bustled through her bedroom in Vienna, excitedly preparing for a trip to London. "Very striking," with "a wealth of dark hair" and deep, dark eyes, she prided herself on a "supple, slender figure," and moved with a deliberate, almost feline grace.[1] A maid fluttered about, laying silk stockings, satin shoes, and elaborate gowns from the exclusive Viennese couturier Maison Spitzer across a bed watched over by a painting of the Madonna. Sunlight spilled through gaps in the beaded curtains covering the windows; bangles were pulled off in anxious fits by the room's nervous occupant. Crystal bottles filled with scent jostled with the silver toilette set on a dressing table crowded with velvet-lined jewelry cases—all the accoutrements needed to ensure a beautiful, polished, and sparkling appearance.[2] In a few weeks Queen Victoria would celebrate her Golden Jubilee, marking fifty years on the British throne; though rank as a minor noble would keep her from truly royal functions, the young Viennese lady anticipated balls in London's aristocratic palaces, and splendid dinners and receptions at the Austro-Hungarian Embassy. Though only sixteen, Baroness Mary Vetsera meant to impress and conquer.

Across Vienna, Crown Princess Stephanie fumed. She, too, had planned to travel to London for the Golden Jubilee, to join her husband in representing Franz Josef during the ceremonies. Stephanie didn't know Mary Vetsera, but she'd heard much about her in the last few weeks, rumors repeated by her sister Princess Louise, by Rudolf's former tutor Latour von Thurmberg, and by her husband's relatives. Mary, according to these sources, had met the crown prince at a Viennese ball a few months earlier. Playing the coquette, the young lady had so brazenly flirted with the notoriously temptation-prone heir to the throne that gossips were soon speculating about her intentions.[3]

Then, in early May, Stephanie heard that the young baroness was leaving for London. Ostensibly Mary Vetsera was off to visit her aunts Elizabeth, Lady Nugent, and Marie—who lived in London with her second husband, Count Otto von Stockau. Her real motive, gossips insisted, was that she hoped to renew her acquaintance with Rudolf and pursue a liaison with him while they were both in England. "This was too much for me," Stephanie confided to Katharina Schratt. "I refused to go. It could only have meant a new series of humiliations for me!"[4]

Stephanie's refusal to attend the celebrations horrified Franz Josef; he implored his daughter-in-law to change her mind, but to no avail. There was "a most unpleasant scandal," with Rudolf furious and even Queen Victoria supposedly angered at this slight.[5] And so Rudolf went alone to London, participating in the regal processions, the Te Deum at Westminster Abbey, and the state banquet at Buckingham Palace to pay tribute to the continent's longest-reigning monarch, though he spent most of his time with his British counterpart Albert Edward, the Prince of Wales, who equaled him in sexual appetites and a taste for dissipation as they lingered at posh clubs until the early morning hours.[6]

One afternoon the Prince of Wales took Rudolf out to Windsor Castle, where Queen Victoria named her distinguished caller a knight of the Order of the Garter. The queen, Rudolf reported, "was very friendly," pinning the order on his tunic and "fondling me as she did so, so that I could hardly refrain from laughing."[7] But if Rudolf made a good impression at Windsor, elsewhere he seemed out of sorts. Count Karl Kinsky, secretary at the Austro-Hungarian Embassy in London, couldn't help notice how visibly nervous Rudolf seemed during official functions. "There is no mistaking it," he recorded. "I was aware of it before and cannot help noticing it now."[8] The wife of an American diplomat who had previously met Rudolf now saw that he "was changed, looked older, had lost his gaiety, was evidently bored with the official entertaining, and used to escape from all the dinners and receptions as soon as he could."[9]

Perhaps he had good reason to be uneasy. Dinners and receptions at the Austro-Hungarian Embassy meant greeting the guests—and in this case, those guests included Mary Vetsera and her socially ambitious mother, Helene. As Austrian nobles visiting London, they pressed for invitations, knowing that they couldn't be denied without considerable scandal. Not that scandal was an alien concept to the Vetseras: Helene's reputation was so bad that Countess Lajos Károly, the ambassador's wife, let it be known she was disgusted that she had to receive "such people."[10] Rudolf scarcely knew Mary; the idea of meeting her again wouldn't have bothered him. But he had history with her mother, the sort of tangled, sordid history that kept gossips dangerously busy spinning out the lethal web of innuendos on which Viennese society seemed to thrive.

Eight years earlier twenty-year-old Rudolf had been spending the summer with his parents at Gödöllö in Hungary. The surrounding lands teemed with aristocratic country estates, usually filled with members—and would-be members—of the empress's equestrian circle. Among the latter—wealthy, ambitious and always looking for opportunities to advance themselves—were the darkly exotic Baltazzi brothers. All were mad about horses. Alexander, the eldest, owned a renowned stable that included Kisbér, which had won the Derby in 1876; Hector was a lavish gambler and a gentleman jockey of some accomplishment; an officer at Vienna's exclusive Jockey Club, Aristide raised fine thoroughbreds at Napajedla, his Moravian stud; and even Heinrich, the youngest of the four and described as "the most elegant gentleman in the monarchy," was so mad about horses that he built his own jumping course near Pardubice for the family's prized stallions and mares.[11]

The Baltazzis, charming and free with their money, were welcome members of equestrian society: In England they moved in the Prince of Wales's circle, and it was while hunting at Belvoir Castle in Leicestershire in 1874 that Empress Elisabeth had apparently met them for the first time.[12] Alexander Baltazzi was smart enough to befriend the empress's favorite riding companion, Bay Middleton, thus ensuring imperial attention.[13] The brothers deployed the same suave tactics in Hungary, gradually winning an ally in Prince Nikolaus Esterházy, whose estate adjoined Gödöllö. A shared love of horses again brought them to Empress Elisabeth's attention, much to the horror of her lady-in-waiting Countess Marie Festetics. "Great caution is necessary," Festetics had written in her diary. The Baltazzis were "clever people . . . intelligent, rich, and all having the same beautiful, interesting eyes; no one knows exactly where these people come from with all their money, but they are pushing and make me feel uncomfortable. The brothers are devoted to sport, ride splendidly, and shove themselves in everywhere; but they are dangerous to us, because they are quite English, and because of the horses!"[14]

Festetics had her own grudge against the family. That summer of 1879 Aristide and Hector were again staying with Esterházy along with their sister, thirty-two-year-old Baroness Helene Vetsera. As darkly exotic as her brothers were dashing, the married Helene had a troubling reputation: She'd already bedded—at least according to rumor—not only Prince Paul Esterházy but also Marie Festetics's brother Vilmos.[15] Now, learning that Rudolf was staying at Gödöllö, she set her sights on a new prize, renting her own nearby villa and openly pursuing the crown prince.

"Madame Vetsera is in hot pursuit of the Crown Prince," Countess Festetics wrote in her diary. "This ought not to be so very dangerous, for heaven knows she is not good looking, but she is so sly and so glad to make use of everyone. . . . She means to get to Court and advance herself and her family." Even the usually detached emperor was disgusted: "The way that woman goes on about Rudolf is outrageous," he complained. "She chases him wherever he goes. Today she has even given him a present. She will stop at nothing."[16]

Always susceptible to feminine flattery, Rudolf played along with the baroness's game. One night he asked Countess Festetics to invite Helene to Gödöllö. Festetics was horrified. "Oh no, Your Imperial Highness!" she flatly told him. "I cannot allow it. She may make assignations with Your Imperial Highness elsewhere, but not in my sitting room. I have no desire for her society. I have kept her at arm's length so far, and shall continue to do so."[17] The determined baroness apparently succeeded in her quest and bedded a willing Rudolf, but her triumph was short-lived.[18] At first Empress Elisabeth had looked on benignly, knowing—as she explained—that her son found Helene "extremely sympathetic when his thoughts first turned to love."[19] But the baroness's indiscretion and overt ambition led to outrage, and the empress soon brought the relationship to an end.

How had this momentary coup come about? From her birth in 1847, ambition had been bred into the former Helene Baltazzi. The Baltazzis, of Levantine origin, had spent centuries as merchants and bankers; like the Habsburgs, they extended their influence and fortune through propitious marriages. Helene was one of ten children born to Theodor Baltazzi, personal banker to Sultan Abdul Aziz I, and his second wife, Eliza Sarrell, daughter of the English vice consul in Constantinople. Though born in Marseilles, Helene spent much of her youth in the Ottoman capital, where she enjoyed great popularity. This wasn't so much for her appearance: Helene, it is true, was unusual, with dark eyes and hair, but her features were just a bit too sharp, her shoulders a bit too stooped, to be deemed truly beautiful.[20] Rather, her father's immense fortune was Helene's greatest asset; Theodor Baltazzi left his children an estate estimated at 10 million gulden (approximately $64 million in 2017), and Helene was believed to be the wealthiest young woman in Constantinople.[21] There was more than a whiff of ambition on all sides when in 1864—a year after her mother's death—she married her legal guardian, Albin Vetsera, twenty-two years her senior; as Helene was Anglican, the marriage was performed in the chapel of the British Embassy.[22] The thin, balding Vetsera was the Austrian Embassy's secretary to the Ottoman court; Franz Josef had not only named his father, Georg, assistant director of the Imperial and Royal Court of Appeals in Hungary but had also promoted Albin's rise in the diplomatic corps. That kind of imperial attention was promising to an ambitious woman like Helene Baltazzi, while Vetsera no doubt recognized that her fortune would open doors in the future.[23]

Vetsera's diplomatic career kept him moving: counselor and then chargé d'affaires at St. Petersburg in 1868; minister extraordinary at Lisbon in 1869; and Austro-Hungarian minister to the grand duke of Hesse at Darmstadt in 1870.[24] Yet Albin refused to deploy what were arguably his greatest assets: his wife's social ambitions and her fortune, which could cement a diplomat's reputation and standing. Inexplicably Helene apparently never joined her husband at any of his posts and only rarely visited him. This would seem a curious omission, but perhaps a wise one: A diplomat's wife had to be discreet, and Helene had something of a reputation for extramarital intrigues that might have blemished her husband's career with unwanted gossip. Vetsera avoided scandal and reaped the rewards for loyal service to the Habsburgs. In 1867 Franz Josef gave him the Imperial Order of Leopold and raised him to the rank of a hereditary knight in the empire; three years later, on January 30, 1870, he named him a hereditary baron, with the honorific "von" attached to his surname.[25] This was a distinction to be sure, though one that carried little social cachet. "The title of baron," wrote Walburga Paget, "is almost unknown in this society; it is reserved for *haute* finance and is considered especially Semitic."[26]

Throughout his career Vetsera kept his wife in considerable comfort, providing her with a large house at 11 Schüttelstrasse in Vienna in which to raise their two children, a son, Ladislaus, born in 1865, and a daughter, Johanna (called "Hanna" in the family), born in

1868. A second son, Franz (called "Feri"), arrived in 1872, but the most famous of Helene's children was born in the house on Schüttelstrasse on March 19, 1871. Eight days later, at the Church of Saint John Nepomuk, the infant received the names Marie Alexandrine.[27] At the time Vienna, like much of Europe, was caught up in the craze for everything English: Imported scents, soaps, and sweets were the rage; sportsmen hunted in English tweeds; and proper British nannies looked after children. This fad soon transformed Marie Alexandrine into the prosaic but eminently more fashionable Mary.

Custom and expectation dictated a young girl's education in the Victoria era. Even a member of the empire's minor nobility like Mary would never be called upon to fend for herself: The goal was to shape the young girl into a proper—and eligible—young lady. Independent thought and precocious intelligence were discouraged: It was better to be demure, versed in the social niceties needed to attract a future husband than to be threateningly pretentious. In Mary's case tutors tended to reading, writing, history, arithmetic, and religious lessons; Gabriele Tobias offered lessons in singing while her sister Hermine taught piano. Mary learned English from her mother and French from a Paris native, Gabriel Dubray.[28] Dubray later remembered the young Mary as having "a heart of gold," a girl who once handed him a box of candy she had just received as a present, in keeping with her "spirit of generosity."[29]

Albin Vetsera seems to have played little part in his daughter's life. After he retired from the diplomatic service in 1872, his health declined; suffering from what was described as weakness of the lungs, Albin began spending winters in Egypt, away from his family.[30] He was in Egypt when, in 1880, Franz Josef appointed him Austrian commissioner to the Public Debt Commission in Cairo; Helene remained in Vienna. To placate his socially ambitious wife, though, Albin provided his family with a new house, renting an ornate little baroque palace on the Salesianergasse in Vienna's elegant Third District, home to many of the city's foreign embassies.[31]

Left to her own devices, Helene set out to conquer. As minor nobles the Vetseras existed on the very fringes of proper Viennese society, tolerated but excluded from the most prestigious circles. No amount of Baltazzi money could atone for their lack of princely ancestors: Only those boasting the infamous "sixteen quarterings"—eight uninterrupted generations of paternal and maternal noble ancestors—could be received at the imperial court. "The only passport to upper society is pedigree," one diplomat recorded. "Without this passport a native might as well think of getting to the moon as getting into society."[32]

Denied access to the most elite circles, Helene Vetsera pushed her way into the new, more-accepting second tier of society, a nouveau but cosmopolitan mixture of civil servants, low-ranking courtiers, minor nobles, wealthy industrialists, many of them Jews.[33] They used their money to lavish effect, renting palaces along the Ringstrasse, filling them with fine paintings and sculptures, sporting Parisian clothing, and giving expensive dinners and balls.[34] Much of Vienna's entrenched aristocracy looked on such endeavors with suspicion. Regarding this "smart set" as avaricious, scheming social climbers, the old aristocracy turned "away their faces with an expression of disgust and dismay" at the very mention of their names.[35]

Baltazzi money won Helene Vetsera a recognized place in this shadowy world. "All smart Vienna," recorded one aristocrat, "went to the Vetsera Palais, and if the women said horrid things about their hostess, they enjoyed her dinner parties, for she was a thoughtful and tactful woman, who contrived that her guests should always be asked to meet the very people they desired to see. Madame Vetsera's reputation was not what is usually termed good but . . . much is forgiven a woman who spends money in lavishly entertaining other people."[36]

Clad in expensive gowns, armed with a French chef, and profligate in her hospitality, Helene Vetsera soon earned a reputation as one of Vienna's most intriguing, if still suspect, social figures. Her parties, reported the *Wiener Salonblatt*, "were of great interest" to fashionable society.[37] Some of the more adventurous elements willingly crossed Helene Vetsera's threshold, and there were even reciprocal invitations from the German and British ambassadors, but few among Vienna's entrenched aristocracy returned the favor.[38]

And those who did were often seeking entertainment of the sort that irreparably damaged Helene's reputation. Any number of lovers, according to rumor, enjoyed her favors, among them at least one Habsburg archduke.[39] There were whispers of a liaison with either Rudolf's wayward cousin Archduke Otto or the young Archduke Eugen, an affair that supposedly ended in January 1886 with the birth of a daughter, Ilona, who was quickly spirited out of the Vetsera palace and raised by a discreet couple in exchange for financial compensation.[40]

An unexpected tragedy brought Albin back to Vienna at the end of 1881: As a reward for exemplary service, five cadets from Vienna's Rudolf Friess Military Academy—among them sixteen-year-old Ladislaus Vetsera—received complimentary tickets for the December 8 performance of Offenbach's *The Tales of Hoffmann* at the Ringtheater. Gas from the stage lights exploded, and a devastating fire swept through the crowded auditorium. Unable to jam through the exits, people leaped from windows or were trampled in the crush. Ladislaus Vetsera was among the 386 unfortunates burned alive in the conflagration; his body could be identified only after Helene recognized the cuff links her eldest son had worn.[41]

Mary was ten when her brother died, though she seems to have recovered quickly through the buoyancy of youth. To escape any unpleasant memories, the Vetseras took a long lease on Schloss Schwarzau, a seventeenth-century baroque villa in the mountains outside Vienna. There Mary regularly spent her summers, and there, ironically, Austria's last emperor, Karl, would wed his bride, Zita, in 1911.[42] Returning to Vienna in the autumn of 1882, Mary embarked on her secondary education at the Sacre Coeur Institute for Young Ladies, a convent school.[43] In addition to academics, the nuns offered instruction in art and dancing and classes in needlework and etiquette—all that was deemed necessary to arm a young noble lady for her future as a wife and mother.[44]

Mary emerged from her formative years as a young lady of medium height, elegant and self-assured. "Extraordinarily beautiful," was how Princess Catherine Radziwill described her, with "the most magnificent pair of eyes it has ever been my fortune to see."[45] Those eyes were dark—almost as dark as the luxuriant hair Mary kept coiled atop her head to emphasize her neck and shoulders. The solemn, stiff formal photographic portraits of the Victorian era rarely captured undeniable beauty, but surviving images suggest that contemporaries tended to exaggerate Mary's physical attributes. "The Baroness," declared one newspaper, "was not what one would call a classical beauty."[46] Her nose was a bit too small, too retroussé, to be deemed really attractive; her lips were just a bit too full, too red, and her teeth a bit too sharp.[47] Her eyes, it is true, were her best feature, but they were set in an oval face atop a thick neck. "Short and rather stumpy, with one shoulder higher than the other," declared the British ambassador's wife.[48] And Mary had developed rapidly and just a bit too much: Her overgenerous bosom, perhaps captivating to men, lent a slightly unbalanced impression to her figure.[49]

Helene Vetsera, recalled Princess Nora Fugger, "loved Mary very dearly" and favored her over her other children.[50] This caused a good deal of resentment: Mary, said a friend, was "always bickering" with her more sober sister, Hanna, who found her coquettish behavior exasperating.[51] It was the era of the notoriously termed "Pushy Mama," of ambitious women like the American Gilded Age hostess Alva Vanderbilt, who ruthlessly negotiated advantageous marriages for their often unwilling daughters to unite fortunes and ascend the social ladder. Helene's preening attentions using Mary were scarcely maternal, though: Her "one ambition," said Princess Fugger, "was to marry off her youngest daughter well in Viennese society. To this end she used every means."[52] This wasn't lost on

Mary, who from childhood had been relentlessly drilled in the idea that she must marry well and raise her family's social status. "Mama has no love for me!" Mary once complained to a friend. "Ever since I was a little girl, she has treated me like something she means to dispose of to best advantage."[53]

Quick-witted and sharply sly, with a mischievous sense of humor and a light, melodic voice, Mary undoubtedly possessed a certain allure, a magnetic quality that made her the center of attention—much to her delight.[54] But years of favored indulgence had gone to her head: A friend deemed Mary "a spoilt child," with an "impulsive Oriental temper" and an "unstable, nervous and irritable" quality that often led her to indulge in tantrums.[55] "Silly" and "vain," said Walburga Paget, while a courtier remembered Mary as "exceptionally excitable and ambitious."[56] She could play the piano and compose verses in French, but Mary had "literally no intellectual interests."[57] The lack of depth was scarcely Mary's fault: Education and expectation had discouraged such unfashionable pursuits. Aside from expensive clothing, Mary's only passion was secretly devouring the "immoral and highly colored French novels" that her maid, Agnes Jahoda, smuggled to her—"the only reading that interests me," as Mary once confessed to Gabriel Dubray.[58]

This was the singular young woman who arrived in London shortly before Queen Victoria's Golden Jubilee, and whose presence so unnerved Stephanie that she preferred causing scenes and creating offense to watching the baroness chase her husband. Nothing apparently came of the visit, though undoubtedly Rudolf and Mary crossed paths during receptions at the Austro-Hungarian Embassy. Together with her parents and siblings, Mary spent seven hours crowding a windowsill to watch the impressive royal processions to and from Westminster Abbey.[59] Then it was on to Paris, where the family stayed at the Hotel du Rhin on the Place Vendôme. "I am suffocating from the heat in your capital!" Mary wrote to Gabriel Dubray in Vienna. She visited the Louvre, shopped along the Champs-Élysées, and drove through the Bois de Boulogne with other fashionables, though she complained that she only saw "the same people, with the same big hats."[60]

Mary was with her mother and siblings at Schloss Schwarzau that autumn when an urgent telegram arrived from Cairo: On October 28 Albin Vetsera had suffered a stroke. Although Helene and her children left immediately for Egypt, the journey took two weeks. They arrived in Cairo on November 15 only to learn that Albin had died the previous day. Rather than bring the body back to Vienna, Helene had her husband buried in a Catholic cemetery in Cairo.[61]

Settling Vetsera's estate kept Helene and her children in Cairo for three months, months that witnessed Mary's stunning transformation from innocent schoolgirl to sexually provocative young lady. She wasted little time mourning her father: A British diplomat recalled often watching the smiling Mary playing tennis on the court at Shepheard's Hotel.[62] When not thus occupied, she hurled herself with abandon into a series of flaunted love affairs that left gossips scandalized. There was now an "arresting, sensual grace" to her movements as she discovered her power over men.[63] The convent-educated Mary soon prided herself on her seductive gaze, the deliberate sway of her hips, and the "breath of hot sensuality" she radiated.[64]

Mary, said a friend, "was a coquette by instinct . . . immoral in her tendencies" and "amorous by nature," qualities that blossomed beneath the hot Cairo sun.[65] She dressed provocatively, flirted openly, and spoke "quite freely many things that a much older person would have felt embarrassed to speak about," recalled the visiting Princess Catherine Radziwill. Mary's habit of boasting about her romantic conquests not only "jarred on the sense of propriety" but also left the distinct impression "that love, far from being a mystery, was known to her in all its details." While the men fawned, the women condemned: Rather than be shamed, Mary "simply laughed and snapped her fingers at the judgments passed upon her and her conduct."[66] In "romantic and indiscreet letters" to a friend in Austria, Mary bragged of her conquests: By the time she returned to

Vienna in early 1888, as another friend delicately referred to her sexual experiences, Mary was "no longer the innocent girl she had once been."[67]

It was now time to conquer the Habsburg capital; reality, though, was about to teach Mary a harsh and unwelcome lesson. Coveted invitations to court balls or the most exclusive aristocratic parties never came. Wrapped in elegant new ensembles from Paris, a determined Mary joined other young fashionables promenading or parading in carriages each morning and evening along the Ringstrasse and the fashionable Kärntnerstrasse; adorned in extravagant gowns from Maison Spitzer, she attended the opera and theater, though aristocratic tradition kept the Vetseras from taking a box in the exclusive parterre circle.[68] Society columns inevitably recorded her presence at parties and noted her smart clothing. "Baroness Vetsera no longer favors the fox," the *Wiener Salonblatt* informed its readers, reporting that she sported a sable wrap at one event.[69]

But no amount of press could win Mary or her family entrance to functions at the imperial court. In this atmosphere of thwarted ambition, she made a name and reputation for herself—and not the sort of reputation that would help her social advancement. Mary flouted the rules: At a time when even the wealthiest banker in Vienna would never dream of taking tea at exclusive Demel's or dining at the Hotel Imperial for fear of offending aristocratic sensibilities, the young baroness had no such hesitations.[70] She threw herself into the role of demimondaine, a young woman who "satisfied the surface requirements of respectability," wrote the historian Frederic Morton, "while remaining tactically mobile in her attachments. A man could leave her, just as he could leave the sweet girl, but this girl he always left at a higher price than when she had been found."[71]

Mary flirted outrageously, spoke in alluring whispers, and smiled beguilingly, earning a reputation for "amorous frivolity."[72] Viennese gossips entertained themselves with stories of her romantic conquests: Young or elderly, married or single—Mary apparently made no distinctions in her pursuits.[73] Stories hinted about this or that gentleman—a Hungarian, a Pole, an Austrian—liaisons, as Lady Paget noted, that condemned Mary as "a very rapid girl" and that "could only have had one object."[74] Aristocratic Vienna deemed her "a horror, avoided by all," undoubtedly the "fastest" of the city's "fast" women, and condemned as "quite without religion or principle."[75] Mary loved to ice-skate, but prim mothers warned their daughters to avoid her at all costs. If they were skating and the young baroness suddenly appeared, they should flee the ice if they hoped to save their own reputations.[76]

Mary was no innocent, but neither was she a cold, calculating adventuress. A sixteen-year-old schoolgirl, ruled by emotion, driven by excitement, and flattered by the attentions she received, she fell victim not only to her own desires but also to her mother's ambitions. Helene Vetsera, far from evincing concern over her daughter, seems to have deliberately flung Mary at a succession of potential conquests. One day she lured the handsome and eligible Prince Fugger to her palace with assurances that her young daughter was highly sympathetic. In a Victorian age in which chaperones were an indispensable guarantee of moral propriety, Helene played by her own rules. As soon as the prince was seated in her drawing room, Helene introduced Mary and quickly left them alone, shutting the doors behind her. And the moment the doors closed Mary bolted from her place on the sofa and jumped into the prince's lap. It didn't take long before the prince's family objected to such visits, complaining that he was compromising their reputation.[77]

Aside from fashion and romance—the melodramatic, torrid affairs of her favorite French novels and the real-life dangerous games she played with Vienna's male population—Mary's only other interest was horse racing, a taste cultivated by her Baltazzi uncles. Mary haunted the racecourse at Freudenau, at the end of the Prater's long, chestnut-lined Hauptallee. Each spring smart carriages and elegantly attired riders promenaded past wild meadows filled with violets and primroses to the distant music of military bands serenading open-air cafés crowded by society.[78] Freudenau was the place to see and be seen, as sartorial reputations were won or lost and fortunes wagered. The "Turf Angel," people called Mary, a young lady hovering in the stands, sipping Champagne as she admired the handsome horses. And on April 12, 1888, wearing a black cape embroidered with gold panels, she found something else to admire: Crown Prince Rudolf, watching a race from the imperial box.[79]

A renewed acquaintance over Champagne: She flashing her dark eyes and flirting, he taking in the young lady with her overdeveloped bosom—a passing moment for the jaded prince but one rich with fantasies for the teenage baroness, who, like other girls her age, had collected souvenir postcards of Rudolf.[80] Some fiery passion overwhelmed Mary: She rushed home, noted the encounter in her engagement book, and breathlessly told her maid, Agnes, "Today I have seen the Crown Prince. He was so beautiful."[81] She suddenly began speaking about Rudolf "with great enthusiasm," remembered Gabriel Dubray. There was a lightness to her step, a "noticeable change in her attitude and mood."[82] Here was a new, exciting challenge, fraught with the sort of romantic drama that Mary found most appealing. The chase was on.

CHAPTER FIVE

A fever burned in Mary Vetsera's brain as spring turned to summer. Infatuated and intrigued after her encounter with Rudolf, she let her girlish fantasies blossom. Every afternoon she visited the Prater, circling its broad, lushly canopied avenues hoping to spot Rudolf's carriage. The slightest glance or exchanged smile filled her with hope, but as yet there was no real relationship.

In her pursuit of the crown prince, Mary soon found a willing ally in Rudolf's cousin Countess Marie Larisch. The illegitimate daughter of Empress Elisabeth's brother Duke Ludwig in Bavaria and his lover, the actress Henriette Mendel, Marie was born in 1858, a year before her parents finally contracted a morganatic, or unequal, marriage, and King Maximilian II of Bavaria created her mother Baroness Wallersee. Elisabeth felt sorry for her pretty young niece condemned to social ostracism and gradually drew Marie into her enchanted web. Soon the golden haired young lady with "lovely, reckless eyes" became the empress's constant companion, traveling with her, riding with her, and sharing her embittered confidences.[1]

Carefully nurtured to be her aunt's willing slave, Marie acted the part of obedient and mindless companion, all the while existing "in a state of impotent and angry revolt" and "smoldering hatred of the life that she was forced to lead."[2] Countess Marie Festetics resented the Baltazzis; she also resented Elisabeth's niece. "There is something about her that I find uncomfortable," she confided to her diary. "I have a feeling that she is not true, not sincere."[3] Perhaps Festetics had reason to worry: Sixteen-year-old Marie endlessly flirted with her cousin Rudolf: Although the illegitimate daughter of a morganatic union, she seems to have taken the empress's favor as evidence that she would be an acceptable bride for the crown prince. Although she later claimed to dislike Rudolf, Marie apparently showed herself more than amenable to his attentions. With his relaxed approach to appropriate behavior, Rudolf is said to have reciprocated his cousin's affections—a dangerous situation that Empress Elisabeth finally ended in 1877 by arranging Marie's quick marriage to Count Georg von Larisch, a minor aristocratic army officer.[4]

The new Countess Larisch found her husband "disfigured by spots" and "hopelessly dull," but she had no say in the matter and did as the empress demanded.[5] At first she kept herself amused gambling away her husband's minimal fortune; when this ran out and her debts swelled, Marie turned to Rudolf. She knew her cousin's secrets—indeed, she knew where all the family skeletons were buried—and she wasn't shy in deploying gossip to accomplish her goals. Those "lovely, reckless eyes," Rudolf knew, concealed an unlovely, reckless, and spiteful spirit: Larisch was eager to repeat every rumor and cause trouble if it kept her entertained, advanced her position, or brought her money.

Given this vindictive record, it is not surprising that Rudolf was soon handing over money to his unpredictable cousin to cover her debts and keep her quiet. Although Larisch later deemed it "ridiculous" to suggest such a thing, evidence discovered after Rudolf's death proved otherwise.[6] The crown prince's payments bought temporary peace of mind, but he managed to make the episode even more sordid by asking Marie Larisch for favors in return. Introducing new lovers to Rudolf, along with arranging for his liaisons, were said to be among the "certain services" she now provided in exchange for her cousin's financial assistance.[7]

Marie Larisch was no stranger to Mary Vetsera and her family:

Ironically, Empress Elisabeth had first introduced her niece to Helene Vetsera at Gödöllö a decade earlier, and she often saw the baroness on visits to Hungary. By 1883 the morally flexible Marie had embarked on an affair with the baroness's married brother Heinrich, whose hussar regiment was stationed near the Larisch estate at Pardubice.[8] Soon enough Larisch found herself pregnant with Baltazzi's child, though jealousy erupted when she learned that he was simultaneously carrying on an affair with the actress Jenny Gross. One night in the winter of 1883, according to Marie Festetics, both of Heinrich Baltazzi's lovers unexpectedly came face-to-face at the opera in Vienna. No shrinking violet, the pregnant Larisch hurled insults at the actress, and startled onlookers had to separate the two women as they literally came to blows on the staircase.[9]

In November 1884 Larisch gave birth to Baltazzi's daughter, Marie Henriette; his son, Heinrich Georg, followed in February 1886. The compliant Georg von Larisch never questioned their paternity, though many in the capital knew of his wife's infidelity.[10] Friends with Helene, lover of Heinrich Baltazzi, and mother to Mary's two illegitimate cousins—Marie Larisch was thus deeply tied to the Vetseras, who were not shy in attempting to use her privileged entrée to the imperial court to advance their social positions and higher goals.

These two ambitious, morally bankrupt women, Helene and Marie, formed a dangerous and ultimately deadly alliance. Although Helene Vetsera later declared that the countess had "abused her trust" and acted "under false pretexts" by facilitating a liaison between Rudolf and Mary, the baroness knew what Larisch was doing.[11] Having apparently succeeded in bedding the crown prince a decade earlier, Helene Vetsera now seems to have pushed her youngest daughter to follow in her footsteps. One thing, as Larisch wrote, seems clear: Helene Vetsera was "fully aware" of Mary's infatuation and treated it "as a great joke."[12] Count Anton Monts, counselor at the German Embassy in Vienna, which regularly opened its doors to the Vetseras, also agreed that Helene Vetsera was well informed about the affair from its inception.[13]

Larisch, for her part, insisted that Mary had sought out Rudolf on her own and that she was surprised to learn of their relationship.[14] This is nonsense. Marie Larisch was more than willing to promote an affair—in exchange for money. Helene Vetsera showered her with bribes and expensive gowns from the leading Paris couturier, Charles Worth: When even these rewards proved insufficient for the avaricious Larisch, she blackmailed Mary, once demanding that the young girl give her 25,000 gulden (approximately $159,750 in 2017) if she ever wanted to see Rudolf again. As soon as she received the money, though, the countess demanded another 10,000 gulden ($63,900) to further the liaison—all while she continued to bleed Rudolf of considerable sums as well.[15]

The only true innocent in this sordid affair, if any innocence indeed existed, was Mary herself. Victimized and used by her mother and Marie Larisch, she became an unwitting—if naively willing—pawn in their dangerous misadventure. And, despite what both Helene Vetsera and Marie Larisch claimed, that misadventure began in the spring of 1888.[16] For a time Mary was completely reliant on Larisch to facilitate meetings with Rudolf. The countess usually collected Mary from her mother's palace every few days, either in the late morning to go shopping or in the afternoons to join her in the Prater, but inevitably these excursions took her to see the crown prince.[17] "Marie Larisch has departed," she confided to Hermine Tobias, "and so I could not see him. I am dying of longing and cannot wait until she returns. . . . I count the hours, because since meeting and talking to him my love has only deepened. I've been thinking day and night how I could see him."[18]

Every encounter only fueled Mary's imagination. "I cannot live without having seen or spoken to him," she confessed to Tobias. There were "accidental" encounters while driving in the Prater. Rudolf, Mary insisted, came only to see her.[19] The blossoming affair was scarcely a secret: Once Stephanie discreetly followed her husband to the Prater and saw him with Larisch and Mary.[20] "Rudolf is meeting this girl here in Vienna!" she complained to Katharina

Schratt. Mary, the crown princess declared, "ought to be packed off to school or somewhere where she'd be taught to respect the holy commandments!"[21]

In June 1888 Helene Vetsera took her two daughters off to England. Mary was reluctant to go, and Rudolf was never far from her mind. To Gabriel Dubray she confessed: "I am still in a dream state after having left Vienna, and now being so far away, so far away. I left with a heavy heart, and hope to return soon to the homeland. It is funny, when you are away, to see things how they are."[22]

English society had always proved less difficult to crack than the archaic and ossified aristocracy of Vienna. Helene's sister Elizabeth had married Albert, 3rd Baron Nugent, and Baltazzi connections to the racing crowd opened doors to the fashionable circle dominated by the Prince of Wales. One Austrian diplomat met the Vetseras at Claridge's Hotel in London and arranged for them to attend several balls being given by the Prince and Princess of Wales at Marlborough House; Mary, "a striking looking girl, with beautiful eyes and a charming manner," the prince recalled, "enjoyed herself immensely."[23] When the heir to the British throne left for a holiday at Bad Homburg in Germany in August, the Vetseras followed, Helene renting the elegant Villa Imperiale to ensure social prominence. Maureen Alleen, a visiting American, briefly befriended Mary at the resort. The young baroness, she thought, was "highly approved of by society, but was very serious. Although unselfish in her manner, people gave her credit for not taking love lightly but rather quite seriously."[24] Just how seriously Mary took her romantic quest that summer remains a mystery, but she certainly made an impression on the Prince of Wales. Mary, he wrote, was "a charming young lady, and certainly one of the prettiest."[25]

By early September, with Mary back in Vienna, her mother thought that the fire smoldering in her heart for the crown prince had "fanned into a bright flame."[26] "Do not think that I have forgotten him," Mary wrote to Hermine Tobias. "I love him even more intimately."[27]

Returning from Pardubice early that autumn of 1888, Marie Larisch found that the affair had flourished in her absence. Mary admitted that she'd written to Rudolf confessing her love, and that one September midnight a meeting had quickly been arranged. To evade nosy servants, she'd taken her maid, Agnes—whose father was the porter at the Vetsera Palace—into her confidence. Mary had slipped out and gone to Rudolf wearing only a fur coat over her filmy nightgown. Mary claimed it was innocent, but Larisch wasn't convinced.[28] The fur coat over the nightgown was a salacious detail that, with a stunning lack of gentlemanly tact, the crown prince freely shared with his brother-in-law, Prince Philipp of Coburg, and his cousin Archduke Otto.[29] It all must have seemed quite amusing to his rather dissolute confidants, but also suggests that Rudolf had little regard for Mary's reputation.[30]

According to Larisch the entire Vetsera household was in an uproar over the relationship. Helene Vetsera complained that Mary "is really not well," while Hanna called her sister "a stupid child" to believe "she is in love with the Crown Prince. You can't imagine anything so silly, and she has no idea how ridiculous it is." If their mother had any sense, Hanna announced, she "would thrash Mary."[31] Mary positively bubbled with excitement over the relationship: "I know it is only a happy dream from which I shall have to awaken one day," she confessed. Larisch was furious. Losing control over the situation lessened her importance as an agent for the liaison and her ability to extort money. All this "happily ever after" talk was too absurd. She was even more irate that Mary had taken Agnes into her confidence. Larisch had heard rumors that Agnes was openly sleeping with several of Mary's Baltazzi uncles—perhaps even the countess's own lover, Heinrich.[32]

Helene tried to conceal her daughter's liaison behind Mary's rumored romance with Duke Miguel of Braganza, a handsome, thirty-five-year-old Portuguese widower and a Habsburg relative then serving in the Austrian army.[33] His ties to the Habsburgs were strong: One sister, Maria Josépha, had married Empress Elisabeth's brother Karl Theodor, while another, Maria Theresa, became the third wife of Franz Josef's brother Karl Ludwig. In 1877 Miguel had married the empress's niece Princess Elisabeth of Thurn und Taxis, a first cousin to both Rudolf and Larisch. Elisabeth bore him two sons but died in 1881 shortly after giving birth to their daughter. In the 1880s Miguel's dragoon regiment was stationed at Schwarzau, and he began spending holidays with Helene and her children at their villa there.[34] By 1888 he seems to have turned his amorous attentions to Mary, who, true to her reputation, is said to have shared the lonely duke's bed.[35]

It was all temporarily diverting; Mary even once derided the duke as "stupid" and insisted to Larisch that he "knows all about my affair with the Crown Prince."[36] Yet Helene seems to have had other ideas. Knowing that the liaison with Rudolf would inevitably end, she cynically used the duke of Braganza to divert attention from her daughter's affair with the crown prince while at the same time hoping that the widowed Miguel might think Mary a suitable wife. This was unlikely. Although he'd assured the succession with two sons, Miguel was titular head of the House of Braganza. "I am sure my grandfather," says his grandson Dom Duarte de Bragança, "never intended to marry Miss Vetsera, since his family, the Portuguese royalists, and his Austrian friends would not have accepted it."[37]

Spurred by her ambitious mother and fed by a taste for steamy French novels, Mary began to see herself as the heroine in an epic royal romance. Although she may not have read such classics as Alexandre Dumas's *La Dame aux Camélias* or Gustave Flaubert's *Madame Bovary*, their themes of suffering, melodramatic love, and atonement by death had infused even the most excessive of Gallic novels and likely influenced Mary's overwrought romanticism. For her it didn't matter that Rudolf was fast losing his youthful vigor and pleasing appearance: He was still the heir to the throne, wealthy, and at the top of the social ladder. Girlish fantasies began to fill Mary's head: Rudolf would annul his marriage to Stephanie and ask her to share his throne. "That stupid Crown Princess knows

I am her rival!" Mary smugly told Larisch.[38] She delighted in mocking Stephanie and her sister, Louise: "Did you ever see anything so ugly as those two Belgians?" she demanded of the countess. "They've no figures; they are just like bundles of hay tied in the middle."[39] Mary's eyes "looked positively evil" whenever she mentioned Stephanie's name.[40]

A lot of ink has been spilled to explain Rudolf's apparently enduring interest. With more than a hint of misplaced misogyny, those who loathed Stephanie contended that Mary offered a potent counterbalance to Rudolf's cold, imperious, and unsympathetic wife, who "nagged and pushed" him into more convivial arms.[41] Rudolf's increasingly troubled state, insists another argument, left him unable to "resist the spell" of Mary's "charm and passion."[42] Mary, Frederic Morton speculated, "kindled in the Crown Prince a necessity unknown to him until then. He had begun to need a woman who could offer him more than surrender. He needed to be embraced by a mystery."[43]

But what mystery could a willing, immature seventeen-year-old girl possibly hold for the worldly crown prince? Rudolf didn't need a sympathetic feminine confidante and lover: He already had one in Mitzi Caspar, whom he continued to see regularly throughout his affair with Mary. Rudolf certainly found Mary attractive and entertaining. She offered her companionship and her body—and Rudolf took both. But Mary wasn't an intellectual who could share Rudolf's dilettantish political ideas, discuss philosophy, or argue about the future of the monarchy. In truth Rudolf treated this new liaison in much the same way as those that had come before it, taking whatever Mary gave in an effort to find temporary escape. His youth was behind him: He had no meaningful role to play and increasingly viewed his life as a failure. Mary's credulous fawning not only offered assurance that he mattered but also appealed to Rudolf's vanity. Even so he admitted to Marie Larisch that Mary's breathless romanticism was often more of an annoyance than a reward, adding that it was difficult not "to despise this poor little girl's affection." Mary, Rudolf explained forthrightly, was "just a woman who loves me. I've known many far more beautiful, but I have never met with one more faithful."[44]

The lovers met throughout the autumn of 1888, "much more frequently" than they admitted, Larisch recalled in annoyance.[45] Rudolf and Mary would "accidentally" encounter each other while the latter was with Larisch in the Prater; as soon as she spotted Rudolf's carriage, Mary fled her chaperone and climbed into the privacy of his fiacre as Bratfisch drove through the park.[46] The countess offered use of her suite at the Grand Hotel, but, suspicious of his cousin's motives, Rudolf wanted something with more privacy. One day he cornered his friend Eduard Palmer, a Viennese banker who kept an apartment on the Ringstrasse across from the Grand Hotel. "Please give me the key to your rooms," the crown prince asked Palmer. "I have a discreet rendezvous and should like to use your rooms. But take care that nobody is there."[47] Palmer loyally complied, and soon Rudolf and Mary were regularly meeting at the banker's apartment.[48]

That autumn of 1888 the Prince of Wales paid an extended visit to Vienna. Attending a race at Freudenau with Rudolf, the British heir spotted Mary Vetsera strolling about the tea pavilion. Having previously met and admired her in Homburg, the prince pointed Mary out to Rudolf and offered to introduce them; aware that the crowd was watching, Rudolf bowed his head politely and quickly moved away.[49] He repeated this charade a few days later. On October 12 Rudolf and Stephanie attended the final performance at the old Burgtheater. By now most of aristocratic Vienna had heard of the affair, and the audience seemed most amused when Mary Vetsera took her seat in the theater and stared quite openly and obviously at the imperial box.[50]

Two days later the Prince of Wales joined the imperial family for the inaugural performance at the new Burgtheater. Architects, builders and artists had labored for fourteen years to create this elaborate building, with its four thousand electric lights and stairway ceilings decorated by Gustav Klimt. A uniformed Franz Josef appeared in the imperial box to the strains of "God Save Our Emperor"; Empress Elisabeth was, as usual, absent, but Rudolf, wearing the uniform of the 10th Infantry Regiment, and Stephanie—in a blue brocade gown trimmed with white lace and adorned with diamonds at her throat and in her hair—escorted the Prince of Wales to the row of gilded armchairs.[51] A triumphant Mary Vetsera watched the scene from her mother's box; she wore a décolleté white tulle gown, with a diamond crescent in her dark hair. "Many an admiring glance," reported the following day's *Wiener Tagblatt*, was cast in her direction, and Mary's appearance "provoked widespread admiration."[52] But when the Prince of Wales pointed her out to Rudolf, saying "how handsome" Mary looked, the crown prince evinced disdain and "spoke, I thought, disparagingly of her."[53]

On November 5 Larisch collected Mary in her carriage from the Vetsera Palace. They went shopping, then drove to the studio of the fashionable Viennese society photographer Adele, where, dressed in black, they had their pictures taken, "*for him*, of course," Mary confided to Hermine Tobias. Bratfisch waited with Rudolf's carriage at the Grand Hotel's rear entrance; the pair climbed in, wrapping feather boas around their necks to shield their faces, and, "at a great pace" set off for the Hofburg. The carriage stopped at the palace's old Augustiner Bastion, where Rudolf's *Kammerdiener* (valet) Karl Neuhammer waited by a small iron door. The two ladies followed the same circuitous route that Rudolf used to escape the Hofburg: along a dark corridor and up a steep staircase to a rooftop terrace and a glassed-in porch opening into the crown prince's bachelor apartments.[54]

Although Larisch omitted this visit from her narrative, Mary described the event in her letter to Hermine Tobias.[55] As the two women entered Rudolf's rooms a pet raven swooped down with fluttering wings, alerting his master to their arrival. "Won't you please come in, ladies," he called from his Turkish salon. The trio, or so Mary claimed, chatted idly about Viennese society before

Rudolf asked to speak to Larisch privately. Left alone to examine the exotic room, Mary walked over to Rudolf's desk. A revolver lay on the blotter, but it was a polished human skull that riveted her attention. Mary was turning the skull over in her hands when Rudolf reappeared and quickly took it from her. "When I said that I was not at all afraid," she reported to Hermine, "he smiled." In her "happy letter" to Hermine, Mary swore her former piano teacher to secrecy, melodramatically protesting that if her mother or sister learned of the visit, "I would have to kill myself."[56]

Was this Mary's first visit to the Hofburg? This, at least, is what both Mary's mother and Rudolf's friend and hunting companion Count Josef Hoyos later suggested.[57] Hoyos—perhaps out of loyalty—insisted that Mary only visited the Hofburg five times, but Bratfisch later estimated that he secretly delivered her to the palace on at least twenty different nights.[58] This must have included the time she came to Rudolf in September, wearing only a fur coat over her nightgown. Her visits were so frequent that, even today, a small flight of steps leading to Rudolf's former apartments is known as the Vetsera Staircase.[59] And, if "accidental" encounters in the Prater were innocent, it's unlikely the same can be said of Rudolf and Mary's midnight meetings, assignations in Eduard Palmer's apartment, or reunions in the privacy of the Hofburg. Sometime that autumn Rudolf seems to have commissioned a portrait of his latest lover, a painting depicting a nude Mary Vetsera in all her seductive glory—a provocative bit of art that left little doubt as to what he temporarily found so diverting in the young baroness.[60]

Mary convinced herself that Rudolf was desperately in love. As evidence, she wrote to Hermine Tobias that, in a letter, he had insisted that "he could not live without her and would go mad if he could no longer see her." But she couldn't provide the actual letter: Larisch, Mary complained, took all of Rudolf's correspondence back from her as soon as she'd read it.[61]

"If we could live together in a hut we would be happy," Mary wrote to Tobias. "We always talk about how happy it would make us. But unfortunately it is not to be. If I could give my life for him I would gladly do so, for what does my life mean to me? We have made a pact toward this possibility."[62] And Rudolf apparently commemorated this pact—however loosely made or unrealistic it may have been—by giving his lover a ring made of plain, inexpensive iron. Mary prized the trinket, wearing it on a chain around her neck and referring to it as a "wedding ring." Engraved inside the band were the initials ILVBIDT for the phrase *In Liebe Vereint bis in den Tod* (United by Love Until Death).[63]

Triumph drove Mary's behavior in these months as she spiraled out of control. The affair, conducted according to Rudolf's terms and schedule, thrived in a hothouse atmosphere that amplified every development. It isn't surprising that the immature young woman took a perverse delight in causing deliberate public scenes. When Rudolf attended a performance by Sarah Bernhardt at the Theater an der Wien, Mary was front and center in her mother's box, staring openly at her lover as the audience watched her every move.[64] Then there was the night she appeared at the opera in an extremely low-cut gown of white crepe de chine accented with diamonds. "I think you display very questionable taste in flaunting yourself," Larisch warned the young baroness, but to no avail: Mary was determined to attract attention, knowing that Stephanie would also be present. When Rudolf entered the imperial box with his wife, Mary fixed the crown princess with "an insolent gaze." Not to be outdone, and "with a refinement of maliciousness," Stephanie proudly leveled her opera glasses and stared back as the auditorium erupted in whispers.[65]

Nor was Rudolf discreet. One evening he and Stephanie attended a dinner party given by her sister Louise and her husband, Prince Philipp of Coburg. "There was naturally much gossip current in Vienna about the liaison that existed between Rudolf and Mary Vetsera," Louise recalled. "I was not afraid to mention this delicate subject to Rudolf, and I expressed my hopes that the gossip was exaggerated." Yet, with Stephanie sitting across the table from him,

Rudolf quietly pulled out a cigarette case and opened it for Louise: Within he'd placed a miniature of Mary Vetsera. Louise was horrified—not that Rudolf had acted so brazenly but because he had done so "with the servants present."[66]

On December 11, 1888, Richard Wagner's Ring Cycle opened with a performance of *Das Rheingold* at the Imperial Opera House; claiming that she hated Wagner, Mary excused herself from joining her mother and sister. Instead she waited until they left for the opera and then slipped out of her mother's house. Bratfisch waited in a fiacre around the corner and took her to see Rudolf at Schönbrunn, the Habsburg summer palace on the outskirts of Vienna.[67] She repeated this ploy on December 17 and again four days later, when Bratfisch delivered her to the Hofburg.[68] It was the last time the lovers met that year. When they reunited a month later, the affair would take an ominous, ultimately fatal turn.

CHAPTER SIX

On August 21, 1888—in the midst of his affair with Mary Vetsera—Rudolf had turned thirty. "The age of thirty marks a dividing point in life," he had written to a friend, "and one that is not too pleasant, either. Much time has passed, spent more or less usefully, but empty as far as real acts and successes are concerned. We are living in a time of slow, drawn-out rottenness. . . . Each year makes me older, less fresh, and less efficient. . . . And this eternal preparing of oneself, this constant waiting for great times of reform, wears out one's creative power. . . . However, I must believe in the future. I hope and count on the next ten years."[1]

Three days earlier Rudolf had suffered through a stifling charade of familial happiness when Franz Josef celebrated his fifty-eighth birthday at Bad Ischl. With his graying, bushy whiskers and mustache, the emperor personified the unchanging traditions his son despised; unable to contain his irritation, Rudolf offended everyone by denouncing his father's beloved alpine resort as "a frightful hole."[2] The empire's crown prince was tired of waiting—waiting for his father's approval, waiting for a meaningful role, waiting for a change in the country's cautious, conservative politics. On the morning of his own birthday Rudolf gave vent to long-simmering frustrations with a gesture of contempt, shaving off his beard and leaving only a long mustache modeled on those worn by Hungarian hussars.[3]

The rebellious meaning was clear: Rudolf had broken with his father, with his conservative politics, and with Austria.

This rebellion had been long in coming. Great hopes burdened Rudolf's thin shoulders. He would be "a Habsburg philosopher on the throne," the "head of all modern thought," someone who would use his "striking intellectual gifts and unusual abilities" to fundamentally transform his father's archaic empire.[4] "He knew," insisted a courtier, "that his father's policy of hesitation and half measures could be pernicious to the monarchy," and wanted "to open wide the firmly closed windows of the Imperial Palace and let in bright, refreshing air."[5] Viewing intellectuals and a prosperous middle class as guarantors of the empire's survival, Rudolf entertained himself with visions of breaking Vienna's centralized power in favor of increased regional and ethnic autonomy. He rebelled against anything that smacked of conservatism or carried a whiff of religious influence, and summed up this mood in his first will, written in April 1879: "I have trodden a different path from that of most of my relations, but always from the purest motives. Our age requires new points of view. Everywhere, especially in Austria, there is reaction, which is the first step toward a downfall. Those who preach reaction are the most dangerous enemies."[6]

Among those "dangerous enemies" was Franz Josef's prime minister, Count Eduard von Taaffe, who held the post from 1879 to 1893. Taaffe hailed from an Irish family that had immigrated to Austria during the Thirty Years' War and served at court and in the military. The emperor had known him since childhood, when the two boys often played together; Taaffe was the only person outside the imperial family allowed to call the emperor by his first name, though he was rigidly correct, addressing him publicly as "Your Majesty."[7] Taaffe walked a fine line between mild reform and reactionary repression. "Muddling along in the old rut," was how one wit characterized the prime minister's opportunistic program of granting illusory autonomy to competing nationalities to keep them dependent on the throne.[8] This brought temporary stability but at a price:

Taaffe ruthlessly crushed opposition and unwelcome hints of liberalism: In his first year as prime minister, 635 newspapers alone were seized and destroyed.[9]

"Taaffe's manure heap," Rudolf called the prime minister's political alliances, composed of "crafty schemers" filled with "fanaticism, delusion, stupidity, infinite cunning, lack of principle, every unpatriotic feeling, Jesuit adroitness and boundless lust for power."[10] In December 1881 Rudolf had boldly given his father a twenty-page memorandum outlining the dangers he perceived in Taaffe's policies and asked that the prime minister be removed from office.[11] "I can see plainly the slope down which we are slipping backwards," he had confided to Latour von Thurmberg; "I am intimately connected with affairs but can do absolutely nothing; I may not even speak up to express my feelings and beliefs." Taaffe, he complained, did not "even admit my right to hold an independent opinion," and dismissed him as "insolent and a rebel." His father's attitudes—"clerical, intransigent, distrustful"—led Rudolf to fear for the future. The memorandum, he insisted, contained "nothing of rebellion: it is not the voice of one who desires the limelight but is the voice of distress, giving counsel. . . . Will the Emperor take this little work seriously, or will he just glance through it in the evening before retiring and lay it in a file, taking it as the eccentricity of a dreamer?"[12]

As Rudolf had feared, Franz Josef did not even bother to acknowledge his son's memorandum. Rudolf fought back. His network of friends and advisers included not only professors and philosophers but also radicals and his father's political opponents. Now he used his friendship with Moritz Szeps, the Jewish editor of the popular liberal newspaper *Neues Wiener Tagblatt*, to advance his own agenda. Rudolf had first met Szeps in 1880; intrigued by the editor's liberal ideas, he began writing anonymous articles for the newspaper critical of the empire's policies and foreign alliances. This didn't remain a secret for long: Rudolf's every move was shadowed. "They are becoming very watchful and suspicious of me," he confided to Szeps, "and every day I see more clearly the narrow circle of espionage, denunciations and supervision surrounding me."[13]

Rudolf had a tendency toward paranoia, but in this case his fears were well founded. One particularly watchful enemy was his own great-uncle Archduke Albrecht, Inspector General of the Imperial and Royal Armed Forces. Humorless and deeply conservative, he regarded it as a sacred duty to preserve Habsburg honor and prestige.[14] Rudolf had a prickly relationship with the elderly archduke: Albrecht, the crown prince complained to his cousin Franz Ferdinand, "loves poking his nose about, picking quarrels, intriguing, and doing harm, for he is malicious."[15] Rudolf soon learned that Albrecht was actively spying on him, intercepting most of his correspondence and forwarding it to the emperor. "All journalists," Albrecht warned Franz Josef, "are Jews conspiring against man's most sacred heritage"; Szeps, "a thief and a swindler," was filling the crown prince's head with untenable political notions.[16]

Officialdom retaliated: To silence Rudolf, the government closed Szeps's newspaper. "We have embarked on a catastrophic policy and it seems that no one can alter it now," Rudolf complained. "We are being driven into darkness by fate, and it's partly the work of the Jesuits, who are closely connected with all the most influential members of the Imperial Family."[17] In 1885 a mob led by Georg von Schönerer, head of the anti-Semitic German National Party, broke into the offices of the *Neues Wiener Tagblatt*, vandalized equipment, and beat the employees. Szeps was actually found guilty of having libeled Schönerer and spent several months in prison. Rudolf felt responsible: When Szeps was released, the crown prince gave his friend money to found a new newspaper, the *Wiener Tagblatt*, in which he continued to promote his liberal ideas.[18]

"In Austria," Rudolf complained, "I belong to the least informed group."[19] He was pointedly "excluded from all political information"; the lowest chamberlain at court, he believed, "has a wider influence on activities than do I. I am condemned to idleness."[20] Franz Josef tried to appease his son by ordering Austria's foreign minister, Count Gustav Kálnoky, and the departmental head of the Ministry of the Royal Household and of Foreign Affairs for Hungary, Ladislaus von Szögyény-Marich, to begin briefing his heir on the empire's foreign policies.[21] He also named Rudolf inspector general of the infantry in early 1888. But neither effort succeeded. Rudolf indiscreetly began sharing confidential political information with Szeps and others in his circle, and diplomatic secrets leaked out and appeared in the pages of Vienna's newspapers. When word of this inevitably got back to the Hofburg, Franz Josef ordered that his ministers were to brief his son only on minor issues and provide him with outdated documents.[22] And Rudolf's post as inspector general of the infantry carried no power, only demands that he attend reviews and visit regiments: It was busywork, meant to occupy his time and keep him out of trouble.[23] This much Rudolf learned when his father barred him from military councils and refused him any say in important decisions.[24]

Franz Josef never understood his son or appreciated his talents, which were considerable. In 1878, working with the economist Karl Menger, Rudolf had produced a provocative—and anonymously published—critique of Austria's aristocrats, deriding their idleness and deeming them frivolous hedonists unfit to serve whether as army officers or as high government officials.[25] Rudolf was able to put his name to the 1883 publication of *Fifteen Days on the Danube*, an engaging chronicle of one of his hunting expeditions, which won him an honorary doctorate from Vienna University.[26] In 1884 he published an account of his 1881 journey to the Middle East, in which he more fully displayed a gifted literary style, but he soon turned his attention inward, producing the first part of a multivolume encyclopedic work, *Die Österreichisch-ungarische Monarchie in Wort und Bild* (The Austro-Hungarian Monarchy in Words and Pictures), meant to chronicle his father's empire. Franz Josef was so surprised by the erudite tone of his son's introduction that he insultingly asked if Rudolf had really written the words.[27]

Rudolf's complaint was that of royal heirs the world over: lack of a "proper" job. Queen Victoria, disappointed in her eldest son's wayward behavior, refused to allow the Prince of Wales any meaningful role, while in Prussia the elderly Kaiser Wilhelm I clung tenaciously to his throne as his ambitious, liberal-minded heir, Friedrich Wilhelm, languished in the shadows of power even as cancer consumed him. A life of indolence, with Rudolf reduced to the role of decorative prop at his father's court, stretched out before the crown prince.[28] His own belief in the providential nature of his position made Franz Josef temperamentally unsuited to share power, and he expected his heir to conform to and support his ideas. But father and son were poles apart when it came to their political views: Rudolf's embrace of liberalism, though born of conviction, seemed a personal affront, a rejection of all that the emperor believed and held dear. Franz Josef had treated his brother Maximilian in much the same way. "My individuality," the archduke once declared, "does not fit the views of my older brother; he lets me feel this on every occasion in a most unequivocal, inconsiderate and insulting manner."[29]

"The Emperor," Latour von Thurmberg complained, "could have intervened most successfully if he had kept the Crown Prince's mind occupied, initiated him into the business of government, and made him play his part. Serious, productive work would have taken up the whole of the Crown Prince's time."[30] Latour von Thurmberg, though, was being too optimistic. Although Rudolf posed as a deep-thinking intellectual, his political convictions were often rashly formed and poorly considered. He had vision and talent, but he was too impatient and never appreciated his father's steadfast approach—born of experience—to political issues. Rudolf wanted immediate change. While promoting himself as an enlightened prince seeking equality, he could not see beyond the narrow scope of preserving Habsburg rule as necessary for the empire's continuation. In publicly agitating against his father, and by sharing sensitive political and diplomatic information, Rudolf destroyed his father's trust and undermined Franz Josef's one attempt to involve his son in governmental affairs.

Rudolf remained a man without power or influence. Heir to one of Europe's oldest royal dynasties, he was forbidden to exercise his intellect or explore his political ideas. Convinced that nothing would change, that he was—until his father died—condemned to a twilight world as a passive onlooker, Rudolf grew embittered and sank into depression. Temporarily reunited with her mercurial husband on a joint visit to Sarajevo in the summer of 1888, Stephanie saw "an alarming change" in Rudolf: "It was not only that he was more restless and distraught than before," she wrote. "In addition he had become prone to outbursts of fierce anger upon the most trifling occasions. I had long become accustomed to the fact that the conventionalities of our life together as husband and wife, especially as our relationship found expression in his letters, contrasted glaringly with Rudolf's actual everyday behavior. Now however he was often quite unrecognizable. His inward disorganization led to terrible attacks of wrath, to intolerable and undignified scenes. It was as if, with the loss of inward stability, he had also lost any sense of good form. On such occasions he would not hesitate to talk to me openly about his distasteful amours."[31]

It wasn't just an embittered wife who noticed the change. A few months earlier Marie Valerie had confided to her diary: "Rudolf stares at us, particularly at Mama and me, with glances of such deep and bitter hate that one is overcome with a feeling of anxiety. Even Gisela, whose sober views certainly don't lend themselves to imagination and whose love for Rudolf tends always to embellish his behavior, confessed . . . she was frightened herself by his stare and eventually all three of us broke out in tears. . . . This odd, unexplainable hatred of Rudolf's casts a dark shadow over our future."[32]

A growing sense of menace now surrounded Rudolf. Restless and irritable, he rarely slept more than four or five hours a night.[33] Headaches, painful joints, and eye infections—symptoms of his gonorrhea—recurred with uncomfortable regularity.[34] Rudolf was now giving himself half-gram injections of morphine several times a day; when his court physician, Hermann Widerhofer, suggested that he cut the amount to a quarter gram, Rudolf ignored him and actually increased the dosage.[35] He was also downing copious amounts of Cognac and Champagne until drunk; more than once members of his suite had to intervene and whisk the crown prince away from some ceremony before he caused a scandal.[36]

Rudolf's life spiraled into chaos that autumn of 1888. There had been no invitation to attend the spring Army High Command conference, and he was excluded from the autumn meeting as well.[37] Frustrated, Rudolf submitted a report to his father suggesting military reforms; Franz Josef passed it on to Archduke Albrecht, who in his reply derided the crown prince's ideas as attempts to "make up" for his own "deficiencies" as inspector general of the infantry.[38]

An incident that autumn reinforced Rudolf's sense of despair. He'd once placed great hopes on the accession of his Prussian counterpart, the liberal Crown Prince Friedrich Wilhelm, envisioning a time after Franz Josef's death when together they could reshape European politics. Unfortunately fate intervened. When old Kaiser Wilhelm I died in 1888 and his son took the throne as Friedrich III, the new emperor was already dying of throat cancer. After a reign of just three months, Friedrich's premature death placed his son on the German throne as Wilhelm II. Rudolf had long despised the brash, militaristic new kaiser, and the feeling was mutual. Rudolf, Wilhelm rather hypocritically complained, "did not take religion at all seriously and it pained me when he poured out his mordant wit not only on the church and clergy but also on the simple faith of the country folk."[39]

Kaiser Wilhelm II visited Vienna that October of 1888. During a routine military inspection he belittled Rudolf's infantry and complained that their newly adopted Mannlicher rifles were unfit for use in any armed conflict. As the head of Austria-Hungary's principal military ally, the kaiser wanted Rudolf stripped of his position as inspector general. Unwilling to provoke the volatile young kaiser, Franz Josef gave in and asked his son to resign. Rudolf angrily refused.[40] Soon a spate of unflattering articles highly critical of Rudolf began appearing in the German press. There were veiled references to an unnamed "august personage" in Austria who not only hated Germans and Germany but who was also leading a remarkably dissolute life—charges picked up and reprinted in certain French and Italian journals. True to form, Rudolf fired back, anonymously writing anti-Prussian articles for the *Wiener Tagblatt* and for a new Austrian journal, *Schwarz-Gelb* (Yellow-Black), which he helped fund.[41] Rudolf also let his friend Moritz Szeps know that the young kaiser was then embroiled in an affair with an Austrian woman of dubious reputation, who had stolen Wilhelm's monogrammed cuff links as proof. If the attacks in the German papers didn't stop, Rudolf suggested, Szeps should publish the damning information about Wilhelm II.[42]

"I no longer find it within me to worry about anything at all," Rudolf confided to Latour von Thurmberg that October.[43] His mental detachment from previous interests, friends, and pursuits increased as the months passed.[44] "The pursuit of high ideals has died within me," Rudolf wrote to Szeps in November.[45] And his behavior had grown increasingly reckless. In January he'd been out shooting with his father at Höllgraben when he carelessly discharged his rifle: The bullet missed Franz Josef by mere inches and seriously wounded a beater in the arm.[46] Furious, the emperor barred his son from shooting the following day and refused to speak to him. According to Stephanie he suspected that Rudolf had meant to kill him and disguise it as an accident; afraid of his son, the emperor now avoided Rudolf and would see him only if others were present.[47]

By the autumn of 1888 the few remaining members of Rudolf's circle found him nervous and antagonistic.[48] "The Crown Prince recently took supper with me," wrote Franz Karl, Prince Khevenhüller-Metsch. "He then lay on the sofa in the library smoking and drinking sherry. He babbled away incongruously about liberty and equality, railed against the nobility for representing an attitude whose time had passed and stated that his preferred position would be president of a republic. I thought, You are either intoxicated or you are a fool."[49]

Stephanie got an unwelcome taste of Rudolf's decline when she returned to Vienna from a holiday: "His decay was so greatly advanced as to have become conspicuous. He was frightfully changed: his skin was flaccid, his eyes were restless, his expression was completely changed. It seemed . . . as if a process of internal dissolution was going on. I was profoundly sorry for him and wondered how the devastation would end." Concerned and anxious to "save us both from disaster," Stephanie went unannounced to the emperor. "I began," she recalled, "by telling him that Rudolf was extremely ill, and that my husband's appearance and behavior caused me great anxiety. I earnestly begged the Emperor to send his son on a journey round the world, which might remove him from a life that was wearing him down." But Franz Josef interrupted. "You are giving way to fancies, my dear," he condescendingly told his daughter-in-law. "There is nothing wrong with Rudolf. I know he is rather pale, gets about too much, expects too much of himself. He ought to stay home with you more than he does. Don't be anxious." With this he arose and embraced Stephanie. "I had been dismissed, and had not been allowed to pour out my heart in the way I expected." An official soon called on Stephanie: In the future the emperor wanted her to follow protocol and approach him only by asking his adjutant for a formal audience.[50]

Empress Elisabeth, too, worried about her son, though unlike Stephanie she failed to act. That autumn her youngest daughter and favorite child, Marie Valerie, was about to become engaged to Archduke Franz Salvator. Something about Rudolf's behavior unnerved her. "Never be nasty to Valerie," she warned her son.[51] Visiting Vienna from her married home in Bavaria, Gisela found that "the whole family" now regarded Rudolf "as a person to be treated with caution."[52] For her part Marie Valerie was so afraid of her volatile brother that she kept word of her impending engagement from him until the middle of December. Rudolf, she confided to her diary, had an "unstable, often bitter, sarcastic expression" that made her fear being alone with him.[53]

Thoughts of death increasingly filled Rudolf's head. Vienna celebrated its supremacy in coffee, pastries, and waltzes, yet it also held the unwelcome distinction of having Europe's highest suicide rate.[54] "At the slightest difficulty these people meet," Walburga Paget recorded in astonishment, "they at once resort to suicide. There must be something in the air of Vienna that makes people do this."[55] Servants, she noted, "kill themselves because they break a plate, children of seven or eight hang themselves because they cannot do a lesson, soldiers because they do not like the army, girls because they cannot marry their first loves." The situation was so bad, she remembered, that officials actually warned her to avoid early-morning rides in the Prater before they could cut down the previous evening's suicides hanging from the trees.[56]

Rudolf eagerly consumed florid accounts of the latest suicides that Vienna's newspapers spun out to shock their readers.[57] There was the handsome young couple who, having enjoyed a last luncheon of chicken and Champagne, entered a cemetery and shot themselves; the woman aboard the express to Budapest who changed into a wedding dress before leaping to her death from the speeding train; and the young student who poisoned himself and his girlfriend after receiving low marks at school.[58] One woman loyally sang the national anthem, then leaped from her third-floor Vienna apartment; a tightrope walker hanged himself from a window, declaring in a note, "The rope was my life and the rope is my death"; in the middle of his performance a trapeze artist who had quarreled with his wife deliberately let go and plummeted to his death.[59] When the Hungarian sportsman István Kégl shot himself, Rudolf could talk of nothing else, devouring all the details, including the fact that Kégl had used a small hand-held mirror to adjust his aim.[60] The more theatrical the exit, the more Vienna's newspapers lingered over the details. Suicide had become entertainment, obsession with death the latest fashion.

By the autumn of 1888 Rudolf's fascination with death had shifted to an unwholesome embrace. "From time to time," Rudolf wrote to Latour von Thurmberg in October, "I look for an opportunity to see a dying person and attempt to enter into his sensations as he draws his last breath. I also make it a practice to intensely study dying animals, and attempt to accustom my wife to such sights, for one must learn to reckon with the last necessities of life."[61]

A devastating escalation of circumstances and events, both minor and major, began to prey on Rudolf's mind. "You know how badly Stephanie and I get on," he once confided to Marie Larisch. He had infected his wife with venereal disease, caused her sterility, and deprived himself of an heir. Painful symptoms of his gonorrhea came and went without warning, fueling Rudolf's escalating descent into alcoholism and drug addiction. Depression, anxiety, and feelings of inadequacy left him alienated and embittered. "Altogether I'm in a bad way," he told Larisch. "I'm tired of life." He was a "despicable puppet," someone "dressed up to please the people," with no purpose in life other than to await his father's demise.[62]

Rudolf took his repeated exclusion from the Army High Command conferences, his clashes with Archduke Albrecht, and his father's request that he resign his post as inspector general of the infantry as humiliating personal and professional failures. The death of the liberal German emperor Friedrich III tore away at Rudolf's hopes for the future, while a chance political victory by Prime Minister Taaffe in the autumn of 1888 cemented his bitter enemy in power and ensured that his opinions and ideas would continue to be rejected. On top of this the persistent attacks on Rudolf in the German press shamed the crown prince by presenting him as the disreputable "other," an unbalanced man unfit for the Habsburg throne.

The accumulated blows led to talk of suicide. At first it was loose talk, the kind of talk that consumed suicide-mad Vienna. In his erratic, unpredictable way, Rudolf spoke of suicide to his cousins Archdukes Johann Salvator, Franz Ferdinand, and Otto, as well as to the Duke of Braganza.[63] Once he even pointed to Franz Ferdinand during a shoot, announcing, "That man walking toward us will become Emperor of Austria."[64] It seemed like a bad joke: No one took him seriously. There was something so lighthearted, so cavalier, about Rudolf's manner—even Mitzi Caspar thought so when, in the midst of his affair with Mary Vetsera, he'd suddenly talked about killing himself. But Mitzi laughed off the idea as the result of too much alcohol and morphine.[65]

But the loose talk solidified that autumn as Rudolf began asking members of his staff to join him in a suicide pact. Lieutenant Viktor von Fritsche, Rudolf's personal secretary, was stunned when the crown prince asked if he would die with him; although he considered it a great honor, Fritsche explained, he was unwilling to kill himself. Rudolf then turned to *Flügeladjutant* Baron Artur Giesl von Gieslingen, one of his staff officers; but Giesl, like Fritsche, had no wish to die and politely declined the request.[66] This unnerving state of affairs led many men on the crown prince's staff to ask for reassignment.[67] Rudolf even threatened Stephanie, raging that he was going to shoot her and then himself.[68]

In December Rudolf again asked Mitzi to join him in a suicide pact, saying that honor demanded that he kill himself: They would shoot themselves in the Husarentempel at Mödling in a spectacularly symbolic coup de théâtre. Erected to the glory of hussars who had fallen in the emperor's service, the temple offered Rudolf an altar on which he could make the ultimate gesture of contempt for his father's conservative ideas of heroic loyalty.[69] This time Mitzi didn't laugh off the suggestion. Something about Rudolf's manner scared her, and she apparently reported his request to the Viennese chief of police, Baron Franz von Krauss. Krauss was not receptive: Ignoring her information, he threatened to prosecute Mitzi if she repeated a word of the crown prince's plea to anyone else.[70]

Three aromatic blue fir trees, branches alight with wax candles and bedecked with gilded ornaments, stood over tables crowded with gifts when the imperial family gathered at the Hofburg to celebrate Christmas. Rudolf had bought toys for his young daughter at Vienna's traditional *Christkindlmarkt*, or Christmas market; for his mother he had purchased some original letters written by her favorite poet, Heinrich Heine—a thoughtful gift that the empress all but ignored.[71] Indeed, Elisabeth seemed most taken with showing off her latest, unlikely acquisition: Much to her husband's horror, she'd had her shoulder tattooed with an anchor.[72]

Smiles and gifts couldn't conceal the undercurrent of tension. Something was so obviously wrong with Rudolf that Elisabeth pulled Marie Valerie aside and again warned her of her brother's malicious behavior. Then she turned to her son. After making him promise that he would be kind to Marie Valerie, Elisabeth embraced Rudolf and said that she loved him. Hearing this, Rudolf collapsed into agonized sobs; his mother, he cried, hadn't said those words "for a long time."[73] Franz Josef and Elisabeth were embarrassed at the display; neither recognized their son's emotional breakdown as a last, dramatic cry for help as Rudolf slipped ever closer to the edge of an abyss.

PART II

CHAPTER SEVEN

All seemed well that January of 1889 as revelers flung themselves into the social season; mourning for Empress Elisabeth's father had canceled the court ceremonies, but aristocratic Vienna went on with its celebrations. Strauss led his musicians through waltzes at the annual Opera Ball; society crowded the Industrialists' Ball, the Coiffeurs' Ball, the Laundresses' Ball, the Bakers' Ball, the City of Vienna Ball, and the undoubted highlight of the season—the Fourth Dimension Ball, where trees and flowers bloomed upside-down from a garden on the ceiling and malevolent-looking witches and warlocks moved among the guests.[1] But beneath the surface an ominous sense hung over the city, a "general air of discontent," a "breath of melancholy" that rippled through society.[2]

Rudolf and Stephanie spent the last week of 1888 together at the Villa Angiolina in the Adriatic resort of Abazzia; on December 29, he decided not to remain through the New Year but instead return to Vienna.[3] From the Hofburg he dispatched a letter to his wife: "I send you every possible good wish for the New Year, health and pleasant days, cheerful times, the fulfillment of all your desires."[4] But Rudolf's tone when writing to Moritz Szeps was dark: "The current peace that now reigns is ominous, like the calm before the storm. It can't go on like this; that is my consolation."[5] In his reply Szeps did what little he could to counter Rudolf's depression:

> The oppression cannot last forever, and soon a year of change will arrive. When that which is rotting, faded, and old gives way to that which is fresh and run, it is really an act of rejuvenation, which is necessary for the world. . . . Your task is to keep your spirit and your flesh strong for the day of action. . . . You have had to experience malice and treachery but have shaken it off with fortitude. All know that you desire great things, that you are capable of achieving them. . . . You have many enemies. But rely on yourself, on your genius and talents, your strength and endurance . . . and you will accomplish great things.[6]

The empire's semiannual Army High Command conference was scheduled for January 1, 1889; as usual Rudolf had not been invited, but this time he ignored the slight and appeared unannounced, adding his unsolicited opinions as his uncle Archduke Albrecht scowled in silence.[7] Rudolf lived a confused, schizophrenic existence in these weeks: regimental duties and visits by Prince Leopold of Bavaria, Prince Alexander of Battenberg, and a group of Russian dignitaries kept him busy by day; at night he slunk away to seedy cafés, called on Mitzi Caspar, and shot himself full of morphine when already intoxicated with Champagne and Cognac. When Stephanie returned to Vienna on January 11, she was "struck by the change in the Crown Prince, and this time more strongly than ever. He was rarely sober, he did not get home to the Hofburg until dawn; and as for the company he kept, the less said the better. His restlessness and nervous irritability had become intensified. He spoke menacingly of horrible things and in my very presence would cruelly toy with the revolver he always carried about. Indeed, I had become afraid to be alone with him."[8]

Not that Stephanie had to worry about being alone with her husband—Rudolf did as much as humanly possible to exclude her from his life. On January 20, while shooting eagles at Schloss Orth, the country estate of his cousin Archduke Johann Salvator, he asked his friend Hoyos to join him at his hunting lodge of Mayerling in the Vienna Woods—he thought he'd probably go there at the beginning of February.[9] When Stephanie learned of this, Rudolf "expressly informed me that my presence was not wanted."[10] No fool, she worried that he planned to take Mary Vetsera with him. One morning she appeared unannounced at the Coburg Palace, "anxious and disturbed," as her sister Louise recalled. "Rudolf," Stephanie told Louise, "is going to Mayerling, and intends staying there some days. He will not be alone. What can we do?"[11] But Louise, whose husband, Prince Philipp, had also been invited to the lodge, could offer no suggestions.

Not until the evening of January 13 did Rudolf again see Mary, when Bratfisch delivered her to the Hofburg. "Oh, it would have been so much better had I not gone to see him today!" Mary cried to her maid, Agnes, on returning home. "Now I no longer belong to myself alone but exist only for him. From now on I must do everything he asks."[12] And to Hermine Tobias, Mary explained: "I must confess something to you that will make you very angry. I was with him yesterday from seven to nine. We both lost our heads. Now we belong to one another body and soul."[13] Two days later Mary used 400 gulden ($2,556 in 2017) she had received as a Christmas gift from her uncle Alexander to purchase a gold cigarette case from the exclusive Vienna jeweler Rodeck's. She had it engraved with the date January 13, and the words *Dank dem Glücklichen Geschicke* (in gratitude to kind fate) before giving it to Rudolf.[14]

After the tragedy at Mayerling, those most closely involved with Rudolf, Mary, and their liaison made concerted efforts to erase history, insisting that the relationship only began on November 5 and that January 13 marked the affair's consummation. But circumstance weighs heavily against this. The relationship began in April 1888, much earlier than previously suspected; there were regular assignations at Eduard Palmer's apartment, and Bratfisch had delivered Mary to the Hofburg on at least twenty nights throughout the autumn of 1888, including the time in September when she provocatively arrived with only a fur coat covering her lingerie. With his sense of entitlement and relentless pursuit of pleasure, Rudolf was not the sort of man to long delay gratification "once his desires were in question," as Larisch recalled.[15] Rudolf's sexual conquests were legion, and he was not accustomed to being denied. Nor was Mary the type of woman to stand on moral propriety: With her "fast" reputation and string of past lovers, she had already abandoned any claim to virginal innocence. Given their characters and desires, it is extremely unlikely that Rudolf and Mary waited nine months to consummate their relationship.

A disapproving Hermine Tobias had repeatedly warned Mary against pursuing her relationship with the married crown prince. "I know everything you say is true," Mary had replied, "but I cannot change the facts. I have two friends, you and Marie Larisch. You work for my soul's happiness, and Marie works for my moral misfortune."[16] Given this, it is likely that Mary was not entirely forthcoming in her previous letters to Tobias, evading the truth and concealing the sexual nature of the liaison until she believed that circumstances finally compelled her to do. It now seems that January 13 marked not sexual consummation but rather some shared confidence, some new secret that, in Mary's impressionable mind, cemented the personal romantic fairy tale she had woven around the liaison and inexorably tied her to Rudolf.

Mary soared in elation for a week. On Saturday, January 19, she ignored a previously accepted invitation to attend a ball and slipped away to the Hofburg to see Rudolf.[17] She briefly saw him again in the Prater on the afternoon of January 24, and a happy mood the following evening sent her ice-skating.[18] As she left the ice Mary spotted a fortune-teller and, over her maid's protests, disappeared into the tent for a reading. A few minutes later Mary emerged looking "shocked and excited." She was unusually quiet, but Agnes found her tossing and turning later that night. "God, I am feverish," Mary sobbed. "I keep thinking of what that woman told me." The seer, she said, had warned of an impending death—probably a suicide—within her family. Mary seemed horrified by the idea.[19]

Tired and anxious, Mary watched the following morning as her mother searched her room. Increased gossip about the affair, Mary's reckless behavior, a sense of impending danger, Agnes Jahoda's confession that her mistress had purchased an expensive cigarette case the previous week—something drove Helene Vetsera into a sudden panic. Helene later claimed that she only now suspected the affair; in fact she'd been behind the liaison for months, bribing Larisch with cash and expensive gowns and even joking about the romance. Breaking open Mary's locked jewelry case, Helene found some photographs of Rudolf; a will Mary had made and dated on January 18; and a silver cigarette case engraved with Rudolf's name—his standard farewell gift to one of his sexual conquests.[20]

An argument between mother and daughter ensued, and Mary fled to the Grand Hotel, seeking refuge with Marie Larisch. Mary, the countess saw, "was deathly pale and her eyes seemed far too big for her face; she looked as if something dreadful had happened." She collapsed into an armchair and erupted in tears. "Oh, Marie darling, do get me away from Vienna! I shall die if I have to remain at home!"[21]

Larisch eventually calmed Mary and returned her to the Vetsera Palace. But, entering her mother's house, Mary promptly fainted and had to be put to bed, "deathly pale and speechless," as Helene remembered. "What have you done to her?" Larisch demanded of the baroness, but Helene was too angry to answer questions. To appease her Larisch lied, saying that the case engraved with Rudolf's name had originally been given to her; she had merely passed it on to Mary as a gift.[22]

While this drama at the Vetsera Palace played itself out, a far more momentous confrontation was taking place at the Hofburg. Two days earlier Rudolf had attended a dinner given by the British ambassador, Sir Augustus Paget. According to Lady Paget he "seemed somehow different, less sarcastic, less down on people, and for the first time he looked me in the eyes when speaking."[23] His good mood disappeared a few hours later, however, when he went to the opera to see *Die drei Pintos*. The emperor had not been expected, yet everyone noticed that he soon arrived in the imperial box and had a strained conversation with his son. Having said what he meant to say, Franz Josef rose and abruptly left the theater after the second act.[24]

Whatever drove a worried Franz Josef to this sudden confrontation erupted again that Saturday. As usual the emperor arose a little after four, dressed, and was at his desk by five to read the latest reports and newspapers. Something that morning shocked him into action: He sent word through an adjutant demanding that Rudolf appear before him in a formal audience at nine. The order left Rudolf tense and agitated. He put on his full-dress uniform as inspector general of the infantry, walked through the marble halls from his bachelor apartment to his father's rooms, was announced, and entered Franz Josef's study. Controversy surrounds precisely what took place behind those closed doors, but something left Franz Josef infuriated. The "stormy" and "violent" interview went badly.[25] The emperor, Latour von Thurmberg asserted, was "overwhelmed with grief and rage" and spoke to Rudolf "in terrible agitation and with brutal candor."[26] When Rudolf finally opened the study doors, it seemed obvious to a courtier that "something frightful" had taken place between father and son. Sophie von Planker-Klaps, Stephanie's principal *Kammerfrau* (lady of the bedchamber), or lady-in-waiting, saw Rudolf rush back to his own apartment through the halls. He "looked terribly upset, on the point of collapse, and his hand carrying his general's hat shook visibly."[27]

Thoroughly unnerved, Rudolf decided that it was best if he left Vienna. He wouldn't wait for February, but would go to Mayerling on Tuesday, January 29. He told Rudolf Püchel, his *Kammerbüchsenspanner* (personal gun loader), to head out to Mayerling on Monday with a small domestic staff and make preparations for the crown prince's arrival Tuesday.[28] Rudolf also sent word to Franz

Wodicka, a huntsman attached to Mayerling, to relay the change to Hoyos, bidding him to come out to the lodge for two days, January 29–30.[29]

Plans made, Rudolf went unannounced on Sunday morning to see Larisch in her suite at the Grand Hotel. "I want you to bring Mary tomorrow to the Hofburg. You must persuade the Baroness to allow Mary to go out with you." He was, Larisch recalled, "very excited" and looked pale and nervous as he spoke.[30]

That same Sunday morning, an anxious Mary had begged her mother to let her go out driving in the Prater with Larisch, saying that "this was her only pleasure."[31] Mary, Helene thought, still looked "deathly pale" after the previous day's contretemps; nevertheless she kissed her and "implored her to see reason and to end all of this nonsense" before finally giving her permission to see Larisch.[32] It was half past two when the countess called at the Vetsera Palace and collected Mary. Princess Louise also happened to be in the Prater when she spotted her brother-in-law's carriage stopped along the main avenue; he was speaking to Larisch and Mary.[33] As soon as Rudolf saw Louise, he waved Larisch off and went to speak to his sister-in-law. He had a "peculiar look," "pale and feverish," and "seemed on the verge of a nervous breakdown." Before leaving he asked Louise to tell "Fatty"—the nickname he had ungraciously bestowed on his brother-in-law—that he would be expected at Mayerling on Tuesday.[34]

That evening Larisch wrote a short letter to Rudolf assuring him that she would bring Mary to the Hofburg the following morning. The tone undermined her later assertions that she loathed her cousin: "You know that I am blindly devoted to you and that I will *always* obey your command whenever you call me! I shall naturally come along under these threatening circumstances, I cannot expose her to unpleasantness on her own—I shall therefore *certainly* come, no matter what happens!"[35]

Letter dispatched, Larisch then returned to the Vetsera Palace. That evening the German ambassador, Prince Heinrich Reuss, was holding the soiree at his embassy to celebrate Kaiser Wilhelm II's thirtieth birthday. As a loyal ally—and despite the court mourning still in place for his father-in-law—Franz Josef and his family, except for the empress, would attend—and so would the Vetseras. Larisch found Mary drinking tea with her mother and Hanna, though Mary had laced hers with rum and sat smoking as Helene Vetsera chastised her. Larisch followed Mary to her bedroom, watching as the young woman donned her light-blue gown trimmed in yellow. "Do I look nice?" Mary asked, smiling and "coldly" saying that Stephanie was sure to notice her and be jealous. "Her eyes," Larisch recalled, "looked positively evil."[36]

Mary's antagonism was on full display when she snubbed Stephanie that night at the soiree: The contemporary press reported "a violent scene" in the ballroom, presumably when Helene had to pull her daughter into a reluctant curtsy.[37] The humiliation was too much: Stephanie sent for Karl von Bombelles, Rudolf's lord high chamberlain, and asked him to tell her husband that she wanted to leave. She bade a gracious farewell to Prince Reuss and approached the ballroom door, but Rudolf stood motionless in the center of the hall as Mary walked up to him and began to speak. Rudolf hesitated before finally joining his wife. "The whole scene," recorded one witness, "was so strange that it struck everyone present." As they descended the crimson-carpeted staircase, several witnesses supposedly heard "a violent exchange of words" between Rudolf and Stephanie that left everyone in the ballroom embarrassed.[38]

Rudolf had asked his friend Moritz Szeps to meet him at the Hofburg late that night. He found the crown prince "in a dreadful state of nervous excitement." The previous day's confrontation with his father had left Rudolf shaken. Now he complained that during the soiree Franz Josef had deliberately turned away and thus publicly humiliated him. If this indeed happened it must have been so quick as to escape notice, though perhaps the emperor had briefly expressed his displeasure at seeing Mary Vetsera strutting about the ballroom. Rudolf was clearly embittered, fixated not on the scene caused by his mistress but by his father's apparent slight. "The Emperor," he told Szeps, "has openly affronted and degraded me. From now all ties between us are broken. From now I am free."[39]

At midnight, after bidding Szeps farewell, Rudolf went to see Mitzi Caspar. His mood was black: Entering her house, he grabbed a bottle of Champagne and drank for the next two hours. Alcohol loosened his tongue. Now Mitzi listened as Rudolf announced that he planned to "shit on the government." Honor, he insisted, demanded that he kill himself while at Mayerling; his cousin Archduke Franz Ferdinand could take his place as heir after his death. Mitzi had heard such drunken talk of suicide before, but the last time she'd gone to the police they'd threatened her with prosecution if she said anything. All she could do was listen as her lover rambled on incoherently. Rudolf finally left at three that morning. As he stood in the doorway he raised his hand and made the sign of the cross on Mitzi's forehead—something he had never done before and a gesture completely out of character for the atheistic Rudolf.[40]

CHAPTER EIGHT

Monday, January 28, 1889, dawned cold and clear in Vienna: A sheen of frost glistened over the frozen snow banking the broad avenues. That morning Rudolf rang for his servant Püchel and announced a sudden change of plan. Rather than travel to his hunting lodge on January 29, Rudolf explained, "I am going to Mayerling today." Püchel needn't see to the arrangements: Rudolf had already dispatched some servants to the lodge earlier that morning. "I am only waiting," Rudolf told Püchel, "for a letter and a telegram." When the letter arrived, Püchel brought it to his master. He found Rudolf standing at his bedroom window, staring out vacantly and "quite lost in thought. He held his watch in his hands, turning the winder. He did not seem to have noticed me." Püchel silently placed the letter on a desk and left. Some thirty minutes later the expected telegram arrived. Püchel found Rudolf still standing at the window, watch still in hand, and still staring out. The crown prince scanned the contents, remarking enigmatically to himself, "Yes, it has to be."[1]

At a quarter past ten that morning, Larisch climbed into a carriage at the Grand Hotel and asked the driver, Franz Weber, to take her to the Vetsera Palace. There she collected Mary, telling Helene that they planned to go shopping.[2] Mary wore an ice-skating ensemble from the imperial couturier Josef Fischer to guard against the cold: an olive-green pleated skirt and tight, matching jacket trimmed with black lace over a silk blouse; a small green felt hat trimmed with black ostrich feathers and a thin veil; and an ostrich-feather boa wrapped around her neck.[3] "I thought she had never looked so handsome," Larisch recalled. Once settled in the carriage, Larisch said she turned to Mary, imploring her to "finish this episode, otherwise I fear the results of it will be disastrous for us all." But Mary merely smiled. They first went to the Weisse Katze to shop for lingerie; after this Weber drove to the Hofburg, stopping at Larisch's directions at the iron door in the Augustiner Bastion, where a servant waited to lead them up to the crown prince's apartments.[4]

Mary, Larisch thought, seemed "strangely well acquainted" with this circuitous route through the palace. According to Larisch, while waiting for Rudolf, Mary kissed her, saying, "I want you to forgive me from the bottom of your heart for all the trouble I have caused you. Whatever happens, don't think I wished to deceive you or play you false."[5] This seems an unlikely declaration; more probably Larisch invented the conversation as "proof" that the lovers had "used" her and abused her trust.

Soon Rudolf appeared and asked to speak to Mary privately; after some minutes he returned, this time alone. Mary, he told his cousin, had already left the Hofburg. Larisch was to return to the Vetsera Palace and report that Mary had disappeared while they were shopping. Larisch later claimed to be horrified. When she objected Rudolf grabbed her violently and, waving a revolver in her face, growled, "Do you want me to hurt you? Unless you swear to be quiet, I'll kill you!" He needed to speak to Mary: "A great deal may happen in two days," Rudolf explained, "and I want Mary to be with me. I stand on the edge of a precipice." He gave his cousin 500 gulden (approximately $3,200 in 2017) with which to bribe her driver to back up her story about Mary's "disappearance."[6]

Rudolf had told his coachman Bratfisch to wait with his carriage at the iron door in the Augustiner Bastion. Shortly before eleven Mary Vetsera came out of the Hofburg, and Bratfisch beckoned to her. Soon they were speeding through the city, toward the Roten

Stadl, the Red Barn Inn, some ten miles outside Vienna, where Rudolf planned to meet them.[7] A few minutes later Larisch drove to Rodeck's on the Kohlmarkt. Apparently armed with a bribe, Franz Weber later insisted to officials that Mary had been with the countess, and had disappeared from his carriage while Larisch was shopping.[8]

As soon as the two ladies had gone, Rudolf made a rare excursion to his wife's rooms. He hadn't come for Stephanie; instead he asked her lady-in-waiting to go and find his young daughter: he wanted to see her before leaving for Mayerling. Sophie von Planker-Klaps returned in a few minutes. Little Elisabeth's nanny, she sheepishly explained, had said the girl was otherwise occupied and could not see her father.[9] Rebuffed, Rudolf left the Hofburg at half past eleven, driving himself in a phaeton through Vienna and out into the country to keep his rendezvous with Mary at the Roten Stadl. He wore a knee-length Hungarian lancer fur coat over his hunting tweeds, with a flat cap atop his head.[10]

Mary, Bratfisch remembered, had been unusually quiet during the drive to the Roten Stadl and hadn't said a word to him. They arrived early, and Bratfisch drove back and forth for nearly an hour, waiting for Rudolf. When he finally did appear, the crown prince left his phaeton and quickly slipped into Bratfisch's carriage: With a smile he apologized for having kept them waiting, and then asked Bratfisch to drive them to Mayerling. He didn't want to go via the normal route, instead asking that Bratfisch take a series of back roads and that he drive slowly enough so that they would not arrive before dusk.[11] They bypassed the old resort village of Baden, where both Beethoven and Mozart had once spent summers, and disappeared along little-used roads slippery with snow. Several times the carriage wheels slid into ruts; Rudolf had to get out and help Bratfisch push the vehicle back onto the roadway.[12]

It was late in the afternoon when the carriage rumbled through a forest of pine and spruce, emerging into the Vienna Woods' Helenenthal (valley) as the sun was rapidly fading from a cold clear sky. Ahead, nestled in a hollow fringed by gently rolling hills and open fields some sixteen miles southwest of the imperial capital, Mayerling lay in shadow. There in the fourteenth century, monks from the nearby Cistercian Abbey of Heiligenkreuz had laid out a farm and built the Church of Saint Laurenz. Over the centuries the estate had passed into private hands and grown to include several small villas for guests, a kitchen block, and stables. Though the surrounding forest offered superb hunting, the estate itself was a rather ramshackle collection of buildings that fell decidedly short of the usual imperial standards.[13] But there were other attractions: It was probably no accident that Rudolf bought Mayerling from Count Reinhard von Leiningen-Westerburg in 1887. The count lived in a villa on the estate with his beautiful wife, Anna—who just happened to be the former actress Anna Pick, who had shared the crown prince's bed and who had accompanied him to Brussels when he went to ask for Stephanie's hand. Having the new, sympathetic countess near at hand only added to Mayerling's attraction.[14] Spending more and more time there, Rudolf added a bowling alley and a rifle range along one side of the walled garden to the south. At the center stood the main lodge, a simple, whitewashed two-storey building dotted with shuttered windows, capped by a steeply hipped gray roof, and protected by gateways to the east, south, and west.[15]

Rather ungallantly Rudolf stopped the carriage at the edge of the forest and asked Mary to wait there while he went ahead to the lodge. She stood hidden in the snowy copse until Bratfisch returned, collected her, and quickly drove her through the southern gate, where she was able to slip inside through a service door without attracting any notice.[16] Her destination was Rudolf's private apartment at the southeastern corner of the ground floor. East of the lodge's main corridor, a door opened to an anteroom, where Rudolf's desk sat beneath an impressive set of antlers; beyond, reached by a white enameled door, was his corner bedroom, with two shuttered windows on each of its outer walls and a small gas chandelier hanging from its ceiling. Sofas and chairs covered in red velvet stood grouped around a tiled stove; against the center of the eastern wall stood a double bed of dark oak, its high headboard decorated with turned spindles. A second door to the right of the bed opened to a small hallway, where a private staircase ascended to Stephanie's apartments above.[17]

As ungallantly as he had arranged Mary's arrival, Rudolf kept her hidden away in the bedroom, beneath its vaulted ceiling and behind its heavily draped and shuttered windows. Concealing her from inquisitive eyes demanded seclusion: In addition to Bratfisch, twenty-four others were at the estate, including three policemen who might jot any comings and goings in their little notebooks.[18] Yet aside from Bratfisch, only one member of the staff apparently knew of Mary's presence: Johann Loschek, who had come out to Mayerling earlier that afternoon. Born in 1845, Loschek had joined the imperial court as a gamekeeper at eighteen; in 1883, he was named *Saaltürhüter*, or hall porter, to the crown prince and acted as his occasional valet. Like Bratfisch, Loschek knew all of his master's secrets: In addition to stories that Rudolf used him to obtain morphine, Loschek had also regularly delivered letters to and from both Mary and Larisch.[19] He too settled in at Mayerling, taking a small bedroom just off the anteroom so that he would always be close at hand to serve Mary's meals and answer her summons if needed.

The apparent calm at Mayerling stood in stark contrast to the chaos that Rudolf and Mary's sudden departure caused in Vienna that Monday. After leaving Rodeck's, Larisch went to the Vetsera Palace, arriving about half past eleven that morning. She burst in, said Helene Vetsera, "as if demented." "I lost her!" Larisch shouted dramatically. "She left me!" The countess claimed that she had gone into Rodeck's alone, leaving Mary in her carriage; the young woman had disappeared when she returned—having slipped out of the carriage and, said Larisch, climbed into another vehicle that sped away.[20]

Hearing this, Helene turned pale and said, "I was certain that she would do something rash."[21] In her memoirs Larisch claimed that Hanna Vetsera searched Mary's room and discovered a letter, but according to Helene, the countess handed it over, explaining that she had found it in the carriage: "I cannot go on living," Mary had written. "Today I have gained a lead on you; by the time you catch up with me I shall be beyond saving, in the Danube, Mary."[22]

This note, Larisch insisted, was yet another example of Mary's theatrics. "Don't you believe it," she told Helene of the ominous message. "She is much too fond of life. Perhaps she disappeared with the Crown Prince." At this Helene later claimed to have protested: "But she does not know him at all!"[23] This bit of retroactive whitewashing was clearly meant to save her own reputation. But Helene, too, calmly dismissed the note as "folly," adding, "Let us see whether she will return. I will not have any scandal; it would be fatal to our position in Vienna." This "dread of gossip," Larisch later wrote, "seemed to affect her far more than the loss of her daughter, and I could not help feeling sorry for Mary when I saw how little real affection her mother seemed to have for her."[24]

Deeply implicated in the liaison, Larisch hoped to conceal the truth when she now volunteered to intervene with Chief of Police Krauss. "Let me go to him alone," she told Helene. "I will secretly tell him all my conjectures. If you go, and someone saw you, there would be talk."[25] To Krauss, Larisch was careful to repeat her tale about Mary's disappearance from the carriage while she had been shopping in Rodeck's, and feigned ignorance of the affair; as for Mary's letter, Larisch insisted it wasn't to be taken seriously.[26] "The chief object," she claimed, "is to persuade the girl to return to her mother at once." But then Larisch dropped a bombshell: Mary's disappearance was probably connected to the crown prince: Would the baron please help her locate Rudolf and resolve the situation? Hearing this, Krauss immediately said that he could not possibly interfere in Rudolf's private affairs.[27]

Krauss had little sympathy: Any scandal might well fall on the aggravating Vetseras and drive them from Vienna in disgrace. By the time Larisch returned to the Vetsera Palace and reported this interview, Helene had summoned her brother Alexander to a hasty family conference. Baltazzi, Larisch recalled, "was perfectly furious over his niece's behavior." Something seems to have left him unhinged. Baltazzi declared that he meant to find the crown prince and confront him over the affair, even as Helene kept repeating that there must be no public scandal. Finally, said Larisch, Baltazzi asked her to accompany him to see the chief of police early that evening and request that his department search for Mary.[28]

This second interview went no better. Mayerling, Krauss explained, was an imperial residence and thus outside his jurisdiction. "If I were to mix myself up in the love affairs of the Imperial House," the chief of police declared, "I should have my hands full. Indeed, I dare not." Hearing this, Baltazzi erupted. "What?" he shouted. "Are the Habsburgs allowed to behave like common ravishers and yet go unpunished? Is there no justice in Vienna?"[29] But any investigation, Krauss explained, meant that word of Mary's disappearance would inevitably leak to the press—something Helene Vetsera was desperate to avoid.[30] Finally Krauss agreed that he would make some discreet inquiries; after they left a suspicious Krauss recorded of Larisch: "She came not to make a statement, but because she wanted to exculpate herself."[31]

Fear that investigation would expose her role in the liaison drove Larisch to write Krauss an urgent letter as soon as she returned to her suite at the Grand Hotel. Helene Vetsera, she warned:

> will probably turn to His Majesty the Emperor as a last resort—I request you *urgently* to keep silent about my confidences even in that case. It cannot be avoided that the *future* will be investigated, but one's wish is to have the past remain as *un-elucidated* as possible, and I ask you therefore to do your *utmost*; besides the events that have taken place are of no use—and as for the *future* events there is nothing left but to go on in the *usual* way! My request is merely to treat the matter up to the present day *with consideration*. Because no one wants a lot of innocent people to be implicated.[32]

Not content to stop there, Larisch followed this with a second letter, which Krauss did not receive until the morning of January 30:

> I am speaking to you *completely frankly* in the knowledge that you will treat my information as *private* but it is necessary that I should tell you the full truth because I fear that the matter will turn out more serious than it seems! I do not know if I told you that in addition to the note, which I handed over to the lady's uncle, there was also a letter in the cab—which was the real reason for my coming to see you at all and making my report to you on those lines! Although—no more than the family, I had no suspicion whatsoever—of the lady's possible relations—an occurrence like that of yesterday never came into my head at all, and I probably do not have to tell you that as far as this escape—I stand entirely outside and was only most reluctantly involved in this affair![33]

Something was clearly wrong. Perhaps Larisch had heard some loose talk about suicide. Her rising panic, though, stemmed less from worry about Rudolf and Mary than it did from fear for her own reputation and position. Krauss had no doubt as to the intent behind the letters: Larisch was covering her tracks.

•

The night's snow had turned to rain when Philipp of Coburg and Josef Hoyos left Vienna early on the morning of Tuesday, January 29. A train took them to Baden, where a carriage waited for the short journey to Mayerling. Arriving at half past eight, they saw that all the shutters were still closed, "as if the place was uninhabited," Hoyos later wrote. But a servant opened the gate and led them into the lodge's billiard room on the ground floor. Rudolf soon appeared, still wearing a dressing gown, and took a "very cheerful" breakfast with them. But Rudolf declined to join his companions in the day's shooting, explaining that he'd caught a cold the previous day after his carriage had become stuck crossing a snowy mountain pass and he'd had to help push it back onto the roadway. Hoyos found this odd route to the lodge "incomprehensible" and "very mysterious," but said nothing. Rudolf remained at the lodge while Coburg and Hoyos set off into the surrounding forest.[34]

Franz Josef and Elisabeth planned to leave for Budapest on January 31, but at six that Tuesday night they were giving a family dinner at the Hofburg to celebrate Marie Valerie's engagement.[35] Both Rudolf and Coburg were expected.[36] But when Coburg returned to the lodge at half past one, he found Rudolf looking embarrassed and wringing his hands; finally he told his brother-in-law that he would be staying at Mayerling. He asked Prince Philipp to kiss the emperor's hand and explain that he had a cold.[37] Coburg left just before three; Rudolf waited until 5:10 to send Stephanie what must have been an unwelcome telegram: "Please write to Papa that I respectfully beg his pardon for not appearing at dinner, but I have a bad cold and think it best that I should not make such a journey this afternoon but instead stay here with Josl Hoyos. Embracing you all warmly, Rudolf."[38]

"Oh God, what shall I do?" Stephanie cried out on reading the message. "I feel so strange."[39] Perhaps she understood just how significant and calculated Rudolf's decision really was. His absence was not only a silent rebuke to both his father and to Marie Valerie's favored position in the family, but in waiting until the last minute to cancel his appearance and throw the careful arrangements of the imperial court into disarray, Rudolf struck at the traditions Franz Josef held so dear.[40] Stephanie attended the dinner alone; she could not shake the nagging sense that something was very wrong.[41]

The melodrama surrounding Mary's disappearance continued to unfold in Vienna on Tuesday. That morning Helene Vetsera and Alexander Baltazzi called on Chief of Police Krauss. Helene claimed that, until Mary's disappearance, she had no reason "to attach any importance to her daughter's infatuation" with Rudolf, but now

Larisch was certain that the crown prince was somehow involved. Was it possible, Krauss asked, that Larisch had been lying to Baroness Vetsera about the relationship? No, Helene insisted, she'd known Larisch "for fifteen years." Krauss had spoken to cab driver Franz Weber, who had confirmed Mary's "disappearance" while Larisch was in Rodeck's, but the police chief suspected that "he has probably been bribed." When Helene pressed for further investigation, Krauss again explained that if he launched an official inquiry, Mary's name would inevitably appear in the press; apparently by this time the baroness was worried enough to consent, leaving a photograph of Mary with the baron, who promised to keep the situation "as secret as possible."[42]

Aware of the family's rather sordid reputation, Krauss called on Prime Minister Taaffe that afternoon and briefed him on the situation. But the prime minister seemed unconcerned, saying that he thought Helene Vetsera "was herself involved in this business, since her own life, and that of her daughter, are not free from wild escapades." He ordered Krauss to do nothing.[43]

By nightfall Alexander Baltazzi managed to work his sister into a frenzy over Mary's disappearance; soon after Krauss's visit Helene Vetsera stormed into the prime minister's office, demanding an audience. At first Taaffe was politely patronizing, explaining that he was in no position to speak directly with the crown prince about the issue as he was "not on good terms with him and had no standing to raise his private affairs." The crown prince was expected back in Vienna that evening; if he failed to appear, Taaffe would then have detectives make some inquiries, "though this made him very uncomfortable."[44] Until and unless Rudolf failed to return, the prime minister warned, the baroness should keep her silence. When Helene threatened to go directly to the emperor, however, Taaffe's tone immediately changed. After all, he gleefully asked her, what made Helene think that Mary, profligate as she apparently was with her favors, was with the crown prince? All Vienna knew of the young lady's reputation: Rudolf, Taaffe told her, certainly couldn't have hoped to deflower Mary Vetsera. When he went further and named Prince Heinrich von Liechtenstein as one of Mary's "very intimate admirers," Helene blushed "blood red" and quickly left the prime minister's office.[45]

Six o'clock arrived, and Rudolf did not appear at the Hofburg. Learning this, Taaffe again met Krauss. Now the prime minister advised the chief of police to quietly send an inspector out to Mayerling the following morning. He also wanted to know if the crown prince had confided in Mitzi Caspar. Krauss was to send for police agent Florian Meissner and have him question Rudolf's mistress about his plans, and especially about his relationship with Mary Vetsera.[46]

Rudolf had spent most of that Tuesday in his rooms at Mayerling, where Mary remained hidden and took her meals. Late that afternoon he summoned one of the gamekeepers, Hornsteiner, and said that he would not participate in the next day's hunting. Something about his manner struck Hornsteiner as strange. "What's up with the Crown Prince?" Hornsteiner asked Loschek. "He just spoke with me now, but seemed to be thinking of something else entirely."[47]

Hoyos returned to Mayerling at half past five that afternoon: He'd managed only a bad shot at a single stag, and gamekeepers had to chase the wounded animal most of the afternoon before finishing it off.[48] At seven he left his room in the old gamekeeper's lodge and walked across the courtyard to join Rudolf for dinner in the billiard room—the usual spot for informal meals. Mary remained in Rudolf's bedroom; Hoyos later insisted that he had no idea she was at the lodge. Rudolf seemed to be in a good mood: He ate the soup, goose pâté, roast beef, venison, and pastries "with considerable appetite," and "drank plenty of wine." After the meal the two men chatted and smoked. Talk turned to the following day's hunt, but at nine and complaining of his cold, Rudolf said that he wanted to retire early. He rose, shook his friend's hand, and disappeared into his own apartments, while Hoyos returned to his lodgings some thousand feet away.[49]

But Rudolf did not retire. He apparently called for Bratfisch and asked him to wait with his carriage early the following morning: Mary, he said, would be returning to Vienna.[50] Loschek tended to the lovers as they retreated to Rudolf's bedroom. "You are not to let anyone in," Rudolf warned him, "not even the Emperor!"[51] Mary took a small gold watch set with diamonds from her pocket, handed it to Loschek, and said, "Take this as a keepsake of this last time."[52] With these ominous words Rudolf and Mary disappeared into his bedroom and closed the door behind them.

CHAPTER NINE

Flurries of snow fell throughout the night at Mayerling; by the morning of Wednesday, January 30, 1889, a fine powder cloaked the lodge's steep roof in a blanket of white. Dawn broke late, gray, and gloomy, the dark fringe of forest ringing the estate standing in dim shadow against a leaden sky.

Loschek was up early that morning. At ten past six Rudolf—dressed in his usual hunting clothes—came into the small anteroom, closing the bedroom door behind him. He asked Loschek to see to the horses and carriages needed for the day's hunt, and to order breakfast for half past eight, by which time he expected Prince Philipp to have returned from Vienna. Until then Rudolf wanted to get a little more sleep, and he asked Loschek to wake him at half past seven. Rudolf's mood seemed lighthearted as he turned and disappeared back into his bedroom: He was, Loschek remembered, whistling a tune.[1]

Within a few minutes, Loschek later claimed, he heard two gunshots, fired in quick succession. Running back to the anteroom, he thought he smelled gunpowder in the air. Seeing nothing obviously wrong, he tried the door to Rudolf's bedroom: It was locked on the inside. This was odd: Rudolf normally left his bedroom unlocked. Yet Loschek did not alert anyone; hearing nothing further, he walked across the courtyard to order breakfast and carriages for the hunt.[2]

Loschek passed Bratfisch, who sat on the box of his carriage, waiting to take Mary back to Vienna.[3] At seven, as the imperial huntsman Franz Wodicka crossed the courtyard to prepare for the day's shooting, Bratfisch called him aside, announcing, "No good rallying the beaters! There will be no shoot!" When a puzzled Wodicka asked what he meant, Bratfisch declared, "The Crown Prince is dead."[4] The remark remained unexplained at the time.

Half past seven arrived, and Loschek went to wake the crown prince; there was no response to his repeatedly insistent knocking. The door was still locked from within, and Loschek could not find the key. Increasingly worried, the valet left the anteroom, climbed the main staircase, walked through Stephanie's apartments above, and descended the smaller staircase to the corridor that gave access to Rudolf's bathroom. There another door opened to the crown prince's bedroom; when Loschek tried to open it, he found that this, too, was locked on the inside. Returning to the anteroom, Loschek grabbed a length of firewood and used it to bang against the closed bedroom door. It was not unusual for Rudolf to pass out from drinking or overindulgence in morphine, but he'd been up ninety minutes earlier; even if the crown prince was now unresponsive, surely Mary Vetsera would answer the door.[5]

But after twenty minutes Loschek had worked himself into a panic, and he sent Alois Zwerger, the *Schlosswärter* (lodge warden) at Mayerling, to fetch Hoyos.[6] Hoyos was preparing for breakfast when his valet knocked on the door a few minutes before eight: Zwerger now explained that Loschek was unable to wake the crown prince.[7] Hoyos was unconcerned. Rudolf, he told Zwerger, was "probably tired, let him sleep."[8] Zwerger, though, insisted, and Hoyos accompanied him back to the lodge.[9]

Loschek was still in the anteroom, banging on the door, when Hoyos entered. Was the bedroom, Hoyos asked, heated with a coal stove, and could fumes have overcome Rudolf? No, Loschek replied, the bedroom stove used wood for fuel. Hoyos rapped loudly against the door, yelling out Rudolf's name; still, there was no reply. The "death-like silence in the bedroom," Hoyos thought, gave "obvious reason for suspecting disaster." Loschek refused to break down the door; when Hoyos insisted, the valet confessed that Rudolf was not alone but had Mary Vetsera with him. "This news naturally caused me the greatest embarrassment," Hoyos later unconvincingly claimed, "all the more as I had neither suspected the presence of the Baroness at Mayerling nor had I known of her relations with the Crown Prince."[10]

Hoyos looked at his watch: 8:09 a.m. Prince Philipp should soon be returning from Vienna for the morning's shooting; it was better, Hoyos decided, to wait and let Rudolf's brother-in-law take responsibility for breaking into the room. Ten minutes ticked by before Coburg's carriage arrived. Hoyos flagged him down, pulled him into the billiard room, and quickly explained the situation. The prince ran to the anteroom, closed the door to the corridor behind him, and ordered Loschek to break into the bedroom; because of "the exceptionally delicate circumstances," Hoyos said, they asked Loschek to enter the room alone and report back to them.[11]

Loschek fetched an ax, but his blows couldn't break the lock. Finally he turned the blade to the upper panel, chopping a hole through the bedroom door. It had been dark when Rudolf came out of his bedroom a few minutes after six; he must have lit a lamp or a candle, and it was in this poor light, with the curtains drawn and the windows shuttered, that Loschek first peered through the smashed panel. Yet with a quick glance, before having entered the room and without a moment's hesitation, Loschek announced that both Rudolf and Mary were dead.[12]

"Our horror and grief," Hoyos said, "were beyond words." But what if Loschek was wrong? Should a doctor be called? Coburg and Hoyos finally asked Loschek to enter the room and look more closely.[13] Loschek reached through the panel, found the key, and opened the door. "An appalling sight" met his eyes: Mary Vetsera was on the right side of the bed, closest to the door, while Rudolf sat on the opposite side, his legs extended over the side of the bed and torso bent forward. Both of their heads, Loschek said, were hanging down, and it was obvious that both were dead. The top of Rudolf's skull was gone; brain tissue oozed from the cranium, spattering the headboard, and blood had poured from his nose and mouth. His revolver lay on the bed. A single bullet wound to Mary's left temple had shattered the right side of her skull.[14]

"It was clear at first view," Loschek recalled, "that Rudolf first shot Mary Vetsera and then killed himself. There were only two well-aimed shots."[15] Yet Hoyos claimed that the valet stumbled from the room declaring that Rudolf and Mary had died after taking strychnine, insisting that this often caused bloody hemorrhages.[16] This story sounds suspicious: Loschek, a former gamekeeper, had seen Rudolf's shattered skull and the revolver—why would he think that the crown prince had died by poison? As for Hoyos, he later insisted that he never entered the room, but this isn't convincing: Would he and Coburg, two of Rudolf's closest friends, really leave all examination to Loschek?[17] The German ambassador, Prince Reuss, who seemed remarkably well informed on events at Mayerling, confidently reported to Berlin, "I know for certain that Count Hoyos and the Prince of Coburg saw the two bodies immediately after the door was broken down."[18] To diplomat Count Eugen Kinsky, Hoyos confessed that he and Coburg had briefly entered the room and looked at the corpses.[19] Coburg also admitted, in a letter to Queen Victoria, that he "saw everything."[20] And, to his friend Justice Adolf Bachrach, the prince confided: "Hoyos and I found the Crown Prince already dead. We were the first to see his body. Poor man! His head was terribly disfigured."[21] Neither could have missed the obvious gunshot wounds to the corpses.

Hoyos and Coburg held a quick conference: It was obvious that both Rudolf and Mary were beyond assistance, but what should they do? The most important thing was to keep word of what had happened secret until Franz Josef had been told. Coburg "was so broken with grief that he was hardly capable of action," and so the unfortunate duty of taking news of the tragedy to Vienna fell on Hoyos. The count told Loschek to telegraph Rudolf's court physician, Dr. Hermann Widerhofer, asking him to come immediately to Mayerling on a matter of grave urgency; a servant brought the count's fur coat, and at 8:37 a.m. Hoyos climbed into a carriage, ordering Bratfisch to drive him quickly to the station at nearby Baden, where he could board a train and travel to the capital. Prince Philipp was left to stand guard over the scene at Mayerling.[22]

Throughout the drive, Hoyos recalled, Bratfisch "tried to question me," but the count insisted that the crown prince was merely indisposed. He warned Bratfisch to say nothing about the situation. At the Baden station Hoyos ordered Bratfisch to wait with his carriage for Widerhofer and then ran into the telegraph office, where he sent a message to Prince Constantine von Hohenlohe, lord high chamberlain of the imperial household, warning that he was on his way to the Hofburg on a matter of great urgency. Hoyos then checked with the stationmaster: The next train, the express from Trieste, would pass through the station at 9:18. Ordinarily it didn't stop, but Hoyos demanded that it do so, saying that "I was traveling on the most important official business and I was given permission to board the express." According to Hoyos, his "greatest care was to keep everything as secret as possible, and neither in Mayerling itself nor during my journey did anyone learn anything from me."[23]

In fact, to persuade the stationmaster to stop the train and allow him to board, Hoyos told him that "the Crown Prince has shot himself."[24] This confession demolishes any idea that Hoyos actually believed Rudolf had been poisoned. As soon as Hoyos boarded the train, the stationmaster ran to the telegraph office. Baron Nathaniel Rothschild, and not the Austrian state, owned the Southern Railway, on which the Trieste express traveled; within minutes the baron had a telegram informing him of Rudolf's death at Mayerling. Rothschild immediately telegraphed the news to his youngest brother and head of the family business Baron Albert Rothschild, who rushed to the German Embassy and informed Prince Reuss of the tragedy; Reuss in turn summoned Count Anton Monts, his embassy counselor, and broke word of the crown prince's suicide.[25] Albert Rothschild then ran to the British Embassy. "I have come to tell you a very sad thing," he told Sir Augustus and Lady Paget. "Your Crown Prince is dead."[26] Diplomatic Vienna thus learned of Rudolf's suicide before the emperor did.

On the journey from Baden to Vienna, Hoyos apparently realized that, having just come from the lodge, he would be pressed for details at the Hofburg. Although he'd seen the bodies and blurted out to the stationmaster that Rudolf had shot himself, the idea of having to break such awful news to the emperor or empress—not to mention that Rudolf had apparently also shot Mary Vetsera—was simply too unnerving. With Widerhofer on his way to Mayerling, the facts would emerge soon enough. Until then Hoyos seems to have decided to obfuscate. At this point the poisoning story probably entered his head; later it would be easy enough to claim confusion and blame any misunderstanding on the dead crown prince's valet. But for now Hoyos almost certainly believed that it was best to spare the emperor and empress the terrible truth—and himself the odium of having to inform them of Rudolf's suicide.

After arriving in Vienna, Hoyos went straight to the Hofburg; it was, he recalled, 10:11 a.m. as he raced through the Schweizerhof to the rooms of Karl von Bombelles. Hoyos quickly briefed Bombelles on "the terrible state of affairs" at Mayerling and asked him to tell the emperor. "I cannot possibly," the count insisted. "Her Majesty is the only person who can tell His Majesty such a thing." The oppressive Spanish etiquette of the Hofburg kicked in: Bombelles decided that Baron Ferenc Nopcsa, lord high chamberlain of the empress's household, should inform Elisabeth of the tragedy. But Nopcsa too protested that etiquette prevented him from acting, and so the trio shuffled off to ask Prince Hohenlohe what to do. Rudolf had been a lieutenant general in the imperial army; only a military man, Hohenlohe insisted, could approach the emperor.

And so they went to ask Count Eduard Paar, Franz Josef's *Flügeladjutant*. Like the others, Paar wanted no responsibility in breaking the news: Only the empress, he declared, could tell the emperor of such a tragedy. Nopcsa, he pronounced, must inform Elisabeth and let her tell her husband.[27]

Empress Elisabeth was having a Greek lesson that morning; Nopcsa sent for her reader, Ida von Ferenczy, and asked that he be announced at once. Elisabeth was obviously irritated at the interruption, saying that Nopcsa "must wait and come back again later." But the countess pressed, confessing, "He has bad news, grave news, about His Imperial Highness the Crown Prince!" Hearing this, Elisabeth dismissed her Greek tutor, and Ferenczy ushered Nopcsa into the room. The baron now repeated what Hoyos had said: Rudolf was dead at Mayerling, and Mary Vetsera with him; it seemed likely that she had poisoned him and then, consumed with guilt, taken her own life. A few minutes later, when Ferenczy returned, she found the empress sobbing loudly. But Elisabeth quickly dried her tears and kept a stoic face as an unsuspecting Franz Josef was ushered into the room. A few minutes later the emperor emerged, face ashen and head bowed at word of his son's death.[28]

By coincidence Katharina von Schratt arrived at the Hofburg that morning to see the emperor. Overwhelmed by her own grief, Elisabeth decided the kindest thing she could do was let the actress provide Franz Josef with the emotional comfort she could not give him.[29] "You must go to him," Elisabeth told her. "You must try to help him. I can do nothing more."[30]

No one had yet told Stephanie of her husband's death; it says something about the empress's loathing of her daughter-in-law that, rather than send for the unsuspecting widow, Elisabeth next called for her favorite child, Marie Valerie. The archduchess found her mother weeping in her bedroom. "Rudolf is very, very ill," the Empress sobbed. "There is no hope!" Marie Valerie was no fool: "Has he killed himself?" she asked. Elisabeth recoiled: "Why do you think that? No, no. It seems probable, even certain, that the girl poisoned him."[31] Soon Franz Josef joined them and, as Marie Valerie wrote, "The three of us held each other close and cried."[32]

Stephanie, meanwhile, was in her apartments having a singing lesson, when a lady-in-waiting interrupted and said she had grave news. "I realized instantly that the catastrophe I had so long dreaded had taken place," Stephanie later wrote. "He is dead!" she cried out, and the courtier nodded silently before withdrawing. Stephanie would remain understandably bitter that the emperor and empress had ignored her and let a lady-in-waiting break news of the tragedy.[33] "God have mercy on the soul of my dearly beloved husband!!" she wrote in her diary after receiving the "dreadful" news.[34]

The now-widowed crown princess had to wait for a formal summons from the emperor before Franz Josef and Elisabeth received her later that morning. When she finally called on her parents-in-law, she found Elisabeth had already dressed in black, "her face pale and rigid," standing beside Franz Josef, who sat on a sofa. Rather than offer sympathy, Stephanie remembered, "they looked on me as a criminal. They assailed me with a crossfire of questions, some of which I could not, and others would not, answer." Sensing that she was being blamed for the tragedy, Stephanie spoke of Rudolf's erratic behavior and how Franz Josef had dismissed her warnings; Elisabeth refused to listen: "In her eyes, I was the guilty party."[35] It was all so sordid: the crown prince apparently poisoned by his young lover who had then killed herself. Nothing of the kind, Franz Josef and Elisabeth quickly decided, must ever be admitted. Before Stephanie was dismissed, they seem to have told her that officially Rudolf's death would be ascribed to a heart attack. This only aroused her suspicions. Returning to her apartments, Stephanie cried out to Sophie von Planker-Klaps, "Have you heard that the Crown Prince died today at Mayerling of heart failure? Do you believe that?" It all proved too much: Stephanie collapsed, and a doctor sedated her and put her to bed.[36] She was, she confided to her sister, "broken by the pain of this terrible misfortune," and begged Louise to "pray for me and for *him*, who was so good."[37]

One last bit of lugubrious business was enacted that morning at the Hofburg. Earlier, before word of the tragedy reached Vienna, Helene Vetsera had again called on Taaffe, asking what progress he had made in finding her daughter. The prime minister had nothing to report; if she believed the matter was so urgent, he finally suggested, Helene should seek an audience with the empress and ask her to intervene with Rudolf.[38] The baroness agreed, but when she arrived at the Hofburg, Ferenczy tried to dismiss her, saying, "What do you want here? Kindly go away." Helene, though, refused to leave: "I have lost my child," she cried, "and she alone can restore her to me." Eventually an irritated Ferenczy informed the empress of her insistent caller. "Does she know anything yet?" Elisabeth asked. On being told that she did not, the empress remarked, "Poor woman. Very well, I will go to her." Elisabeth drew herself up and, "full of grandeur," finally faced the unsuspecting mother, saying flatly: "Collect all your courage, Baroness. Your daughter is dead."

"My child!" Helene cried out. "My dear, beautiful child!"

"But," Elisabeth coldly said, her voice rising in anger, "do you know that my Rudolf is dead as well?"

Hearing this, Helene collapsed to the floor in sobs, clutching at the empress's skirt and muttering, "My unhappy child! What has she done? Can this be her doing?" Elisabeth was silent. She freed herself from the baroness's grasp and coldly dismissed her with the warning, "Remember, the Crown Prince died of heart failure!"[39]

A cover-up had been set in motion. No one wanted to admit that Rudolf had, presumably, been poisoned by his mistress or, worse, joined her in a suicide pact. While gossip filtered through Vienna's foreign embassies, no one on the streets knew that anything had happened. It was, to all appearances, an ordinary winter Wednesday morning. A little after noon, a regiment of soldiers marched through the snowy streets as usual: The changing of the palace guard at the Hofburg was, at might be expected at Franz Josef's court, a precise ritual, accompanied by rousing music. At half past twelve a regimental band launched into a noisy rendition of the march from Giacomo Meyerbeer's opera *Les Huguenots* as smartly uniformed soldiers presented arms, clicked boot heels, and saluted in the Hofburg courtyard. Then, for the first time that anyone could remember, the music suddenly stopped without explanation.[40]

CHAPTER TEN

"Bleak, desperate excitement" gripped Vienna as word of Rudolf's death swept through the city's smoky coffeehouses and aristocratic palaces.[1] At the Stock Exchange, people whispered of a hunting accident or murder.[2] The early afternoon edition of the *Wiener Zeitung* confirmed Rudolf's death at Mayerling, attributing it to a stroke.[3] The story had changed by the evening. Prime Minister Taaffe had heartily disliked Rudolf; deep down he might have relished the idea of spreading word that the unstable heir to the throne had killed himself and his mistress. Taaffe, though, owed his first allegiance to the emperor. And so, at three that Wednesday afternoon, he released a terse bulletin: "His Imperial and Royal Highness the Most Serene Crown Prince the Archduke Rudolf died between 7–8 in the morning at his hunting lodge Mayerling of heart failure."[4]

A stroke? A heart attack? Few believed the official bulletins, and the shifting explanations only fed conspiracy theories. By noon most of the city's diplomatic corps had heard whispers of Rudolf's alleged suicide, and as the hours passed, the rumors only increased. "Breathlessly," recalled a military cadet, "we caught at every speck of detailed news. The words 'hunting accident,' 'murder,' and 'suicide' were flying about. The news of such an unexpected disaster threw everything out of order."[5]

Theaters closed; black-draped photographs of Rudolf went up

in shopwindows. An immense crowd soon surged around the Hofburg, sobbing and demanding, "Is it true?" of even the lowliest servants. "Vienna," reported *Le Figaro*, "is in a fever."[6] There was, Marie Larisch remembered, "a somber stillness, like a funeral pall, over everything and everybody . . . a sense of horror and mystery in the very air we breathed."[7]

At half past one on the afternoon of January 30, Prime Minister Taaffe met with Baron Krauss. "The Crown Prince was found dead in bed with the Vetsera woman this morning," Taaffe told the police chief. "They had poisoned themselves." A commission had already left for Mayerling; the most important thing, Taaffe warned, was to conceal Mary Vetsera's death at the lodge, get her body away from Mayerling, and bury her in secret.[8]

Vienna thrived on gossip, and it was not long before word of Helene Vetsera's anxious visit to the Hofburg that morning leaked out. Rudolf's affair with Mary Vetsera was no secret, and people quickly assumed that the young baroness might somehow have been involved in his death. By early afternoon journalists jostled along the iron railing ringing the Vetsera Palace, shouting questions at anyone who dared appear.[9]

Panic erupted in the Hofburg: The truth had to be suppressed. A crown prince who had an affair, aided by the empress's illegitimate niece, with a young woman of scandalous reputation and died at her side under suspicious circumstances was too humiliatingly distasteful ever to admit. It wasn't only inquisitive journalists who might uncover and publish unwelcome details: With Helene Vetsera's reputation, who knew what she might do? Unwilling to take the risk, Franz Josef met with Taaffe: He wanted Helene Vetsera out of Vienna immediately.[10] And so that afternoon the emperor dispatched his adjutant Paar to the Vetsera Palace. Still relying on what Hoyos had said, the count told Helene that Mary had poisoned an unsuspecting crown prince and then herself. Helene Vetsera was to leave Vienna that evening and remain out of the country until the emperor decided otherwise.[11]

Curious disbelieving crowds had also begun gathering outside Mayerling. Inspector Eduard Bayer, ordered by Krauss early that morning to investigate Mary Vetsera's whereabouts, was refused admittance to the lodge. Sure that something dramatic had taken place behind those shuttered windows, he pulled out his notebook and slyly began questioning servants. The lodge, a few confided, had blazed with light throughout the night—presumably some kind of party had taken place.[12]

It was a little after noon when the imperial physician Dr. Hermann Widerhofer, accompanied by Bombelles, arrived at Mayerling from Vienna; only then did Widerhofer learn that Rudolf and his mistress were dead. Loschek led him into the corner bedroom, opened the shutters, and drew the curtains back. "I hope I may never see such a sight again," Widerhofer later told Larisch. "There was blood everywhere. It stained the pillows, it bespattered the walls, and it had flowed in a sluggish stream from the bed to the floor, where it had made a horrible pool."[13]

The two corpses were still on the bed. Mary was in full rigor mortis, but Rudolf was only in the beginning stages; he had survived his lover by at least six hours.[14] Rudolf wore his usual hunting clothes, but the information about Mary is contradictory. Loschek said that she was "fully dressed," while Hoyos claimed she wore a black dress.[15] Yet the only clothing Mary brought to Mayerling was the olive-green ice-skating ensemble she wore out to the lodge; this was found neatly folded on an armchair in the bedroom.[16] There was no black dress: Loschek and Hoyos were probably attempting to conceal the lurid fact that Mary was naked.[17]

Standing on the left side of the bed, Widerhofer visually examined Rudolf's corpse: His legs still hung over the side of the bed, his torso upright but bent forward and his head bowed. Blood had gushed from his nose and mouth, congealing on his lap and around the bed in an ugly crimson pool. A single bullet hole, singed around the ragged edges, gaped in his right temple: The projectile had pierced the brain, blowing out the left top and rear of Rudolf's head. Fragments of bone, hair, and brain tissue had sprayed against the headboard and the wall behind the bed; decimated brain tissue oozed from the shattered skull and covered the sheets.[18]

Mary's head, too, hung down, loose hair falling about her neck and shoulders. Open eyes, "protruding in a fixed stare," gazed vacantly; congealed blood entirely covered her upper torso and had pooled at her waist. A single shot disfigured Mary's left temple; the area around the wound was singed by gunpowder. The bullet had passed through the brain, exiting above the right ear and splintering the skull; she still held a handkerchief in her left hand.[19] Rudolf's sister Marie Valerie supposedly recalled that Widerhofer found both bullets in the room.[20] The bullet which killed Rudolf was supposedly handed over to Franz Josef—certainly a grisly relic to pass on to a grieving father.[21]

Darkness had fallen by the time the seven-member court commission, led by Dr. Heinrich Slatin, court secretary in the lord marshal's office, arrived at Mayerling from Vienna late that afternoon.[22] They crowded into the bedroom, examining the grisly scene. A crystal tumbler on the bedside table still held brandy; a broken coffee cup and two smashed Champagne glasses apparently lay on the floor.[23]

Loschek remembered that the gun had been by Rudolf's side, presumably lying on the bed, something echoed by the official *Wiener Zeitung*.[24] Hoyos, though, wrote that Rudolf still held the revolver in his hand: "It was no longer possible," he insisted, "to straighten out the right index finger, which was crooked round the trigger."[25] Widerhofer told Larisch that it was still in Rudolf's hand when he arrived, but other accounts reported that the gun was found on the floor at the side of the bed.[26] By the time of the court commission's arrival, though, someone—presumably Loschek or Widerhofer—had moved the gun; Slatin saw it resting atop a small table or chair to the left of the bed.[27]

Slatin also noted that a small hand mirror lay on the table next to the gun.[28] Later Slatin learned of Rudolf's interest in the suicide of the Hungarian sportsman István Kégl using a hand mirror to better adjust his aim. This led Slatin to speculate that Rudolf had used the mirror when he shot himself; if so, it—like the gun—must have been moved after his death, given that the bullet to his brain was instantly fatal and left no time for Rudolf to set the mirror down calmly.[29]

The commission found a number of notes and letters in the bedroom. Rudolf had written four. Near the bed was a note addressed to Loschek: "Dear Loschek, Fetch a priest and have us buried together in a grave at Heiligenkreuz. Please hand over my dear Mary's valuables to her mother. Thank you for your invariably loyal and devoted services throughout the many years you have served me. See that the letter to my wife reaches her by the shortest route. Rudolf."[30] He had added a postscript: "Greetings to Count Hoyos. The Baroness asks him if he remembers what he said to her about Mayerling during the evening reception of German Ambassador Prince Reuss. Hoyos is not to telegraph Vienna, but send to Heiligenkreuz for a priest to come and pray by our sides."[31] Rudolf had also drafted a telegram to Abbot Heinrich Grünböck, prior of the monastery at Heiligenkreuz, asking him to come and pray over the bodies.[32]

These notes were obviously written at Mayerling, as was the letter Rudolf left for his mother. The precise wording of the latter remains something of a mystery. Elisabeth later asked her reader and trusted companion, Countess Ida von Ferenczy, to destroy it; what little is definitely known came from the countess and from Marie Valerie.[33] In 1934 Egon Caesar Conte Corti published his pivotal biography *Elisabeth von Österreich*, which appeared in an English translation two years later as *Elisabeth, Empress of Austria*. Corti consulted Ida von Ferenczy's papers, which apparently included an extensive transcription of Marie Valerie's diary.[34] This related conversations at the Hofburg, described the scene at the lodge, and gave the wording of Rudolf's last letters to his mother and to his youngest sister. Subsequent historians, believing that Marie Valerie's diaries were either lost or inaccessible, have all drawn on these apparent transcriptions, which were partly reproduced in Corti's book and survived in his personal archive. Yet questions surround the material. Marie Valerie's actual diary ended up in the Bavarian State Library and was published in 1998. This revealed serious discrepancies between Corti's version of the diary as recorded by Ferenczy; Marie Valerie's actual entries related to events at the Hofburg; and the content of Rudolf's final letters. It is possible that Ferenczy heard the details she recorded from Marie Valerie and mistakenly attributed them to her diary, but the differences suggest that readers employ a degree of caution.

The letter to Empress Elisabeth thus remains a frustrating mystery. Referring to his father, Rudolf apparently wrote, "I know quite well that I am not worthy to be his son." According to notes left by Ferenczy, the letter ended with a plea that Rudolf be buried at Heiligenkreuz alongside Mary, whom he called "a pure, atoning angel."[35] In her diary Marie Valerie recorded only that her brother made some reference to "the necessity of his death to save his stained honor."[36] Yet Empress Eugénie of France later recalled that Elisabeth told her the letter began with the words "I no longer have any right to live: I have killed."[37]

The fourth of Rudolf's letters likewise bore no date; the content suggests it was likely written in Vienna and brought to the lodge. This was addressed to Count Ladislaus Szögyény-Marich, chief of the Hungarian section of the Imperial Foreign Ministry, and written in Hungarian:

> Dear Szögyéni! I must die—it's the only way to leave this world like a gentleman. Have the goodness to open my desk here in Vienna, in the Turkish Room, where we so often sat together in better times, and deliver the papers as set out in my last will enclosed herewith. With warmest regards and with all good wishes for yourself and for our adored Hungarian fatherland. I am yours ever, Rudolf. Departmental

> Chief von Szögyény-Marich will please open my writing desk in the Turkish Room in Vienna at once and alone. The following letters to be delivered: 1) Valerie; 2) To my wife; 3) To Baron Hirsch; 4) To Mitzi Caspar. Any money that is found please hand over to Mitzi Caspar—my valet Loschek knows her exact address. All letters from Countess Marie Larisch and the little Vetsera girl to me should be destroyed immediately.[38]

A fifth letter was supposedly found in a desk drawer. Allegedly written by Rudolf to an unknown recipient and bearing the date January 30, it read: "Time is running short. I conclude: the Emperor will not abdicate in the foreseeable future. He is heading for decline. Eternal waiting with deeply injurious slights and repeated conflicts unbearable! Aspirations with regard to Hungary magnificent but dangerous. Be watchful! No understanding anywhere for crushing matrimonial relations! Young Baroness chooses the same way because of hopelessness of her love for me. Expiation! Rudolf."[39] Yet this letter has never been seen, and serious doubts surround its authenticity.[40]

Mary, too, had written a number of letters. Until recently their content was known only from Helene Vetsera's privately published booklet on Mayerling. The originals, it has often been said, were destroyed after her death on Helene Vetsera's instructions.[41] But in the summer of 2015, the letters to her mother, sister, and brother were discovered in a bank vault in Vienna, among other papers related to the Vetsera family that had been mysteriously deposited there in 1926.[42]

All of Mary's letters were written at the lodge, on stationery embossed "Jagdschloss [Hunting Lodge] Mayerling," with a crest of antlers at the top. After her death Rudolf tucked three of these into a single envelope with his crest, and addressed it to Baroness Helene Vetsera. "Dear Mother!" Mary wrote. "Forgive me for what I have done; I could not resist love. In agreement with Him I wish to be buried by his side in the cemetery at Alland. I am happier in death than in life. Your Mary."[43] According to what one of Helene Vetsera's friends told Hoyos, the letter contained the line, "We are already very curious to know what things are like in the next world."[44] But these lines do not appear in the recently discovered original.

"We are both going happily into the unknown beyond," Mary wrote to Hanna. "Think of me now and again, and marry only for love. I could not do so, and as I could not resist love, I am going with him. Your Mary. Do not cry for me. I am going to the other side in peace. It is beautiful out here." It has been said that this letter contained an additional postscript, asking Hanna to put a gardenia on her grave every January 13, and ensure that their mother provided for Mary's maid, Agnes Jahoda, "so that she does not suffer from my faults," though these sentences do not appear in the original.[45]

Another letter to Hanna was supposedly found tucked into Mary's clothing: "Today he finally confessed to me that I could never be his; he gave his father his word of honor that he will break with me. Everything is over! I go to my death serenely."[46]

To her brother Franz, Mary wrote: "Farewell, I shall watch over you from the other world because I love you very much. Your faithful sister, Mary."[47]

Mary wrote two further letters. One, to the duke of Braganza, has never been published. It was, said Hoyos, "cheerful" and concerned a feather boa Mary left Braganza, with the request that he hang it over his bed as a reminder of their time together.[48] A week after the tragedy, *Le Figaro* claimed that Rudolf had written the letter to Braganza: "Dear Friend, I must die. I cannot do otherwise. Farewell, Servus, your Rudolf."[49] This seems apocryphal, but Rudolf did add a postscript to Mary's letter: "Cheers, Wasser!" This was a reference to Braganza's nickname of Wasser, or Waterboy, derived from his habit of wearing red scarves like the boys who washed Vienna's cabs.[50]

A final letter was addressed to Marie Larisch. Undated, it was finally shown to the countess some three weeks after Mary's death: "Dear Marie, Forgive me all the trouble I have caused. I thank you so much for everything you have done for me. If life becomes hard for you, and I fear it will after what we have done, follow us. It is the best thing you can do. Your Mary."[51]

Bodies bathed in blood, skulls shattered, brains spattered against walls, the glinting steel of a gun, aching farewell letters—Mayerling was a tableau of horrors. As the wind whipped against the lodge, Mary's cold, naked, and bloody body was carried into a storeroom and hastily hidden beneath her clothing. A dozen hours had passed since Rudolf's death; now Widerhofer carefully wrapped his shattered skull in a length of white cloth, hoping to conceal the terrible wound and prevent more brain tissue from oozing onto the bed. This done, he gently eased the stiffening body back against the crimson-splotched mattress and covered Rudolf with a sheet.[52]

Gathered around braziers for warmth, a crowd of curious spectators—their faces illuminated by flickering flames—watched as a squad of police surrounded Mayerling that evening. "Silent, lost in thought, all eyes turned to the white walls of the lodge that conceals a terrible mystery," reported *Le Matin*.[53] Soon snorting horses appeared out of the dark forest, pulling a hearse that quickly disappeared through a lodge gate. Nothing in nearby Baden had been deemed suitable for the crown prince, and so officials had dispatched a bronze casket by rail from Vienna. It was midnight when the hearse reappeared, now carrying Rudolf's body past the silent crowd and out into the stormy night.[54]

A special train adorned with black crepe bunting waited to carry the crown prince from Baden station back to Vienna. Soldiers loaded the coffin, and at 12:20 a.m. the train finally steamed out of the station. A small crowd ringed Vienna's Südbahnhof (South Station) as the train arrived; a guard of honor stood in the chilly early-morning air along the platform, presenting arms as four court valets carried the casket, covered in a black pall embroidered with a gold cross, to a hearse drawn by six horses. At half past one the grim cortege set off for the Hofburg; thousands stood in "great silence," blanketed in fresh snow, as the hearse made its way down the Ringstrasse. Six mounted lifeguards trotted alongside the hearse; behind walked Dr. Laurenz Mayer, chaplain to the imperial court in the Hofburg; Prince Constantine von Hohenlohe; and Rudolf's *Flügeladjutant* Baron Artur Giesl von Gieslingen and his ordinance officer, Major Count Maximilian Orsini und Rosenberg.

The clock in the Schweizerhof was chiming two when the cortege finally reached its destination. A crowd stood in the courtyard; when they caught sight of Rudolf's coffin, many knelt in the snow. Valets eased the pall-draped casket from the hearse and carried it up the double staircase of honor into the palace.[55] Rudolf's parents were absent: Fearing his wife's unpredictable emotions, Franz Josef made Elisabeth remain in her rooms.[56] In death as in so much of his life Rudolf was alone.

Emperor Franz Josef,
about 1875

Empress Elisabeth in her Hungarian
coronation gown, 1867

The Hofburg in the nineteenth century

(All images courtesy the authors' collection unless otherwise noted)

Crown Prince Rudolf, about 1872

Rudolf in Prussian uniform

Engagement photograph of
Rudolf and Stephanie

Rudolf and Stephanie, about 1882

Stephanie with her daughter Elisabeth, 1890

Prince Philipp of Coburg (Credit: Arturo Beéche/Eurohistory Collection)

Princess Louise of Coburg (Credit: Arturo Beéche/Eurohistory Collection)

Mitzi Caspar

Josef Bratfisch

Moritz Szeps

Rudolf in the hunting ensemble
he wore to Mayerling

Albin and Helene Vetsera

Mary and Hannah Vetsera

Alexander Baltazzi in 1876

Heinrich Baltazzi in 1885

Mary in fancy dress

Mary in the ice skating ensemble she wore to Mayerling

Marie Larisch and Mary, photographed at Adele's, November 5, 1888

Archduchess Marie Valerie with Marie Larisch

Duke Miguel of Braganza

Mayerling, 1889

Johann Loschek

Count Josef Hoyos

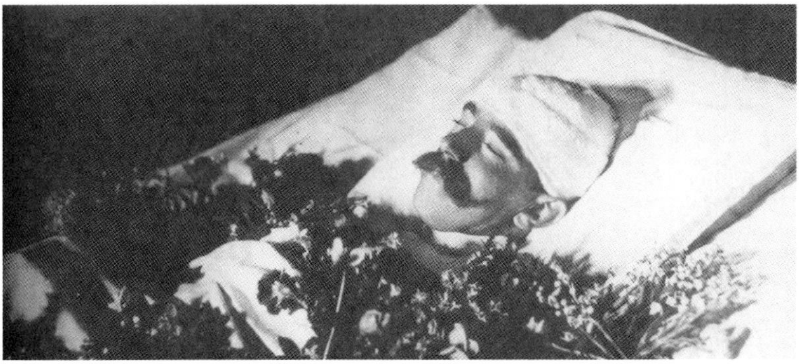

Rudolf in death

Mary's grave at Heiligenkreuz (Credit: Denise C. Clarke/Alfred Luckerbauer)

Mayerling today, showing the church built onto the original lodge (Credit: Denise C. Clarke/ Alfred Luckerbauer)

Altar of the church at Mayerling, built atop the spot where Rudolf and Mary died (Credit: Denise C. Clarke/ Alfred Luckerbauer)

CHAPTER ELEVEN

Vienna struggled to make sense of its crown prince's mysterious death. No one knew what to believe. On the evening of January 30, the *Neues Wiener Tagblatt* reported that Rudolf had been shot in a hunting accident, or that he had died during a drunken orgy.[1] When the *Neue Freie Presse* repeated rumors that a gamekeeper had killed Rudolf after the crown prince seduced his wife, the government confiscated all copies.[2] It was a hint of things to come: Over the next few weeks Taaffe ordered more than five thousand newspapers, magazines, and journals seized in a futile effort to suppress unwelcome speculation.[3]

"With the deepest sorrow," Franz Josef had cabled to Stephanie's parents that Wednesday afternoon, "I must inform you that our Rudolf died suddenly this morning, probably from heart failure, at Mayerling where he had gone to hunt. God give us all strength."[4] The emperor went to bed that night believing that Mary Vetsera had poisoned Rudolf and then herself. By six the next morning, and keeping to his inflexible schedule, he was at his desk when Dr. Widerhofer came to report on his findings at Mayerling.[5]

"Tell me everything frankly," Franz Josef supposedly said to the physician. "I want to know all the details."

"I can assure Your Majesty," Widerhofer replied, "that His Imperial Highness the Crown Prince did not suffer for a moment. The bullet went straight through his temple absolutely straight, and death followed instantaneously."

"What bullet are you talking about?" Franz Josef asked in confusion.

"Yes, Your Majesty, we found the bullet, the bullet he shot himself with," Widerhofer replied.

"He did?" the emperor stammered. "He shot himself? That's not true! Surely she poisoned him! Rudolf did not shoot himself!"[6]

Widerhofer now had to break the truth: Rudolf had killed Mary Vetsera first, sat with her body for hours, and finally shot himself. Hearing this, Franz Josef broke into sobs. Finally, he asked, "Did Rudolf leave a letter of farewell?"

"Several letters," Widerhofer told him. "But none for Your Majesty."[7]

This last insult from a disillusioned son against a distant father snapped Franz Josef out of his temporary shock. "My son," the emperor commented bitterly, "died like a *Schneider*."[8] What did this mean? The word *Schneider*, or "cutter," could have been a derisive reference to the Hungarian tailor János Libényi, who had attacked him in 1853. But more likely Franz Josef was thinking of another association. In hunting "*Schneider*" was used to describe a coward, a stag that hid itself rather than charge forth in challenge.[9]

Franz Josef wanted to see his son's body, but he insisted on changing his clothing first: Etiquette demanded that he pay his respects to an Austrian general by donning the appropriate uniform, complete with ceremonial sword and white gloves.[10] "Is he much disfigured?" he asked Rudolf's adjutant Baron Giesl von Gieslingen.

"No, Your Majesty," the baron assured him.

"Please cover him up well," Franz Josef said. "The Empress wishes to see him."[11] But he was irritated that the body had not yet been dressed in the uniform of an Austrian infantry general; the baron thought that he wanted to get through the ordeal of seeing his son as quickly as possible.[12]

The former Grand Duke Ferdinand IV of Tuscany arrived at the Hofburg shortly before seven that Thursday morning.[13] A collateral Habsburg relative, the grand duke was one of Franz Josef's few trusted friends; he found the emperor "so stunned" that he could only murmur, "Rudolf . . . Rudolf . . . ," again and again. Finally Franz Josef took the grand duke's arm and led him to the bedroom where Rudolf's body was laid out.[14] A blanket had been drawn up to Rudolf's neck; his face seemed serene, but the top of his head was still shrouded in a white wrapping to conceal his shattered skull. For fifteen minutes Franz Josef stood silently by the bed, head bowed, hand clutching the hilt of his sword.[15]

Rudolf's last act horrified and humiliated Franz Josef. His brother Archduke Karl Ludwig found him "deeply shaken and weeping" when he visited him at the Hofburg.[16] The crown prince had not only killed himself but had also committed murder, even if Mary had apparently been a willing partner. His son's suicide, as Stephanie's nephew noted, was "a heavy blow to the Emperor's personal pride, and more especially to his prestige in the Catholic world as Apostolic King."[17] The kings of Saxony and Serbia, newspapers reported, planned to travel to Vienna to attend the funeral, along with the Prince of Wales and Tsarevich Nicholas of Russia; but Franz Josef, hoping to avoid unwelcome questions, wanted no foreign royal representatives at the funeral.[18] "His Majesty," an official assured inquiring embassies, "is most sincerely grateful for all the proofs of sympathy but desires to have around him at this profoundly moving ceremony of mourning none but the closest members of his family."[19] This was understandable. Less sympathetically, Franz Josef dispatched a cable to Stephanie's parents on January 31; even though their daughter was still in shock, the emperor asked them to stay away from Vienna. But the king and queen of Belgium ignored the request and left Brussels the following day.[20]

Late that Thursday morning Stephanie brought five-year-old Elisabeth to see her father's corpse. The room was dim: Curtains shielded the winter sun, while a sea of candles cast eerie shadows over the macabre scene; Stephanie, remembered the emperor's brother Archduke Karl Ludwig, was "weeping bitterly."[21] Elisabeth carried a bouquet of white carnations, rosebuds, and lilies and laid it against the foot of the bed, but she screamed when she saw the bandaged head. "That is not my father!" the little girl sobbed as she hid behind her mother, who quickly led her from the room.[22]

Marie Valerie dreaded the ordeal: "I had never seen a dead body," she wrote. She found Rudolf laid out on his bed, "dead, dead. He was so beautiful and so peaceful, the white sheet pulled up to his chest and flowers ringed around him. The narrow bandage on his head did not disfigure him; his cheeks and ears had a healthy, youthful red glow, and the erratic, bitter expression that he so often had in life had given way to a peaceful smile. . . . He seemed to be asleep, quiet, and happy."[23]

Count Ladislaus von Szögyény-Marich spent that morning in Rudolf's Turkish salon, sorting through the contents of his locked desk drawer.[24] It is said that he found an onyx ashtray: "A revolver, not poison, a revolver is surer," Mary had supposedly scrawled on its basin in violet ink.[25] The last person to see it was apparently Count Artur Polzer-Hoditz, head of Emperor Karl's chancellery, when in 1918 he found the ashtray hidden in a leather suitcase stashed away among some official files.[26] If this was some kind of suicide note, it was certainly a strange one: Why would Mary write these lines, and how would ink remain unmarred and legible on an onyx surface?

This was not the only discovery. Franz Josef had sent Rudolf Kubasek, court secretary in the lord marshal's office, to retrieve anything deemed damaging; this included letters from Mary and from Marie Larisch that Rudolf wanted destroyed. Along with a number of other documents, they were seized and handed over to the emperor.[27] One envelope bore the inscription "Contents: 100,000 Florins" (gulden) ($639,000 in 2017) in Rudolf's hand. When opened, though, it contained only 30,000 gulden ($191,700).[28] The missing 70,000 gulden had probably gone to pay Marie Larisch's gambling debts and ensure her silence about her cousin's affair; in accordance with Rudolf's last wishes, the remaining 30,000 gulden presumably went to Mitzi Caspar.[29] At least one of Larisch's letters to Rudolf, written in the third week of January, informed him that Mary could meet him in a carriage on the Maximilianstrasse at a certain time.[30]

Szögyény-Marich also found the four envelopes described by Rudolf in his letter left at Mayerling, addressed to the financier Baron Maurice Hirsch; Mitzi Caspar; Marie Valerie; and to Stephanie. The letter to Hirsch probably concerned the 150,000 gulden Rudolf had borrowed from him to pay for Mitzi Caspar's house and jewelry.[31] The letter to Mitzi was dated June 1888; she later destroyed it, but Szögyény-Marich told Hoyos that the letter was "overflowing with love."[32]

The undated letter Rudolf left for Marie Valerie has also disappeared. In her diary Marie Valerie noted only that Rudolf had written "of the need to do what he had done, but gave no reason." He also warned her to leave the country after Franz Josef's death, as he feared what would happen to the empire.[33] But Ida von Ferenczy, at least according to Empress Elisabeth's early biographer Corti, recorded that it included the line, "I do not die willingly, but must do so to save my honor."[34] Confusingly, though, in his published work Corti quoted only the first half of this sentence.[35]

The last letter was handed over to Stephanie that afternoon, two pages filled with crowded writing that sloped off the page:

> Dear Stephanie! You are freed henceforth from the torment of my presence. Be happy in your own way. Be good to the poor little girl who is the only thing I leave behind. Give my last greetings to all my acquaintances, esp. to Bombelles, Spindler [Lt. Heinrich von Spindler, chief of the crown prince's secretariat], Latour, Wowo, Gisela, Leopold, etc., etc. I face death calmly—death alone can save my good name. With warmest love from your affectionate Rudolf.[36]

"Every word," Stephanie wrote, "was a dagger thrust in my heart." She continued:

> A storm of indignation and revolt raged within me. What I had foreseen in the quiet, agonizing dread of many lonely hours had now come to pass. My whole personality rose in revolt against the impiety, the wicked frivolity with which a life had been thrown away. . . . I had dreaded this act of self destruction, had (in veiled terms), warned others that it was imminent and nevertheless on this day when the news came it remained an enigma to me. Again and again I asked myself why he had committed suicide. In this moment of profound loneliness my reasoning powers seemed to have deserted me. Thoughtlessly, cruelly, the man had forsaken me, to whom eight years before I had been handed over as a child. I was wounded to the quick and reacted with all my energy against the monstrous cruelty of the fate that had befallen me after lying in wait for me for years. True, death relieved me from a conjugal life which was full of anxieties, cares and sorrows but at what a cost! My own future and that of the country, for which I had endured so much with unfailing patience, seemed to have been shattered.[37]

•

Not a word about Mary Vetsera had appeared in the press but, as Princess Nora Fugger recalled, "all of Vienna spoke about her, said that she was implicated, and was not among the living." Princess Fugger was refused entry when she went to the Vetsera Palace early on the morning of January 31; Mary, the doorman insisted, had a bad cold and was indisposed.[38] The death of one of Rudolf's usual amours might have been concealed, but Mary was a member of the nobility. Explaining away her sudden disappearance from the face of the earth would be impossible. But the imperial court would never admit to her presence at Mayerling, or her death with the crown prince.

Hoping to confine any scandal, Franz Josef had ordered Helene Vetsera out of Vienna. She'd left aboard a train for Venice on the evening of January 30, believing that Mary had poisoned Rudolf and then herself and, as she wrote, "without having seen her tenderly beloved daughter after her death, and without being able to fulfill her last maternal duties." She was "horrified on the journey to think of her daughter's corpse, and agonized by tortured thoughts, wondered if her daughter had been so insane in her adoration for the Crown Prince that she had murdered him."[39]

Early that Thursday morning, as Helene's train rumbled south, officials in Vienna summoned her brother-in-law Georg von Stockau, husband of her sister Eveline, to a meeting; only then did the family learn that Rudolf had killed Mary and then himself. On no account was this news to be made public. The Vetseras could not publish any notice of Mary's death: The family must temporarily act as if she were still alive. Mayerling was an imperial residence; as such, Prime Minister Taaffe decided, events there were not subject to governmental or legal jurisdiction. The imperial court would settle all issues.[40]

Helene Vetsera was still on her way to Venice when a telegram from Alexander Baltazzi rather indiscreetly informed her of these revelations. Suspecting that she'd been deliberately lied to, the baroness abruptly returned to Vienna.[41] She arrived at her palace, "expecting to find her daughter's corpse brought to her house."[42] Instead Stockau told her of the imperial court's orders that "everything was subject to arrangements made by His Majesty." Mary was to be quietly and secretly buried in the cemetery attached to the Cistercian Abbey of Heiligenkreuz near Mayerling; "fearing that otherwise her child might even be buried in secret and without any of her relatives present," the baroness reluctantly agreed.[43] Helene was now handed the envelope, "addressed by the Crown Prince, in his own hand," containing the letters Mary had written to her, to Hanna, and to Franz.[44]

When Taaffe learned that the baroness had returned—and suspecting that she would make trouble and expose the conspiracy—he ordered police agents to stake out her palace and shadow her movements.[45] That evening an official arrived and asked the baroness to leave again and remain away until after the crown prince was buried. Tired of being toyed with, Helene said she would go only if the order came directly from the emperor; a few hours later Taaffe arrived and, in Franz Josef's name, again made the request. For the second time in two days, Helene Vetsera departed the Habsburg capital.[46]

The rights or feelings of the Vetsera family meant nothing to officials. Alexander Baltazzi and Count Stockau would be allowed to escort the body from Mayerling to Heiligenkreuz only under certain conditions: There must be no hearse; her uncles would have to take her body away in a regular carriage. Slatin, along with Police Superintendent Habrda and Inspector Gorup, were sent ahead to convey Taaffe's orders—orders that, as Slatin recorded, "did not correspond literally to the legal requirements." Calling on the district governor of Baden, they insisted that Mary's family wanted her immediately buried at Heiligenkreuz and won his authorization to forgo the legally required inquiry.[47]

Gorup found Abbot Heinrich Grünböck at Heiligenkreuz less agreeable. "I realized that the Abbot would refuse the Church's blessing and burial in a Catholic cemetery," the inspector recalled, "and that it needed all my questionable diplomatic skill to make him change his mind." As Gorup had feared, Grünböck refused to bury a suicide in his cemetery. The inspector tried again, adding Franz Josef's name as leverage: The emperor wanted Mary Vetsera immediately buried in this remote spot to avoid any scandal. Grünböck was still unmoved. Finally Gorup confessed the truth: The imperial court had ordered the finding of death by suicide to hide the fact that the crown prince had shot the young baroness. Hearing this, the abbot finally agreed to allow Mary's burial in his cemetery.[48]

Baltazzi and Stockau left Vienna for Mayerling early that evening of January 31. A storm raged as their carriage rumbled through the dark forest surrounding Baden, pelted by crashing rain, buffeted by gusts of wind, and accompanied by the howling of distant dogs. Finally a flash of lightning revealed the lodge, still ringed by remnants of a curious crowd and a string of journalists who, the police noted warily, "suspect that the dead Baroness Vetsera is still hidden within."[49] The wooden gates swung open, and the carriage rolled to a stop at the main door. Baltazzi and Stockau had to wait for the arrival of Slatin and Police Superintendent Habdra; when their carriage finally stopped in the courtyard, warden Alois Zwerger, a flickering lantern in his hand, led the men through the silent lodge to a small storeroom and flung open the door.[50]

Mary's body had been dumped into a large basket, covered with her clothing, and then ignored. Now, in the dim light, Baltazzi and Stockau saw their niece's cold, naked corpse, "still in the same state in which it had been found the day before."[51] The scene, Slatin recalled, reminded him of some gothic penny-dreadful.[52] Mary's eyes were "wide open and protruding in a fixed stare, the mouth half open, with a stream of congealed blood having poured from it to cover part of the body." No one, Helene later complained, "had done anything" to the corpse, "as if she was unworthy of any help from good, human hands."[53]

After a shocked Baltazzi and Stockau confirmed their niece's identity, they likely left the room as the court physician Dr. Franz Auchenthaler examined the body. He found a small wound, measuring 5 by 3 cm, high on the left temple where the bullet had entered the head; the surrounding skin was ragged and the hair was singed, indicating that the gun had only been a few inches away when fired. The bullet traversed the brain from left to right, shattering the skull. When it exited the head some 2 cm above the right ear canal, it blasted out bone and brain tissue, leaving a gaping wound surrounded by protruding splinters of the skull. There were no other injuries.[54] Auchenthaler also reportedly later found that Mary was suffering from gonorrhea, presumably after being infected by Rudolf.[55]

At the end of his examination Auchenthaler washed the body and called in Mary's uncles. It was up to them to dress the corpse in the same ice-skating ensemble she had worn to Mayerling.[56] This horrific task over, the doctor presented Baltazzi and Stockau with his signed report. Mary had been right-handed; she'd been shot in her left temple. It was obvious that Rudolf must have pulled the trigger, but officials had ordered Auchenthaler to rule her death a suicide.[57] Baltazzi confronted Court Commissioner Heinrich Slatin, who had come from Vienna to supervise the macabre transfer. Surely, Mary's uncle argued, the church would refuse to bury a suicide at Heiligenkreuz. But if Mary wasn't listed as a suicide, Slatin said, judicial authorities would investigate her death, and the imperial court had forbidden any such inquiries; everything had already been settled.[58] Hearing this, Baltazzi and Stockau reluctantly signed the protocol.[59]

Baltazzi and Stockau were ordered to take Mary to their carriage, "and to support the body between you in such a way as to make it appear that the Baroness still lives." The men were horrified; this "loveless desecration of the corpse," Helene Vetsera complained, "cruelly injured the family's feelings."[60] They each took a side and picked up the corpse; Mary's head fell forward and her body sagged to the floor. This would convince no one: She was obviously dead. Not knowing what else to do, someone fetched one of Rudolf's walking sticks and rammed it down inside Mary's jacket to keep her erect. Baltazzi and Stockau again lifted the body, but their niece's head slumped forward. A handkerchief was tightly wound around her neck and tied to the walking stick to keep Mary's head from falling to her chest, with her feathered boa used to provide additional support. Finally Baltazzi and Stockau managed to raise the corpse to its feet. It took both of their efforts, half-carrying, half-dragging Mary's body, to manhandle the corpse into the carriage and onto the rear seat. To keep it from falling over, Baltazzi sat on one side and Stockau on the other, arms wrapped around their niece's body to prevent it from falling forward.[61]

Shortly before ten, with Slatin and Auchenthaler leading the way in a separate carriage, the cortege finally left the lodge and disappeared into the dark, wild night. To avoid attracting any unwanted attention, the commissioner decided to take a longer route to the monastery at Heiligenkreuz, along rarely used roadways.[62] Wind howled mournfully through the forest; sleet pelted the vehicles, and the windows soon frosted over. Mary's corpse swayed and jostled each time the horses bolted and the carriage wheels sank into a rut, falling forward, then back, knocking first against Baltazzi and then against Stockau for two hours as the agonizing ride played out.[63]

The bells at Heiligenkreuz Abbey were just tolling midnight when the carriages finally reached the complex; two monks opened the gates and motioned the procession into the courtyard.[64] Inspectors Habrda and Gorup helped Baltazzi and Stockau lift Mary's body from the carriage and carry it to a small chapel.[65] Officials in Vienna had assured Stockau that they would send a coffin to Heiligenkreuz; but no coffin waited, and the men roused the monastery carpenter to hastily knock together a plain pine box. Mary's corpse was finally laid inside, on a bed of sawdust shavings; Baltazzi cut a lock of his niece's hair for his sister, and Stockau placed Mary's folded hat beneath her head as a pillow. Finally they placed a small silver crucifix in her cold hands.[66] Mary, her mother complained, "was treated like a criminal."[67]

Officials in Vienna had wanted Mary buried under cover of darkness, but the storm made it impossible to dig a proper grave until early the following morning. Shortly before nine on February 1, Father Malachias Dedič read the funeral service over the body, watched by Baltazzi, Stockau, Slatin, Auchenthaler, Gorup, Habrda, and several others. Despite the veil of secrecy imposed by the imperial court, somehow word of the burial had leaked out, and a small crowd stood beyond the cemetery walls, craning their necks and trying to see what was taking place. Rain poured from the gray sky as the quartet carrying Mary's casket slipped and slid over the muddy ground; the wind whipping through the tombstones made lowering the coffin difficult but finally, at half past nine that Friday morning, Mary Vetsera was buried in an unmarked grave, the earth shoveled in, Stockau complained, "with almost feverish haste."[68]

Two weeks after Mary's death, her mother was finally allowed to publish an obituary in the provincial *Illustriertes Grazer Extrablatt*, but only after she agreed to the official lie. Mary Vetsera, it was announced, had died suddenly while traveling to Venice; her body had been taken to Bohemia for burial on a Baltazzi estate.[69] Then the court-imposed veil of silence descended: As if she had never existed, the name of Mary Vetsera, which had filled the capital's fashionable periodicals and passed from tongue to tongue by censorious gossips, would never again appear in any Viennese newspaper until after the fall of the Habsburg monarchy in 1918.

CHAPTER TWELVE

The billiard-room windows in Rudolf's bachelor apartments blazed with light, spilling shadows across the Hofburg forecourt throughout the last night of January 1889. The same storm that enveloped Mary Vetsera's last journey now fell on Vienna, rattling the palace windows.[1] A little after eight, four physicians gathered there to conduct the crown prince's autopsy: The court doctor Professor Eduard Hofmann, director of the Institute of Forensic Medicine in Vienna, supervised Hans Kundrath, director of the Institute of Forensic Medicine's Pathology Department, and court physicians Hermann Widerhofer and Franz Auchenthaler. The commandant of the palace, Ferdinand Kirschner, and Nikolaus Poliakowitz, representing the Lord Chamberlain's Office, stood in a corner, watching as the grim scene unfolded.[2]

Carried in from his bedroom, Rudolf's corpse was stripped of its clothing, laid out on his billiard table, and the white bandage removed from his shattered skull.[3] The complete autopsy report is missing; what little is known of its findings comes in an excerpt released by the imperial court and published in Vienna's newspapers on February 2:

> Firstly, His Imperial and Royal Highness Crown Prince Rudolf died from a skull fracture and destruction of the

> front portion of the brain; this fracture was caused by a shot fired against the right anterior temporal area at close range. A bullet fired from a medium caliber revolver would likely produce the injuries in question; the projectile was not found, as it exited through a hole discovered above the left ear; there is no doubt that His Imperial and Royal Highness fired the shot himself and that death was instantaneous. The premature fusion of the sagittal and coronal sutures, the remarkable depth of the skull cavity, and the so-called fossae impressions on the inner surface of the skull bones, with evident subsidence of the brain passages and distention of the ventricles, are pathological circumstances, which experience has shown are usually accompanied by abnormal mentality, and therefore justify the assumption that the deed was committed in a state of mental derangement.[4]

This offered the public a summation but few specifics. The revolver had been found; why, some asked, did the autopsy not note the specific type and caliber of the gun that had been used? A number of guns were available to Rudolf, from his 9 mm Gasser-Kropatschek infantry officer's revolver to the 11 mm revolver used in the army.[5] Prince Philipp of Coburg inexplicably claimed that Rudolf somehow shot himself with his hunting rifle, presumably by stepping on the trigger—a bit of highly unlikely gossip Empress Friedrich of Germany picked up and repeated to her mother, Queen Victoria.[6]

According to Rudolf Püchel, who saw the body, "the entire upper right side" of the skull was shattered.[7] It seems likely, however, that Püchel's memory failed him. Rudolf probably had his head slightly bowed and bent to the right when he shot himself: The bullet entered the right temple and traversed the brain before blowing out the top left side and rear of his skull. But in the absence of hard fact, speculation ran rampant. On February 1, Moritz Szeps's

Wiener Tagblatt reported that Rudolf had aimed the gun against his lower-right jaw and shot upward, blowing out the top of his forehead and skull; Taaffe quickly had the newspaper confiscated.[8] A few months later one of the first books on the tragedy measured the entrance wound at 7 cm in diameter and placed it 3 cm above the right ear, while Baron Krauss's granddaughter asserted that Rudolf had shot himself in the mouth—claims contradicted by both the autopsy excerpt and by witnesses who actually saw the body.[9]

The autopsy ended at two on the morning of February 1, and the body was embalmed. By tradition Rudolf would lie in state before the public, but his shattered skull presented a problem, and no one knew quite what to do. Officials toyed with the idea of having a sculptor make a model of Rudolf's head and fit it to a fake corpse, dressed in the appropriate uniform, which could then be displayed.[10] This, though, would take too long, and so a mortician was called in to reconstruct the head. It took several hours of work and a copious supply of peach and pink wax before the damage was concealed; as the top of Rudolf's head had been blasted into pieces, it seems a hairpiece was fitted onto the skull and any remaining holes daubed over with dark brown paint.[11] The end result fooled no one: A scar from the torn skin still pocked the right temple, and the face had an unnatural look that led some correspondents to report that it was actually a wax mask.[12]

For the second time in twenty-four hours, an uncomfortable Widerhofer had to stand before the emperor and deliver a devastating bombshell. But Franz Josef seemed surprisingly receptive to the declaration that his only son had been suffering from mental illness. For the unimaginative emperor, it explained so much: his troubled relationship with Rudolf; his son's wayward behavior and questionable decisions; and even his death could all be laid at the door of an organic imbalance, absolving Franz Josef of any personal responsibility. "God's ways are inscrutable," the emperor said calmly. "Perhaps He has sent me this trial to spare me yet a harder one."[13] Parental grief there certainly was, but the remark also hinted at a certain pragmatic sense of relief that Franz Josef no longer need worry over his son's eventual rule.

The declaration that Rudolf had been mentally deranged benefited everyone except the empress; the finger of genetic blame inevitably pointed away from the Habsburgs and toward Elisabeth and her eccentric Wittelsbach relatives. "The Emperor should never have married me!" she cried. "I have inherited the taint of madness!"[14] Marie Valerie wrote of her mother's "rigid anguish" in fearing that "her Bavarian blood had risen to Rudolf's mind."[15] Hysterical sobs alternated with bitter recriminations: Elisabeth blamed Rudolf for not having confided his troubles, refusing to admit that her absences and apparent lack of concern had left him alienated and alone. "Now all the people who spoke such nastiness about me from the first hour of my arrival," she complained bitterly to Marie Valerie, "will have the consolation that I shall disappear without leaving a trace in Austria."[16]

The questionable finding that Rudolf had been mentally deranged at the time of his death owed more to expediency and religious considerations than medical reality. As the historian Baron Oskar von Mitis noted, the examining physicians "had gone to the greatest possible lengths in their judgment on these pathological points."[17] Onerous and humiliating rules imposed by the imperial court had dictated Mary's secret burial; now the Habsburgs faced a similar dilemma in winning Rudolf his last rites. A crown prince who had murdered his mistress and then killed himself would be denied a Catholic funeral, but the Church accepted mental derangement as a mitigating factor when considering the burial of suicides. And so, on the emperor's authority, the imperial court issued a new bulletin: "His Imperial and Royal Apostolic Majesty the Emperor wishes to take His People into His confidence about the circumstances that make even more tragic the disaster at Mayerling." The statement went on to announce that Rudolf had indeed killed himself, while alone and in a state of mental derangement.[18] As supporting evidence the excerpt from his autopsy report was released to the press. By the evening of February 1 Vienna's newspapers published and expanded this newest version of events. The *Wiener Zeitung* told its readers: "We cannot conceal that several persons in His Imperial and Royal Highness's closest entourage had, in recent weeks, repeatedly observed signs of a pathological nervous excitement in his exalted person, so that one must embrace the view that this terrible event was the result of momentary confusion of his mind."[19]

Many found this explanation too convenient. "The latest news that Rudolf's death is attributed to suicide has hardly met with belief," reported one foreign newspaper from Vienna.[20] Moritz Szeps took issue with the official announcement in the pages of his *Wiener Tagblatt*. It was, he loyally insisted, beneath Rudolf's dignity as a prince to have killed himself. He protested against the declaration of insanity; the facts about Mayerling, he thought, were being concealed.[21] "They are still hiding something!" people complained to a French correspondent, who noted that "the most contradictory rumors circulate."[22]

Franz Josef had waited some twelve hours after the first official announcement to telegraph word of Rudolf's death to Pope Leo XIII: "With the deepest sorrow I must inform Your Holiness of the sudden death of my son Rudolf. I am sure of your deepest sympathy in this cruel loss. I offer up this sacrifice to God, to whom I render without a murmur what I have received from him. I beg your Apostolic blessing for myself and my family."[23] The pope was less than sympathetic: According to Vatican Secretary of State Mariano Rampolla, Leo XIII was "greatly offended" that the king of Italy learned of the tragedy first.[24]

But now the emperor had to appeal directly to a put-out Leo XIII: Having admitted suicide, he needed papal dispensation to have the crown prince buried according to Catholic rites. On February 1 and again the next day, Franz Josef sent two personal letters to the pope.[25] Neither has ever surfaced, though they almost certainly raised Rudolf's alleged mental illness and warned of an unthinkable scandal if the Church objected to a Catholic funeral. What is known of the discussions between Vienna and Rome comes from a diplomatic dispatch Prince Reuss sent back to Bismarck in Berlin. On this point at least Reuss had an impeccable source: Monsignor Luigi Galimberti, the papal nuncio in Vienna and a man squarely in the middle of negotiations with the Vatican. Galimberti, "one of the handsomest, cleverest, most cultivated, and affable men in Europe," recorded an aristocrat, "enjoyed society immensely" and had a nose for gossip.[26] Relying on Galimberti, Reuss reported:

> The Papal Nuncio told me of the great embarrassment in which the Pope found himself concerning his consent to the church burial of the Crown Prince. Had this consent not been forthcoming, and had it been necessary to bury the suicide without the blessing of the church, the population of Vienna would undoubtedly have given itself over to the very worst excesses. His Majesty was therefore supremely worried until the autopsy was completed, and the doctors and court officials made the declaration of probable insanity. The Emperor immediately dispatched Kálnoky [the Foreign Minister] to submit a report of the official findings to the Nuncio. Monsignor Galimberti reported this by telegram to Rome, and thus dispelled the church's scruples. In this country, too, the Nuncio has met with many inquiries from bishops as to the attitudes they should adopt. He pointed out that insanity excuses suicide in the eyes of the church. "My official conscience is clear," the Nuncio added to me. "I only have to believe what the Foreign Minister tells me. Nevertheless, this is probably the first time in history that a Papal Nuncio will attend the funeral of a murderer and a suicide representing the Pope."[27]

The declaration of mental derangement won Rudolf his Catholic funeral, but the uproar was immense. Cardinal Rampolla protested, and persuaded the entire College of Cardinals to boycott the Vatican's requiem for the crown prince. The pope argued that such a public snub would evoke hostile comment and unnecessarily wound Franz Josef's feelings, but Rampolla remained unmoved.[28]

At nine on the evening of Sunday, February 3, a black-robed choir sang Palestrina's mournful *Miserere* as soldiers carried Rudolf's coffin through the Hofburg to the Hofkapelle, the royal chapel, where he would lie in state. The white-and-crimson chapel had been transformed into an unrelieved sea of black: Crepe cloaked walls, adorned the little galleries ringing the interior, and draped the altar and the pews; a black carpet covered the floor. Silver-and-gold escutcheons bearing Rudolf's coat of arms hung on the walls; floral wreaths heavily scented the air. Silver candlesticks circled a seven-foot-high bier, set before the altar and beneath black crepe cascading from a baldachin above. Four soldiers, two Austrians in crimson-and-gold jackets and two Hungarians with leopardskin dolmans draped over their shoulders, stood frozen at the corners, ceremonial swords in hand and silver-helmeted heads bowed. Rudolf rested in an open coffin. He had been dressed in the uniform of an Austrian general: a white tunic with red collar and cuffs adorned with gold stars, over red trousers and shining black boots. The red-and-green sash of the Order of Saint Stephen stretched across his chest; his gloved hands clutched a small ivory cross. Velvet cushions around the bier displayed Rudolf's princely crown, his archducal crown, his green-plumed general's hat, his ceremonial saber, and his orders and decorations. The court choir chanted as priests blessed the body and prayed through the night.[29]

It was a bitterly cold night, but more than one hundred thousand people braved the weather to pay their respects to the dead crown prince when the doors of the Hofkapelle opened to the public at eight on Monday morning. No one had anticipated such crowds: Cold, tired, and anxious to see Rudolf's body, they pushed through the Schweizerhof attempting to reach the Hofkapelle. The few officers lining the entrance had to draw their swords to prevent a stampede; excited women beat back at them with fists or umbrellas, and a number of people were injured in the crush.[30] Although Franz Josef extended the viewing by three hours that evening, and allowed another four the following morning, only thirty thousand of his subjects gained admittance to the small chapel.[31]

Hidden away behind the Hofburg walls, the imperial family seemed to be in a daze. Franz Josef, Marie Valerie recorded, "was quiet, godly, and sacredly heroic" in his acceptance of Rudolf's death, but Elisabeth could only sob about predestination and a nagging sense that she had tainted her son with Wittelsbach madness.[32] Gisela, who arrived from Bavaria "nervous and anxious," insisted, "It is impossible that Rudolf is dead!" She was kept from viewing the corpse only with great difficulty.[33]

Stephanie, too, seemed lost: For the first time the emperor and empress asked her and her daughter to join them for meals, but this proved unnerving as Franz Josef and his wife kept breaking into tears at the sight of their granddaughter.[34] But they seemed curiously cold toward Stephanie, who couldn't escape the feeling that the couple, especially the empress, blamed her for Rudolf's death. When her parents arrived from Belgium on the evening of February 3, they found their daughter in despair but the emperor and empress "less ill and stricken than we expected."[35] The empress treated the visiting king and queen with the same cold disdain she reserved for her daughter-in-law: Elisabeth had no wish to share her grief with others.[36] It got to Stephanie. She was tired of the perpetual blame, the desire that she act contritely, as if her husband's suicide had been her fault. There was, Marie Valerie noted, a "horrific dinner," during which "Mama and I could not hold back our tears, while Stephanie, cold and—God forgive me—heartless, spoke of all and sundry." Elisabeth abruptly interrupted the meal to chastise her daughter-in-law in front of the startled guests, saying that she was ashamed of her behavior.[37]

Tuesday, February 5, dawned cold and gray in Vienna. An icy wind howled along the Ringstrasse, whipping black mourning banners and bunting stretched across facades into grotesque shapes. Deep crowds lined the streets: That afternoon the funeral procession would travel from the Hofburg to the Kaisergruft, the imperial crypt beneath the Capuchin Church on the Neuer Markt—the traditional resting place of the Habsburgs since the sixteenth century. As the city's bells began their mournful tolling, a weak winter sun finally broke through the leaden sky, shimmering over tiled roofs still glistening with patches of snow.[38]

"I have before me the hardest task of all," Franz Josef wrote that morning to Katharina Schratt.[39] Threats had restricted the ability of Mary's family to grieve openly; nor could the Habsburgs mourn Rudolf without considerations of protocol and appearance. Franz Josef would face the ordeal of his only son's funeral without his wife. Elisabeth's mental state was so fragile that, fearing she might make some public outburst, Franz Josef asked her not to attend the service: Instead she remained closeted at the Hofburg with Marie Valerie. Nor could Stephanie bear the condemnatory looks and silent recriminations she feared would come her way. And so Franz Josef entered the Hofkapelle at four that afternoon with his daughter Gisela, followed by a string of archdukes and archduchesses who crowded into the black-draped pews as the court choir sang the *Libera Me*. Flickering candles surrounding the bier shimmered as Cardinal Prince Archbishop Ganglbauer incensed the coffin and prayed for the dead crown prince.[40]

At the end of the service, soldiers carried Rudolf's coffin—now closed and covered with a pall embroidered with his coat of arms—out of the Hofkapelle and into the Schweizerhof, placing it on an elaborate, Baroque-style hearse replete with gilded cherubs and twisted columns supporting an arched canopy topped by a gold crown.[41] Instead of the customary black horses, six young gray Lipizzaners caparisoned with fluttering black ostrich plumes pulled the hearse as it took Rudolf from the Hofburg for the last time.[42]

The clip-clop of hooves, the sharp clicks of regimental boots on the cobbles, and the muffled drumbeats announced the start of the procession beneath a sky growing dim with impending twilight. A detachment of hussars opened the cortege, followed by mounted divisions from the elite Imperial and Royal Guards Regiments. Swaying ranks of priests marched ahead of a contingent of courtiers and state and municipal authorities in black carriages. Franz Josef was barely visible behind the windows of his state carriage as he rode with Gisela; grooms in elaborate mourning liveries and tricorne hats walked in measured pace, leading black horses drawing court equipages filled with Habsburgs and members of Rudolf's suite and household. Clad in medieval Spanish costume, a rider appeared atop a single Lipizzaner—a visible reminder of the imperial court's former Iberian ties. Finally the hearse came into view, flanked by pages in medieval liveries holding aloft flaming torches. Six members of the Royal Archer Guard, attired in crimson coats and silver helmets with waving plumes, galloped at one side of the hearse, balanced by six members of the Hungarian Life Guards Regiment in red tunics and fur dolmans draped over their shoulders on the other. Holding shining halberds, a contingent of mounted bodyguards in medieval dress led hundreds of soldiers and sailors drawn from the empire's military and naval services, marching in tribute to their dead crown prince.[43]

The procession halted before the door of the inconspicuous sixteenth-century Capuchin Church. Soldiers lifted the coffin from the hearse and carried it to the closed door, where Karl von Bombelles, armed with his golden staff of office as Rudolf's lord high chamberlain, stood waiting. Raising his staff, Bombelles rapped loudly against the doorway three times.

"Who is there?" asked a voice from within.

"His Imperial and Royal Highness the Most Serene Crown Prince, Archduke Rudolf of Austria-Hungary," Bombelles replied.

"We know him not!" the voice declared. Bombelles again knocked three times on the closed door.

"Who is there?" came the query.

"Archduke Rudolf!" Bombelles cried out.

"We know him not!"

Bombelles rapped on the door a third time. "Who is there?" came the question.

"A poor sinner!" Bombelles announced.

"He may enter," the voice answered, and the doors were flung open to receive the coffin.[44]

The cardinal prince archbishop of Vienna sprinkled the coffin with holy water and incensed the body, then led the procession to the altar, where another bier waited to receive the crown prince. Franz Josef followed, taking his place in the first pew next to Gisela and Stephanie's parents. As members of the black-robed court choir intoned the *Libera Me*, Franz Josef "kept a fixed gaze" and stared stoically ahead.[45] With the solemn absolution ended, Franz Josef's brothers Archdukes Karl Ludwig and Ludwig Viktor; his nephew Archduke Franz Ferdinand; his son-in-law Prince Leopold of Bavaria; Marie Valerie's fiancé, Archduke Franz Salvator; and Rudolf's brother-in-law, Prince Philipp of Coburg, followed him as soldiers carried the coffin to the crypt's entrance.[46]

By tradition Bombelles was to head the procession below, but at the last minute the emperor stepped forward and led his son to his final resting place. Down the staircase and through the maze of vaulted chambers forming the Kaisergruft, the cortege moved toward a side niche, its shadows illuminated by flickering lanterns. Franz Josef had maintained his mien of studied calm throughout the ceremonies; standing in the crypt and surrounded only by his family, he admitted, "I could endure it no longer.[47] He fell to his knees, sobs racking his body as he embraced the coffin and repeatedly kissed its lid.[48]

"The heaviest blow which could hit a father's heart," read the emperor's message to his subjects, "the immeasurable loss of My Dear Son, had filled with the deepest mourning Myself, My House, and My Faithful Peoples. Shaken to My very depths, I bow My head in humility before the unfathomable decision of Divine Providence."[49] Past events replayed themselves constantly in his mind as he sought answers and absolution; the fact that Rudolf had pointedly left him no farewell letter stung deeply.[50] "There is no purpose in going over it all again," he admitted to Schratt, "but one cannot think of anything else."[51] Life became a charade, with Franz Josef acting the part of stoic emperor, but to Marie Valerie he admitted, "I am becoming sadder with every passing day."[52]

Franz Josef not only buried Rudolf in the Capuchin Crypt but also, as one historian noted, under "a cloak of fictive recollection."[53] Never, the emperor insisted, had there been any trouble between them: Rudolf's death, he said, was "the first vexation my son has caused me."[54] For Franz Josef death had suddenly transformed Rudolf into "such a clever man, with such a good heart."[55] To Schratt he described Rudolf as "the best of sons" and the "most loyal of subjects."[56] It was the only way he could make peace with the situation and with himself.

All investigation into Rudolf's death was called off. "The Emperor has expressed the desire that silence be maintained about the tragedy at Mayerling," an official warned the press, appealing to "feelings of loyalty and decency" in asking that newspapers stop reporting the story.[57] Those papers and journals that questioned the official story continued to be confiscated and destroyed. Secrecy descended over events at Mayerling. "Anything," Franz Josef declared, "is better than the truth!"[58]

PART III

CHAPTER THIRTEEN

Rudolf's interment did nothing to stop the onrush of escalating rumors about events at Mayerling. Within twenty-four hours of his funeral, newspapers had managed to ferret out the basic circumstances, describing the movements and actions of Loschek and Hoyos at the lodge.[1] But few were convinced by the official version. "The story that someone killed Rudolf is as of much value as the carefully elaborated account of his suicide," *The New York Times* reported on February 3. "Berlin, Brussels, and Paris are full of rumors, all discrediting the theory that the Prince took his own life."[2]

It didn't take long for the foreign press to learn of Mary Vetsera and spin out a tale of tragic romance. On February 2 Munich's *Neuesten Nachrichten* reported that the young baroness had committed suicide with Rudolf at Mayerling.[3] The following day *Le Figaro* noted "much talk about of a single disappearance: the Baroness Mary W[*sic*], who has not been seen since Tuesday. The family claims she is at Schloss Pardubitz [Pardubice, the Larisch estate in Bohemia] but no one has seen her and the public does not believe it."[4] By February 5 *Le Temps* was reporting that "the death of a beautiful young girl, whose father was a baron, has produced a great sensation in Vienna."[5] But the rival French paper *Le Matin* scooped its competitors with "the fantastic tale of the mysterious disappearance of Baroness Vetsera related to the tragic drama of

Mayerling." Mary, it declared, was "among the most beautiful women in Vienna, with velvety eyes, a queenly attitude, and a romantic character; her appearance was very admired in worldly circles, which always welcomed her with murmurs of admiration." Hours after the public learned of Rudolf's death, "word got around that the young lady had committed suicide and been mysteriously buried at night."[6]

Vienna was still reeling. "It is all too sad and dreadful," recorded Walburga Paget. "They are most anxious to believe it was Mary Vetsera who inveigled the Crown Prince into all this. But how so silly a girl could have persuaded so clever a man as the Crown Prince of Austria to end his life in such a stupid, dirty, undignified and melodramatic way I cannot conceive. I cannot see the logic—it was not baffled on love. The fact is he was a maniac and she a vain, unprincipled girl who wanted the world to speak of her."[7]

Those privy to the intimate details unanimously echoed Franz Josef's insistence that "anything" was "better than the truth." "It is horrible, horrible," Prince Philipp of Coburg cried to his wife. "But I cannot, I must not, say anything except that they are both dead."[8] Rudolf's death, Coburg wrote to Queen Victoria, was "a terrible, frightful, unspeakable misfortune. It is a mystery to me how such a talented, clever man, who was so revered in Austria-Hungary, who so clung to Emperor and country, could commit such a deed! I, who was at Mayerling, who saw everything, can assure you that only the assumption of a disturbed state of mind can make this terrible thing comprehensible."[9]

To his brother Philippe, count of Flanders, King Leopold II of the Belgians confided: "It is absolutely imperative to maintain the suicide version. It may seem difficult, in the eyes of our Catholic people, to see the House of Habsburg insisting on the suicide story. But suicide while of disturbed mind is the only way to avoid an unheard of scandal."[10] Franz Josef's brother Ludwig Viktor insisted that "the whole truth is so frightful that one can never confess it!" Hoyos used the same word—"frightful"—to describe what he had seen, adding, "I have given the Emperor my word that I shall not say a word."[11]

No one knew what to believe. The British prime minister, Lord Salisbury, assured Queen Victoria that he was positive Rudolf and Mary had been murdered. The Prince of Wales, though, was equally adamant: "It seems poor Rudolf has had suicide on the brain for some time," he reported to his mother; sources in Vienna assured him that Rudolf's action had nothing to do with Mary Vetsera. The entire episode, the Prince of Wales wrote, "is like a bad dream."[12]

Authorities moved quickly to tie up loose ends. Several courtiers were ordered back to the lodge to destroy any remaining trace of Mary's presence there.[13] Coburg, Hoyos, Widerhofer, Rudolf's servants, and members of the court commission had originally been asked to answer questions during a meeting on the evening of January 31.[14] Loschek was discussing the tragedy with Prince Constantine Hohenlohe shortly before five that afternoon when Prime Minister Taaffe strolled into the room. He was "in exceptionally high spirits" as he announced that the session was cancelled. Two days later the emperor ordered Taaffe to preside over a secret meeting; Widerhofer was present, but Loschek was surprised that Coburg, Hoyos, the court commissioners, and Rudolf's other servants were excluded. Taaffe read out a short summary of events—so quickly, Loschek recalled, that he could scarcely follow what was being said. At the end Taaffe confiscated all official files and papers concerning Rudolf's death and warned everyone to keep silent about events at Mayerling.[15]

Taaffe kept his promise to the emperor: The confiscated files seem to have been shuffled off to his Bohemian country estate, Schloss Ellischau, for safekeeping.[16] After his death in 1895, his son, Heinrich, took control of the Mayerling papers. Heinrich claimed to have deposited them in a wooden chest handed over to his Viennese lawyer; in 1912, when he asked for the return of the box, the files had allegedly been removed.[17] The Mayerling historian Fritz

Judtmann thought it was likely that the box never held any of the contentious papers: The clumsy story of their disappearance was simply meant to throw future historians off their scent.[18] That this was the correct interpretation was later shown by two facts: In 1919 Countess Zoë von Wassilko-Serecki was staying at Schloss Ellischau. Her grandfather, Baron Franz von Krauss, had been Vienna's chief of police at the time of the Mayerling tragedy; she also happened to be a cousin of Heinrich Taaffe's second wife. While at Ellischau, the countess recalled, Taaffe abruptly asked if she would like to read the missing Mayerling files before he destroyed them. She spent the entire night examining the documents before handing them back to Heinrich Taaffe, presumably to be burned.[19]

But Heinrich Taaffe did not burn the papers, as he told the countess: in 1922—three years after their supposed destruction—he allowed Professor Artur Skedl of Prague University access to a selection of the files for inclusion in a book on Prime Minister Taaffe—proof that they continued to exist after allegedly being destroyed.[20] In 1926 fire swept through the library at Schloss Ellischau, and the press reported that the conflagration destroyed the missing Mayerling papers.[21] But the documents had been kept, as Countess Wassilko-Serecki recalled, in the castle archives, which were not harmed in the blaze. Heinrich Taaffe died in 1928. Nine years later his widow told the *Neues Wiener Tagblatt* that she believed her husband had destroyed the Mayerling papers to ensure that "the confidence placed by the Emperor in his father was not betrayed."[22] This was more obfuscation. Possession of the papers passed to Heinrich's son, Eduard, who in 1937 moved to Ireland—presumably with the documents. In correspondence with Fritz Judtmann in the 1960s, Eduard Taaffe did not deny that the Mayerling papers still existed, but he refused to allow access to them, explaining that he had given "a solemn promise" never to reveal their contents. "The circumstances of the Mayerling affair," he added, "were far more frightful than was imagined."[23] When Eduard Taaffe died in 1967, the papers apparently passed to his cousin Rudolf Taaffe, who both confusingly denied any knowledge of their whereabouts and then later hinted obliquely about the possible contents.[24] Whatever secrets Rudolf Taaffe possessed went with him to his grave in 1985. It seems likely that the enigmatic Taaffe papers do indeed still exist, frustratingly hidden away somewhere and apparently destined to remain so—the "holy grail" of Mayerling materials—suspected of containing momentous secrets surrounding events at the lodge.

Bribes in the form of pensions and monetary gifts also helped suppress the truth. Loschek received some of Rudolf's clothing and his guns; although only forty-five years old, he was immediately pensioned off with the promise of 1,300 gulden a year ($8,307 in 2017).[25] Josef Bratfisch, who knew all of Rudolf's secrets, proved more troublesome. On behalf of the imperial court, Lord Chamberlain Prince Alfred Montenuovo discreetly approached the carriage driver and asked him to leave Vienna in exchange for a considerable amount of money.[26] Bratfisch refused, insisting that he could be trusted. No one was convinced, and Chief of Police Krauss warned the prime minister that his agents had Bratfisch under constant surveillance. "I have also ordered them," he wrote, "to see that no journalists should get in touch with him." He worried that Bratfisch, "who occasionally goes in for excessive drinking," might become inebriated and in that state begin to spill his secrets.[27] Two months after Mayerling, Bratfisch suddenly bought a house and started his own cab company complete with horses from the imperial stables—developments suggesting that the court had bought his silence with a sizable amount of money.[28]

No one in Vienna, though, worried as much as Countess Marie Larisch. She'd accepted Helene Vetsera's bribes of gowns and money to facilitate the affair; she'd blackmailed Mary in exchange for arranging meetings; and she'd extorted enormous sums from Rudolf to do his bidding and ensure her silence. She'd lied to the police, denied any involvement, and desperately tried to exculpate herself when the house of cards threatened to come tumbling down. Married to a minor aristocrat, the empress's illegitimate niece lived on the fringes of society, accepted only because she was in favor at the Hofburg—and now that imperial favor threatened to evaporate.

Trapped in the web she had helped spin, Larisch could only sit helplessly in her suite at the Grand Hotel, hoping that the storm would pass. Then, on the morning of February 5—the day of Rudolf's funeral—a group of officials arrived to question her about her role in the liaison. Larisch tried to deny everything, but it was futile. Several of her letters to Rudolf, offering to arrange meetings between her cousin and Mary Vetsera, had already been found in the crown prince's desk; two days earlier Frau Wolf—Mitzi Caspar's madam—described to police agent Florian Meissner how Larisch had been acting as a go-between for the crown prince and Mary Vetsera, information Rudolf had apparently confided to Mitzi.[29]

At first Larisch insisted that Loschek and Bratfisch had actually arranged everything; she had only been following her cousin's orders. But then officials brought Mary's maid, Agnes Jahoda, into the room and the accusations began to fly as each woman blamed the other for encouraging the young baroness. The empress had sent a courtier to ask her niece about Rudolf's state of mind; sensing an opening, Larisch admitted that her cousin had been behaving strangely.[30] This confrontation—and details of Larisch's involvement in the affair—were reported back to the Hofburg; when Larisch went to see her aunt, she was stunned to find herself abruptly turned away. Empress Elisabeth refused ever to receive her niece again.[31]

Suspicion turned to anger after Rudolf's funeral, when an accidental discovery sealed the countess's fate. Tadeusz Ajdukiewicz, a Polish artist who had been painting an equestrian portrait of the crown prince, still had the dolman Rudolf had worn to his last sitting; a search of the pockets disclosed a highly compromising letter from Larisch to her cousin, detailing her complicity in the liaison and exposing her persistent blackmail. Ajdukiewicz turned the letter over to Franz Josef; from that moment, Larisch complained, "a vicious circle enveloped me."[32] Orders came from the Hofburg: Marie Larisch was forbidden ever to appear at the imperial court again. The empress, Larisch insisted, had "made use of me, and she threw me aside without a regret."[33]

Now designated the "crown princess widow," Stephanie, too, was a victim caught in the web of her husband's misadventure. Her marriage had existed only in name, and she soon made her peace with Rudolf's actions. Stephanie even developed a kind of sympathy for Mary Vetsera, viewing her as yet another of her husband's victims. Rudolf, she complained, had "traded upon Mary Vetsera's passion" in seeking death at her side. In turn Mary's "profound and sincere love" for him, however immature, excused her "poor, misguided" actions.[34]

The emperor and empress continued to blame Stephanie for Rudolf's suicide and slowly but surely excluded her from their circle. Although she had basked in perpetual mourning following Prince Albert's death, even Queen Victoria worried that the young widow needed a reprieve from an oppressive, opprobrium-filled Vienna. Would Stephanie, she asked, care to come and stay with her at Windsor Castle for a few weeks? But, as if exacting whatever punitive retribution against their daughter-in-law they could find, Franz Josef and Elisabeth flatly vetoed the proposal. Humiliated and insulted, feeling trapped amid her dead husband's embittered family, Stephanie soon took young Elisabeth and retreated to Schloss Miramar in distant Trieste.[35]

•

The Austrian government had moved heaven and earth to hide Mary Vetsera's death at Mayerling. Despite her secret burial, the continued confiscation of newspapers, and the lies her family were forced to repeat, though, inevitably word leaked out, and soon curious crowds began haunting the cemetery at Heiligenkreuz, searching for Mary's unmarked grave. Within a week of the tragedy Helene Vetsera leaked two of Mary's farewell letters to *Le Figaro* in Paris.[36] "The mother of the young girl is now in Venice," Prince Reuss reported on February 9, "where she is parading her daughter's disaster without making any secret of the romance. This throws a clear light on this person, who claims to have received a promise that, provided she disappear and keep quiet before the burial, everything could be published later. Blackmail cannot be excluded here."[37]

By the end of March, as Countess Eleonore Hoyos wrote in her diary, "the snake, the viper, the horrific" Helene Vetsera was back in Vienna.[38] Helene was still careful to conceal her role in the affair, even from her own family. To her sister Elizabeth in England, she wrote:

> I am so much ashamed of myself not having written to you up to now. . . . You see, in the beginning, I really could not. This thunderbolt that fell on me felled me to the ground. You know how I worshipped Mary, perhaps too much, and that is why I have been cruelly punished. I can assure you that my grief is worse than ever; I cannot see how I am ever to forget all this dreadful past and as long as I do so my life and my thoughts can only be full of anguish. . . . She left us three such beautiful letters, childish, but also showing that faith that there must be a world the other side more beautiful than this one. . . . The last fortnight her nerves must have been very broken; we saw there was something the matter with her, but had no idea as I did not know they knew each other until they were both dead. . . . I spent six weeks in Venice to patch up my broken nerves and then I came back here to go and see her grave which I had not been able to do before leaving. The coming back into this house was dreadful. From morning to night she was about me (except for the few times she left the house with that bad woman Countess Larisch, who knew everything and who might have saved them through a word) that now I miss her every hour of the day.[39]

Larisch, for her part, was fighting her own battle against Helene and her Baltazzi brothers. It was, she complained, "a scandal" that they were attempting to "roll everything onto me" and blame her for the liaison. Heinrich had abruptly broken with her—"for him to rant against me," Larisch raged to one of Helene's relatives, "is a vile, shameful thing." Now she was "bitterly set against him," and she wanted her former lover to know that he "may tremble before my revenge" when she exposed "how the Messrs Baltazzi behave toward women."[40]

Worried about the scenes at Heiligenkreuz, Prime Minister Taaffe tried to bribe Helene, offering her a considerable sum of money if she exhumed Mary's body and took it away for secret burial elsewhere. Infuriated, she refused. Scheming social climber though Helene Vetsera may have been, she felt that she'd been treated appallingly. Brimming with resentment, she now decided to make a spectacle of her daughter's grave as a permanent irritant to the imperial court. On May 16 she had Mary's plain pine casket exhumed, placed within a large, ornate copper casket, and reburied in a more prominent grave at Heiligenkreuz, "the most beautiful spot in this world of God's creation," Helene wrote, "a heavenly spot, one can call it."[41] An elaborate wrought-iron grille surrounded the new grave's monument:

MARY
FREIIN V. VETSERA
GEB. 19 MÄRZ 1871
GEST. 30 JÄNNER 1889
WIE EINE BLUME SPRIEST DER MENSCH AUF
UND WIRD GEBROCHEN
(MAN COMETH UP LIKE A FLOWER AND IS CUT DOWN)
JOB 14:2.[42]

Not content to stop with the grave, Helene commissioned a Romanesque-style marble memorial chapel in the cemetery. A large stained-glass window above the altar depicted the Virgin Mary; Helene originally asked that her face be modeled after Mary's, but officials vetoed this proposed bit of effrontery, nor would they allow any mention of the Vetsera name. Instead artisans worked Mary's features, and those of her brother Ladislaus, who had perished in the 1881 Ringtheater fire, onto the faces of angels kneeling on either side of the Virgin. Denied use of the family name, the Latin inscription on the chapel's memorial plaque read:

In pious memory of
Ladislaus and Mary,
Her sweetest children snatched away prematurely,
The grief-stricken mother,
Redeeming a vow,
Built this chapel,
In the year of Our Lord 1889.[43]

Helene Vetsera's provocative actions came amid her ongoing struggle against the imperial court. Since returning to Vienna, she'd deluged the emperor with plaintive letters. Everyone, she complained, knew the truth about Mayerling, and everyone unfairly blamed her daughter. Society had followed the court's lead, punishing the Vetseras and Baltazzis for Rudolf's actions. The baroness wanted Franz Josef to issue a statement absolving her of responsibility for the tragedy and warning that her remaining children should not be ostracized.[44]

Franz Josef pointedly ignored the baroness's pleas. With no satisfaction forthcoming, Helene decided to take revenge by writing and publishing an account of Mary's liaison with the crown prince and its tragic denouement, drawing on her daughter's letters and personal papers. She secretly delivered the manuscript to the Viennese publisher Johann N. Vernay at the beginning of May, and by the end of the month 250 copies of *Der Vetsera Denkschrift* went out to bookstores and newsagents. Just as quickly, police raided the publisher and news stalls, seizing every copy they found.[45]

Despite their best efforts, however, a few dozen escaped destruction and were smuggled out of Austria. When the Austro-Hungarian ambassador in London heard that *The Times* was about to print a translation, he intervened and had the publication quashed. But *Le Temps* in Paris published extracts on August 26, while both *L'Éclair* and the *Liverpool Daily Post* printed the complete memoir on September 3.[46] This booklet was, of course, meant to present Mary and her mother in the best possible light. Helene unconvincingly claimed complete ignorance of the affair until a few days before the tragedy; she blamed Larisch for having conspired with her daughter and the crown prince and facilitated the liaison behind her back. Later the baroness's surviving daughter, Hanna, made a handwritten copy of her mother's original manuscript, adding details about Larisch's blackmail schemes that did not appear in the published version.[47]

The Habsburg court took a dim view of these developments; Helene Vetsera won not imperial compliance but scorn. By July, Franz Josef had enough, and ordered his chief of protocol to reply to the baroness's constant stream of pleading letters. At first the communiqué seemed conciliatory: "Even from the very first moment," it assured Helene, "the thought that you might have been an accomplice in this terrible tragedy never entered His Majesty's head." But this was the only olive branch extended. The letter went on to chide the baroness for becoming "entangled in the accusations" surrounding Mayerling. She would "have been better advised to have refrained from attempting to excuse [herself] in public" by publishing her memorandum and "taking the law into your own hands." By doing so she had "compromised [her] own child and flaunted the matter in public." As such, societal retaliation against the Vetsera family was only to be expected. The emperor was sorry if her maternal feelings had been wounded by Mary's hasty burial, but the tragedy had demanded secrecy. The baroness would do well to "bear with calm devotion the heavy sorrow that Fate has placed upon you."[48]

There the matter rested. Helene Vetsera would be shunned, but she had the satisfaction of knowing that crowds regularly flocked to her daughter's grave at Heiligenkreuz, tearing away pieces of ivy from the headstone as treasured souvenirs.[49] It was a place evocative of tragic romance, at least until the spring of 1945, when Heiligenkreuz came under heavy fire by Soviet artillery as they advanced against the retreating Nazis. One shell landed atop Mary's grave, smashing through the top of the coffin.[50] Occupying Soviet troops spent the next year ransacking the cemetery and pilfering graves. Using a garden hoe, they hacked away at Mary's casket, smashing in the top and sides, severing her skull from the body in the process, and searching the remains for jewelry and valuables. The grave was left open to the elements, Mary's bones in disarray, her skull thrown to one side of the coffin, and the hoe haphazardly tossed in before the soldiers abandoned their quest.[51]

Authorities at Heiligenkreuz could do nothing until the Soviets left. In 1948 the grave was sealed with a new stone slab; then, in 1959, an Italian lady heard of the terrible state of Mary's grave and volunteered to pay for a new coffin. The grave was exhumed on July 7, 1959. When the stone slab was lifted, it revealed the shattered bronze coffin beneath, its lid dented and awry.[52] Water had filled the casket, and it was impossible to raise it; the gravedigger Alois Klein descended, opened the lid, and tried unsuccessfully to bail out the brackish water. Finally Klein simply ripped pieces of the skeleton from the muck and placed them in buckets. Hauled to the surface, the skull, vertebrae, femurs, pelvis, and other disarticulated bones—"all coated with a fine layer of black slime"—were laid out "randomly" in a new metal coffin, along with clumps of hair and the remnants of Mary's clothing, hat, and shoes.[53]

In transferring the remains, Klein managed to examine the skull. It was shattered and fragmented, though it was impossible to determine if this dated from Mary's death or if the Soviets had caused the damage during their clumsy exhumation. Despite its poor condition, Klein thought he "clearly" saw two small gunshot wounds, one on the left temple, the other above the right ear.[54] Yet the local physician Gerd Holler later claimed to have seen only a small oval hole, measuring approximately 5 by 7 cm, at the top of the head.[55]

Holler developed a startling theory: Mary, he suggested, died as the result of a botched abortion, with Rudolf killing himself out of remorse. Larisch, Holler claimed, engaged the services of the midwife Theresia Miller to perform an abortion—at least this is what the midwife's grandson, Emil Miller, told him. This procedure supposedly took place at the Hofburg on the morning of January 28, when a catheter was inserted into the uterus; this was to be left in place for twenty-four hours, and Rudolf and Mary went to Mayerling so that she could rest. The next night, according to Holler, an unknown woman arrived at the lodge, presumably to remove the catheter. But something went wrong, and Mary bled to death; in despair, Rudolf then shot himself.[56] Aside from the fact that serious questions surround some of Emil Miller's claims, Holler largely ignored troublesome evidence contradicting his theory, including Mary's suicide letters and the accounts of those who saw the bullet wound to her head.

But the theory only played into larger accusations of conspiracy. Then, in 1991, the story took a truly bizarre turn. Helmut Flatzelsteiner, a middle-aged furniture salesman from Linz, first read Gerd Holler's book, *Mayerling: Die Lösung des Rätsels—Der Tod des Kronprinzen Rudolf und der Baroness Vetsera aus medizinischer Sicht*, in 1988 and became obsessed with the case. Flatzelsteiner apparently believed he was in psychic communication with the dead couple.[57] One July night in 1991 he crept into the cemetery at Heiligenkreuz and, aided by two confederates, secretly exhumed Mary's remains. "I had anticipated something pretty," Flatzelsteiner said of the remains, "but it was all wet, dirty, and smelled awful."[58]

After cleaning the skeletal remains, Flatzelsteiner said he approached several forensic experts, claiming that the body belonged to a relative who had died a century earlier. He wanted to know if they could determine the cause of death. Professor Dr. Klaus

Jarosch at the University of Linz concluded that the remains belonged to a woman approximately eighteen years of age. The skull was incomplete: Portions of the jaw were found in the coffin, but little remained of the cranium from the tops of the eye sockets down. Jarosch couldn't determine with certainty if there had been a bullet wound—the skull was simply too fragmented. He did, though, believe that it had been subjected to multiple fractures, which might have led to death.[59]

Thinking that he had a blockbuster mystery, Flatzelsteiner began shopping his story around to journalists. After being approached, though, the writer and historian Georg Markus went to the police with the tale of grave robbing, and authorities quickly seized the remains.[60] After examination, Professor Dr. Johann Szilvássy of the Institute of Forensic Science at the University of Vienna agreed that the remains likely belonged to an eighteen-year-old female; she had probably died a hundred years earlier. He agreed that the skull was too fragmented to accurately determine any possible injuries.[61] Yet conflicting reports kept the press speculating. A small, semicircular groove in the left temple might have been caused by a bullet, but press reports insisted that it was impossible to make any definitive finding.[62]

Although the use of DNA as a forensic tool was then still in its infancy, genetic testing could have established that the remains belonged to Mary. Rumor hinted that Vetsera and Baltazzi descendants would donate blood to enable the necessary examinations, yet no genetic testing ever took place.[63] This only led to more speculation, including stories that the genetic material was too deteriorated to obtain an uncorrupted sample. An order suddenly came from the family prohibiting further inquiries. "It's incomprehensible to me," complained Professor Georg Bauer, who had been examining the remains in Vienna, "why, more than a hundred years after the tragedy, the tools of modern forensic sciences and corresponding investigations are being prevented."[64] In the end the remains were placed in a new coffin and on the morning of October 28, 1993, reburied in Mary Vetsera's grave at Heiligenkreuz.[65]

Unlike Mary, the Mayerling controversy refused to rest quietly. Stories that her skull bore no trace of a bullet wound in 1959 had stoked the flames of conspiracy theories: Modern examinations only added fuel to the fire. Was the severed skull found in the coffin really Mary's, or had the Soviets simply tossed a random head into her grave? And if not, what was the explanation? Was there really no trace of a bullet wound to the skull, or was the small groove at the side of the head evidence that Mary had been shot in the head? Did the extensive fracturing mean that Mary had been killed in an argument with Rudolf? Or, as increasingly popular theories suggested, had Rudolf and Mary been murdered? For more than a century confusing claims have cloaked events at Mayerling; to solve the mysteries it is necessary to return to January 1889 and examine how the seemingly impenetrable layers of rumor first consumed the story.

CHAPTER FOURTEEN

What really happened behind those locked bedroom doors at Mayerling? When Rudolf closed them, he and Mary were still alive; the following morning both were dead. The answer seems obvious: Rudolf killed Mary as part of a suicide pact, and then turned the gun on himself. Horrified and humiliated by events at Mayerling, Franz Josef ordered inquiries stopped and Mary's death at his son's side concealed, actions that only fed the rumors. The official story changed no fewer than three times in forty-eight hours, and newspapers questioning the facts were seized. Investigation into events at Mayerling was abruptly cancelled and the findings concealed—all giving rise to a widespread belief that something was wrong, something was being hidden from the public.

"I do not believe that it could have been simply a love affair," wrote Princess Nora Fugger, "because the Crown Prince of a powerful empire has many means at his command to terminate or continue love affairs with young girls as he sees fit."[1] The theories ranged from the plausible to the outrageous, including claims that Rudolf did not die at all. Unlike the famous Grand Duchess Anastasia of Russia, who was long rumored to have miraculously escaped the execution of her family in 1918, Rudolf supposedly planned his own apparent death to escape an empty life as heir to the throne. In 1937 an obscure book appeared called *He Did Not Die at Mayerling*. This laid out the theory that Rudolf was involved in a conspiracy against his father; when the emperor confronted his son, Rudolf decided to stage his own death to escape punishment. He supposedly fled to America, where he worked as a lawyer in New York City before dying in the 1950s.[2] Or, according to another version, Rudolf actually fled to El Salvador, where he lived under the name Justo Armas until his death in 1936.[3]

In 1992 the late Archduke Otto, son and heir of Austria's last emperor, Karl I, said, "I believe most in the version of a double suicide," but then added enigmatically, "As long as I live, the secret of Mayerling will not be completely solved."[4] To what "secret" was the archduke alluding? This evocative turn of phrase encapsulated a century of suspicions. The imperial court's shifting explanations undermined its credibility; even when it admitted that Rudolf had shot himself, it concealed Mary's presence and death at the lodge—something most of Vienna had already learned through pervasive gossip.

Rumor replaced fact in the days after Rudolf's death. "The truth is that no one knows anything," declared *Le Figaro*.[5] And the correspondent for *Le Temps* warned, "I am obliged to convey the rumors, but do so with the utmost reservations, as there is a lot of exaggerated fantasy in the air."[6] This fantasy proved dangerous: On the day of Rudolf's funeral Viennese police swarmed through cafés, arresting anyone overheard questioning the official version of events.[7]

Within twenty-four hours of Rudolf's death, tales of his murder by a vengeful gamekeeper at Mayerling swept Vienna. When the *Neue Freie Presse* dared mention the rumor on February 1, the government confiscated the edition.[8] Unencumbered by imperial censorship, however, *The New York Times* picked up and elaborated on the tale: "Rumor says that he was shot through the window by a person employed on his estate who afterwards committed suicide," it reported.[9] And the next day, citing a report from Berlin, the paper wrote that the gamekeeper's corpse had been secretly burned and buried in the woods.[10]

The French press, similarly free to repeat the prevalent gossip, continued the story: "New information confirms the view that a jealous ranger killed Rudolf," *Le Matin* told its readers on February 4. "For some time, this ranger at Mayerling suspected his wife's relationship with the Prince. The woman is said to be very pretty." Having shot Rudolf, the gamekeeper then "blew his own brains out."[11] The next day *Le Gaulois* named the culprit as a forester called Werner. Having discovered his wife's affair with Rudolf, Werner supposedly attacked the crown prince; Loschek, according to this account, found Rudolf's body in the snow outside the lodge, "his skull broken and his side pierced; nearby lay the body of gamekeeper Werner, with his rifle—which he had used to commit suicide—by his side."[12] Additional stories in *Le Temps* speculated that, on returning from his rounds, Werner had seen a mysterious figure climbing out of his bedroom window and fired at him; he shot himself on discovering that he had killed the crown prince.[13] Unfortunately for this theory, no man named Werner was ever employed at Mayerling, nor did any member of the lodge staff die at the time.[14]

Yet the gossip was so prevalent that even Prime Minister Taaffe remarked on it. He dismissed it as nonsense, saying, "An Austrian forester who surprises the Emperor's son with his wife does not shoot, but starts to sing *God Save Our Emperor*!"[15] Taaffe's remark was more reflective of wishful thinking than reality, and it did nothing to quiet speculation. According to Bay Middleton, Empress Elisabeth confided that Rudolf had been killed over a love affair, though not with Mary Vetsera.[16] Franz Josef's adjutant Albert von Margutti heard, through a bit of secondhand gossip, that servants had found Rudolf in the snow outside the gamekeeper's lodge on the morning of January 30, with his head battered. Some years later Margutti mentioned this to Count Ludwig Apponyi, the Hungarian grand chamberlain at court. Finally Apponyi said, "Well, it's the solemn truth! But keep it to yourself. We had it straight from a member of the hunting staff at Mayerling immediately after the Crown Prince's death." According to Apponyi, Mary had earlier killed herself after Rudolf ended their liaison.[17]

After the fall of the Habsburg monarchy, Margutti spoke to Rear Admiral Ludwig Ritter von Hohnel, who had served as an adjutant to Franz Josef in 1889. Hohnel repeated the same tale, but claimed he'd learned of it after seeing a letter Hoyos had written to a Hungarian relative detailing the affair. Franz Josef, according to Hohnel, somehow learned of this letter and ordered Hoyos to retrieve and immediately destroy it.[18] The story seems to have been popular at court: Franz Josef's valet Eugen Ketterl repeated the details in his own memoirs, saying he'd learned of them thirdhand.[19]

Rudolf's amorous exploits lend the story a certain ring of plausibility, although a more likely object of his affection at Mayerling was his former mistress Anna Pick, who lived on the estate with her husband, Count Reinhard von Leiningen-Westerburg. This makes it theoretically possible that the crown prince continued his amorous relationship with her, but the count certainly didn't kill himself in the aftermath of Mayerling, nor did he suffer any social stigma.[20] Yet if Rudolf was killed by a wronged husband, how to explain his suicide letters? Why would the imperial court and the government conceal the fact, especially if the culprit had then killed himself? Admitting death at the hands of a man bent on revenge would certainly have been far less damning to the Catholic Habsburgs than a cover story that Rudolf had shot himself.

Equally popular in the days immediately following Rudolf's death was the rumor that he'd been shot in a duel. Once again it was the unencumbered French press that took the lead in printing what was only whispered in Vienna. On February 2 *Le Figaro* reported rumors that Rudolf had "caused serious offense to someone almost as noble as he," a young woman from a prominent aristocratic family. As a result one of her relatives challenged him to a duel, during which Rudolf was killed.[21] That same day *Le Matin* noted that talk in Vienna "traced the origin of the mystery to the seduction of a young girl of princely family who was an intimate of Archduchess Marie Valerie." According to this, her brother had shot Rudolf during a duel.[22] More details emerged over the next few days: The young woman was a princess and had found herself pregnant with Rudolf's child. When she confided her situation to her brother, he challenged Rudolf to a duel; Rudolf refused to fire his gun, but not so the outraged brother, who killed him. A lot of hints were dropped about "one of the first families of Austria," but not until February 9 did *Le Temps* finally mention the name Auersperg in connection with the gossip.[23]

Princess Aglaia von Auersperg had indeed been one of Marie Valerie's confidantes. According to these stories, Rudolf seduced her. When she confessed her pregnancy to her brother Karl, ran the tale, the outraged prince challenged Rudolf to something called an American duel: Two balls, one black, the other white, were placed in a sealed box. When Rudolf blindly pulled out the black ball, he had a set period of time to do the honorable thing and kill himself.[24] There was, in this absurd story, no explanation as to Mary's demise or of her suicide notes. No one took it seriously except the Auerspergs: As late as 1955 the princess's descendants sued one Viennese newspaper for repeating the salacious gossip.[25]

Nothing, it seemed, could suppress the wild tales spreading through Vienna. On learning of the tragedy, Papal Nuncio Luigi Galimberti had rushed to Mayerling on the afternoon of January 30. Ostensibly he came to pray over Rudolf's body, but Court Commissioner Heinrich Slatin thought that Galimberti was more interested in chasing down rumors that Mary Vetsera was there and might also be dead.[26]

In the week following the tragedy Galimberti seems to have absorbed all the stray bits of gossip circulating in Vienna and passed them on to the German ambassador. On February 9 Prince Reuss reported to Bismarck on the "increased support for the rumor that the Crown Prince, as well as the young lady found on his bed, were murdered." If true, Reuss speculated, the imperial court had been forced to lie as any judicial investigation would have revealed "the entire, rather immoral circumstances" of Rudolf's death. "To avoid this, the Emperor is said to have made the possibly much worse and more damaging admission of suicide, which could then be exonerated by insanity." Then Reuss repeated the rumors about Rudolf that Galimberti had shared: "The bullet did not pass from right to left, as officially stated, but from back left behind the ear upwards, where it left the head. Moreover, other wounds were found on the body." According to the papal nuncio, the revolver found hadn't belonged to Rudolf, and its chambers were empty, suggesting that all six bullets had been fired. As for Mary, Galimberti confided that her wound was "not at the temple, as has been maintained, but at the center top of her head. She, too, is said to have had other wounds."[27]

This dispatch has loomed large in Mayerling conspiracies, yet closer examination suggests that Reuss was merely passing along what was at best thirdhand gossip—albeit highly placed gossip—as whispered by Papal Nuncio Galimberti. Speculation about the number of bullets fired, for example, circulated in Vienna: In a February 15 article, the correspondent for *Le Temps* traced them to an unnamed Hungarian aristocrat, who seems to have repeated the claim freely.[28] While reporting the tales to Berlin, even Reuss noted that they did "not fit in with the fact that a great many circumstances point to suicide."[29]

Galimberti, Reuss noted, heard these rumors from Grand Duke Ferdinand of Tuscany "and from other quarters."[30] Not that these were the only claims circulating: A spurned Mary, went one, castrated Rudolf and then killed herself; he'd suffered numerous wounds fighting off some unnamed assassin, claimed his aunt Archduchess Maria Theresa and Duke Miguel of Braganza to various courtiers; his hands were so injured that they had to be gloved, he had a broken jaw, he was "frightfully mutilated"—on and on the rumors went.[31]

On July 3, 1907, the Milan newspaper *Corriere della Sera* noted the death two days earlier of the former Italian ambassador to Vienna, Count Constantine Nigra. The obituary included some startling claims about Mayerling. Nigra, it was said, had accompanied Papal Nuncio Galimberti to the lodge on the afternoon of January 30 and was taken to see Rudolf's body. A bandage swathed the head; without a word Loschek supposedly unwound the wrappings, and Nigra saw that the skull "was shattered, as if it had been hit with a bottle or a thick stick. Hair and splinters of bone penetrated the brain. A wound gaped under and behind the right ear."[32]

In fact some serious questions surround the story attached to Nigra's name. Between January 31 and February 7, the ambassador sent a total of seven official dispatches back to Rome; in none did he mention having visited the lodge or viewed the corpse—curious omissions if, in fact, the count possessed such vital first-hand information.[33] The article also claimed that Nigra accompanied Professor Widerhofer to Mayerling—something patently untrue—and that Franz Josef had arrived at the lodge that afternoon and thrown himself into Nigra's arms, a touching scene that never happened, as the emperor remained in Vienna.[34] The most that can be said is that Nigra *may* have been at the lodge that afternoon with Galimberti and *perhaps* viewed Rudolf's body. But his official dispatches, and the fictitious details attributed to Nigra only after his death, undermine the controversial claims advanced in his name.

The most persistent of all Mayerling theories, though, whispers of a raucous party gone wrong, with Rudolf beaten over the head—usually with a Champagne bottle—and Mary shot by a drunken guest. The next morning, so these stories go, the lodge was in a shambles, with furniture overturned and broken glass strewn across the carpets.[35] In 1942 a carpenter at Mayerling named Friedrich Wolf insisted that there were signs of "a bitter struggle" in Rudolf's bedroom. Blood, he claimed, was spattered over the walls and floor, chairs were overturned and broken, and at least five bullet holes pocked the walls and furniture—evidence that apparently eluded every other person who inspected the room.[36]

Death by Champagne bottle first appeared in the 1897 German booklet, *Der Mord am Kronprinzen Rudolf*.[37] The story soon took on a life of its own. The anonymous *Society Recollections in Paris and Vienna* repeated the story in 1907, claiming information from Archduke Franz Ferdinand's adjutant.[38] Then, in 1910, a curious article appeared in *The New York Times*, quoting an enigmatic "Doctor H"—described as a confidant of Stephanie's sister Louise, who had supposedly confessed all to him. According to this bit of secondhand gossip, a drunken party at Mayerling, having "reached the point when it was about to turn into an orgy," took a deadly turn when Rudolf boasted of Mary Vetsera's physical charms and demanded that she display them to his guests. When she refused, he ripped the bodice from her dress; insulted, she hurled a heavy Champagne glass at his head. Injured and infuriated, Rudolf pulled out his revolver and shot her. Fearing for their lives, the rest of the party fell on Rudolf, battering him over the head—albeit with a candlestick.[39] As Princess Louise actually insisted that Rudolf had killed himself, this suspicious tale only further muddied the waters.[40]

When the theory next arose, it came from a source undeniably close to the Habsburgs: Princess Louisa, daughter of Grand Duke Ferdinand of Tuscany. In her 1911 memoirs Louise described her father's visit to the Hofburg on the morning of January 31. When Franz Josef took him to view Rudolf's body, Louisa wrote, the grand duke "was horrified to see that the skull was smashed in, and that pieces of broken bottle glass protruded from it. The face was quite unrecognizable, and two fingers of the right hand had been cut off." When the grand duke questioned Loschek, the valet supposedly spoke of "a very uproarious dinner" at Mayerling on the night of January 29, during which Rudolf was fatally injured in a drunken brawl. Louisa speculated that Mary had struck him over the head with a Champagne bottle, after which some crazed guest shot her.[41]

Thereafter the essentials of the story—a drunken brawl with Rudolf beaten over the head with a Champagne bottle, and Mary then shot dead by someone else—regularly cropped up in the accounts of Habsburg courtiers. Young Elisabeth's governess repeated them in her 1916 anonymously published memoirs, as did Count Roger de Ressegtier, son of one of Franz Josef's chamberlains, in his 1917 book.[42] Laurenz Mayer, the Hofburg court chaplain at the time of Rudolf's death, repeated the claim to several people, including Artur Polzer-Holditz, head of the Court Chancery under Austria's last emperor, Karl I.[43] Karl Wagemut, chaplain to the family of Duke Robert of Parma—whose daughter Zita became Karl I's consort—echoed the tale, as did a forester at Mayerling and the son of a policeman who had been on duty at the lodge.[44]

In 1932 Princess Louisa's brother Archduke Leopold agreed with his sister's account of Grand Duke Ferdinand's visit to the Hofburg. "Standing by the bedside, very cool and collected was the Emperor's chief physician Dr. Widerhofer," he wrote, "and Father could hardly restrain himself from crying out in horror when he saw the doctor drawing out of Rudolf's skull with most business-like precision large pieces of broken green glass. The skull was obviously fractured, for it had several ugly gashes from which the brains were protruding and it was evident that the wound which had been inflicted must have caused instantaneous death." According to his son, the grand duke believed that some unnamed man—identified only as one of Mary's admirers—arrived at Mayerling to protest her presence there. An inebriated Rudolf insulted him, and the mysterious visitor picked up a Champagne bottle and struck him over the head, accidentally killing him. On learning of this Mary poisoned herself. "The whole thing," Leopold quoted his father as saying, "was so frightful that it had to be hushed up."[45]

Grand Duke Ferdinand of Tuscany certainly arrived at the Hofburg on the morning of January 31, and seems to have accompanied

Franz Josef when the emperor went to view his son's corpse. He spread any number of rumors questioning the official version of events at Mayerling, principally to Galimberti, but the one thing he apparently *never* did was to make any claim about seeing glass pulled from Rudolf's head. That story comes only from two of his children and, under closer examination, collapses.

One problem involves the timeline: Franz Josef received Widerhofer at 6:00 on the morning of January 31; the audience was over by 6:40, when the grand duke arrived at the Hofburg, and shortly after 7:00 Franz Josef—and presumably Ferdinand—entered Rudolf's bedroom. Widerhofer had wrapped Rudolf's head at Mayerling; the doctor would have had to race through the Hofburg after meeting Franz Josef, hastily rip the bandage from Rudolf's skull, and immediately begin extracting glass in order for the grand duke to see him at work. But Widerhofer had no need to examine the head that morning: He'd done so the previous afternoon, and would assist at the autopsy that night. Nor does it make any sense that the emperor would be admitted to view his son's body if a medical procedure was taking place, much less when Rudolf's shattered skull was unwrapped and his lacerated brain exposed.

More problematically, as Archduke Leopold admitted, it was "some years later" when the grand duke supposedly confided these details to his children, likely placing it at a time after the Champagne-bottle theory had already appeared in print.[46] Princess Louisa published her book in 1911, three years after the grand duke's death. By this time her family had all but disowned her after she left her husband, Crown Prince Friedrich August of Saxony, and ran away to Switzerland with her children's French tutor. Her husband divorced her, and in 1903 Franz Josef deprived Louisa of her Austrian rank and titles. Four years later she abandoned the tutor to marry the musician Enrico Toselli; she sought her revenge against the Habsburgs in her memoirs.

Nor did her brother, who confirmed her account several decades later, enjoy a stellar reputation. Like his sister, Archduke Leopold had fallen from favor when, in 1902, he ran off with a woman of notorious reputation and married her, renouncing his rank and titles in the process and adopting the name Leopold Wölfing. Divorce followed in 1907, and thereafter the former archduke moved swiftly from scandal to scandal. Wölfing's 1932 memoirs are filled with the most absurd, demonstrably false information. Perhaps he simply repeated and elaborated what his sister had claimed in 1911 in an attempt to bolster her story. But their contradictory accounts and varied theories reveal that Louisa and Leopold—like many others—were merely repeating gossip and speculating on what may have happened at Mayerling.

Who, according to these tales, killed Rudolf? On the morning of January 30, Princess Louise of Coburg wrote, an unnamed courtier arrived at her Vienna palace with the alarming news that her husband had murdered the crown prince. Prince Philipp had attended the dinner for Marie Valerie on the evening of January 29 and then promptly disappeared; he did not return home until the afternoon of January 31.[47] In a bit of secondhand gossip, it was later said that Duke Miguel of Braganza confided to an official—while intoxicated—that Coburg had killed Rudolf by striking him with a Champagne bottle.[48]

In 1963 Karl Albrecht, whose policeman father, Thomas, had been on duty at Mayerling, claimed that the duke of Braganza had been responsible for the deaths at Mayerling, apparently acting out of jealousy. According to Albrecht, "Prince Lónyay"—presumably a reference to Elemér Lónyay, who in 1900 became Stephanie's second husband—had joined the duke in this misadventure.[49] In fact the duke of Braganza was with his regiment in Graz on January 29–30.[50]

But most of these tales name one of Mary's uncles—usually Alexander or Heinrich Baltazzi—as the man who allegedly wielded the Champagne bottle. Storming into Mayerling to rescue Mary, and finding her in bed with the crown prince, Baltazzi supposedly erupted in anger, battering Rudolf over the head with a bottle and either accidentally shooting his niece as she tried to protect her lover or else killing her in a fury.[51] More than a few of these versions insisted that Baltazzi was seriously injured in the battle over Mary's honor and either quickly succumbed to his wounds or was forcibly exiled from Austria when his crime was discovered.[52] Both claims are demonstrably false. Mary's uncles lived on for several decades, and in Vienna, where they continued to dominate smart society.

Stories of vengeful Baltazzis have a certain appeal but, like the rumors of a murderous forester, they collapse under scrutiny. Who, under this scenario, wrote the suicide letters? And what of the fact that Mary died hours before Rudolf? Few but the most conspiratorially minded took the notions seriously: Had a Baltazzi killed Rudolf, there would have been no reason to obfuscate the truth. The imperial court could certainly have put forward a more convincing—and morally acceptable—story than the version that Rudolf had killed himself. This didn't stop Baltazzi descendants from strenuously objecting. As late as 1976 Mary's nephew Heinrich Baltazzi-Scharschmid threatened to sue for libel one author who had repeated the claim.[53]

Death by Champagne bottle has lingered on in Mayerling theories for more than a century. But, if true, why would the imperial court resort to the far more damaging story that he had killed himself? How would a blow to the head, under any circumstances, be worse for the Catholic emperor than admitting to the suicide of his only son? Three things are apparent. Accounts of drunken parties and glass in Rudolf's head began to appear only after the 1897 publication of the German booklet *Der Mord am Kronprinzen Rudolf*, and all are, at best, second- and often third- or fourth-hand versions of supposed events at Mayerling. Then, too, nearly all stemmed from Habsburg relatives or their courtiers. Under ordinary circumstances their intimate proximity to events and actors would lend such tales an aura of credibility. Here, though, it's hard to escape the sense that these stories originated in a shared goal: to undermine the idea that Rudolf had killed Mary and then himself, and thus free his memory from the moral odium of murder and suicide.

A strong sentimental romanticism still surrounds the Habsburgs in modern Austria; many refuse to accept that Rudolf shot himself, much less that he killed Mary Vetsera.[54] And so, in a quest for more morally palatable alternatives, theories that Rudolf died in a political assassination have increasingly taken hold.

CHAPTER FIFTEEN

Over the decades tales have emerged from the shadows of history, tales suggesting that Rudolf was murdered for political reasons. Unlike some of the more imaginative stories surrounding his death, these, at least, offer a motive firmly grounded in one of Rudolf's more troubling misadventures.

Hungary looms large in several of these alternative theories. Although Rudolf had once insisted that the country must forever remain part of the Habsburg empire, his views softened over time and he discreetly threw his support to those aligned against the liberal Hungarian prime minister Kálmán von Tisza.[1] Hoping to counter Rudolf, Tisza sought to neutralize the crown prince with a powerful appeal to his vanity. The Ausgleich of 1867 preserved, at least in theory, Hungary's right to demand its own king; in 1883 Tisza suggested that Rudolf could assume the throne. Hungary would remain part of the Habsburg empire, but Rudolf would take Franz Josef's title as Apostolic King of Hungary.[2]

Agents shadowed Rudolf's every movement, and a network of spies regularly intercepted, read, and reported his private correspondence to his great-uncle Archduke Albrecht. The humorless Albrecht was aghast on learning of the Hungarian proposal. "I must warn you against it," he counseled Rudolf, "because the title of Majesty that you would acquire would only flatter your vanity."[3]

And so the crown prince let himself be talked out of the idea—a move he deeply regretted as the years passed and political power and influence remained elusive.

Rudolf nursed his regret for five years, until the autumn of 1888, when he joined a shooting party at Sáromberke, the Transylvanian country estate of his close friend Count Samuel Teleki von Szék. One alcohol-fueled evening, the story goes, talk turned to Hungarian independence, with Teleki making a plea for Rudolf's cooperation. A document was supposedly produced, and an inebriated Rudolf signed his name, pledging to support a rebellion that would give him the Hungarian crown.[4]

The idea that Rudolf was actively plotting against his father is certainly startling, yet the remaining evidence seems conclusive. In his last weeks of life he was reading books about the coup against Paul I of Russia, led by his son and heir, Alexander.[5] According to Stephanie, Rudolf was indeed involved in "secret plans" that she found "wholly repugnant." While Rudolf had "great respect for the Emperor, he was ready to fling this respect to the wind as soon as anyone reminded him that he himself would one day mount the throne. His conviction was that he was predestined to inaugurate a new era, and he was ready to hazard everything on a single cast of the dice."[6] Stephanie would go no further, at least in public; privately, though, she was more direct, referring to a "conspiracy" in which "the Crown Prince acted against the Emperor."[7]

This conspiracy seems to have been something of an open secret among the Habsburgs. According to Karl I's private secretary, Karl von Werlmann, Rudolf "had involved himself in a Hungarian adventure. Later on, he wanted to withdraw from it, but he could not find a way out." Werlmann's source, someone who "knew all the details personally from Franz Josef," was almost certainly Emperor Karl himself.[8] Artur Polzer-Hoditz confirmed this view, writing that Rudolf's death stemmed from "an affair of a political nature" and adding: "From everything that has hitherto come to light about this tragedy of the Imperial House, we may infer with a probability that almost amounts to certainty that Crown Prince Rudolf regarded death as the last and only solution of a terrible conflict of a political nature."[9] In 1983 Karl's elderly widow, Empress Zita, suggested that Rudolf had been murdered as part of a conspiracy against his father; it seems likely that the fantastic details she relayed originated in her late husband's knowledge of a Hungarian scheme.[10]

The issue was to be pressed in late January 1889, when Prime Minister Tisza laid a new army bill before the Hungarian parliament. Among the proposals was Vienna's demand that use of Magyar be outlawed in the military: German was to be the exclusive language. This infuriated Hungarian nationalists, among them Count István "Pista" Károly, a prominent member of parliament and a vocal proponent of Magyar independence. Károly opposed the bill; if the debate became contentious—as everyone assumed it would—it could be used to challenge Tisza's liberal coalition and bring down his government.[11]

Károly, as everyone knew, was one of Rudolf's closest Hungarian advisers; it didn't take much imagination to believe that Austria's crown prince backed the Magyar nationalists, and Károly did nothing to challenge the idea. Before the debate Károly let slip that he was in regular telegraphic communication with Rudolf. He added that "a very trustworthy source" had assured him that Hungary would soon be independent—presumably with Rudolf's full support.[12]

In her book Marie Larisch told a curious story. On Sunday, January 27, Rudolf had stormed unannounced into her suite at the Grand Hotel: he was, she said, "very excited," and seemed pale and shaken. "You cannot possibly realize the trouble in which I am plunged," he told his cousin, adding that he was "in very great danger" from a "political" problem. He handed her a sealed box, explaining, "It is imperative that it should not be found in my possession, for at any moment the Emperor may order my personal belongings to be seized." This was surely a reference to the Hungarian conspiracy, for he added, "If I were to confide in the Emperor, I should sign my own death warrant."[13] Larisch, for her part, was convinced that her cousin was "actively engaged" in some "mysterious political intrigues" related to a possible coup d'état against his father.[14]

After Mayerling, Larisch wrote, a note arrived asking her to bring the locked box to an isolated spot in the Prater. The writer had given the same secret code that Rudolf had warned her to expect—RIUO, supposedly an acronym for *Rudolf Imperator Ungarn Österreich* (Rudolf King of Hungary Austria).[15] When Larisch went to the Prater, she was surprised to find Rudolf's cousin Archduke Johann Salvator of Tuscany waiting for her.[16] A career army officer six years older than Rudolf, Johann Salvator had become something of a Habsburg black sheep. His public calls for liberal reform and tendency to publish criticisms of the military eventually earned the emperor's wrath.[17] Johann, the emperor complained in a veiled warning to his son, had acted in a "manner irreconcilable with discipline and subordination," and he ordered the archduke into semipermanent exile in Linz.[18]

According to rumor Johann Salvator was involved with Rudolf's Hungarian plans, supposedly entrusted with secret negotiations between the crown prince in Vienna and rebels in Budapest.[19] The Hofburg chaplain Laurenz Mayer even named him as Rudolf's killer, insisting that he had gone to Mayerling and confronted his cousin over the Hungarian scheme. When Rudolf refused to honor his previous promise to support the rebels, the archduke killed him with a Champagne bottle to the head.[20] Artur Polzer-Hoditz too suggested that Johann Salvator had somehow been involved in Rudolf's death.[21] Unfortunately for this theory, Johann Salvator was in Fiume when Rudolf died.[22]

When Larisch handed over the box in the Prater, the archduke confirmed that it held secrets related to a Hungarian conspiracy. "If the Emperor had found these papers," he supposedly confessed, "matters would be infinitely worse. The Crown Prince has killed himself, but if the Emperor had known all, it would have been his duty to have had him tried by military law and shot as a traitor."[23]

Before leaving, the archduke told Larisch, "I'm going to die without dying," explaining that he was going to leave the country and disappear.[24] In October 1889 Johann Salvator duly renounced his archducal titles and, assuming the name Johann Orth, left for South America. His ship later disappeared between ports; although he was presumably lost at sea, many Habsburgs were convinced that he'd deliberately vanished and lived out the rest of his life in exile.[25]

The box Larisch handed over to the archduke—like Johann Salvator—soon disappeared, though Marie Stubel—sister of his lover Ludmilla "Milli" Stubel—later confirmed that he had indeed received it.[26] In 1993 newspapers reported that a locked box, said to contain a revolver, several of Rudolf's suicide letters, and missing files, had been discovered in Canada; the owner handed it over to the late Archduke Otto, the son of Emperor Karl I. The archduke freely admitted that he had received the box but refused to comment on the contents.[27]

Any of Rudolf's papers related to his Hungarian plans also disappeared. At one time a mysterious File No. 25 existed in the Austrian Foreign Ministry: This held correspondence between Rudolf and Count Károly related to the Army Reform Bill. It sat on the shelves for less than a decade before officials culled it from the archives.[28] Károly also destroyed all his letters from Rudolf; nothing remains documenting their contacts during the momentous last month of the crown prince's life.[29]

Though authorities did their best to systematically erase damning evidence of Rudolf's Hungarian plans, enough solid information remains to elevate the idea beyond mere speculation. The Mayerling historian Fritz Judtmann, a sober analyst of the tragedy, confirmed the plot's essentials with Count Teleki's descendants.[30] Rudolf's apparent conspiracy against his father was not merely an act of rebellion; it reflected his fading grasp of reality. He knew his movements were followed and his correspondence read, and yet he plunged recklessly forward, oblivious to the probable results when his treachery was inevitably discovered.

Discovery of the Hungarian conspiracy looms large in at least one murder theory. According to this, Franz Josef learned of his son's scheme in the third week of January 1889 and confided details to his uncle Archduke Albrecht. As a loyal Habsburg, Albrecht knew his duty: He planned to confront Rudolf at the dinner for Marie Valerie and force his withdrawal from the plan. When Rudolf failed to appear, the archduke decided that it was too late for an appeal to reason; instead, he dispatched a small group of trusted soldiers to Mayerling, where they were to arrest the crown prince for treason. A scuffle broke out: When Rudolf pulled out a revolver to defend himself, a soldier grabbed a Champagne bottle and beat him over the head, while Mary was killed by a stray bullet.[31]

In the 1970s the historian Judith Listowel picked up and expanded this theory. Her grandfather, a former aristocratic parliamentary figure in Budapest, told her that Rudolf's death had "something to with Hungarian independence."[32] Further investigation led her to Rudolf Taaffe, whose late cousin Eduard had safeguarded the Mayerling files confiscated by his grandfather, Prime Minister Eduard von Taaffe. According to Rudolf Taaffe, his cousin had shared details of the tragedy before his death. Listowel then spoke to a person she identified only as one of the crown prince's descendants, who confirmed that Archduke Albrecht had been behind events at the lodge. The elderly archduke, ran this claim, sent ten members of his Roll Commando sharpshooters unit to Mayerling to confront Rudolf with evidence of his treachery; the crown prince was given a few hours to do the honorable thing and kill himself. When he refused, soldiers broke into his bedroom and shot him.[33]

Listowel believed that this theory was "credible and correct." She declared that not only was Archduke Albrecht behind the operation but also suggested that Prime Minister Taaffe himself had been involved—a startling assertion that his descendants were unlikely to welcome. It is true that Taaffe heartily disliked Rudolf; from various reports and interventions with Chief of Police Baron von Krauss, Taaffe knew that the crown prince had threatened to kill himself and had likely gone to Mayerling with Mary Vetsera, yet he did nothing. This, Listowel believed, was proof that "Rudolf's death suited Taaffe both from a political and a personal point of view. From deciding deliberately to refrain from preventing a planned suicide it is but a short step to deciding to give the coup de grace if the victim failed in his own purpose."[34]

This isn't convincing. Doing nothing is far removed from a loyal prime minister actively participating in the murder of his emperor's son. And the theory, it must be said, also suffers from some extraordinary lapses in logic. Franz Josef supposedly learned the truth soon after Rudolf's death, yet he continued to pour out his favor on Archduke Albrecht, who remained inspector general of the imperial army until his death in 1895. What soldier in the Austrian army would have dared kill the crown prince without the emperor's direct order? What guarantee was there that Loschek, Hoyos, or Bratfisch would not immediately come running and return fire in an effort to save Rudolf? Under this scenario Mary was presumably killed to silence her; how, then, to explain her death six hours before Rudolf's, or her suicide letters? Or, for that matter, Rudolf's suicide notes? Listowel suggested that Albrecht's plot just happened to erupt as Rudolf and Mary were preparing to kill themselves and after they had both written their letters—an extraordinary coincidence and one that, if true, completely negated the need for anyone to further complicate matters and murder them.[35]

Yet the suggestion that Rudolf was murdered for political reasons has become fashionable in conspiratorial circles, and the finger of suspicion has long pointed toward Berlin and German chancellor Otto von Bismarck. This isn't surprising: Rudolf's antagonism toward Prussia was scarcely a secret. Like many Austrians, he despised Prussian aggression, growing militarism, and its humiliating usurpation of previous Habsburg dominance over European

Germans. "Germany needs this alliance more than we do," Rudolf once wrote to Szeps. Bismarck's goal, he believed, was "to isolate Austria more and more from all other powers and make it dependent upon German help."[36] Bismarck, for his part, made no secret of the fact that he feared Rudolf's eventual accession to the Habsburg throne. Although he praised the crown prince's "mental powers and the maturity of his opinions and conceptions" to an Austrian official, privately he expressed concern over Rudolf's "close connections with literati and journalists," adding that "if the Crown Prince continues in this way it must fill us with apprehension for the future."[37]

Rudolf, Bismarck feared, would cast aside Austria's alliance with the German empire in favor of a new pact with England and France. With an eye to discrediting the crown prince, the chancellor had almost certainly approved the autumn 1888 German newspaper campaign against him. He also relied on a series of agents to keep him abreast of Rudolf's indiscretions and anti-German sentiments. The Viennese police informer Florian Meissner, for example, supposedly also sold his damning information on the crown prince to the German ambassador, Prince Reuss.[38]

Accusations that German agents killed the crown prince were certainly in circulation at the time. On February 2 the *New York Times* reported rumors that some unnamed assassin had torn away gratings over the bedroom window and shot Rudolf.[39] But the story really got going during World War I, when anti-German sentiment was at its height and two books, published in quick succession, blamed Berlin for the crown prince's death. The first, written by Dr. Armgaard Karl Graves, a former member of the Prussian secret service, contained an imaginative scene of sudden attack at Mayerling, replete with invented "servants" who, though grievously wounded, managed to relate later that Rudolf had been murdered. As to responsibility, the book hinted obliquely: "Prussian diplomacy had gained such an ascendancy over the House of Habsburg and the affairs of Austria that Austria has been and is a staunch ally and supported by Germany in all its aims and ambitions. This alliance is developed to such an extent that even an heir apparent to the Austrian empire, unless acceptable to and identified with Prussian-Germanic interests, finds it impossible to ascend the throne. . . . Rudolf of Habsburg had to the full the proud instinctive dislike to, and rooted disinclination against, the ever increasing Germanic influence in and over his country. He died."[40]

The second work, the anonymously published *The Last Days of Archduke Rudolf*, laid out a most comprehensive scenario. The author claimed that he was Rudolf's personal secretary; that he was born between 1861 and 1863; that his father was a courtier; that he attended school in England; and that he entered the archduke's service in 1887.[41] From these few clues several possible candidates emerge as the author. The first is Artur Giesl von Gieslingen, a soldier who worked in military intelligence before his 1887 appointment as Rudolf's *Ordonnanzoffizier* (orderly officer in attendance). Although his 1887 appointment to court matches the date given for the anonymous author of *The Last Days of Archduke Rudolf*, other details do not. Born in 1857, Gieslingen was older than the book's supposed author; he was not educated in England, nor did he serve as Rudolf's secretary. Another possibility is Heinrich Ritter von Spindler, head of the crown prince's secretariat; Spindler, though, was even older than Gieslingen, and entered Rudolf's service much earlier than the putative author of the book. The final candidate is Lieutenant Viktor von Fritsche, who was indeed several years younger than Rudolf and who served as the secretary to his chancellery. Fritsche was the most likely author of the book, if it was indeed written by a member of Rudolf's staff.

The Last Days of Archduke Rudolf insisted that the crown prince had been murdered for political reasons. The enigmatic author claimed to have seen a secret letter about "a man of the first importance who, the context allowed an intelligent person to assume, constituted an obstruction in the path of those whom the writer represented, as well as a thorn in the path of other important persons."[42] He wove this together with a story that in November 1888, Bismarck had taken a special train to Laxenburg to confront Franz Josef with rumors that he planned to abdicate in Rudolf's favor.[43] There was little doubt, the author claimed, that the chancellor was behind events at Mayerling.[44] A forged letter from Rudolf, the book claimed, brought Mary to the lodge. She traveled by train from Vienna to Baden, but in fact her arrival at Mayerling was a complete surprise to the crown prince.[45] Ominously, the book contended, some German hunters were seen roving the forests around Mayerling just before the tragedy.[46] In a final flourish, the anonymous author repeated a bit of thirdhand gossip that, on the morning of January 30, Bratfisch had heard two shots: When he went to investigate, he saw four men in hunting clothes sneaking away from the lodge.[47]

In 1969 the author Victor Wolfson again raised claims of a German assassination in *The Mayerling Murders*. He eagerly seized on *The Last Days of Archduke Rudolf* as a factual chronicle of events because, as he explained, "one welcomes corroboration for one's own point of view."[48] Wolfson had no doubt that Bismarck had ordered Rudolf's death, suggesting that Rudolf's suicide letters could be traced "to the forgery apparatus in Berlin," which, having planned to murder the crown prince, wanted to "make certain" that his intent was clear.[49]

This assertion echoed *The Last Days of Archduke Rudolf*, which declared that all the suicide letters found at Mayerling were clever forgeries.[50] The claim wasn't new. On February 10 the Viennese journal *Schwarz-Gelb* raised questions about the letters and their authenticity: "If bank notes can be forged, why cannot a Prince's letters be forged as well, and his handwriting imitated with deceptive accuracy?" it mused.[51] The problems posed by this idea are staggering. If there was some chicanery involved and the alleged forgers planned to kill Rudolf, why would the conspirators then involve Mary as an additional victim? If some foreign government forged the letters found at Mayerling, how did it then get access to the locked drawer of Rudolf's desk in the Hofburg to plant the ones discovered there?

Though *The Last Days of Archduke Rudolf* contained enough accurate information to suggest a degree of veracity, it also served up a healthy dose of inaccuracies regarding Mary's journey to Mayerling and events at the lodge. Wolfson's attempts to dismiss evidence contrary to his theory were likewise unconvincing: He suggested, for example, that officials forced Mitzi Caspar to invent stories of Rudolf's suicide proposals, while ignoring the crown prince's repeated overtures to many others.[52] Bismarck certainly worried about Rudolf's accession to the throne, but no compelling evidence has emerged to support the idea that he ordered his assassination.

The highest-profile claim that Rudolf died as a result of a political assassination, though, came from a seemingly unimpeachable source: Empress Zita, the widow of Austria's last emperor, Karl I. Zita was born three years after Mayerling, but no one doubted that she knew all the Habsburg secrets. In 1983 the ninety-one-year-old former empress insisted that Rudolf had not committed suicide but instead had been murdered as part of an international conspiracy against Franz Josef.[53] According to this the French, not the Germans, were behind Rudolf's death. The future French prime minister Georges Clemenceau supposedly approached Rudolf with a plan to stage a coup against his father, so that once on the throne the new emperor could sever the alliance with Germany and form a pact with the French Republic. Zita claimed that Rudolf refused to act in so dishonorable a fashion, and that Clemenceau then arranged for his assassination.[54]

On its face this seems absurd. That Rudolf admired France was no secret. "We are indebted to France," he wrote to Szeps, "as the source of all liberal ideas and constitutions in Europe. And whenever great ideas begin to ferment, France will be looked to for an example.

What is Germany compared to her? Nothing but an enormously enlarged Prussian regimental barbarism, a purely militaristic state."[55] Rudolf's friendship with the Prince of Wales also influenced his friendly views toward France. An idea grew that if Austria severed its alliance with Germany, it would then be free to tie itself to both Great Britain and France; Germany would thus be encircled and contained. To this end Szeps even arranged a secret meeting between Rudolf and Clemenceau in December 1886, at which the potential realignment was discussed.[56]

Erich Feigl's 1989 biography of Empress Zita fleshed out this extraordinary claim of French involvement. The Habsburg loyalist wrote that the former empress insisted she'd learned details of the plot from Rudolf's sisters, Gisela and Marie Valerie: According to this, Cornelius Hertz, a Jewish banker, had led the French assassination squad.[57] She even declared that Franz Josef knew all but had said, "I could not act in any other way. The monarchy was at stake. The truth would have shaken the foundations of the Empire. Everything will be published after my death. Then poor Rudolf will be entirely rehabilitated."[58]

No such publication ever took place, though in 1983 Zita promised that she'd soon release secret family documents confirming her tale.[59] But when the historian Gordon Brook-Shepherd attempted to pursue this pledge, the former empress backpedaled and changed her story. "Alas," she wrote to him, "all proofs, that is documentary proofs, have either disappeared or cannot be found." Instead she insisted that the Christian burial Rudolf received proved that the Vatican knew he had been murdered.[60]

Empress Zita died in 1989. No evidence supporting her claim has ever surfaced. Although convinced that she genuinely believed her story, the former empress's family expressed embarrassment and bewilderment at her allegations. Her eldest son, the late Archduke Otto, even gently refuted his mother's allegations in public interviews.[61] Many regarded Zita as a woman of great integrity who would never have descended to gossip; unfortunately, in her last decade, she was given to any number of questionable statements, and it seems most likely that she later conflated stories she had heard about the Hungarian conspiracy and embellished them with her own prejudices. For the staunchly Catholic Zita, Rudolf's suicide was anathema, a blemish on the house of Habsburg. It is likely no coincidence that her claim coincided with the onset of an ultimately successful campaign to see her husband, Karl, beatified by the Catholic Church as a man who sought peace during World War I.[62]

The war, in fact, likely also explains the former empress's zeal to blame Clemenceau for Rudolf's death. In 1917, without consulting his ally Germany, Emperor Karl asked Zita's brother Prince Sixtus of Bourbon-Parma to enter into secret negotiations with France over a separate peace. In the spring of 1918, the Austrian foreign minister, Count Ottokar von Czernin, unaware of the emperor's overtures, attacked Prime Minister Clemenceau for refusing to end the war. Furious, Clemenceau revealed Karl's overtures; when Germany protested, Karl lied, saying he had never authorized his brother-in-law to negotiate with the French. Clemenceau produced the documents, and revelation of the affair, which left Karl dishonored and Austria weakened, which undoubtedly fueled the revolution that autumn that drove the Habsburgs from their throne. Zita never forgot this humiliation. It is difficult not to believe that her claims against Clemenceau ultimately stemmed from lingering personal animosity.

Stories of Rudolf's political assassination remain popular in Mayerling literature. Aside from lack of proof, most share similar dismissals of all contrary evidence: The suicide letters are deemed forgeries; Rudolf's previous declarations of suicide are put down to coercion of witnesses after the fact; and the differing times of death for Rudolf and Mary are questioned or ignored. These assertions soon amass a wealth of contradictions, implausible scenarios, and claims of vast conspiracies that put the imperial court's efforts at a cover-up to shame. Like tales that Rudolf was killed by blows from a Champagne bottle or shot by a jealous forester, it is surely no accident that many stemmed from Rudolf's descendants, members of the Habsburg family, or from former courtiers—those most determined to rescue his memory and proclaim him innocent of murder and suicide.

PART IV

CHAPTER SIXTEEN

A century has transformed the bloody scene at Mayerling into romantic tragedy: star-crossed lovers who preferred death together than to be parted by cold unfeeling propriety. The story has been replayed countless times, in histories and in novels, in movies and musicals, and through ballet. For too long, rumor has displaced fact. The time has come to rend the veil of gauzy romanticism and bizarre conspiracies, revealing—as much as is possible—the byzantine truth that led to tragedy.

In the end evidence suggests that only two people were responsible for the events at Mayerling: Rudolf and Mary. Yet exactly what took place between them behind that locked bedroom door can never truly be known. From the distance of more than a century, both emerge as deeply flawed, emotionally damaged, high-strung, and desperate actors. But the question of motive remains: What drove Rudolf and Mary to such a tragic end? Did they, as sentimental historians suggest, find the idea of life without each other simply too much to bear? Or did Rudolf and Mary die for reasons that may have had no connection to each other? A new look suggests a far more plausible—and ultimately more shocking—scenario surrounding Mayerling.

"There is no doubt," Queen Victoria wrote of Rudolf after Mayerling, "that the poor Crown Prince was quite *off his head*."[1] The official declaration of mental instability likely stemmed from religious expediency, but few doubted that Rudolf had been a deeply disturbed man. The question of just how disturbed he may have been—and what role this played in his ultimate end—has long plagued history. But new analysis suggests some startling possibilities.

Generations of incestuous marriages brought physical and mental infirmities to Rudolf's ancestors. "With us," his cousin Archduke Franz Ferdinand once complained, "man and wife are always related to each other twenty times over. The result is that half of the children are idiots or epileptics."[2] The archduke wasn't exaggerating. Rudolf's parents were first cousins; his grandmothers were sisters; and Franz Josef and Elisabeth shared the same grandfather in King Maximilian I Josef of Bavaria.[3] The crown prince's genealogical tables, as his official biographer Baron Oskar von Mitis so delicately phrased it, revealed "a scarcity of ancestors."[4]

The Habsburg inheritance was not untroubled. Emperor Ferdinand I has often been described as "an epileptic idiot," a man who "could hardly put two sentences together," while his sister Archduchess Marie displayed signs of mental instability.[5] Varying degrees of eccentricity exhibited themselves in Rudolf's paternal relatives: His uncle Ludwig Viktor haunted Vienna's bathhouses to seduce young male soldiers and liked to be photographed in elaborate ball gowns; Archduke Karl Ludwig, an otherwise sober and serious uncle, had a reputation as a religious fanatic who terrorized his third wife, Maria Theresa. And Rudolf's favorite cousin, Archduke Otto, was an overt sadist who delighted in torturing both animals and the soldiers in his regiment.[6]

Stephanie's memoirs deemed Rudolf "more of a Wittelsbach than a Habsburg. He was clever, indeed brilliant, highly cultivated, with a broad, generous mind. He was as sensitive as his mother. He was impulsive, mercurial, highly strung. He had terrific outbursts of temper, moods."[7] This Bavarian heritage was particularly troubling. King Maximilian I Josef's brilliant but highly eccentric son

King Ludwig I lost his throne over his stunningly indiscreet liaison with the notorious dancer Lola Montez; Ludwig's sister Alexandra went through life believing she had once swallowed a piano made of glass. The king's grandson Prince Otto was declared insane in 1878 and spent the rest of his life locked away in a castle, howling at imaginary voices, tearing apart his food, and smashing flies against the windows.[8]

Then there was King Ludwig II of Bavaria, Empress Elisabeth's unfortunate second cousin. He'd come to the throne at the age of eighteen, tall, handsome, and decidedly odd, envisioning himself as a hero in one of the Wagner operas he so loved. After a disastrous engagement to Elisabeth's sister Sophie ended in 1867, the homosexual king flung himself into a world of nocturnal fantasies, building his famed castles, picnicking in the snow, holding conversations with phantoms, and cavorting with handsome young soldiers. His delusions led the Bavarian government to depose him as insane in 1886; a day later Ludwig's body was found floating in an alpine lake along with that of his doctor, the former monarch apparently having drowned his keeper and then himself rather than endure life locked away like his brother Otto.[9]

Finally, of course, there was Empress Elisabeth. Her paternal grandfather, Duke Pius, had been feebleminded and lived in isolation; after marrying his second cousin Ludovika, Elisabeth's father, Duke Max in Bavaria, grew noticeably eccentric. Of Max and Ludovika's children, the eldest son, Ludwig—Marie Larisch's father—was a recluse with a reputation for restlessness, while daughters Elisabeth and her sisters Helene, Sophie, Marie, and Mathilde all suffered from serious depression, feelings of persecution, and occasionally erratic behavior.[10]

As Baron von Mitis noted in his biography of the crown prince:

> What effect, if any, this genetic inheritance may have had on Rudolf remains a mystery, but there is no denying the accumulated psychological and physical forces that, by the beginning of 1889, led him to tragedy.

> The profound incentive to his actions was not formed by one single motive. A mass of personal irritations and tragic associations of a higher order, which were often inter-related, fostered the germination of a seed, which was already biologically present in his being. The unbearable burden of the whole dragged him down to the depth of life and made him covet death. Each individual of the component causes might seem to a cool observer hardly sufficient in itself to destroy the joy of living but in a sick mind and all being united they can develop the lurking consent to death until only the moment of release is needed to stage the last scene of the tragedy.[11]

Rudolf had always been psychologically fragile, subject to anxiety and depression. Franz Josef was too preoccupied with the business of ruling, too consumed with exalted conceptions of his role, too emotionally aloof, and too judgmental to offer his son any real guidance or affection, and his disapproval likely fueled in Rudolf a sense that he was a disappointment. Rudolf was two when his mother first fled Vienna, and she was frequently absent for months thereafter. When Elisabeth did appear, she was often battling Rudolf's grandmother Archduchess Sophie, tearing the young boy's affections in differing directions. Although he idolized Elisabeth, she was too elusive a presence to provide Rudolf with the love and acceptance he craved. His forced separation at six from his sister Gisela and his nanny undermined any stability, while the empress's obvious favoritism toward Marie Valerie likely reinforced Rudolf's sense of inadequacy and resentment.[12] The educational regime instituted by Gondrecourt was physically and emotionally abusive, and the trauma manifested itself in Rudolf's persistent bed-wetting, wild mood swings, and nightmares.

Early on Rudolf developed an unhealthy fascination with death. When his grandmother Archduchess Sophie died in 1872, he insisted on hearing every detail of her last moments over and over again. Walking through a park one day, he saw a man drink caustic soda and die in agony; Rudolf was so obsessed with the episode that for days he talked of little else.[13] He also showed a tendency to aggression, not only when denied something but also in his artwork. Childish drawings and paintings of dead animals, decapitated heads, and men dueling—with splotches of crimson vividly slashed into the wounds—suggest a propensity toward violent thoughts.[14] Marie Festetics remembered how even as a child Rudolf compulsively shot bullfinches from his window. "Every creature that breathes or has wings is doomed to death," she wrote, adding that Rudolf had "become possessed by a sort of lust for killing."[15] This wasn't a passing fancy: Rudolf had a disconcerting and dangerous habit of waving his guns around—in 1878 he'd accidentally shot himself in the hand.[16] And, shortly before his wedding, Rudolf amused himself by having caged animals set loose in the palace courtyard so that he could cold-bloodedly shoot them down.[17] Yet no one seems to have expressed any concern over his obsessive behavior.

A journal entry Rudolf wrote at the age of fifteen is telling: "Thoughts of all kinds race through my head; it seems confused, all day long my brain boils and toils the whole day long; one goes out, another comes in, and each possess me, each tells me something different, sometimes serene and happy, sometimes black as a raven, full of fury; they fight and from the struggle truth slowly develops."[18] Retrospective analysis is a tricky and inexact thing, but some evidence suggests that Rudolf may have suffered from Bipolar I disorder; his mention of racing thoughts is indicative of a manic episode, one of the symptoms usually attributed to the disorder. Others include depressive episodes; grandiosity; restlessness; irritability; aggression; paranoia; pronounced decrease in sleep; reckless personal and sexual behavior; and increased suicidal thoughts. Rudolf displayed elements of all these symptoms throughout his life.[19]

Rudolf's sense of political impotence gnawed away at his

self-esteem and left him depressed: Neither his father, government officials, nor his extended family took him seriously. His constant complaints of being ignored and excluded likely emphasized Rudolf's sense of despair.[20] When, on his thirtieth birthday, he wrote to Szeps of his "empty" life, his growing frustration, and his increasing weariness at "waiting for great times of reform," Rudolf gave vent to the suppressed hostility raging within.[21] Repeated exclusion from the Army High Command conferences, his clashes with Archduke Albrecht, and his father's request that he resign his post as inspector general of the infantry fell on Rudolf as personal and professional failures, leaving him humiliated. The death of the liberal German emperor Friedrich III tore at Rudolf's hopes for the future; the persistent attacks in the German press that autumn of 1888 shamed the crown prince by presenting him as the disreputable "other," an unbalanced man unfit for the Habsburg throne.[22] In the last months of his life Rudolf isolated himself from former friends and lost interest in writing, hunting, and scientific pursuits.

At the beginning of 1889 a new outbreak of gonorrhea left his eyes infected and added to the crown prince's depression.[23] The painful symptoms came and went without warning, fueling Rudolf's escalating spiral into alcoholism and drug addiction. Suffering from insomnia, headaches, and joint pains, Rudolf grew thin and pale, his face ashen, his restless eyes rimmed with dark circles. The regimen of Champagne, Cognac, and morphine not only rendered his behavior increasingly unstable but also took a toll on Rudolf's sense of masculinity by frequently leaving him impotent. It is impossible to verify what precisely Rudolf was told about his disease, but with his tendency to hypochondria and overreaction, he may have feared that he was infected with syphilis. This would have been a death sentence, the shameful idea of gradual madness preying on a mind already burdened with emotional turmoil.[24] After Mayerling, Queen Elisabeth of Romania hinted at this in a letter to Stephanie, writing, "I think that he himself, being a man of outstanding intelligence, saw the approach of destruction and despairingly flung himself into the abyss, hastily seizing all life could give him before the night came."[25]

Stephanie chronicled the "nervous unrest," "violent temper," and "complete mental decay" that characterized Rudolf's final years.[26] His mind was filled with grandiose ideas for the future, but his inability to put them into practice left him restless and irritable. Although the trait had been present since childhood, in the last years of Rudolf's life Stephanie, Marie Larisch, Empress Elisabeth, and Marie Valerie, among others, all noted his hostile demeanor. Soon after their marriage Stephanie recalled that, while her husband often kept late hours, he was always ready for work the next morning; in the last few months of his life he was sleeping only four or five hours a night—another sign of possible Bipolar I disorder.[27]

And Rudolf was increasingly reckless in the last year of his life. There was the 1888 incident in which he nearly shot his father, and the numerous occasions on which he appeared intoxicated in public and had to be quickly rescued by anxious courtiers before he caused a scandal. Then there was Rudolf's sexual behavior. Not only did he indiscriminately bed any number of women, sometimes fathering their children, but he was careless enough to pick up a case of gonorrhea and then infect his wife with the disease. By 1889 his private life was in a shambles, his marriage existed only in name, and Rudolf had few intimates with whom he could share his disappointments.

An increase in suicidal thoughts grew as hope faded. Rudolf's fascination with death and avid interest in reports of the latest suicides was not only a reflection of an imperial Vienna consumed with such things: Unhappiness eventually drove him to ponder death as preferable to an unfulfilling life. This despair took dangerous form when Rudolf asked Mitzi Caspar to die with him that summer of 1888. When she laughingly dismissed his request, he asked members of his staff, and even threatened to kill Stephanie and then shoot himself. While these all seem to have been genuine declarations of intent, perhaps subconsciously Rudolf hoped that someone would intervene, assuring him that his life and future mattered.

These threads unfortunately wove together in January 1889. Rudolf's Hungarian misadventure was bad enough, an unmistakably traitorous act driven by political despair and personal failure, but it had no connection to his liaison with Mary Vetsera. That relationship, begun as nothing more than another temporary diversion, at first kept the crown prince occupied, but with the passing weeks it became an intricate web of intrigue, pushed ever further by Marie Larisch, Helene Vetsera, and by Mary herself.

Kept on the social sidelines because of her illegitimacy and perpetually in debt from gambling, Larisch was already intimately tied to Mary's family, not merely by friendship but through her affair with her uncle Heinrich Baltazzi, who fathered her third and fourth children. Ever on the lookout for possible financial rewards—and attendant chances at blackmail—Larisch may have suggested an affair to Helene Vetsera, letting it be known that she was amenable to using her position and influence to facilitate a liaison in exchange for financial consideration. Certainly someone, either Larisch or Helene Vetsera, pushed—and pushed hard—given that Mary and her mother went to London in 1887 and let it be known that while there, the young baroness would prove sympathetic to the crown prince's amorous needs.

Nothing apparently came of the visit to England, but the efforts were renewed in the spring of 1888. Despite her later claims of ignorance, Helene Vetsera not only knew of her daughter's liaison with Rudolf but also helped engineer it. She'd made little attempt to disguise her ambitions, chasing after the imperial family and, more particularly, Rudolf, a decade earlier at Gödöllö. Her behavior stretched the bounds of propriety, but Helene seemed unconcerned. And now Mary became her tool for advancement, as Helene became submerged in her daughter's romantic career. The mother assured men that her daughter was sympathetic, boldly invited them to her palace, and pushed Mary toward them as she left the room—unsubtle hints that few mistook. This wasn't a search for potential husbands: Gentlemen didn't marry young ladies who acted so outrageously and bore such terrible reputations. Helene's calculated actions promoted Mary to various potential lovers in exchange for coveted invitations to social events, introductions to important aristocrats, rewards of money or, more ominously, perhaps blackmail to keep word of any indiscretions from spreading through Vienna.

Mary was no innocent: A string of romantic conquests lay behind her when she first met Rudolf. Yet it is impossible to view her as calculating. She was only sixteen, a teenage girl, immature, erratic, and accustomed to maternal obedience. Without moral guidance, propelled by fantasy, and pushed by her ambitious mother, Mary easily gave in to the exciting new adventure of pursuing Rudolf. That she came to care deeply for him over time seems likely. Perhaps in her girlish imagination she believed that he was desperately in love with her; it was, after all, just the sort of forbidden and dangerous romance that filled the lurid French novels she regularly devoured, and she began to envision herself as the heroine in some epic royal love story.

Rudolf was oblivious to the women manipulating his affair. All he saw was a pretty, willing young woman who evinced nothing short of hero worship where he was concerned. Mary temporarily cemented her hold by appealing to his vanity. Rudolf was accustomed to fawning adoration and breathless romanticism among his conquests: It was all part of the game, a fire that briefly burned bright before inevitably being extinguished. And he was practiced in the illusion of participating in the passing charade as long as he was entertained and amused. For him the affair became yet another well-acted, diverting, but ultimately ephemeral romance.

The affair played itself out across the autumn of 1888, with meetings in the Prater, assignations at Eduard Palmer's apartment, and Mary's repeated visits to Rudolf at the Hofburg. Although history often portrays Rudolf as so desperately in love with Mary that he regarded death at her side as preferable to life without her, the truth is that by the end of 1888 the liaison had run its course.

Evidence disputing the romantic myth is clear: There is no doubt that in the last months of his life Rudolf was slowly but surely pulling away from Mary. This wasn't an unexpected development. "He loved many women in his time," recalled Rudolf's cousin Archduke Leopold of Tuscany, "but no one woman for long, and I am convinced in my own mind that he knew well enough that the infatuation he felt for poor Mary would very soon pall." He would "pluck at every fair flower within his reach, and cast it aside as soon as he was done with it."[28]

On December 21, 1888, Bratfisch collected Mary and took her to see Rudolf at the Hofburg. This was the last time the lovers met that year. It also seems to have marked the beginning of Rudolf's attempts to distance himself from Mary, attempts ironically spurred on by her own mother. Increasingly Mary's flagrant and erratic behavior unnerved Helene Vetsera. There was too much gossip about her daughter in Vienna now: Everyone, it seemed, knew of her relationship with Rudolf—that might have been acceptable had Mary's immaturity not driven her to cause constant public scenes, especially when the crown princess was present. Helene wasn't stupid: A liaison with the crown prince could be mined for potential financial and social rewards, but she knew it would one day end. When that time came, she pinned her hopes on the duke of Braganza; she erroneously believed that, as a widower, he might be amenable to a young lady of damaged reputation.

But Mary's behavior threatened these plans. She'd turned a discreet liaison with the crown prince into a delicious society scandal. If Helene hoped to salvage anything of the future, Mary had to be reined in. Given her romantic flights of fancy and conviction that Rudolf was desperately in love with her, Mary wouldn't willingly end the relationship, and so her mother tried to force the issue and contain the damage. It is said that she actually wrote to Rudolf in December 1888—surely an odd letter, coming from a woman he had apparently slept with a decade earlier, and whose daughter now shared his bed—asking him to put an end to the affair.[29]

This alleged request coincided with Rudolf's waning interest in the affair. By December, according to the anonymously published *Last Days of Archduke Rudolf*, the crown prince's "attachment to Mademoiselle Vetsera, renewed and broken again by intervals of absence or, indeed, of disagreements—which were not infrequent—was undergoing its inevitable denouement."[30] In the wake of Mayerling, a police investigation revealed that Rudolf had recently embarked on another affair with a chorus girl named Glaser at the Karl Theater, and given her a diamond ring worth 1,200 gulden ($7,668 in 2017).[31] Artur Polzer-Hoditz, who served as head of the imperial chancellery to Karl, Austria's last emperor, later wrote of a collection of telegrams exchanged by Rudolf and Mary Vetsera at the end of 1888 that had been briefly deposited at a government archive in Vienna. These telegrams, he said, revealed that, "the Baroness's love had become an inconvenience to the Crown Prince. This was obvious in spite of the careful language in which his refusals were couched."[32] And the exceptionally well-informed Walburga, Lady Paget, stated "as a positive fact" that she'd learned Rudolf "was not the least in love" with Mary, "and only wanted to get rid of her, but that she would not let him go."[33]

Rudolf had come to realize that the ambitious Helene Vetsera was using the liaison to attain social status and financial security—"Mary represents the last throw of the dice," he once commented bitterly.[34] Particularly telling were his remarks about Mary to Louise of Coburg during the soiree given by Prince Reuss on January 27: "Oh, if somebody would only deliver me from her!"[35] On more than one occasion Rudolf implored Marie Larisch to take Mary away from the capital. He even mentioned the idea to Mary, who sobbed, "I know what that means!" "Goodness knows I have tried my utmost to persuade her to accept Miguel of Braganza," Rudolf confided to Larisch. "It would suit me admirably."[36] A man who desperately tried to get rid of his current mistress, wanted to send her away, and attempted to marry her off to another, was unlikely to have been besotted beyond all reason. His remarks to

Marie Larisch and Louise of Coburg and his apparently curt telegrams suggest that Rudolf was attempting to end the liaison.

Rudolf, having enjoyed the fruits of the affair, was now consumed with other interests: his new chorus girl, and especially the impending Hungarian conspiracy. He was usually adept at ending his liaisons, abruptly dispatching farewell letters and gifts once his interest had waned. And most of his conquests accepted this arbitrary cessation of imperial favor. But most of his conquests weren't unpredictable teenage nobles given to causing public scenes. With Mary, Rudolf lacked the courage of his convictions: He'd always resorted, Latour von Thurmberg complained, to prevarication and avoidance to escape confrontation. But ending his current affair was fraught with potential dangers. With her breathless romanticism, and her spectacular capacity for attracting unwelcome attention at the opera, theater, and at balls, Mary was something of a loose cannon; pushing back against her idealized version of reality might lead to some uncomfortable display or, worse yet, propel her into some scandalous action. Rather than make a clean break, he simply withdrew, made himself unavailable, and became terse in his communications. And, sometime after December 21, perhaps driven to act by Helene Vetsera's letter, he sent his young lover a cigarette box engraved with his name—his standard farewell present when concluding a liaison.

But Helene did not wait for imperial action. That December she also discussed the situation with her brothers, asking them to intercede and help end the affair—though in typically tangled fashion this involved a bit of duplicitous chicanery. Aware of Franz Josef's liaison with Katharina Schratt, Hector Baltazzi had cultivated a friendship with the actress, hoping that his flatteries and offers of fine thoroughbreds might convince her to push for his acceptance at court.[37] In the summer of 1888 a concerned Franz Josef warned Schratt that it was best that she not go riding with Hector or be seen with him in public. Although he admitted that he had occasionally spoken to Baltazzi and that the empress had once been quite friendly with him and his brothers, the emperor wrote to Schratt that Hector "does not have an entirely correct reputation in racing and in money matters."[38]

When Hector's overtures failed, his brother Alexander apparently took over: Dashing and elegant, Baltazzi supposedly charmed his way into the actress's bed hoping to win her influence. But by December 1888 what Baltazzi most wanted was for Schratt to speak to Franz Josef about the liaison between Rudolf and Mary, asking if the emperor would end the affair.[39] Surrounded by a wall of courtiers who kept him shielded from anything unpleasant, Franz Josef was likely the only aristocratic man in the capital who had no idea about the liaison. Schratt agreed, but because of an illness and the Christmas holiday she was not able to see the emperor until the middle of January; by that time unforeseen circumstances had intervened, setting the stage for the tragedy at Mayerling.

CHAPTER SEVENTEEN

After their December 21 meeting at the Hofburg, three weeks passed before Rudolf again saw Mary. He was, it is true, away from Vienna for five days after Christmas, but his lack of interest in his lover only underscores his desire to gradually pull away from the liaison. Then, on the evening of January 13, he agreed to see Mary in his bachelor apartments at the Hofburg.

Something critical happened that night, something that—for Mary at least—seemed to cement her place in Rudolf's life. Two days later Mary purchased the gold cigarette case from Rodeck's and had it engraved with the date of January 13, and the words *Dank dem Glücklichen Geschicke* before giving it to Rudolf.[1] What "kind fate" was Mary commemorating? Almost certainly she now believed that she was pregnant. As with most things surrounding Mayerling definitive proof is lacking, but the theory is not without evidence.[2] A few days after the tragedy, the Italian ambassador Count Constantine Nigra reported to Rome that Mary had "been pregnant, or thought that she was," a bit of information he likely picked up from Papal Nuncio Galimberti. Nigra added a caveat: Examination supposedly disputed this idea.[3] Stephanie's memoirs, though, offer a cryptic hint, asserting that had Rudolf and Mary lived, "the consequences of their liaison might have been the birth of a child."[4] Citing conversations with Rudolf's mother, Empress

Eugénie of France later confided to a diplomat that Mary had been pregnant at the time of her death.[5] Then, in 1955, Countess Zoë Wassilko-Serecki recalled that, according to the Taaffe papers she'd read in 1919, Mary had been either three or five months pregnant at the time of her death.[6]

All of this might be dismissed as yet more gossip surrounding the story, but there is one critical piece of information that lends the idea particular weight, and it came from Mitzi Caspar, Rudolf's longtime mistress. She was a woman with no particular ax to grind and no reason to lie. Mary, she told police agent Florian Meissner on February 3, had been four months pregnant at the time of her death.[7] What makes this especially compelling is that Mitzi can only have heard the news from Rudolf himself.

Given her experience and reputation, Mary was unlikely to have been ignorant of birth-control practices. But if she actually believed herself to be in love with Rudolf, she may have been less cautious than usual, perhaps intentionally. A pregnancy, and not sexual consummation of the affair, is likely the "fate" Mary commemorated with the cigarette case. In her exalted state of mind, she would indeed have believed that fate now tied her to the crown prince: Giving birth to Rudolf's child would forever connect her to her beloved.

Rudolf was unlikely to have welcomed such news, particularly when his attention was elsewhere and he was attempting to end his affair with Mary. He already had a number of illegitimate children—a situation that never seems to have troubled him. He had used the unlimited resources of the court to cover up indiscretions, pay off mothers, provide for the children, and ensure a veil of silence. But this was worryingly different. Mary wasn't some unknown actress or singer who could disappear into obscurity without unwanted questions being asked. She was unlikely to go quietly, if at all: There'd be a price to pay to keep her silent and avoid scandal, and who knew what the ambitious Vetseras might demand? With Helene Vetsera renowned for her lack of scruples, Rudolf might have feared threats of possible exposure parlayed into financial rewards, social connections, and a grudging acquiescence to their demands that they be admitted at court.

And yet, if Mary indeed made a confession to him, Rudolf probably nodded agreeably to appease her and avoid confrontation. With the denouement of the Hungarian conspiracy looming, his future hung in the air. If it failed he might have to flee the country or even kill himself. And, if neither outcome materialized, he could then make whatever arrangements were needed when he finally broke with Mary. Until then it was likely easier to play along with her fantasy than to destroy it.

Illness and the Christmas holidays kept Katharina Schratt from seeing the emperor and conveying Alexander Baltazzi's worries over the crown prince's affair until January 17. Stunned on learning of the relationship, the emperor is said to have summoned Baltazzi to a private audience at the Hofburg a few days later and quizzed him about the details.[8] Unaware of Rudolf's own efforts to end the affair, perhaps told that Mary had visited the Hofburg on January 13, and now confronted with her family's request, Franz Josef probably believed that the liaison was very much alive; he was now determined to stop it.

Rudolf was oblivious to these discussions until the evening of Thursday, January 24, when Franz Josef suddenly entered the imperial box where his son sat listening to the opera. No one had expected the emperor to attend: Ruled by order, Franz Josef had never before disrupted his schedule and appeared at a theater without warning. Something urgent drove him to see Rudolf. Not even the spell of the performance distracted the audience from staring at this unprecedented scene. They watched as Franz Josef spoke intently to his son; the entire conversation seemed strained. Finally, at the end of the second act, Franz Josef abruptly rose and left the opera.[9]

It seems likely that this conversation concerned Rudolf's liaison with Mary Vetsera. Franz Josef was adamant: Rudolf had to end the affair at once. This was not a request but an order: The Emperor even made his son promise "on his word of honor," as Mary would write, that he would do so.[10]

But what was so important that Franz Josef, who had never before interfered in Rudolf's sexual dalliances, rushed to the opera to confront his son? In the 1950s an Austrian official and art historian, Dr. Peter Pötschner, examined Albin Vetsera's diplomatic file for the year prior to Mary's birth. According to the correspondence and dispatches he uncovered, Albin left to take up his post in Darmstadt the second week of May 1870, while Helene remained in Vienna. More than ten months passed before the couple reunited in the spring of 1871, just before Mary's birth on March 19. This time frame made it extremely unlikely that Mary was Albin's daughter.[11] Indeed, when Mary was born her mother allegedly wasn't entirely sure of her paternity: A diplomat slyly reported that, "in Vienna social circles," Mary "was nicknamed *Le Picnic*, because five or six men were regarded as her potential father."[12]

Among those names whispered as her father was one very highly placed individual indeed: Emperor Franz Josef. The rumor has floated through the Mayerling story like a piece of fetid flotsam no one wanted to touch.[13] Stephanie's sister Louise hinted that with the affair, Mary had placed Rudolf "in an impossible position."[14] And Rudolf's cousin Louisa of Tuscany wrote of her belief that the emperor had made "certain disclosures" to his son "in order to prove that an insurmountable barrier existed between Mary Vetsera and himself, and that any affection between them, as lovers, was impossible."[15] This was as close as any member of Rudolf's family would come to hinting at this rather scandalous possibility.

This terrible concern, runs the speculation, led a frantic Franz Josef finally to confront his son over the affair and confess the dark secret that Mary Vetsera might be his illegitimate daughter. In this case the truth was irrelevant: There was, in 1889, no way to know for sure, but the slightest hint that this was indeed a possibility—that Rudolf might now be involved in an incestuous romance with his half sister—would have threatened the monarchy. If word of this got out—and Franz Josef, knowing Helene Vetsera's reputation, may well have worried that it would—the scandal would have been immense. He may even have suspected that Helene had engineered her daughter's liaison with the crown prince to launch an elaborate blackmail scheme. For Rudolf a possibly incestuous liaison would have been bad enough; but if Mary was indeed pregnant, or told Rudolf that she was, the crown prince now faced an untenable situation.

Another crushing blow was about to land on Rudolf's shoulders. Given the empire's extensive network of informers and secret agents, it would not have been difficult to ferret out the crown prince's links with those agitating for independence in Budapest. This would have been worrisome enough, but on January 25, Rudolf's friend István Károly inadvertently blew up the entire affair.

That Friday, Károly had leaked word to the press that he was in regular contact with Rudolf; in a heavy hint he told reporters that "a very trustworthy source" had assured him that Hungary would soon be independent.[16] Károly followed this opening salvo when he rose from his parliamentary seat in Budapest that afternoon and spoke out against the pending Army Reform Bill that Prime Minister Tisza had proposed at Vienna's request. If Károly could win enough support to his side when the vote was taken on Monday, January 28, he could force a no-confidence vote and bring down Tisza's government—and thus set in motion plans for Hungarian independence. Károly's indiscretions left official Vienna in little doubt that the crown prince was involved in a traitorous plot. Indeed, when Count Szögyény-Marich searched Rudolf's desk in the Hofburg on January 31, he did so under the watchful eye of an official sent by Franz Josef specifically to retrieve "a document which relates to the last major controversies in the family," likely a reference to the Hungarian misadventure.[17]

Within hours of Károly's remarks, already saddled with worry over the Vetsera affair and facing his son's disloyalty, the emperor apparently learned of yet another of Rudolf's transgressions: that the crown prince had foolishly asked that his marriage be annulled. This, at least, is what many believed—and not without some evidence; indeed, two weeks after the tragedy at Mayerling newspapers in Berlin were thrilling their readers with tales of "a very violent confrontation" between the emperor and his heir over an annulment request.[18] Although the purge of official documents makes it impossible to verify, some surprisingly consistent and convincing information moves the idea beyond mere rumor. Marie Festetics, Empress Elisabeth's faithful lady-in-waiting, confirmed that Rudolf requested an annulment; so too did Auxiliary Bishop Dr. Gottfried Marschall, chaplain to the household of Franz Josef's brother Archduke Karl Ludwig, and someone with impeccable ties to both the court and Church hierarchy.[19] And few in the Mayerling story were better placed than Princess Louise of Coburg: Intimate information came from both her sister Stephanie and from her husband, Prince Philipp, who, as one of Rudolf's few trusted friends, was undoubtedly privy to the crown prince's secrets. And Louise insisted that Rudolf tried to get his marriage dissolved.[20]

Four others, indisputably in the crown prince's confidence, also confirmed his annulment request. Latour von Thurmberg, Rudolf's faithful friend and former tutor, confidently asserted that Rudolf had written to Pope Leo XIII asking to have his marriage dissolved.[21] Rudolf also apparently discussed the issue with Moritz Szeps, as his daughter Bertha—drawing on private conversations and her father's papers—related.[22] Viktor von Fritsche, his private secretary, later claimed that Rudolf had applied for an annulment on the grounds of Stephanie's infertility, but that Pope Leo had refused the request.[23] Perhaps most convincingly, Ladislaus von Szögyény-Marich, Rudolf's friend and the executor of his estate, told the Russian chargé d'affaires that the crown prince had asked that his marriage be annulled.[24] As the man who sorted through Rudolf's private papers after his death, and handed off any potentially damning documents to the emperor's representative, Szögyény-Marich would have known if such correspondence had once existed.

Prince Heinrich Reuss—having heard the story—decided to tackle it head-on by confronting Monsignor Luigi Galimberti, the papal nuncio to the Habsburg court. In a dispatch to Berlin dated February 5, 1889, Reuss reported that Galimberti "denied all knowledge. Nothing concerning such a matter had passed through his hands." But then Galimberti added a curious caveat: Perhaps, he suggested, the pope had not answered Rudolf directly but instead sent the request on to Stephanie's father, King Leopold II, in Brussels; the king of Belgium, Galimberti said, could then have forwarded it to Franz Josef in Vienna.[25] If no such request had been made, it was unlikely that Galimberti would lay out such a detailed scenario regarding transmission of the pope's alleged nonreply.

Despite intensive searches, no request for an annulment has ever been found, but then, nearly all of the sensitive documents concerning Rudolf's last months and his death have disappeared. In this particular case, absence of evidence cannot be taken as evidence. That Rudolf was unhappy in his marriage was widely known. Having infected Stephanie with gonorrhea and made her barren, he knew that she could never bear him the son and heir he needed. Surely the future emperor of the very Catholic Habsburg empire would have recognized the impossibility of an annulment or divorce—*if* he intended to sit on the Austrian throne. But if Rudolf was indeed involved in a conspiracy aimed at taking the Hungarian crown, it is possible that any annulment request concerned the throne in Budapest. He would establish a new dynasty, and a dynasty must have heirs to cement continuity. Once on the throne, Rudolf would need a suitable consort, some princess from a proud and ancient Magyar family who could then provide him with children clearly Hungarian in dynastic origin. If, as seems likely, Rudolf not only threw in his lot with the rebels in Budapest but also asked for an annulment—an unthinkable action for the future emperor of Austria-Hungary and crown prince of the proudly Catholic Habsburg dynasty—it only underlines just how unstable his thinking had become.

The accumulated weight of these threatening scandals was too much for even the notoriously nonconfrontational emperor to bear. Early on the morning of Saturday, January 26, Franz Josef unexpectedly summoned Rudolf to that urgent audience at the Hofburg. Precisely what was said remains a mystery, but it seems likely that this uncomfortable confrontation, perhaps spurred on by the previous day's developments in Budapest, encompassed not only Rudolf's Hungarian conspiracy but also his requested annulment. The first was not merely a traitorous act: It went against every concept of loyalty and honor that Franz Josef held dear, an overtly hostile effort aimed directly at the emperor. As to the second, both Latour von Thurmberg and Szögyény-Marich repeated that the annulment request infuriated Franz Josef, who may have feared that his son wanted to wed Mary Vetsera once Stephanie was presumably out of the way. "Overwhelmed with grief and rage," Latour von Thurmberg asserted, "he summoned the Crown Prince to his presence and told him in terrible agitation and with brutal candor that on no condition would he sanction such insane behavior."[26] There was, Szögyény-Marich said, a "violent scene" between father and son. "After this I know what remains for me to do," Rudolf was quoted as telling his father. "Do whatever you like," the emperor supposedly replied. "I will never agree to your separation."[27] According to Stephanie, Franz Josef told his son that there was "only one way out" of his predicament.[28] The crown prince left the audience visibly shaken and pale, his father shouting, "You are not worthy to be my successor!"[29] As Rudolf had presumably pledged to end the affair with Mary, these words cannot have referred to that relationship. Instead they seemed aimed at either the Hungarian plot or the annulment request or both. In this context the emperor's later remark to Widerhofer about Rudolf's death is telling: "God's ways are inscrutable. Perhaps He has sent me this trial to spare me yet a harder one."[30] This strongly hinted that, had his son lived, the emperor would have faced some fearful ordeal over his son's behavior.

This confrontation left Rudolf unnerved. From the Hofburg he drove out into the countryside with his cousin Archduke Otto, relieving his frustration by shooting ducks.[31] He was clearly still on edge the following morning, when he stormed unannounced into Marie Larisch's suite at the Grand Hotel: Rudolf, she said, was "very excited," and seemed shaken. "You cannot possibly realize the trouble in which I am plunged," he told his cousin, adding that he was "in very great danger" from a "political" problem. It was then that he handed her the sealed box, explaining, "It is imperative that it should not be found in my possession, for at any moment the Emperor may order my personal belongings to be seized." This was surely a reference to the Hungarian conspiracy, for he added, "If I were to confide in the Emperor, I should sign my own death warrant."[32]

And the troublesome liaison with Mary also preyed on his mind—"I'm in a devil of a mess in more ways than one," he told Larisch. Having agreed to his father's demand that he end the affair, he asked Larisch to bring Mary to the Hofburg the following morning. He explained to his cousin that he'd tried to get rid of Mary but "she won't be shaken off." The situation had become critical. Mary, he complained, was "a perfect little devil" who had "lost her head" and now threatened to "kick over the traces and cause a regular scandal." The affair, he finished, "would not matter so much if it did not clash with far more important things."[33]

The remarks suggest something of Rudolf's shattered nerves. He'd been trying to ease Mary out of his life but she wouldn't go; now she was using her possible pregnancy to force some concession or she would cause a scandal—a possibility made even more worrisome if his father had indeed warned that Mary might be his half sister. The blows had followed rapidly, one atop another over a momentous forty-eight hours: Mary, revelation of his apparent request for an annulment, and exposure of Rudolf's involvement with the Hungarian rebels. The crown prince's world was collapsing.

Mary's world, too, was collapsing around her. Since her January 13 meeting with Rudolf, she had moved blissfully through the month, certain that her future with the crown prince was secure. Then, on Saturday, January 26—just as Rudolf was facing his father at the Hofburg—Mary also found herself confronted. The previous night she'd heard the fortune-teller's dire warning of impending death and agonized over the prediction. Something about Mary's behavior finally unnerved her maid, Agnes Jahoda. She'd been Mary's confidante, had known all about the liaison, had helped Mary slip into Bratfisch's fiacre to keep assignations with Rudolf, and had seen the cigarette case Mary had purchased and sent the crown prince. She kept her silence, at least until that Saturday morning, when something pushed her over the edge. It is likely that, worried about her job—and that of her porter father—Agnes now went to Helene Vetsera and warned her that Mary might be pregnant.

Agnes was not only Mary's confidante but also her maid: She would have known if her young mistress suddenly had no sanitary napkins to be washed. Whatever she suspected or had been told, Agnes no longer felt that she could keep Mary's secrets. This at least helps explain Helene's outburst: Mary's "crazy action," she warned, "could compromise her terribly."[34] Helene had centered all of her considerable ambitions on Mary. The liaison with Rudolf might be parlayed into social recognition, financial gain, and acceptance at court, but it would inevitably end; when that time came Mary would have to make a suitable marriage, perhaps to the duke of Braganza, to advance the family's fortunes.

An unexpected pregnancy threatened these plans. If Mary's reputation had been questionable before her affair with Rudolf, a possible pregnancy would leave her thoroughly damaged. There was also the possibility that an infuriated Franz Josef might exile the troublesome Vetseras from Vienna. After searching her daughter's room, an infuriated Helene apparently summoned her brother Alexander Baltazzi to an urgent family conference before they confronted Mary with a new plan clearly born of desperation. Baltazzi would take Mary away to Constantinople at once and there marry her; this would allow her to give birth as a married woman and disguise the circumstances of the child's paternity. Not that Helene had entirely abandoned her ambitions: After giving birth Mary could return to Vienna and, as she told Princess Nora Fugger, "do whatever she wished without ruining her reputation"—in other words, continue the affair with Rudolf.[35]

Mary was horrified. She had no wish to marry her uncle, nor did she want to abandon her relationship with Rudolf. The scene must have devolved into chaos as a terrified Mary fled her mother's house, seeking refuge with Marie Larisch at the Grand Hotel. Larisch remembered that she was hysterical. "You've no idea what a cruel mother I have!" Mary sobbed. "Mama wants to sell me." Helene, she complained, had "blamed me for bringing disgrace on our family—the virtuous Vetseras!" If Larisch sent her back, Mary declared, "I'll throw myself in the Danube!"[36]

At the hotel Mary must have told Larisch about the confrontation with her uncle Alexander, for the countess wrote to Rudolf of an "incident" that Saturday between Mary and "A"—almost certainly Baltazzi—that left both women frightened. Larisch, in fact, said that she was afraid to leave Mary alone with "A" because she thought him "capable of anything."[37] When Larisch finally managed to return Mary to her mother's house that evening, the unpleasantness started again, with an angry Helene complaining that her daughter was now "openly compromised."[38]

Fate brought Rudolf and Mary publicly together one last time on Sunday evening at the Reuss soiree. Having ordered his son to end the affair, Franz Josef must have been stunned to see Mary Vetsera strutting about the ballroom, her eyes following Rudolf's every move. Perhaps, as Rudolf complained to Moritz Szeps a few hours later, the emperor had turned his back to his son on witnessing the scene. This apparent slight, the scene between Mary and Stephanie, and the bitter words exchanged with his wife as they departed the embassy left Rudolf, as Szeps recalled, "in a dreadful state of nervous excitement."[39] By the time he appeared at Mitzi Caspar's early Monday morning, Rudolf had apparently embraced the possibility that suicide offered the only escape from the avalanche of problems cascading down upon him. Mitzi had heard him speak of suicide before, but now Rudolf told her that he was about to "shit on the government" and kill himself at Mayerling.[40] This interpretation is borne out by Rudolf's final action when he left Mitzi at three that morning: For the first time he made the sign of the cross on her forehead, suggesting that, if the Hungarian plans collapsed, he was resolute in the decision to end his life.[41]

Rudolf and Mary were on two different paths. He had wanted to escape the liaison even before the confrontation with his father; possible revelation of questions about Mary's paternity would have ensured his agreement to end it. If the following day's parliamentary vote in Budapest went against the Magyar nationalists, Rudolf was prepared to end his life. But Mary was still deeply immersed in the personal romance she had woven around the affair. Happily unaware that Rudolf had promised to end their affair, she was triumphant, defiant in the face of family resistance. In less than forty hours these two divergent paths would collide in a shower of blood and gore.

CHAPTER EIGHTEEN

After Saturday's confrontation with his father, Rudolf abruptly changed his plans, deciding to go to Mayerling on Tuesday rather than wait until the middle of the week. Sunday morning he asked Larisch to bring Mary to the Hofburg the following day: He'd assured his father that he would end the relationship, and it is likely that he planned to do so that Monday. As the crown prince complained to his cousin, he had too many other, "far more important things" to consider: "I cannot waste my time on love."[1]

But anxiety seems to have intervened. Mary was no shrinking violet: With her emotional tantrums and penchant for histrionics there might well be a scene—and prying servants with open ears filled the Hofburg. Things might go badly, and leaving a newly spurned Mary in gossip-hungry Vienna, in the clutches of her scheming and unpredictable mother, perhaps seemed too great a risk, especially if Rudolf still held out hope for the Hungarian scheme. The scene at the German Embassy Sunday night probably pushed Rudolf to change his plans. Early the next morning he abruptly decided to go out to Mayerling that afternoon instead of the following day, and to take Mary with him. Retreating with her to the lodge not only postponed the inevitable: Mayerling also offered privacy, ensuring that any outbursts could be contained. Rudolf's decision was so abrupt, in fact, that he ignored everything else. He was so eager to get away from Vienna that he didn't even bother to cancel a Monday-afternoon appointment with Archbishop Count Schönborn-Buchheim—perhaps in reference to his annulment request—nor did he apparently give any thought to a meeting he was scheduled to attend at the army historical museum, the Arsenal, later that same day.[2]

That Monday morning Rudolf awaited two mysterious communications, a letter and a telegram from an unknown correspondent or correspondents. Voting on the Army Reform Bill was scheduled to take place in Budapest; as Count István Károly was in regular telegraphic communication with Rudolf over the next thirty hours, it is possible that this letter and telegram concerned events in Hungary. Perhaps they reported the violent pro-Magyar demonstrations in the streets of Budapest that forced postponement of the parliamentary vote until the following day; perhaps they alerted him that prospects for the vote no longer favored those seeking independence from Austria.[3]

Rudolf Püchel recalled that, on reading the telegram, the crown prince anxiously folded it up and remarked to himself, "Yes, it has to be."[4] Before leaving Vienna, Rudolf sat down and wrote his farewell letter to Count Ladislaus von Szögyény-Marich, which he carried with him to Mayerling. This directed Szögyény-Marich to "open my desk here in Vienna" and deliver the letters found within. "I must die, it's the only way to leave this world like a gentleman," Rudolf added. Yet Rudolf continued to waver. With the Hungarian situation unresolved and the vote pending, it seems that he still harbored some hope of an outcome favorable to his plans. Indeed, that same morning he told Marie Larisch that "a great deal may happen in two days," suggesting that he had not yet made a final decision.[5]

Retreat to Mayerling offered Rudolf brief respite as he awaited word from Hungary and pondered his fate. Yet despite the romantic legend, no evidence suggests that Mary journeyed to the lodge intending to kill herself. In fact it seems likely that Rudolf only asked her to join him at Mayerling during their brief meeting at the Hofburg that Monday morning. She brought nothing with her—no toiletries, and no clothing other than the ice-skating costume she wore to the Hofburg. Unaware of Rudolf's plan to end their affair, she seems to have expected nothing more than a romantic rendezvous.

While Rudolf had long discussed killing himself, evidence that Mary was suicidal is extraordinarily slim: The Mayerling tragedy amplified what little did exist. Helene Vetsera later recounted that, according to the French tutor Gabriel Dubray, Mary had once mentioned the suicide of a student named Henri Chambige. A year earlier, having made a pact with his mistress, Chambige shot her and then turned the gun on himself; having bungled his own death, he was tried and convicted of his lover's murder.[6] Dubray was surprised at Mary's "astonishing familiarity" with details of the case, and by her remark that a friend had told her that Chambige should have used a hand-held mirror to better adjust his aim.[7] Yet Mary was merely repeating what Rudolf—the unnamed friend she mentioned to Dubray—had told her about István Kégl's suicide using a hand-held mirror to improve his aim. Rudolf, not Mary, was obsessed with the case, once interrupting his protesting wife's conversation with a courtier to wallow in the details.[8]

At Christmas 1888 Mary sent Marie Larisch a signed copy of the joint photograph they had taken at Adele's on November 5, writing underneath, "True until Death," and adding in a letter, "This is the last photograph I shall ever have done." This sounds ominous, but Mary then explained that she meant to emulate the camera-shy Empress Elisabeth and avoid future photographs, so that no one would "remember me except as a pretty young girl."[9] Then there was her autumn 1888 letter to Hermine Tobias, in which Mary wrote that she and Rudolf had discussed a suicide pact—compelling except for the next sentences: "But no! He must not die. He must live for his people. Everything surrounding him must be only fame and glory."[10] And on November 5 Mary wrote to Hermine that she would "have to kill myself" if her mother or sister learned the truth about her liaison with Rudolf. Given that both Helene and Hanna were well aware of the affair, this seems to have been a careful bit of dissembling aimed at the morally censorious Tobias.

The emotionally volatile Mary was given to such exaggerated outbursts. In January, according to a bit of thirdhand gossip, she supposedly hinted to a courtier that in a few weeks she would be dead.[11] It says something about the frequency of Mary's histrionic declarations that no one took them seriously. Nor was the note Marie Larisch handed over to Helene Vetsera on January 28 particularly damning. Once again Mary insisted that she could not "go on living," but this was the sort of melodramatic exclamation to which she was prone. Her line that she could be found in the Danube seems to have been nothing more than an attempt to conceal the fact that she'd fled Vienna for Mayerling.

Glamorized in the Viennese press and viewed as enthralling scandal, suicide took on a surreal quality. Boasted about, treated as adventure, and transformed into a macabre form of mass entertainment, it fascinated fashionable elements in the imperial capital. Mary never expressed such interests or made ominous—if all-too-glib—declarations until her affair with Rudolf. The crown prince slowly drew her into his grim and growing fascination with death, until she was repeating his morbid thoughts as her own. As he had done many times before, Rudolf certainly told Mary he had pondered killing himself and, as he had done with many others, asked if she would join him in a suicide pact. It was just the sort of romantic idea that appealed to the emotionally overwrought seventeen-year-old.

This almost lighthearted approach, driven by obsession and stripped of any sense of finality, clashed with reality. On January 18 Mary made out a will and locked it away in her jewelry case—suggesting that on some level she was toying with the possible idea of her own impending death. Yet only a week later, a fortune-teller's ominous prediction of a looming suicide in her family so upset

Mary that she could not sleep—certainly evidence that she had not yet abandoned her thirst for life.

In fact—and in contrast to the despondent Rudolf—Mary passed the last weeks of her life in a state of exaltation. Everything in her actions—her flaunting of the affair, her declaration that she was Stephanie's rival, her confrontation with the crown princess at the Reuss soiree—it all suggests a sense of triumph, not impending tragedy. She was looking not toward the grave but toward the future, one she now imagined that she would share with Rudolf. This almost certainly explains what happened on January 13: If, as seems probable, Mary confessed that she was pregnant with Rudolf's child, she may well have felt that they now belonged to each other "body and soul."

Block by block, Mary's fevered mind constructed a glittering imaginary palace—and Rudolf, fueled by too much alcohol and morphine, likely laid the inadvertent foundation with loose talk of his Hungarian plans and possible request for an annulment. Rudolf wasn't a fool: Marrying a seventeen-year-old minor aristocrat of extremely scandalous reputation would scarcely serve his plans to found a new Hungarian dynasty. But unencumbered by such realities, Mary may have incorrectly filled in the unspoken blanks and believed that the ultimate fantasy was within reach. Already convinced of her hold over Rudolf and starring as the heroine in a liaison she painted as an epic royal romance, the credulous young woman may have envisioned a future at his side: his wife once he was free, mother of his heir, and crowned as his queen in Budapest. Eager to avoid unpleasant scenes and emotional confrontations, Rudolf could nod agreeably and let her believe what she wanted to, knowing that he could wait until fate forced his hand.

And fate, in the guise of Franz Josef's demand that he end the affair with Mary Vetsera, had now indeed done precisely that. The Hungarian scheme, as Rudolf confessed to Larisch, was far more important than any love affair. After avoiding her, after couching his messages to her in increasingly distant terms, after starting a new romance with a chorus girl, after bestowing his customary farewell gift of an engraved cigarette case, after complaining of her and begging Larisch to take Mary away—it all came down to an imperial order. Whether that order came with warnings of a possibly incestuous relationship, whether Mary was pregnant or not, whether worries about potential Vetsera blackmail played into the ultimatum—Rudolf's father had unwittingly come to his rescue and given him exactly what he most wanted: a way out of his liaison with Mary.

The break with Mary was unavoidable, yet Rudolf lacked the courage of his convictions. The unfinished letter to Hanna makes clear that Rudolf waited until Tuesday to tell Mary of his father's order. That Monday evening at Mayerling they were still awaiting word from Budapest: news that would determine his future, and news that she imagined would make her queen of Hungary. It was her misfortune that the liaison with Rudolf reached a climax just as his world collapsed.

On Tuesday, January 29, Rudolf excused himself from shooting at Mayerling with Prince Philipp of Coburg and Count Josef Hoyos. Although he claimed a cold, it is likely that he remained at the lodge awaiting word of developments in Budapest. The Hungarian plot apparently hinged on that morning's parliamentary vote. Even if Franz Josef had learned of the conspiracy, Rudolf might have clung to some sliver of hope that the situation would work itself out.

But then three telegrams arrived at Mayerling, telegrams sent by Károly in Budapest.[12] The parliamentary vote had been taken. Everyone thought that Prime Minister Tisza would be lucky if he could get 60 deputies to support Vienna's Army Reform Bill; instead, a surprising 126 deputies voted in favor. "Down with the traitors!" Magyar nationalists shouted from the floor between loud hisses. "There are 126 traitors!"[13] Defeat of the Magyar cause ended any push for independence: The Hungarian misadventure was over.

Abruptly Rudolf cancelled his plans to return to Vienna and attend his sister's engagement dinner. He wandered about in a daze: A gamekeeper remembered that the crown prince seemed preoccupied that afternoon—and with good reason. Rudolf could no longer avoid the consequences of his impulsive actions. The emotionally volatile Mary couldn't and wouldn't be shaken off despite Rudolf's best efforts, and now she apparently believed that she was pregnant. Franz Josef had ordered him to end the affair with his teenage mistress and possibly revealed fears that she might be his half sister. There'd been the uncomfortable confrontation with Franz Josef, the annulment request, and revelation of the Hungarian conspiracy: Now Rudolf's last tenuous hope for the future had crumbled away in Budapest.

The emperor would never have allowed his subjects to learn of his son's treachery, nor would he have subjected his heir to a court-martial. Franz Josef was too much of a traditionalist to have removed Rudolf from the succession, which would have brought public disgrace on the house of Habsburg. But Rudolf's anxious and unbalanced mind probably amplified the humiliation he imagined loomed in his future. He might be stripped of what little autonomy and authority he possessed, his freedom restricted, and be forced back into the narrow confines of a controlled life beneath his father's roof. Anticipating the worst, as he often did, Rudolf now saw death as the only escape from his escalating troubles. The crown prince's fate was sealed.

CHAPTER NINETEEN

More than 125 years have passed since the tragedy at Mayerling. Shifting stories, deliberate lies, wild theories, and the disappearance of evidence have shrouded the story in seemingly impenetrable layers of mystery. Absent documentation, history can only speculate about what happened between Rudolf and Mary at that isolated lodge. But enough remains, when coupled with modern forensic evidence and psychological analysis, to weave together a plausible version of events, one that not only fits within the framework of known facts but also offers a believable and ultimately devastating reconstruction of those final, fateful hours.

The telegrams from Károly on Tuesday, January 29, persuaded Rudolf to end his life. Having made the decision to die, he now faced the unpleasant ordeal of cutting Mary loose. She waited in his corner bedroom. Lacking courage and disliking emotional confrontations, Rudolf probably took the easiest way out with his volatile and unpredictable mistress. Sometime early that evening he told Mary that the emperor had ordered him to end the affair. "Today he finally confessed to me that I could never be his," she wrote to Hanna that night; "he gave his father his word of honor that he will break with me. Everything is over!"[1]

Rudolf clearly used his father's order as a convenient excuse, a way to cloak the lack of romantic ardor that had been growing within him for the last month. It absolved him of responsibility and relieved him of having to admit so much: that he'd been trying to pull away, that he'd sent Mary his customary farewell gift of a cigarette case, that he'd turned his attentions to a chorus girl at the Karl Theater, and that he was still sleeping with Mitzi Caspar. By blaming a "cruel" emperor, Rudolf probably believed that he could let Mary down gently and direct any emotional outburst away from himself and toward his father. He could protest, commiserate, and portray himself as heartbroken without ever letting Mary know the truth.

But Rudolf hadn't counted on Mary's childish ability to deny reality. He'd discussed his unhappy marriage with her; while inebriated he'd probably revealed something of the Hungarian plot and his requested annulment. Knowing that she'd never be acceptable as a royal consort, Rudolf was unlikely to have made any promises, but the impressionable Mary would have heard only what she wanted to. Her stunningly naive capacity for wishful thinking led to dreams that Rudolf meant to marry her and place her on the Hungarian throne.

Those dreams now shattered, one after another. The affair was over; there'd be no Hungarian throne, and no annulment. The bleak reality must have crushed her, but Mary still had one last trump card to play: her apparent pregnancy. Even if Rudolf couldn't be with her or make her queen of Hungary, a child would unite their futures and prove their love to the world. But any mention of this likely compelled Rudolf's decision. There couldn't be a child, not if it was at all possible that Rudolf and Mary might be half siblings. Arrangements could be made to eliminate the problem, but the risk was too great. In any case there'd be no united future for Rudolf and Mary: He planned to kill himself.

Rudolf had previously sought companions in a suicide pact: Stephanie, Mitzi Caspar, his adjutants—it didn't seem to matter who joined him. But now, in a last, unselfish gesture, he decided that Mary must return to Vienna. Leaving his room at seven to join Hoyos for dinner, Rudolf asked Bratfisch to have his carriage ready to take Mary back to the capital early the next morning.[2] He would face his future alone at the snow-embowered lodge.

While Rudolf dined with Hoyos, Mary remained hidden in the bedroom, alone with her disappointment. She'd never be queen of Hungary, never be his wife; his protection would be gone, and not even her presumed pregnancy offered hope—not if worries about her paternity dictated future actions. She'd entered an enchanted world only to find rejection. Return to a hostile household, to be berated by her mother and threatened that she must marry her uncle to conceal her pregnancy, loomed on the horizon. It was too much for Mary to bear: She wanted no part of her hated former life. Then there was the inevitable public humiliation she would face. Not only would everyone know that her imperial lover had discarded her but once he had killed himself, Mary must have worried that she'd somehow be blamed for his actions.

A situation so long teased about and toyed with suddenly became real. Mary had feared such an outcome when she lightly mentioned a suicide pact to Hermine Tobias, writing, "But no! He must not die! He must live for his people!"[3] But now, with a bleak future in mind, Mary made her own decision. She would not allow herself to be shamed, to be sent back to Vienna; instead she would die with him, dedicated to the romantic fantasy she'd spun out in her head to the very end.

Fashionable Vienna's preoccupation with suicide, its almost lighthearted reveling in the dramatic details, likely exerted a strong pull on Mary's mind. And, somewhere in her fevered imagination, she seems to have envisioned her death alongside the crown prince as the final rung on the ladder of her social ambition, a way to perpetuate the romantic myth in which she believed. If she could not share his life, she could share his death, and thereby prove her love to him, to her family, and to history. If the crown of Hungary could never rest atop her head, she would replace it with a crown of martyrdom and by doing so, ensure her immortality in a grand Wagnerian *Liebestod*.

Mary had romanticized the scene that now stretched out before her. "In some place that no one knows," she had written to Hermine Tobias, "after some happy hours," she would die "together" with Rudolf.[4] The snowbound lodge became the altar on which Mary would sacrifice herself. Outside a chill wind swept down the dark valley, blowing gusts of white powder against the curtained and shuttered windows; inside the bedroom a fire crackled in the stove and light from the gas chandelier blazed across the fussy, overstuffed red velvet sofas and chairs. Mary took up a handful of engraved stationery from the desk and began writing her letters, letters meant to portray herself as the heroine in an epic romance to the last: It was Mary and Rudolf, united in their forbidden love against a cruel and uncaring world. To her mother she claimed that she "could not resist love," and was "happier in death than in life."[5] Mary's letter to Hanna, repeated exactly this phrase, "I could not resist love"; she was happy to go with Rudolf "into the unknown beyond."[6] Only in the unfinished note to Hanna did Mary admit that Rudolf had ended the affair, adding, "I go to my death serenely."[7]

An unsuspecting Rudolf, meanwhile, dined with Hoyos, outwardly calm and charming. He ate heartily and drank a copious amount of wine. "The Vienna woods are beautiful, very beautiful," he commented to the count. Then, as they sat smoking after the meal, Rudolf pulled the three telegrams from Károly from his pocket and waved them in the air. His previously jovial air vanished. He did not let Hoyos read them, but complained that Károly's actions had left him "compromised." According to Hoyos, Rudolf remarked bitterly, "The affair is absolutely disastrous."[8]

A little after nine that Tuesday night, Rudolf left Hoyos and returned to his rooms. After Rudolf warned Loschek to let no one in, "not even the Emperor," Mary handed the valet her gold-and-diamond watch "as a keepsake of this last time."[9] The couple stepped inside, and Rudolf closed the door behind them.

Rudolf had gone to dinner knowing that he would die but expecting that Mary would listen to reason, obey him, and let Bratfisch take her back to Vienna early the next morning. But now he found that she'd written her notes and was resolute in joining him in death. An argument erupted: Loschek later said that he heard Rudolf and Mary "speaking in very serious tones," though he claimed he had no idea what was being said.[10] This doesn't ring true: If Loschek described the conversation as "very serious," he must have heard at least some of what was being discussed.

And there can be little doubt that the conversation turned on suicide: Rudolf's decision to kill himself, his efforts to talk Mary out of joining him, and her adamant stance that she die by his side. The more he argued, the more she insisted: "she probably did not want to be sent home," was the way Franz Josef's adjutant Eduard Paar phrased it to Helene Vetsera, who recorded her daughter's "resistance" to leaving the lodge.[11] Mary seems to have done everything in her power to remain: She undid her hair, took off her ice-skating ensemble, folded the skirt, jacket, and blouse, and neatly placed them on a chair—presumably in the hope that her nakedness would prevent Rudolf from forcing her out of the bedroom, that she might tempt him with her body and thus prolong the illusion of romance. Yet Rudolf apparently resisted. When found he was fully clothed and wore his boots, making it extremely unlikely that he undressed that night.

Countless books and films have portrayed what happened next: a contented Mary quietly lying down on the bed, closing her eyes, and drifting off into an untroubled sleep; a watchful Rudolf, gazing on his beloved, waiting until she was at peace before finally putting his revolver to her head. Yet the evidence tells a very different story. Mary was found completely covered in congealed blood that had erupted from her nose and mouth and gushed down to her waist; her eyes were open and she clutched a handkerchief in her left hand. Had she been supine on the bed at the time of her death, the flow of blood would have been limited to her face, neck, and shoulders. The blood extending to and pooling on her waist meant that Mary was awake, sitting up on the right side of the bed, when she was shot; the handkerchief suggests that she was crying. Loschek confirmed this positioning: Mary's head, he recorded, "hung down"—an impossibility if she was flat upon the bed.[12]

The shot came abruptly and took Mary by surprise. Rudolf seems to have fired his revolver in the midst of the ongoing "very serious" discussion. What may have been said can never be known: perhaps the impulsive Mary, in a last bid to convince Rudolf to let her stay and die at his side, threatened to reveal everything if he forced her to return to Vienna. Something must have suddenly set him off and pushed Rudolf over the edge. The same man who had wanted Mary to leave Mayerling suddenly pulled his revolver and apparently shot her without warning. He must have been at the left side of the bed as he suddenly thrust the gun at Mary's head and pulled the trigger; powder burns around the entrance wound, as well as scorching of her hair, indicate that the revolver was only a few inches from her forehead when she was shot. The bullet traversed her skull at roughly a thirty-degree downward trajectory, passing from the upper left temple through the brain and exiting just above her right ear canal. Death was immediate.[13]

And, despite conflicting stories that emerged after the 1959 exhumation, it is clear that Mary was shot in the head. The evidence is overwhelming: Loschek, Hoyos, Widerhofer, Auchenthaler, Heinrich Slatin, Alexander Baltazzi, and Georg Stockau, all saw the bullet wound in Mary's temple; so too did Alois Klein when he pulled Mary's skull from her shattered coffin in 1959. The Viennese forensic expert Dr. Christian Reiter confirmed this during his own examination in the 1990s. Despite the skull's fragmented state, Reiter located a small groove just above and behind the left eye socket, whose beveled edges indicated the bullet's entrance; a corresponding wound on the right side of the head where the projectile exited had caused extensive fracturing to the skull.[14]

Loschek must have heard the shot that killed Mary. That he knew more than he was willing to admit seems clear. When Loschek dictated his memoirs in 1928, he claimed to have heard two gunshots shortly after six that morning. This seems to have been invention, at least about the number of shots. Not only did Loschek fail to mention hearing any such shots to Hoyos that morning, but he also omitted this claim when speaking to officials: The protocol written by Chief of Police Krauss the following morning repeated the essentials of Loschek's story but made no reference to any gunshots being heard.[15]

Having listened at the bedroom door closely enough to relate that Rudolf and Mary had a "very serious" conversation, and perhaps having heard talk of possible suicide, Loschek may eventually have retired to his own adjacent room. While the outer walls of the lodge were up to three feet thick in places, the inner walls were not: An ordinary masonry wall separated the two bedrooms, and the doors were only an inch thick.[16] Loschek could not have missed the gunshot that killed Mary, fired less than twenty feet away from his bed. His immediate reaction must have been worry, especially if he suspected that the crown prince had suicide in mind: Logically he would have rushed to knock on Rudolf's bedroom door, asking if his master was all right. If this happened, Rudolf must have given Loschek some assurance, speaking to him either through the closed door or cracking it open to alleviate his concerns. Given Rudolf's unnerving habit of carelessly waving pistols around, perhaps he simply explained away the noise as an accidental discharge; perhaps he admitted that Mary was dead and ordered Loschek to say nothing until he could think through the situation. But whatever happened left Loschek open to later charges of incompetence: If he'd heard the first shot and done nothing for six hours, he might be held responsible for not having intervened and saved the crown prince's life. With his master dead, facing investigations, and now reliant on the imperial court for his job and pension, Loschek claimed complete ignorance at the time; only later did he invent his tale of hearing two shots after six that morning, offering a scenario in which he thought history would hold him blameless.

Loschek also likely heard the single gunshot sometime after six that morning—the shot that Rudolf put through his brain. And this accounts for some otherwise inexplicable statements that have haunted the Mayerling story. How else, for example, with just a quick glimpse through the hacked-open door panel and before he actually set foot in the bedroom, was Loschek able to tell Hoyos and Coburg that both Rudolf and Mary were dead? He must have put together the argument he overheard, his master's talk of suicide, the first gunshot, the second, later shot, and the locked bedroom door and concluded that the worst had happened. It also seems likely that early that morning Loschek told Bratfisch—waiting in his carriage to take Mary back to Vienna—that both Rudolf and the baroness had died; this would explain the coachman's startling declaration to Wodicka, ninety minutes before the bodies were found, that Rudolf was dead.

Having likely dealt with a worried Loschek, Rudolf returned to the macabre scene of his lover's corpse. In death, as he wrote to his mother, Mary became a "pure, atoning angel."[17] But the man who for so long had toyed with the idea of death now saw the reality of what he had done in a fit of anger: the singed and bloody entry wound in Mary's temple, the ugly gush of crimson that had poured from her nose and mouth and covered her body. The sight must have unnerved him, for he did nothing to conceal the horror: He did not even close her vacant, staring eyes.

Looking at Mary's increasingly cold body, Rudolf lost his own nerve to act. Had he really desired death with her, had he really believed that his life was meaningless without her, Rudolf would have killed himself immediately. Instead he passed the next six hours drinking, perhaps taking morphine, and writing his own letters as he tried to work up his courage. In one sense Mary's death forced his hand. He was already politically humiliated, shamed by his father, and psychologically overwhelmed. Shooting Mary only added to the burdens crushing him. Yet even at this last minute, had Rudolf truly wanted to live, it wouldn't have been impossible for him to escape the consequences of his actions: Mary's death could be disguised, the true circumstances concealed, and her relatives bribed into silence. But too many disappointments had already fallen on Rudolf's shoulders for him to think clearly. Mary might have been his willing victim, but he'd killed her.

In those lonely hours Rudolf's determination gradually took hold. There was, to be sure, an element of hostility in his act. He had once thought to theatrically kill himself with Mitzi Caspar in a neoclassical temple dedicated to the emperor and his empire, a flamboyant rebuke to all that Franz Josef held dear. While reflecting his disillusion with life, Rudolf's suicide at Mayerling also carried a message of revenge against his father, the inert government, his neglectful mother, and his despised wife.

Unlike Mary, Rudolf wrote only four letters in those early morning hours. With the possible exception of the letter to Marie Valerie, those later found in his locked desk at the Hofburg—to Stephanie, to Baron Maurice Hirsch, and to Mitzi Caspar—were almost certainly written in the weeks and—as with the one to Mitzi, even as early as seven months—before he went to Mayerling.[18] Rudolf had thus been preparing for his possible death for some time. Of the Hofburg letters, only those to Stephanie and Marie Valerie hinted at his motives. "Death alone can save my good name," Rudolf wrote to his wife.[19] To his sister Rudolf mentioned only "the need" to kill himself but, she recorded, "gave no reason."[20] Ida von Ferenczy told Empress Elisabeth's early biographer Count Corti that it also included the line, "I do not die willingly, but I must do so to save my honor."[21]

Rudolf's messages to Loschek and the draft telegram to Abbot Grünböck at Heiligenkreuz said nothing of his motives. Only the letter to Empress Elisabeth offered possible explanations, though they were contradictory. "I no longer have the right to live," he apparently wrote. "I have killed."[22] Only now do these words make sense. Mary had been willing to go to her death at his side, but he'd actually murdered her. She was his victim. After declaring that death was necessary "to save his stained honor," Rudolf wrote of his father, "I know quite well that I am not worthy to be his son."[23] This repeated nearly exactly the emperor's dismissal of his son after their contentious Saturday meeting: "You are not worthy to be my successor!"

The words to Rudolf's mother carry two implications. The first, and most apparent, suggests that exposure of his traitorous behavior finally overwhelmed Rudolf's conscience, and that he truly believed his actions had left him dishonored and unworthy. But there is a second, perhaps more likely, psychological explanation. By using his father's own words in his suicide note, by throwing them back as the driving force behind his desperate act, Rudolf was laying the blame for his suicide squarely at the emperor's doorstep. This explanation seems likely, especially when taken together with the fact that Rudolf pointedly wrote no letter for his father. He wanted Franz Josef to feel responsible for his death, to exact the only revenge he had left against the man he blamed for many of his miseries in life.

These two reasons—saving his name and his honor—again point to the Hungarian conspiracy as the principal motivation behind Rudolf's decision to end his life. He had made a similar claim to Mitzi Caspar in the summer of 1888, indicating that he had begun flirting with the idea far earlier than previously suspected. Yet repeated use of the word "honor" also suggests that Rudolf was suffering from delusions of grandeur, a characteristic of his possible Bipolar I disorder, which led him to exaggerate events and his role in them until they assumed critical importance. "Honor" became an excuse, a means by which Rudolf sought to absolve himself of his own decision.

Rudolf's letter to Count Szögyény-Marich offers the clearest insight into his final thinking. "I must die—it's the only way to leave this world like a gentleman," he explained. That it was written in Hungarian is telling; even more telling was its line, "With warmest regards and with all good wishes for yourself and for our adored Hungarian fatherland."[24] There was no mention of Austria or the empire—only Hungary, confirming that this had been the sole focus of Rudolf's thoughts. Failure of the conspiracy became the final, staggering blow in a life already overwhelmed with disappointments and traumas both physical and psychological.

The later autopsy finding that Rudolf had been of unsound mind when he killed himself was a religious convenience, meant to ensure his Catholic burial. He was not insane, but the physicians unknowingly hit upon a truth that would not become apparent until the advent of modern psychiatry. After having killed Mary, after sitting with her stiffening corpse for hours, after having written his own suicide notes, Rudolf could whistle lightheartedly after speaking to Loschek at 6:10 that Wednesday morning. In the last hours of his life Rudolf may thus have been in the midst of a manic episode caused by Bipolar I disorder.[25] A few minutes later, with the door locked behind him, Rudolf sat on the bed beside his lover's corpse, put his revolver to his right temple, and calmly blew his brains against the wall, finally snuffing out a life begun with such promise and now ending alone and in such misery.

EPILOGUE

In his last will, dated March 3, 1887, Rudolf had named his father as guardian of his young daughter, Archduchess Elisabeth. It was an unsubtle slap at Stephanie, who in the wake of her husband's death found herself pushed aside and ignored as a nonentity. In the empress's absences, Franz Josef asked his sister-in-law Archduchess Maria Theresa to take over Stephanie's previous role as the highest-ranking lady to preside over court functions.[1] However, it did not take Stephanie long to recover from whatever grief she felt over Rudolf's death: In letters to her sister Louise she seemed most upset at the loss of her position as future empress. Scarcely a month after Mayerling, she was again using Louise to arrange meetings with her lover, Artur Potocki, explaining that it was easier for them to reunite in Vienna than elsewhere.[2]

As the crown princess widow, Stephanie kept her apartments at the Hofburg, though feeling unwelcome in Vienna, she lived mainly at Schloss Laxenburg and at Miramar in Trieste. In these years she nursed a growing resentment of her late husband and his family—and not without some justification. Empress Elisabeth still blamed her for Rudolf's death: "You hated your father, you did not love your husband, and you do not love your daughter!" she once shrieked at Stephanie.[3] Entirely dependent on the emperor's financial largesse, Stephanie felt belittled and humiliated. Franz Josef also used young

Elisabeth as a weapon in the battle, refusing to let Stephanie take her out of Austria to visit her relatives in Belgium.[4] The emperor doted on Erzsi, showering her with the gifts that Stephanie could not, and as a result the girl came to resent her mother. Elisabeth had adored her father, and—like her paternal grandmother—unfairly blamed her mother for his death.

A further break came in 1900, when Stephanie did the unthinkable and remarried. Potocki had died of cancer in 1890: "I have lost my best friend," Stephanie confided to Louise, "a man I valued so highly and love so much."[5] By 1900 she had fallen in love with Hungarian Count Elemér Lónyay de Nagy-Lónyay és Vásárosnamény. Franz Josef greeted the news with horror, regarding the marriage as an insult to Rudolf's memory.[6] When, on March 22, 1900, Stephanie married Lónyay at Miramar, the emperor stripped her of her titles of crown princess widow and archduchess of Austria.[7] The newly married couple withdrew almost completely from public life, living at his Schloss Oroszvár in Slovakia. Young Erzsi, now sixteen, followed her grandfather's lead and cut off all contact with her mother.

Erzsi proved herself equal to her difficult parents, falling in love with Prince Otto Weriand von Windisch-Grätz. Not only was he a decade older than Erzsi but he was also engaged to another woman at the time. Elisabeth went straight to her grandfather, insisting that he let her marry Otto despite the scandal. The prince soon found himself summoned to an imperial audience, where the emperor ordered him to break off his current engagement and instead propose to Elisabeth.[8] The prince complied, and he and Elisabeth were married at the Hofburg in January 1902.

While Stephanie essentially disappeared into private life, Elisabeth played out her increasing troubled marriage before the eyes of the public. Soon after the wedding Erzsi learned that her husband was having an affair with an actress from Prague. Ever her father's daughter, she responded by pulling a revolver on the woman and shooting her; the actress later died of her wounds, but Franz Josef managed to hush up the details and protect his granddaughter.[9] Despite this Elisabeth duly gave birth to four children: Prince Franz Josef in 1904, Prince Ernst in 1905, Prince Rudolf in 1907 and Princess Stephanie in 1909. Like her mother, Elisabeth soon responded to her husband's continued infidelities by taking her own lovers.

Elisabeth could do nothing about her marriage while her grandfather lived—and as Rudolf had feared—Franz Josef seemed destined to live forever. While, after Mayerling, Franz Josef retreated further and further into a narrow world dominated by bureaucratic paperwork, Empress Elisabeth continued to wander Europe, a dangerously thin figure habitually draped in black. In 1898 an Italian anarchist stabbed her to death while she was on holiday at Geneva. "No one," the emperor cried on hearing the news, "knows how we loved each other!"[10]

The emperor did his best to forget Rudolf, though every January 30 he faithfully visited his tomb at the Capuchin Crypt to pray. "Tomorrow," he wrote to Elisabeth in 1896, "is the painful day when our thoughts unite us in prayer for our dear Rudolf. Seven years have passed, the pain has eased, but the tragic memory and the irrevocable loss to the future remains."[11] Everyone at court knew never to mention the late crown prince's name. In 1901, when a newly appointed courtier casually spoke of Rudolf, Eduard Paar, the emperor's adjutant, warned him, "Leave that. That's a subject we don't like to talk about."[12] In 1903 Franz Josef took his revenge against Mariano Rampolla, the Vatican state secretary who had objected to a Catholic burial for the crown prince and who, in protest, had persuaded his fellow cardinals to boycott the requiem held in Rome for Rudolf. When Leo XIII died, everyone expected the College of Cardinals to elect Rampolla as pope. But, using an antiquated relic of Habsburg days as Holy Roman Emperors, Franz Josef vetoed his election; instead the conclave was forced to select Cardinal Giuseppe Sarto, who became Pius X.[13]

Franz Josef could never reconcile himself to the fact that his nephew Franz Ferdinand was now heir and stood in Rudolf's place.

A few days after Mayerling the emperor received his nephew: "I shall never be told officially whether or not I am Heir to the Throne," Franz Ferdinand complained after the meeting. "It's as if this stupidity of Mayerling was my fault! I have never been treated so coldly."[14] True to form, the emperor made the same mistakes with the archduke that he had made with the crown prince, attempting to deny him a useful role and keeping him as ignorant as possible about governmental affairs. Some of this antipathy undoubtedly stemmed from the archduke's morganatic marriage in 1900 to Countess Sophie Chotek, which—like Stephanie's second marriage—he regarded as an insult to the dignity of the house of Habsburg; ironically Stephanie became one of the couple's few friends in the imperial family. But Franz Ferdinand proved himself a much stronger character than his cousin Rudolf, and through sheer will and hard work eventually forced the emperor to allow him a substantial role.

In the summer of 1914, Franz Ferdinand and Sophie visited Sarajevo. Twenty-six-years earlier Rudolf and Stephanie had come to the Bosnian city amid worries of possible assassination. The parallels between 1888 and 1914 were eerie: Like Rudolf and Stephanie, Franz Ferdinand and Sophie stayed at the Hotel Bosna in the nearby resort of Ilidže; they followed their footsteps in touring Sarajevo and shopping in its fabled bazaars. But unlike Rudolf and Stephanie, Franz Ferdinand and Sophie didn't leave the city alive: An assassin's bullets finally opened the floodgates to a general European war. The old emperor carried on for two miserable years, but on November 21, 1916, he finally succumbed to pneumonia at the age of eighty-six. His great-nephew, who assumed the throne as Karl I, was more generously inclined toward Stephanie: In 1917 he raised her husband, Elemér Lónyay, to the rank of hereditary prince. But a year later the empire crumbled away: Karl and Zita fled into exile, and Stephanie lost the annual stipend that had enabled her comfortable style of life. By 1921, bereft of funds, the former crown princess was reduced to opening a cinema in Budapest.[15]

Stephanie remained estranged from her daughter, who, in the aftermath of the monarchy's fall, took up her father's political interests and joined the Social Democratic Party, falling in love with the politician Leopold Petznek. In 1924 Elisabeth formally separated from her husband, and Prince Windisch-Grätz unsuccessfully battled her for custody amidst gleeful newspaper headlines. She did not, though, seek a divorce: Petznek was married, although his wife was confined in an asylum; mirroring her father's romantic indiscretions, Elisabeth bought a house in Vienna, where she lived openly with her lover, attending political rallies and marches at his side.[16]

In 1935 Stephanie published her memoirs, *Ich Sollte Kaiserin Werden*, translated into English the next year under the title *I Was to Be Empress*. Written with an aristocratic couple, this was a fairly straightforward look back on her marriage to the crown prince, though undoubtedly it was meant to elicit sympathy for the wronged wife. Stephanie still felt wounded and humiliated by her life with Rudolf; her book carried a certain strain of animosity, though it was not as embittered as many of Rudolf's biographers would insist. Countess Juliana von Stockhausen, one of her ghostwriters, recalled that Stephanie was "torn between a desire to tell the truth and a reluctance to make these matters public."[17] But the book, depicting a dangerously unbalanced Rudolf, was deemed too frank, and Erzsi managed to have it banned in Austria; Stephanie retaliated by cutting Elisabeth out of her will.[18] Not that Stephanie was above resorting to such tactics when it suited her. In 1935 she learned that the director Anatole Litvak was filming an adaptation of Claude Anet's melodramatic 1930 novel *Mayerling*, starring Charles Boyer as Rudolf and Danielle Darrieux as Mary Vetsera. Stephanie immediately objected, and somehow persuaded authorities in both Austria and her native Belgium to ban the motion picture.[19]

Stephanie and her husband continued to live at Schloss Oroszvár as Europe again erupted into war. But the advance of the Soviet army in 1945 forced them to flee, and they sought refuge at the Benedictine Abbey of Pannonhalma in western Hungary. It was there on August 23, 1945, that Stephanie died; her husband followed her to the grave less than a year later. Both are buried at Pannonhalma.

Nor did Elisabeth escape the trauma of World War II. In 1944, the Nazis arrested Petznek and sent him to Dachau concentration camp near Munich, where he remained until the end of the war. His wife had died in 1935, but only in 1948 did Elisabeth finally divorce Prince Otto Windisch-Grätz and marry Petznek. During the Soviet occupation of Vienna she had lost her villa, and was not able to return to it until 1955. After she formally renounced her titles, people referred to Elisabeth as "the Red Archduchess" in recognition of her less-than-conservative political views and work. Petznek died in 1956, and Elisabeth in 1963: At her request she was buried in an unmarked grave in Vienna. Her four children—Rudolf's grandchildren—are now all deceased as well: Prince Rudolf died in 1939, and Prince Ernst in 1952. Prince Franz Josef, the eldest, remained alive until 1981, while his sister, Princess Stephanie, died in 2005 at the age of ninety-five.

•

Fate was not kind to many of those closest to the Mayerling tragedy. Stephanie's sister Louise endured her miserable marriage to Prince Philipp of Coburg until 1895, when she met a young Croatian officer, Count Géza Mattacic, in the Prater. Louise was something less than discreet about the liaison, and her unconventional behavior resulted in Franz Josef barring her from the imperial court. Outraged friends persuaded Prince Philipp to challenge Mattacic to a highly unsuccessful duel, during which the young soldier fired his revolver into the air while Coburg missed his shot. Having failed to dispose of the impudent officer, Coburg soon claimed that Mattacic had been forging Stephanie's name to her sister's bills; authorities arrested him and sentenced him to six years in prison. At the same time Louise was confronted with a choice: Either she return to her husband or be committed to an asylum. She chose the latter, where authorities acting under imperial orders declared her insane. Public pressure won Mattacic's release in 1902, and he soon managed to rescue Louise from the asylum and spirit her out of the empire. In 1906 Louise finally won her divorce from Coburg, but Mattacic died prematurely and thereafter she lived a peripatetic, impoverished existence, pointedly ignored by her relatives—including her sister Stephanie—until her death in 1924.[20] Prince Philipp, Rudolf's great friend, brother-in-law, and hunting companion, died in 1921.

Complicity in her cousin Rudolf's affair with Mary Vetsera condemned Countess Marie Larisch to exile from the Viennese court. Abandoning the socially damaged Heinrich Baltazzi, she transferred her affections to Karl Ernst von Otto-Kreckwitz and, in 1894, gave birth to his son, Friedrich Karl; with his wife's social connections demolished, Georg von Larisch was no longer willing to tolerate Marie's indiscretions, and he finally divorced her in 1896. A mere year passed before Larisch abandoned Otto-Kreckwitz and wed the musician Otto Brucks. This union, too, proved unsuccessful: Brucks found that being married to the infamous Countess Marie Larisch brought no rewards, and he soon became an alcoholic. With her bank coffers empty, Marie began writing about her Habsburg relations; in 1897 Franz Josef gave her a substantial sum of money in exchange for the manuscript about a subject he wanted forgotten.[21] Then, in 1909, her son, Heinrich Georg, killed himself, having learned about his mother's involvement in Mayerling and questions about his paternity. Larisch was bent on revenge. In 1913, working with the British writer Maude Ffoulkes, Larisch published her memoirs, *My Past*. Like the booklet by Helene Vetsera, this was largely meant to rewrite history, in this case revising Larisch's actual knowledge of and role in her cousin's affair. If Helene Vetsera had pointed the finger of blame at Larisch, the countess now returned the favor, insisting that Mary's mother had actually known of the liaison from its start. The book was an entertaining if highly questionable rendering of Larisch's involvement in the Mayerling affair, in which she denounced the "tissue of lies woven around me."[22] She railed against those she believed had wronged her, including the emperor, whom she described as "that stupid old man in Vienna."[23]

Brucks died in 1914; after working as a nurse during World War I, Larisch again turned her attention to her Habsburg past. Learning that the German director Rolf Raffé was making a film about Empress Elisabeth, the "elegantly dressed Countess" appeared unannounced at his Munich studio and offered to tell him "my own theory on the secret—or perhaps I should say, mystery—of Mayerling, and the deaths and burials of Crown Prince Rudolf and Baroness Vetsera, which would not disappoint." Intrigued, Raffé hired Larisch to help with a Mayerling screenplay; until the project was developed, though—and sensing that he had a potential dramatic coup—he asked Larisch to star as herself in his film on the empress. *Kaiserin Elisabeth von Österreich* duly premiered in 1921 but is now unfortunately lost. Lost as well is whatever "theory" Larisch may have propounded about Mayerling. Not until 1928 did Raffé get around to filming the story in his *Shicksal derer von Habsburg* (The Fate of the Habsburgs), which had an unlikely Mary Vetsera in the person of the future Nazi propagandist Leni Riefenstahl. But *Shicksal derer von Habsburg*, too, no longer exists—not even an outline to give a hint as to what Larisch might have said.[24]

By the time the film finally appeared, though, Larisch had already left Europe. Perpetually short of money, she embarked on a third marriage with an American doctor in 1924, but this union, too, turned miserable, and she left him, working as a maid in New Jersey before returning to her native Germany, where she died impoverished in 1940 at the age of eighty-two, having outlived four of her five children. But she achieved an immortality of sorts apart from Mayerling when her friend T. S. Eliot worked her into his great poem *The Waste Land*.

A few days after the tragedy at Mayerling, Rudolf's friend and frequent hunting companion Count Josef Hoyos had an audience with Franz Josef, in which he generously offered to say that he had accidentally shot the crown prince in a hunting accident—an offer the emperor declined.[25] Stephanie never blamed Hoyos for her husband's misadventures or death: Two weeks after Mayerling, she wrote to the count, thanking him for his "true and sincere friendship, both in happiness as well as in sorrow" and asking that he "only recall the happy days" he had spent with "my beloved Rudolf."[26] Shortly after Rudolf's death Hoyos wrote a lengthy memorandum recording his experiences at the lodge and deposited it in the Imperial Haus, Hof-und Staatsarchiv in Vienna, where it lay forgotten for nearly forty years. Hoyos died in 1899.

Josef Bratfisch kept his silence until his death in 1892 from throat cancer. Johann Loschek, too, refused all offers of interviews, though before he died in 1932 he dictated his memoirs to his son. At the time Loschek likely didn't know that Count Hoyos had also left a written record or that it would soon be published; believing that he was the last eyewitness to the tragedy, Loschek thus made numerous claims at variance both with the known facts as well as the count's contemporaneous memoirs.[27] Perhaps some of these discrepancies could be put down to the passage of time, but Julius Schuldes, the former telegraph operator at Mayerling, believed that Loschek's main intention was to "put himself in a favorable light" and "push himself to the forefront of events" while attempting to refute suspicions about his own actions at the lodge that night.[28] Rather than throw light on events at Mayerling, Loschek's statement only served to further muddy the historical waters.

Rudolf's friend Moritz Szeps died in 1908. In 1891 Mitzi Caspar sold the house Rudolf had bought her in the Heumühlgasse and lived in some comfort for the rest of her life. She refused to speak about her affair with Rudolf, and destroyed his last letter to her before her death.[29] Her death in January 1907 has often been attributed to spinal disease, but in fact she died of syphilis.[30]

Despite her battles with the imperial court and government censorship, Helene Vetsera remained in Vienna after publishing her monograph on Mary's liaison with the crown prince. So too did her Baltazzi brothers. In 1890, Franz Josef worried when, amid much publicity, Katharina Schratt joined Alexander Baltazzi for a ride in a hot-air balloon. "I have never objected," he wrote her, "to your social relations with Alexander Baltazzi," but added that, "in the eyes of a wicked world this fact, picked out by the press, will harm you."[31] Alexander Baltazzi died in 1914, as did his brother Aristide; Hector Baltazzi died in 1916, while Heinrich lived until 1929.

As for Helene Vetsera, smart society in Vienna followed the imperial court's lead, and the once-brilliant hostess faded into obscurity. She left the palace on the Salesianergasse for the less-imposing surroundings of an apartment on Vienna's Prinz-Eugen-Strasse, living in the lengthening shadow of the shame heaped upon her. Mary's sister, Hanna, married a Dutch aristocrat, Count Hendrik von Bylandt-Rheydt, but she died unexpectedly of typhoid after suffering a miscarriage in 1901.[32] World War I claimed Mary's younger brother, Franz, who died in 1915 while fighting with the Austrian cavalry on the Russian front. Helene thus survived all of her children. Postwar inflation in Vienna wiped out her remaining fortune, and she ended her days in a small Vienna apartment. It was there, on February 1, 1925, that she died at the age of seventy-seven; Helene was buried with Franz at Payerbach. It has been said that before her death she destroyed her personal papers related to Mayerling.[33] In fact the letters written by Mary were deposited in a Vienna bank vault, where they remained hidden until being discovered in 2015.

Today Rudolf rests in an elaborate brass-bronze-and-copper sarcophagus in Vienna's Capuchin Crypt, next to his parents, with Franz Josef at the center flanked by his wife and his son. Rudolf's death inadvertently precipitated tumultuous events: the assassination of his cousin Archduke Franz Ferdinand in Sarajevo, World War I, and the fall of Europe's great ruling dynasties. A certain nostalgia has developed around Rudolf's modern legacy, depicting him as a liberal visionary of exceptional intellect and talent, a man who could have transformed the Habsburg monarchy and perhaps saved it when Europe's other royal dynasties crumbled into oblivion. This view seems too naively hopeful. Rudolf undoubtedly had a better grasp of democratic aspirations and the necessity of reform than did his father, but he was too impetuous, too impatient, to advance a considered political program for the future. Had he lived, Rudolf would likely have lingered on the fringes of power, impotent to act and feeling oppressed by his father's unimaginative rule.

Rudolf would have been fifty-eight when his father died in 1916. The better part of his life would have been over, and the endless waiting would almost certainly have made him even more bitter and depressed. But by the age of thirty he was already spiraling into self-destruction. He would undoubtedly have fallen further into drug and alcohol abuse to combat the effects of gonorrhea, and his physical and mental health would have deteriorated further. Even without the intervening events of January 1889, it seems unlikely that Rudolf would have managed to hold himself together for another twenty-seven years until his father's passing. The late Archduke Otto concisely summed up the crown prince: "A wasted life," he said, "followed by a needless death."[34]

•

In Graham Greene's 1950 novel *The Third Man*, the unnamed narrator presciently notes, "One's file, you know, is never quite complete; a case is never really closed, even after a century, when all the participants are dead."[35] As ever in the case of momentous tragedies, the apparent confusion surrounding Mayerling gave rise to conflicting theories that transformed events that night into the ultimate locked-room mystery, shrouded in seemingly impenetrable layers of rumors. The facts—if not the motivating factors—were simple enough, but by depriving its people of the devastating truth, the government needlessly fed the sense of intrigue and left itself open to charges of a vast conspiracy.

Even after a century the fallen Habsburgs still hold a sentimental place in modern Austria. The story of Mayerling, along with a series of highly idealized movies about Empress Elisabeth, has transformed Franz Josef's family into cultural icons. Tourists flock to view the rooms where they lived, to see the empress's lavish gowns, and to immerse themselves in a fairy-tale world of royalty and confections, of gilded palaces and elegant uniforms, set in the imagination to the evocative strains of a romantic Strauss waltz.

After Rudolf's death his Turkish room in the Hofburg remained intact, but it was dismantled after the fall of the monarchy. Just beyond it, the narrow wooden ascent that Mary had often used to visit her lover is still known as the Vetsera Staircase.[36] Today these rooms house government offices and are closed to the public, though morbid curiosity can be satisfied with a visit to the Hofmobiliendepot, or Court Furniture Museum, where the bed upon which Rudolf and Mary died remains a prime attraction.

The Vetsera Palace on the Salesianergasse was for a time occupied by the princely Salm family, though it was razed in 1921.[37] But tourists enamored of the Mayerling story can journey a dozen miles southwest of the capital. At Heiligenkreuz, Mary Vetsera's grave still draws crowds, who come to stare at the little plot enclosed by a low wrought-iron fence and the marble monument recording her name.

Having come this far into the Vienna Woods, tourists almost inevitably travel a few more miles to see Mayerling itself. Less than a month after Rudolf's death, Franz Josef took control of the lodge and ordered that it be transformed into a convent for an order of penitential Carmelite nuns. The old Church of Saint Laurenz was pulled down and the area around the lodge transformed with the addition of new wings encircling the courtyard.[38]

Construction was under way by the tragedy's first anniversary, when the emperor, empress, and Marie Valerie made the sad journey out to the complex to mourn Rudolf's death. Only Stephanie and the young Archduchess Elisabeth, staying at Miramar, were absent—a fact that led to a good deal of bitter public comment.[39] But the imperial couple had made no secret of the fact that they held Stephanie responsible for her husband's death—a death she likely had no wish to commemorate with them, especially as they had pointedly ignored her and her daughter just a month earlier by marking Christmas alone with Marie Valerie and her fiancé. The requiem mass in the new chapel was a solemn affair; Elisabeth and her daughter clad in black, the emperor looking stoic as priests intoned prayers.[40] It was, Marie Valerie commented in her diary, "like a bad dream."[41]

Hidden away in its serene forest, Mayerling remains an evocative place of tragic romance. In 2014 the Carmelite nuns opened a visitors' center, featuring some furniture from the lodge as well as Mary's original copper casket and a few planks from her first pine coffin, which the monks at Heiligenkreuz had kept stored away in a cellar following her 1959 reburial.[42] But little remains of the former lodge. The western side of the building was divided into cells, while the new Gothic-revival-style chapel was built directly over Rudolf's former private apartments. In a grisly bit of design, the architect incorporated the outline of Rudolf's bedroom into the new church, with the elaborately carved altar of Istrian marble erected on the precise spot where his bed had once stood.[43] Even today the nuns still follow the emperor's directive, gathering at the very spot of the tragedy to offer daily prayers for Rudolf's unhappy soul.

NOTES

PROLOGUE

1. Cantacuzène, 64.
2. Lansdale, 146; Hamilton, 65.
3. Hamilton, 50.
4. Cited in Crankshaw, 31.
5. Marek, 22.
6. Cone, 119.
7. Marek, 21; Morton, *Thunder*, 29; Radziwill, *Austrian Court*, 131.
8. Cantacuzène, 74.
9. Paget, *Scenes and Memories*, 227.
10. Friedrich, *Der Kriminalfall Mayerling*, 140n850.
11. Louise of Belgium, 103.
12. Stephanie, 240–41.
13. Larisch, *My Past*, 147; Louise of Belgium, 104; Judtmann, 44; Bibl, 78–79.
14. Cantacuzène, 142–43.
15. Ibid., 79.
16. Bibl, 78; Paget, *Embassies*, 2:465.
17. Louise of Belgium, 103.
18. Dr. Konrad Ritter von Zdekauer, in *Neues Wiener Journal*, June 2, 1923.
19. Larisch, *My Past*, 268, 270; *Der Vetsera Denkschrift*, 64, in Markus and Unterreiner, 255.
20. Louise of Belgium, 102–3.
21. Larisch, *My Past*, 271; Judtmann, 47.
22. Hoyos Memorandum, in Haus-, Hof- und Staatsarchiv, Vienna (hereafter HHS), Box 21; also in Mitis, 342.
23. Larisch, *My Past*, 268.
24. Louise of Belgium, 104.

25. Dr. Konrad Ritter von Zdekauer, in *Neues Wiener Journal*, June 2, 1923; *Le Matin*, February 5, 1889.
26. Cited in Listowel, 214.
27. Larisch, *My Past*, 271; Louise of Belgium, 104.
28. *Der Polizeibericht*, 11. This seems to have happened so quickly that it escaped the attention of most of those present. On this point see Judtmann, 47. In her diary Stephanie merely recorded that she attended the event but added no details; however, Stephanie was unlikely to have written of her public humiliation. See Stephanie, 243, and Stephanie's diary for January 27, 1889, in Hamann, *Der Weg nach Mayerling*, 133.

CHAPTER 1

1. Jászi, 34.
2. Mahaffy, 3–4.
3. Taylor, *Habsburg Monarchy*, 47; Hamann, *Reluctant Empress*, 7.
4. Haslip, *Lonely Empress*, 21; Marek, 41.
5. de Weindel, 63; Mahaffy, 8–9, 11–12.
6. Ernst, 45; Listowel, 44.
7. Rumbold, *Austrian Court*, 158.
8. Strong, 49.
9. Harding, 254–57.
10. Jászi, 34.
11. Taylor, *Habsburg Monarchy*, 9.
12. Margutti, 19.
13. Ernst, 187.
14. Margutti, 50.
15. Ibid., 44.
16. Ibid., 38, 49.
17. Taylor, *Fall of the Dynasties*, 93.
18. Margutti, 38.
19. Nikitsch-Boulles, 47–48.
20. Margutti, 216; Corti, *Empress Elisabeth*, 13; Ernst, 20.
21. Crown Prince Rudolf to Josef Latour von Thurmberg, letter of December 2, 1881, HHS, Box 16; also quoted in Mitis, 205–6; and in Hamann, *Majestät, ich warne Sie*, 10.
22. Jászi, 116.
23. Countess Marie Festetics, diary entry of 1873, cited in Marek, 203–4.
24. Taylor, *Fall of the Dynasties*, 89; de Weindel, 27; Palmer, 65.
25. Redlich, 201, 205; Bagger, 248; Corti, *Empress Elisabeth*, 22.
26. Corti, *Empress Elisabeth*, 26.
27. Hamann, *Reluctant Empress*, 45.
28. Haslip, *Lonely Empress*, 74; Hamann, *Reluctant Empress*, 46–47.
29. Corti, *Empress Elisabeth*, 49; Palmer, 78; Hamann, *Reluctant Empress*, 47.
30. Cited in Hamann, *Reluctant Empress*, 72.

31. Cited in Marek, 106.
32. Corti, *Empress Elisabeth*, 49–50.
33. Ibid., 54.
34. Crankshaw, 111.
35. Larisch, *My Past*, 137.
36. Hamann and Hassmann, 18, 30–31.
37. Corti, *Empress Elisabeth*, 81–82.
38. Ibid., 201–2.
39. Hamann, *Reluctant Empress*, 231–32.
40. Corti, *Empress Elisabeth*, 90; Haslip, *Lonely Empress*, 137; Margutti, 64; Vivian, 77; *Martyrdom*, 49; Marek, 128; Larisch, *My Past*, 154–55.
41. Haslip, *Lonely Empress*, 140–41; Listowel, 12–13.
42. Haslip, *Lonely Empress*, 141.
43. Corti, *Empress Elisabeth*, 143–44.
44. Ibid., 206–7.
45. Louisa of Tuscany, 51–52.
46. Larisch, *My Past*, 98–101.
47. Paoli, 6–9.
48. Corti, *Empress Elisabeth*, 411.
49. Cited in Hamann, *Reluctant Empress*, 250.
50. Margutti, 75.
51. Corti, *Empress Elisabeth*, 186.
52. Franz Josef to Katharina Schratt, letter of August 7, 1866, in Nostitz-Rieneck, 1:57–58; Corti, *Empress Elisabeth*, 152.
53. Margutti, 26, 44–45; de Weindel, 243–44; Rumbold, *Francis Joseph*, 329.
54. Beller, 138.
55. Corti, *Empress Elisabeth*, 327; Haslip, *Lonely Empress*, 346.
56. Kürnberg, 99–100.
57. See Morton, *Nervous*, 23; Morton, *Thunder*, 85.
58. Marek, 215.
59. Haslip, *Lonely Empress*, 358–59.

CHAPTER 2

1. Haslip, *Mexico*, 112.
2. Thiele, *Crown Prince Rudolf*, 8.
3. Corti, *Empress Elisabeth*, 77.
4. Ibid.; Listowel, 8; Franzel, 75; Mitis, 15; Salvendy, 8.
5. Judtmann, 14; Marek, 256; Salvendy, 39.
6. Unterreiner, *Emperor Franz Joseph*, 52.
7. Marie Valerie, diary entry of May 29, 1884, cited in Salvendy, 129; Barkeley, 32; Ernst, 186; Lónyay, 25.
8. Lónyay, 20.
9. Haslip, *Lonely Empress*, 16.
10. Listowel, 18.

11. Corti, *Empress Elisabeth*, 102; cited in Salvendy, 15.
12. Unterreiner, *Crown Prince Rudolf*, 2.
13. Rudolf to Latour von Thurmberg, letter of December 2, 1881, in HHS, Box 16; also in Barkeley, 82.
14. Mitis, 23; Listowel, 17, 26; Barkeley, 11; Salvendy, 13, 151; Lónyay, 23.
15. Salvendy, 11.
16. Bibl, 183.
17. Mitis, 16, 43; Franzel, 76.
18. Lónyay, 11–12.
19. Corti, *Empress Elisabeth*, 12; Franzel, 25.
20. Lónyay, 12.
21. Corti, *Empress Elisabeth*, 110; Lónyay, 12.
22. Marek, 166; Salvendy, 14–15.
23. Barkeley, 12; Listowel, 20–21.
24. Empress Elisabeth to Franz Josef, letter of August 24, 1865, cited in Corti, *Empress Elisabeth*, 123–24.
25. Haslip, *Lonely Empress*, 273–74.
26. Hamann, *Reluctant Empress*, 123; Margutti, 88; Mitis, 16; Listowel, 23; Barkeley, 13.
27. Mitis, 16.
28. Cited in Barkeley, 35.
29. Listowel, 29–30; Barkeley, 10; Corti, *Empress Elisabeth*, 125; Mitis, 20; Lónyay, 18; Thiele, *Crown Prince Rudolf*, 12.
30. Mitis, 128–29.
31. Ibid., 22.
32. Ibid.
33. Latour von Thurmberg report, May 1868, quoted in Lónyay, 50; Latour von Thurmberg report, December 15, 1868, quoted in ibid., 49.
34. Rudolf, diary entry of December 1872, cited in Barkeley, 25.
35. Rudolf to Latour von Thurmberg, 1881, cited in ibid., 74.
36. Rudolf to King Ludwig II of Bavaria, letter of March 9, 1878, quoted in Mitis, 198–99.
37. Rudolf, notebook entry, December 1873, in HHS, Box 12; also in Mitis, 26–27.
38. Ibid.
39. Rudolf, last will, April 15, 1879, quoted in Mitis, 200–201.
40. Crankshaw, 294.
41. Margutti, 87.
42. Crankshaw, 293; Morton, *Nervous*, 174; Franzel, 29.
43. Jászi, 120; Ronay, 58.
44. Rudolf, *Notes on Sport*, 2, 28.
45. Corti, *Empress Elisabeth*, 211–12; Listowel, 35.
46. Ronay, 56–57.
47. Margutti, 87.

48. Lónyay, 101.
49. Cone, 147.
50. de Weindel, 104.
51. Margutti, 105–6; Mitis, 33; Listowel, 51; Bibl, 187.
52. Corti, *Empress Elisabeth*, 281.
53. Mitis, 38
54. Rudolf to King Ludwig II of Bavaria, letter of January 1878, quoted in Mitis, 198–99.
55. Cited in Barkeley, 40–41.
56. Cornwallis-West, 106; Barkeley, 44.
57. Corti, *Empress Elisabeth*, 286; Haslip, *Lonely Empress*, 303–4.
58. Mitis, 49; Listowel, 62–63; Lónyay, 56; Franzel, 78.
59. Listowel, 64; Lónyay, 57–58; Mitis, 61–63.
60. Mitis, 63.
61. Margutti, 91.
62. Ibid., 82–83.
63. Radziwill, *Austrian Court*, 121–22; Grant, 36; Louise of Belgium, 106.
64. Stephanie, 23; Radziwill, *My Recollections*, 143.
65. Louise of Belgium, 106.
66. Grant, 36; Wölfing, 50.
67. Radziwill, *Austrian Court*, 122,
68. Marie Festetics, diary entry of June 9, 1881, in Corti, *Empress Elisabeth*, 307.
69. Quoted in Mitis, 31–32.
70. Wölfing, 49.
71. Larisch, *My Past*, 89, 91, 46.
72. Cited, Hamann, *Reluctant Empress*, 323.
73. Marie Valerie, diary entry of December 9, 1887, quoted in Corti, *Empress Elisabeth*, 405.
74. Marie Valerie, diary entry of June 20, 1885, cited in Salvendy, 128.
75. Haslip, *Lonely Empress*, 293.

CHAPTER 3

1. Mitis, 24.
2. Judtmann, 17; Barkeley, 33; Lónyay, 17.
3. Listowel, 118.
4. Corti, *Empress Elisabeth*, 296.
5. Monts, 98.
6. Wölfing, 49.
7. Cited in Listowel, 121.
8. Barta, 27.
9. Lónyay, 134.
10. Grant, 111, 104.

11. Vacaresco, 100–101.
12. Lónyay, 130–33.
13. Hamann, *Der Weg nach Mayerling*, 114.
14. Lónyay, 134.
15. Listowel, 119; Marek, 500n5; Barta, 35. Robert Pachmann, the alleged son, later sued for legal recognition as a Habsburg and moved to America.
16. Barta, 35.
17. Wolfson, 79.
18. Judtmann, 33; Louise of Belgium, 113; Burg, 224; Thiele, *Crown Prince Rudolf*, 51; Haslip, *Lonely Empress*, 379; Defrance and van Loon, 26.
19. Quoted in Beéche, 196.
20. Cantacuzène, 141.
21. Louise of Belgium, 60–62; Ascherson, 205.
22. *Recollections of a Royal Governess*, 141; Ascherson, 206; Vivian, 95.
23. Rudolf to Latour von Thurmberg, letter of January 15, 1879, quoted in Lónyay, 70.
24. Rumbold, *Austrian Court*, 303; de Weindel, 126–27.
25. Larisch, *My Past*, 144–45.
26. Louise of Belgium, 105.
27. King and Woolmans, 38; Schiel, 97.
28. Rappoport, 230–31.
29. Stephanie, 54.
30. Cited in Tuchman, 40.
31. Margutti, 83.
32. Salvendy, 105; Listowel, 126.
33. Stephanie, 88.
34. Ibid., 94.
35. Ibid., 89–90.
36. Barta, 15; Larisch, *My Past*, 146; Wolfson, 81; Ascherson, 213; Stephanie, 23, 92.
37. Rudolf to Latour von Thurmberg, letter of March 7, 1880, in HHS, Box 16; also in Mitis, 68.
38. Rudolf to Latour von Thurmberg, letter of March 11, 1880, in HHS, Box 16; also in Mitis, 68; Lónyay, 72; Rudolf to Latour von Thurmberg, letter of March 13, 1880, in HHS, Box 16; also in Mitis, 68–69.
39. Margutti, 89.
40. Corti, *Empress Elisabeth*, 301; Cone, 148.
41. Haslip, *Lonely Empress*, 320.
42. Marek, 258; Stephanie, 98; Palmer, 221; Harding, 270.
43. Schiel, 124–25.
44. Kürenberg, 92.
45. Stephanie, 110–11; Larisch, *My Past*, 108; de Weindel, 169; *Martyrdom of an Empress*, 179.
46. Stephanie, 112–13.

47. Ibid., 255.
48. Marie Valerie, diary entry of November 26, 1883, cited in Salvendy, 84.
49. Lónyay, 99–100.
50. Rudolf to Latour von Thurmberg, letter of December 2, 1881, in HHS, Box 16; also in Salvendy, 83.
51. Stephanie, 258.
52. Ibid., 29, 144.
53. Corti, *Empress Elisabeth*, 323.
54. Barkeley, 91.
55. Mitis, 70–71.
56. Stephanie, 151–52.
57. Haslip, *Lonely Empress*, 326.
58. Lónyay, 119, 123–24.
59. Larisch, *My Past*, 145–47.
60. Stephanie, 255.
61. Margutti, 87.
62. Listowel, 138
63. Stephanie, 153–54.
64. Friedrich, *Der Kriminalfall Mayerling*, 79n453.
65. Morton, *Nervous*, 114.
66. Lónyay, 130–31; Larisch, *My Past*, 116; Thiele, *Crown Prince Rudolf*, 48; Wolfson, 77–78; Marek, 268; Markus, 101.
67. Larisch, *My Past*, 148–49; Haslip, *Lonely Empress*, 378; *Recollections of a Royal Governess*, 141.
68. Queen Victoria to Princess Victoria of Battenberg, letter of February 20, 1889, quoted in Hough, 87–99.
69. Stephanie, 30.
70. Marie Valerie, diary entry of August 14, 1885, in Schad and Schad, 74; Marie Valerie, diary entry of August 17, 1885, cited in Salvendy, 78.
71. Cited in Hamann, *Reluctant Empress*, 323; Kürenberg, 92–93.
72. Stephanie, 30.
73. Judtmann, 81–82; Barta, 50–52; Unterreiner, *Crown Prince Rudolf*, 16.
74. Stephanie, 31.
75. Ibid., 124.
76. *Martyrdom of an Empress*, 194; de Weindel, 173; Margutti, 90.
77. Listowel, 149; *Neue Illustrierte Wochenschau*, September 18, 1953.
78. Judtmann, 19; Corti, *Empress Elisabeth*, 341; Listowel, 145.
79. Holler, 37.
80. Sulzberger, 163; Listowel, 149. On page 218 Listowel asserted that Franz Auchenthaler, the physician who performed the postmortem examination on Mary Vetsera, found that she—and thus presumably Rudolf—was infected with syphilis. But her cited source for this bit of information, the book by Stephanie's nephew Carl Lónyay, asserted only that Rudolf and Mary were both found to be suffering from gonorrhea, not syphilis. See Lónyay, 193.

81. *Wiener Zeitung*, February 2, 1889.
82. Margutti, 98.
83. *Neue Illustrierte Wochenschau*, September 18, 1955; Judtmann, 19–20; Markus and Unterreiner, 53–54.
84. Judtmann, 19–20; *Neue Illustrierte Wochenschau*, September 18, 1955.
85. Salvendy, 88; Listowel, 147; Markus, 108.
86. Salvendy, 88.
87. Zweig, 129.
88. Letter of Juliana von Stockhausen to Judtmann, January 29, 1968, in Judtmann, 18.
89. Stephanie, 196.
90. Stephanie, draft manuscript in Corti papers, quoted in Judtmann, 18.
91. Listowel, 147; Louise of Belgium, 108; Schiel, 238.
92. Salvendy, 80.
93. Cited in Salvendy, 89; de Weindel, 178; Listowel, 147; Holler, 37.
94. See Markus and Unterreiner, 54–55.
95. Salvendy, 151; Markus, 108.
96. Stephanie, 256, 208.
97. Corti, *Empress Elisabeth*, 373.
98. Rudolf to Stephanie, letter of April 5, 1887, cited in Salvendy, 97.
99. Rudolf to Stephanie, letter of March 31, 1888, quoted in Schiel, 174.
100. Stephanie, 208–9.
101. Salvendy, 99; Hamann, *Der Weg nach Mayerling*, 114; Wolfson, 85; Schiel, 319, 325–27.
102. Salvendy, 171.
103. Fugger, 5–6; Judtmann, 35.
104. Listowel, 164.
105. Monts, 127–28; *Der Polizeibericht*, 47.
106. Mitis, 200–201; Barkeley, 53; Listowel, 288.
107. Mitis, 288–89.

CHAPTER 4

1. *Society Recollections*, 176; Radziwill, *Austrian Court*, 120.
2. Larisch, *My Past*, 268.
3. Margutti, 94; de Weindel, 80–81; Ryan, 33; *Martyrdom of an Empress*, 211; Louise of Belgium, 103; Haslip, *Emperor and the Actress*, 97.
4. Kürenberg, 94.
5. Margutti, 95–96; Kürenberg, 94–95; de Weindel, 184; *Martyrdom of an Empress*, 211.
6. Van der Kiste, 95.
7. Stephanie, 210.
8. Listowel, 166.
9. Waddington, 111.

10. Hollaender, in Hantsch and Novotny, 160n62.
11. Judtmann, 31; Markus, 23; Listowel, 190–91; Markus and Unterreiner, 16.
12. Corti, *Empress Elisabeth*, 254.
13. http://levantineheritage.com/testi47.htm.
14. Corti, *Empress Elisabeth*, 254.
15. *Der Polizeibereicht*, 66; Lónyay, 156; Listowel, 192; Monts, 106; *Recollections of a Royal Governess*, 158; Marek, 269.
16. Corti, *Empress Elisabeth*, 296–97.
17. Ibid., 296.
18. Hamann, *Kronprinz*, 109–10; see also Markus, 79; Haslip, *Emperor and the Actress*, 95; Sulzberger, 163.
19. Larisch, *My Past*, 102–3.
20. Larisch, *My Past*, 213; Markus, 79.
21. Friedrich, *Der Kriminalfall Mayerling*, 43.
22. Ibid., 62. Helene later converted to Catholicism.
23. Judtmann, 30; de Weindel, 181; Listowel, 188–89; Markus, 23.
24. Listowel, 189; Friedrich, *Der Kriminalfall Mayerling*, 50.
25. Listowel, 189; Judtmann, 30.
26. Paget, *Scenes and Memories*, 220.
27. Friedrich, *Der Kriminalfall Mayerling*, 62n306.
28. Ibid., 52.
29. *Le Journal*, February 2, 1939.
30. Friedrich, *Der Kriminalfall Mayerling*, 61.
31. Judtmann, 77–78; Friedrich, *Der Kriminalfall Mayerling*, 40. The house, which later became the Salm Palace, was torn down in 1916. See Judtmann, 30.
32. Motley, 2:124.
33. Listowel, 192.
34. Cassels, *Clash*, 58.
35. Radziwill, *Austrian Court*, 134.
36. Larisch, *My Past*, 215–16.
37. Markus and Unterreiner, 16.
38. Listowel, 192.
39. *Der Polizeibericht*, 66; Lónyay, 156; Listowel, 192; Monts, 106; *Recollections of a Royal Governess*, 158; Marek, 269.
40. See Friedrich, *Der Kriminalfall Mayerling*, 451–52.
41. Markus, 24; Friedrich, *Der Kriminalfall Mayerling*, 55–56.
42. Friedrich, *Der Kriminalfall Mayerling*, 40.
43. Ibid., 52.
44. Marek, 296; Judtmann, 29.
45. Radziwill, *Austrian Court*, 120.
46. *Berliner Börsencourier*, February 24, 1889.
47. Larisch, *My Past*, 219–20.
48. Paget, *Embassies*, 2:467.

49. Ibid.; Vivian, 56; Fugger, 192.
50. Fugger, 205.
51. Larisch, *My Past*, 234–35.
52. Fugger, 205.
53. Larisch, *My Past*, 241.
54. Baltazzi-Scharschmid and Swistun, 170.
55. Quoted in Freisler, 18.
56. Paget, *Embassies*, 2:470; Margutti, 100.
57. Baltazzi-Scharschmid and Swistun, 179; *Berliner Börsencourier*, February 24, 1889.
58. Larisch, *My Past*, 222; cited in Friedrich, *Der Kriminalfall Mayerling*, 357n1941.
59. Friedrich, *Der Kriminalfall Mayerling*, 356n1983.
60. Quoted in ibid., 356.
61. Ibid., 50, 52.
62. Nemec and Nemec-Jirak, 174.
63. Louise of Belgium, 103.
64. Larisch, *My Past*, 210–20; *Berliner Börsencourier*, February 24, 1889.
65. Larisch, *My Past*, 221–22.
66. Radziwill, *Austrian Court*, 120.
67. Larisch, *My Past*, 218.
68. Lansdale, 15; Cantacuzène, 64; Marek, 9; Morton, *Thunder*, 30.
69. Morton, *Nervous*, 83.
70. Marek, 9; *Society Recollections*, 221.
71. Morton, *Nervous*, 78.
72. *Der Polizeibericht*, 67.
73. Hollaender, in Hantsch and Novotny, 150.
74. Ibid.; *Der Polizeibericht*, 19.
75. Judtmann, 108, 203; Fugger, 222; Lónyay, 156; Radziwill, *Dethroned*, 138; cited in Cassels, *Clash*, 209.
76. Baltazzi-Scharschmid and Swistun, 181; Haslip, *Lonely Empress*, 387.
77. Fugger, 206.
78. *Society Recollections*, 155–56; Levetus, 370–72; Paget, *Scenes and Memories*, 226.
79. Morton, *Nervous*, 82; Barkeley, 210; Markus, 24; Thiele, *Crown Prince Rudolf*, 80.
80. Markus and Unterreiner, 19.
81. Ibid., 18–19; *Der Vetsera Denkschrift*, 23–24, in Markus and Unterreiner, 242–43.
82. Markus, 24.

CHAPTER 5

1. Margutti, 93; Corti, *Empress Elisabeth*, 278; Ffoulkes, 305.
2. Ffoulkes, 314–16.

3. Corti, *Empress Elisabeth*, 278, 280.
4. Haslip, *Emperor and the Actress*, 100; Haslip, *Lonely Empress*, 295; Burg, 179; Margutti, 93; de Fontenoy, *Secret Memoirs*, 2:160.
5. Larisch, *My Past*, 104, 106–7.
6. Larisch, *My Past*, 375.
7. Haslip, *Lonely Empress*, 388; de Fontenoy, *Secret Memoirs*, 2:161.
8. Sokop, 152; Larisch, *My Past*, 76, 102; Listowel, 191; Judtmann, 33.
9. Sokop, 156.
10. Ibid.
11. *Der Vetsera Denkschrift*, 23, in Markus and Unterreiner, 242.
12. Larisch, *My Past*, 221.
13. Monts, 277.
14. Larisch, *My Past*, 244.
15. *L'Éclair*, September 3, 1891; Haslip, *Lonely Empress*, 367; Judtmann, 32, 72–73; Listowel, 192; Markus, 103.
16. Baltazzi-Scharschmid and Swistun, 191.
17. *Der Vetsera Denkschrift*, 35, in Markus and Unterreiner, 246.
18. Ibid., 33, in Markus and Unterreiner, 245.
19. Ibid., 25, in Markus and Unterreiner, 243.
20. Schiel, 281.
21. Kürenberg, 95.
22. Baltazzi-Scharschmid and Swistun, 185.
23. Quoted in "Glimpses," *Royalty Digest* 1, no. 1 (July 1991): 20.
24. Markus and Unterreiner, 20.
25. Cited in Barkeley, 207.
26. *Der Vetsera Denkschrift*, 19, in Markus and Unterreiner, 241.
27. Ibid., 25, in Markus and Unterreiner, 243.
28. Larisch, *My Past*, 221–27.
29. Hoyos Addendum, in HHS, Box 21; also in Mitis, 281; Haslip, *Lonely Empress*, 389.
30. Haslip, *Lonely Empress*, 389.
31. Larisch, *My Past*, 220–21, 235.
32. Ibid., 226–27, 235.
33. Larisch, *My Past*, 243; Markus, 24–25, 61.
34. Friedrich, *Der Kriminalfall Mayerling*, 213.
35. Sokop, 120, 182; Friedrich, *Der Kriminalfall Mayerling*, 213.
36. Larisch, *My Past*, 228.
37. Dom Duarte de Bragança to Sue Woolmans, e-mail of February 1, 2016.
38. Larisch, *My Past*, 237.
39. Ibid., 248.
40. Ibid., 269.
41. Barkeley, 208; Listowel, 131; Lónyay, 122–24.
42. Corti, *Empress Elisabeth*, 390.
43. Morton, *Nervous*, 130.

44. Larisch, *My Past*, 260.
45. Ibid., 248.
46. Ibid., 238–39.
47. Fugger, 190.
48. Haslip, *Emperor and the Actress*, 92; Haslip, *Lonely Empress*, 388; Fugger, 191.
49. Barkeley, 207; Morton, *Nervous*, 83–84; *Neue Freie Presse*, August 21, 1921.
50. Morton, *Nervous*, 119.
51. Ibid., 121–23.
52. Quoted in ibid., 123.
53. Cited in Barkeley, 206.
54. Larisch, *My Past*, 249, 303–4; Judtmann, 81; Mary Vetsera to Hermine Tobias, letter of November 5, 1888, in *Der Vetsera Denkschrift*, 29–32, in Markus and Unterreiner, 244–45.
55. Larisch, *My Past*, 303–4; Judtmann, 81.
56. Mary Vetsera to Hermine Tobias, letter of November 5, 1888, in *Der Vetsera Denkschrift*, 29–32, in Markus and Unterreiner, 244–45.
57. *Der Vetsera Denkschrift*, 35–37, in Markus and Unterreiner, 246; Hoyos Addendum, in HHS, Box 21; also in Mitis, 281.
58. Hoyos Addendum, HHS, Box 21; also in Mitis, 281; Krauss report on Bratfisch, February 2, 1889, quoted in Loehr, 106.
59. Judtmann, 82.
60. Barta, 37.
61. *Der Vetsera Denkschrift*, 24, in Markus and Unterreiner, 241.
62. Ibid., 49–53, in Markus and Unterreiner, 251.
63. *Der Vetsera Denkschrift*, 48, 64, in Markus and Unterreiner, 250, 255; Lónyay, 157; Thiele, *Crown Prince Rudolf*, 84; Morton, *Nervous*, 131.
64. Morton, *Nervous*, 153.
65. Larisch, *My Past*, 244–47.
66. Louise of Belgium, 108.
67. Baltazzi-Scharschmid and Swistun, 193; Hoyos Addendum, HHS, Box 21; also in Mitis, 281; Morton, *Nervous*, 175.
68. Friedrich, *Der Kriminalfall Mayerling*, 63.

CHAPTER 6

1. Rudolf to Szeps, letter of August 21, 1888, in Szeps, *Politische Briefe*, 163–64
2. Corti, *Empress Elisabeth*, 350.
3. Lónyay, 142; Judtmann, 21; Salvendy, 125–26.
4. Mitis, 127; Stephanie, 147; Margutti, 83.
5. Chlumecky, 38.
6. Rudolf, will of April 15, 1879, in Mitis, 200–201.
7. Mahaffy, 167–68; Listowel, 155.

8. Taylor, *Habsburg Monarchy*, 156–58; Mahaffy, 170; Jászi, 12, 103.
9. Barkeley, 66.
10. Rudolf to Szeps, letter of November 24, 1882, in Lónyay, 85.
11. Barkeley, 79–81; Listowel, 79.
12. Rudolf to Latour von Thurmberg, letter of December 2, 1881, HHS, Box 16; also in Mitis, 205–7.
13. Szeps, *My Life and History*, 51; Szeps, *Politische Briefe*, 27–32.
14. Cassels, *Clash*, 63; Cassels, *Archduke and the Assassin*, 14.
15. Rudolf to Franz Ferdinand, letter of November 26, 1884, in Nachlass Erzherzog Franz Ferdinand, HHS, Box 5, cited in King and Woolmans, 18.
16. Lónyay, 87.
17. Szeps, *My Life and History*, 66
18. Listowel, 141; Morton, *Nervous*, 61–62.
19. Rudolf to Szeps, letter of November 19, 1882, HHS, Box 17.
20. Szeps, *My Life and History*, 35; Chlumecky, 30.
21. Judtmann, 34
22. Salvendy, 65; Lónyay, 97.
23. Listowel, 173; Stephanie, 230; Morton, *Nervous*, 10; Barkeley, 187; Judtmann, 23.
24. Mitis, 65.
25. Jászi, 151–52; Lónyay, 92–93; Mitis, 90.
26. Listowel, 62.
27. Salvendy, 131.
28. Strong, 58.
29. Cited in Salvendy, 133.
30. Margutti, 90.
31. Stephanie, 239.
32. Marie Valerie, diary entry of April 30, 1888, in Schad and Schad, 142–43.
33. Hamann, *Kronprinz*, 389–90.
34. Lónyay, 140; Salvendy, 150–51.
35. Cited in Salvendy, 168–69; Listowel, 156.
36. Cited in Salvendy, 166.
37. Morton, *Nervous*, 10, 115.
38. Listowel, 199.
39. Wilhelm II, 240.
40. Lambsdorff, 198–99; Listowel, 185; Morton, *Nervous*, 109.
41. Mitis, 107, 268–69; Listowel, 195–96; Barkeley, 198–200.
42. Morton, *Nervous*, 114–15, 177.
43. Quoted in Lónyay, 149; Rudolf to Szeps, letter of November 8, 1888, HHS, Box 17; also in Szeps, *Politische Briefe*, 166.
44. Salvendy, 161; Mitis, 171.
45. Rudolf to Szeps, letter of November 8, 1888, HHS, Box 17; Lónyay, 149.
46. Franzel, 81; Stephanie, 25; Mitis, 48–49.
47. Stephanie, 35–37; Listowel, 170; Markus, 90–91; Salvendy, 140.

48. Salvendy, 161–62.
49. Thiele, *Crown Prince Rudolf*, 73.
50. Stephanie, 240–41.
51. Corti, *Empress Elisabeth*, 373.
52. Marie Valerie, diary entry of May 4, 1886, cited in Hamann, *Reluctant Empress*, 323.
53. Marie Valerie, diary entry of August 2, 1889, in Salvendy, 179.
54. Morton, *Nervous*, 134.
55. Paget, *Linings*, 2:468.
56. Paget, *Embassies*, 2:454–55.
57. Mitis, 201.
58. Morton, *Nervous*, 65–66, 124.
59. Ibid., 86, 133–34.
60. Listowel, 187; *New York Times*, February 4, 1889.
61. Mitis, 236.
62. Larisch, *My Past*, 259–60.
63. Lónyay, 201; Hoyos Addendum, HHS, Box 21; also in Mitis, 282.
64. Listowel, 92.
65. *Der Polizeibericht*, 46; Corti, *Empress Elisabeth*, 390; Bibl, 176; Salvendy, 186–87; Markus, 78.
66. Bibl, 176–77.
67. Lónyay, 155.
68. Stephanie, 249.
69. *Der Polizeibericht*, 46; Corti, *Empress Elisabeth*, 390; Bibl, 176; Salvendy, 186–87; Markus, 78.
70. Bibl, 176; Listowel, 207; Lónyay, 152; Mitis, 226.
71. Hamann, *Reluctant Empress*, 339; Listowel, 207; Morton, *Nervous*, 177–79; Salvendy, 144–45.
72. Morton, *Nervous*, 179.
73. Marie Valerie, diary entry of December 24, 1888, in Schad and Schad, 164–65.

CHAPTER 7

1. Morton, *Nervous*, 185–91.
2. Ibid., 184.
3. Ibid., 213.
4. Rudolf to Stephanie, letter of December 31, 1888, in Stephanie, 242.
5. Rudolf to Szeps, letter of December 27, 1888, in Szeps, *Politische Briefe*, 168.
6. Szeps, *My Life and History*, 117; Mitis, 271–73.
7. Morton, *Nervous*, 214.
8. Stephanie, 245.
9. Morton, *Nervous*, 221; Hoyos Memorandum, HHS, Box 21; also in Mitis, 275.

10. Stephanie, 243.
11. Louise of Belgium, 109.
12. *Der Vetsera Denkschrift*, 56–57, in Markus and Unterreiner, 253; Barkeley, 218; Markus, 29.
13. Mary Vetsera to Hermine Tobias, letter of January 14, 1889, in *Der Vetsera Denkschrift*, 54, in Markus and Unterreiner, 252.
14. Baltazzi-Scharschmid and Swistun, 195; *Der Vetsera Denkschrift*, 57–58, in Markus and Unterreiner, 253; Markus, 29; Hoyos Addendum, HHS, Box 21; also in Mitis, 282.
15. Larisch, *My Past*, 227.
16. *Der Vetsera Denkschrift*, 28, in Markus and Unterreiner, 244.
17. Ibid., 38, in Markus and Unterreiner, 247.
18. Ibid., 42, in Markus and Unterreiner, 248.
19. Ibid., 59–61, in Markus and Unterreiner, 254–55.
20. Ibid., 4–5, in Markus and Unterreiner, 237; Baltazzi-Scharschmid and Swistun, 195.
21. Larisch, *My Past*, 256, 286–88; Larisch conflates and jumbles this event in her memoirs as two separate meetings, but it seems clear that this happened on January 26.
22. *Der Vetsera Denkschrift*, 11–13, in Markus and Unterreiner, 239.
23. Paget, *Embassies*, 465.
24. Morton, *Nervous*, 222–23.
25. Stephanie, 35; Markus, 69; Hollaender, in Hantsch and Novotny, 151; Lambsdorff, 178, Mitis, 156–57.
26. Margutti, 95.
27. Sophie von Planker-Klaps, in *Neues Wiener Journal*, January 27, 1920.
28. Rudolf Püchel, in *Reichspost*, January 31, 1926.
29. Hoyos Memorandum, HHS, Box 21; also in Mitis, 275.
30. Larisch, *My Past*, 277–82.
31. *Der Vetsera Denkschrift*, 63, in Markus and Unterreiner, 255.
32. Ibid., 25, in Markus and Unterreiner, 240.
33. Judtmann, 43–44. In her memoirs Louise mistakenly placed this encounter on the afternoon of January 29, by which time Rudolf had already arrived at Mayerling.
34. Louise of Belgium, 110.
35. In Corti and Sokol, 117–18.
36. Larisch, *My Past*, 267–70.
37. *Le Figaro*, February 3, 1889; *Le Matin*, February 5, 1889; *Le Temps*, February 7, 1889.
38. See Lónyay, 161; Monts, 104–5; *Neues Wiener Journal*, June 2, 1923; Judtmann, 47, for both this story and for a refutation.
39. Szeps, *My Life and History*, 120.
40. *Der Polizeibereicht*, 45–47.

CHAPTER 8

1. Rudolf Püchel, in *Reichspost*, January 31, 1926; Friedrich, *Der Kriminalfall Mayerling*, 108–9.
2. *Der Vetsera Denkschrift*, 17, 86, in Markus and Unterreiner, 240, 262.
3. Markus, 5, 75; Barta, 41; Larisch, *My Past*, 301.
4. Judtmann, 62, 79, 84–86; Larisch, *My Past*, 302–3.
5. Larisch, *My Past*, 304–5.
6. Ibid., 306–12.
7. Judtmann, 74, 93.
8. Larisch, *My Past*, 312–13; Judtmann, 61–62.
9. Sophie von Planker-Klaps, in *Neues Wiener Journal*, January 27, 1929.
10. Judtmann, 91–93; Hamann, *Der Weg nach Mayerling*, 115.
11. Krauss on Bratfisch, report of February 2, 1889, in Loehr, 104–5.
12. Antonia Konhäuser statement, in Friedrich, *Das Kriminfall Mayerling*, 262.
13. Barta, 72; Franzel, 81; Haslinger and Trumler, 124; Judtmann, 115, 119–20; Grant, 255–56.
14. Friedrich, *Der Kriminalfall Mayerling*, 209.
15. Barta, 72; Franzel, 81; Haslinger and Trumler, 124; Judtmann, 115, 119–20.
16. Krauss report of February 2, 1889, in Loehr, 106.
17. Judtmann, 119–24, 140–41; Barta, 72; Friedrich, *Der Kriminalfall Mayerling*, 193.
18. In addition to Rudolf and Mary, twenty-five people were at the Mayerling estate on the nights of January 29–30, 1889: Thomas Albrecht, police sentry assigned to Mayerling; Baumgartner, staff; Josef Bratfisch; Hornsteiner, huntsman; Count Hoyos; Jakob Zak, *kamerdiener* to Hoyos; F. Kathe, cook; August Kianek, personal huntsman to Hoyos; Kubitschka, forester; Karl Laferl, servant; Laurenz Lebert, police official from Baden; Count Reinhard von Leiningen-Westerburg and his wife, Anna; Mauritz Loffler, huntsman; Johann Loschek, *Saaltürhüter* (hall porter) and occasional valet; Karl Ratschek, huntsman; Julius Schuldes, telegraph operator; Sedlak, orderly; F. Strubreiter, lodge caretaker; N. Strubreiter, lodge maid; Leonard Weckerle, gardener; Joseph Wedl, police post commander assigned to Mayerling; Franz Wodicka, *kammerbüchsenspanner* (gun loader); Friedrich Wolfe, carpenter; and Alois Zwerger, *Schlosswarter* (schloss warden). Friedrich, *Der Kriminalfall Mayerling*, 195.
19. Ibid., 104–5.
20. *Der Vetsera Denkschrift*, 65–66, in Markus and Unterreiner, 256.
21. Larisch, *My Past*, 318.
22. Ibid., 320; *Der Vetsera Denkschrift*, 66, in Markus and Unterreiner, 256; *Der Polizeibericht*, 75.
23. *Der Vetsera Denkschrift*, 67, in Markus and Unterreiner, 256.
24. Larisch, *My Past*, 319–21.
25. *Der Vetsera Denkschrift*, 69–70, in Markus and Unterreiner, 70.
26. *Der Polizeibericht*, 8.

27. Larisch, *My Past*, 324–26.
28. Ibid., 322–23.
29. Ibid., 324–26.
30. *Der Polizeibericht*, 13–14.
31. Ibid., 7.
32. Ibid., 15.
33. Ibid., 23.
34. Hoyos Memorandum, HHS, Box 21; also in Mitis, 274–75.
35. Corti, *Empress Elisabeth*, 391.
36. Rudolf Püchel, in *Reichspost*, January 31, 1926.
37. Hoyos Memorandum, HHS, Box 21; also in Mitis, 275.
38. Lónyay, 165.
39. Rudolf Püchel, in *Reichspost*, January 31, 1926.
40. Marek, 275; Salvendy, 146.
41. Stephanie, 244.
42. *Der Vetsera Denkschrift*, 75–76, in Markus and Unterreiner, 259; *Der Polizeibericht*, 14–16.
43. *Der Polizeibericht*, 18.
44. *Der Vetsera Denkschrift*, 77–79, in Markus and Unterreiner, 259–60.
45. *Der Polizeibericht*, 19.
46. Ibid.
47. Loschek, in *Neues Wiener Tagblatt*, April 24, 1932.
48. Mauritz Löffler, statement of 1943, cited in Friedrich, *Der Kriminalfall Mayerling*, 253–54.
49. Hoyos Memorandum, HHS, Box 21; also in Mitis, 275–77; Loehr, 13.
50. Bibl, 67–69.
51. Loschek, in *Neues Wiener Tagblatt*, April 24, 1932.
52. Antonia Konhäuser statement, in Friedrich, *Das Kriminfall Mayerling*, 263; Baltazzi-Scharschmid and Swistun, 222.

CHAPTER 9

1. Loschek, in *Neues Wiener Tagblatt*, April 24, 1932; Hoyos Memorandum, HHS, Box 21; also in Mitis, 277.
2. Loschek, in *Neues Wiener Tagblatt*, April 24, 1932.
3. Listowel, 225.
4. Mitis, 283; Judtmann, 127; Hoyos Addendum, HHS, Box 21; also in Mitis, 284; Listowel, 238–39.
5. Loschek, in *Neues Wiener Tagblatt*, April 24, 1932; Hoyos Memorandum, HHS, Box 21; also in Mitis, 277.
6. Loschek, in *Neues Wiener Tagblatt*, April 24, 1932.
7. Hoyos Memorandum, HHS, Box 21; also in Mitis, 277.
8. Hoyos, letter of March 1889 to his brother Ladislaus, Count Hoyos, Austrian ambassador in Paris, per Count Alexander Hübner, diary entry of March 10, 1889, quoted in Judtmann, 125.

9. Hoyos Memorandum, HHS, Box 21; also in Mitis, 277–78.
10. Ibid.
11. Ibid.
12. Ibid.
13. Ibid.
14. Loschek, in *Neues Wiener Tagblatt*, April 24, 1932; Slatin, *Abschrift*; Heinrich Slatin in *Neues Wiener Tagblatt*, August 23, 1931; Hoyos Memorandum, HHS, Box 21; also in Mitis, 278; Hoyos Addendum, HHS, Box 21; also in Mitis, 284; Count Corti, manuscript copy of Marie Valerie's diary entry of January 30, 1889, per Ida von Ferenczy, quoted in Judtmann, 144; Corti, *Empress Elisabeth*, 391; Countess Zoë Wassilko-Serecki, Protocol of September 5, 1955, quoted in Judtmann, 342, 344; Bibl, 109; Lónyay, 185.
15. Loschek, in *Neues Wiener Tagblatt*, April 24, 1932.
16. Hoyos Memorandum, HHS, Box 21; also in Mitis, 278.
17. Hoyos, letter of March 1889 to his brother Ladislaus, Count Hoyos, Austrian ambassador in Paris, per Count Alexander Hübner, diary entry of March 10, 1889, quoted in Judtmann, 126.
18. Reuss, dispatch of February 9, 1889, in Hollaender, Hantsch and Novotny, 141
19. In "Glimpses," *Royalty Digest* 1, no. 1 (July 1991): 20.
20. Prince Philipp of Coburg to Queen Victoria, letter of February 10, 1889, in Hollaender, Hantsch and Novotny, 148.
21. *Neue Freie Presse*, December 25, 1927.
22. Hoyos Memorandum, HHS, Box 21; also in Mitis, 278–79.
23. Ibid.
24. Judtmann, 134; Monts, 105.
25. Judtmann, 134; Monts, 105–6.
26. Paget, *Embassies*, 2:466–67.
27. Hoyos Memorandum, HHS, Box 21; also in Mitis, 281; see also Corti, *Empress Elisabeth*, 392.
28. Corti, *Empress Elisabeth*, 392.
29. Ibid., 393.
30. Haslip, *Emperor and the Actress*, 101.
31. Corti, *Empress Elisabeth*, 393.
32. Marie Valerie, diary entry of January 29, 1889, in Schad and Schad, 171.
33. Stephanie, 245–46.
34. Stephanie, diary entry of January 31, 1889, cited in Salvendy, 179–80.
35. Stephanie, 246–47.
36. Sophie von Planker-Klaps, in *Neues Wiener Journal*, January 27, 1929.
37. Schiel, 214.
38. Bibl, 105.
39. Corti, *Empress Elisabeth*, 394–95; Corti, manuscript copy of Marie Valerie's diary entry of January 30, 1889, per Ida von Ferenczy, quoted in Hamann, *Reluctant Empress*, 341; Bibl, 105.
40. Bibl, 104.

NOTES

CHAPTER 10

1. Hanslick, 2:248.
2. *Le Figaro*, January 31, 1889.
3. *Wiener Zeitung*, January 30, 1889.
4. Cassels, *Clash*, 202; Marek, 279; *Wiener Zeitung*, January 31, 1889.
5. Margutti, 84.
6. *Le Figaro*, January 31, 1889.
7. Larisch, *My Past*, 335.
8. *Der Polizeibericht*, 25.
9. Corti and Sokol, 122–23; *Der Polizeibericht*, 34.
10. *Der Polizeibericht*, 34–35.
11. *Der Vetsera Denkschrift*, 91–92, in Markus and Unterreiner, 264.
12. Judtmann, 131.
13. Larisch, *My Past*, 341.
14. *Der Polizeibericht*, 77; Lónyay, 193.
15. Loschek, in *Neues Wiener Tagblatt*, April 24, 1932; Hoyos Addendum, HHS, Box 21; also in Mitis, 284.
16. Judtmann, 128; Markus, 5.
17. Slatin, *Abschrift*; Countess Zoë Wassilko-Serecki, Protocol of September 5, 1955, quoted in Judtmann, 344; Baltazzi-Scharschmid and Swistun, 208.
18. Loschek, in *Neues Wiener Tagblatt*, April 24, 1932; Hoyos Memorandum, HHS, Box 21; also in Mitis, 278; Count Corti, manuscript copy of Marie Valerie's diary entry of January 30, 1889, per Ida von Ferenczy, quoted in Judtmann, 144; Corti, *Empress Elisabeth*, 391; Slatin, *Abschrift*; Bibl, 109; Krauss, Protocol on January 31 meeting with Taaffe, in Judtmann, 156; *Wiener Zeitung*, February 2, 1889.
19. Countess Zoë Wassilko-Serecki, Protocol of September 5, 1955, quoted in Judtmann, 344; Slatin and Auchenthaler, Protocol of January 31, 1889, quoted in Lónyay, 185; Judtmann, 138; Count Corti, manuscript copy of Marie Valerie's diary entry of January 30, 1889, per Ida von Ferenczy, quoted in Judtmann, 144; Corti, *Empress Elisabeth*, 391; Hoyos Addendum, HHS, Box 21; also in Mitis, 284; Slatin, *Abschrift*.
20. Corti, manuscript copy of Marie Valerie's diary entry of January 30, 1889, per Ida von Ferenczy, quoted in Judtmann, 144; Judtmann, 190.
21. Fugger, 198–99.
22. Judtmann, 360n16.
23. Slatin, *Abschrift*; Hamann, *Der Weg nach Mayerling*, 129; Judtmann, 138.
24. Loschek, in *Neues Wiener Tagblatt*, April 24, 1932; Hoyos Memorandum, HHS, Box 21; also in Mitis, 277; *Wiener Zeitung*, February 2, 1889.
25. Loschek, in *Neues Wiener Tagblatt*, April 24, 1932; Hoyos Memorandum, HHS, Box 21; also in Mitis, 277; Hoyos, Addendum, HHS, Box 21; also in Mitis, 284; see also Countess Zoë Wassilko-Serecki, Protocol of September 5, 1955, quoted in Judtmann, 344.

26. Larisch, *My Past*, 341; Judtmann, 138; Count Corti, manuscript copy of Marie Valerie's diary entry of January 30, 1889, per Ida von Ferenczy, quoted in Judtmann, 144.
27. Slatin, *Abschrift*; Bibl, 190.
28. Slatin, *Abschrift*.
29. Ibid.
30. Loschek, in *Neues Wiener Tagblatt*, April 24, 1932; Hoyos Memorandum, HHS, Box 21; also in Mitis, 277.
31. Hoyos Memorandum, HHS, Box 21; also in Mitis, 281.
32. Corti, *Empress Elisabeth*, 397.
33. Hamann, *Reluctant Empress*, 342–43.
34. Friedrich, *Der Kriminalfall Mayerling*, 93.
35. Corti, *Empress Elisabeth*, 398; *Neues Wiener Journal*, February 18, 1937; Bibl, 69; Hamann, *Reluctant Empress*, 342.
36. Marie Valerie, diary entry of March 14, 1889, in Schad and Schad, 196.
37. Paleologue, 164.
38. Judtmann, 143.
39. Polzer, 212.
40. The letter was supposedly found by Chief of Police Baron Ferdinand von Gorup, whose account of events at Mayerling contains several demonstrably false claims; Gorup's own son later deemed the letter a forgery. See Judtmann, 151, and Friedrich, *Der Kriminalfall Mayerling*, 251.
41. Judtmann, 31; Baltazzi-Scharschmid and Swistun, 220; Markus and Unterreiner, 78.
42. Österreichische Nationalbibliothek press release, August 2, 2015, Österreichische Nationalbibliothek, http://artdaily.com/news/80422/-Sensational-find—at-the-Austrian-National-Library-reveals-passion-of-one-of-history-s-great-affairs#.Vbzsg3hLrwx.
43. *Der Vetsera Denkschrift*, 145–46, in Markus and Unterreiner, 281. The February 9, 1889, edition of *Le Figaro* printed a variation: "Dear Mother, I am dying with Rudolf; we love each other too much. Forgive me. Farewell from your unhappy Mary. PS: Bratfisch whistled wonderfully last night." Fritz Judtmann believed that Helene Vetsera showed the letter to a friend with the intention of having it leaked to the press. See Judtmann, 261n25.
44. Hoyos Addendum, HHS, Box 21; also in Mitis, 285.
45. *Der Vetsera Denkschrift*, 147–48, in Markus and Unterreiner, 281.
46. Judtmann, 151. The book *Martyrdom of an Empress*, page 229, presented what it claimed was an expanded version of this second letter: "He has told me all. I can never be his now. I knew that something dreadful would happen to prevent our being happy so I brought the poison with me and I am going to drink it. When he returns it will be too late to save me, and I will die in his arms, happy to be with him till the last."
47. *Der Vetsera Denkschrift*, 158, in Markus and Unterreiner, 281.
48. Hoyos Addendum, HHS, Box 21; also in Mitis, 285; Judtmann, 152.

49. *Le Figaro*, February 9, 1889.
50. Fugger, 199–200; Judtmann, 152; Hoyos Addendum, HHS, Box 21; also in Mitis, 285. The current Braganza family no longer has the original letter and has no knowledge of its fate.
51. Larisch, *My Past*, 354.
52. Ibid., 344.
53. *Le Matin*, February 3, 1889.
54. *New York Times*, February 1, 1889; *Le Matin*, February 1, 1889.
55. *New York Times*, February 1, 1889; *Le Matin*, February 1, 1889; *Le Figaro*, February 1, 1889; *Le Temps*, February 2, 1889.
56. Corti, *Empress Elisabeth*, 396; Judtmann, 137, 380.

CHAPTER 11

1. *Neues Wiener Tagblatt*, January 30, 1889
2. *New York Times*, February 1 and February 2, 1889.
3. Barkeley, 3; Lónyay, 212; Judtmann, 192–94.
4. Lónyay, 180; Judtmann, 232; Ernst, 190.
5. Bibl, 105–6.
6. Corti, manuscript copy of Marie Valerie's diary entry of January 30, 1889, per Ida von Ferenczy, quoted in Judtmann, 144. The wording here differs slightly from the version given by Corti in his biography of Elisabeth, 396–97. Problematically none of this alleged conversation actually appears in Marie Valerie's diary as published in Schad and Schad. It is, of course, possible that Ferenczy learned such details and later repeated them, but the variation between Marie Valerie's actual diary entries and the content as recorded in both Corti's unpublished notes and his biography of Empress Elisabeth remains unexplained.
7. Corti, *Empress Elisabeth*, 396–97.
8. Bagger, 492.
9. Haslip, *Emperor and the Actress*, 107.
10. Corti, *Empress Elisabeth*, 398.
11. Ibid.
12. Giesl von Gieslingen, in *Neues Wiener Tagblatt*, December 8, 1937.
13. Judtmann, 266.
14. Wölfing, 51; Louisa of Tuscany, 239.
15. Corti, *Empress Elisabeth*, 398.
16. Karl Ludwig, diary entry of January 30, 1889, in Praschl-Bichler, 96.
17. Lónyay, vii.
18. *Le Figaro*, February 1, 1889; *Le Temps*, February 2, 1889.
19. Morton, *Nervous*, 260.
20. Judtmann, 250–42.
21. Karl Ludwig, diary entry of January 31, 1889, in Praschl-Bichler, 98.
22. Corti, *Empress Elisabeth*, 398–99; *New York Times*, February 4, 1889; Judtmann, 281; *Recollections of a Royal Governess*, 163.

23. Marie Valerie, diary entry of January 29, 1889, in Schad and Schad, 170–71.
24. Loehr, 81.
25. Polzer-Hoditz, 434; Franzel, 61; Judtmann, 126; Fugger, 200.
26. Polzer-Hoditz, 434.
27. Judtmann, 174.
28. Hoyos Addendum, HHS, Box 21; also in Mitis, 285.
29. Judtmann, 40, 73; Markus, 103.
30. Krauss, Protocol of February 3, in *Der Polizeibericht*, 48.
31. Judtmann, 50; Corti, *Empress Elisabeth*, 390.
32. Fugger, 194–95; Hoyos Addendum, HHS, Box 21; also in Mitis, 285.
33. Marie Valerie, diary entry of January 29, 1889, in Schad and Schad, 170.
34. Corti, manuscript copy of Marie Valerie's diary entry of January 30, 1889, per Ida von Ferenczy, quoted in Judtmann, 146.
35. Corti, *Empress Elisabeth*, 397.
36. Stephanie, 248.
37. Ibid., 248–49.
38. Fugger, 188.
39. *Der Vetsera Denkschrift*, 94–95, in Markus and Unterreiner, 265.
40. *Der Polizeibericht*, 26–27.
41. *Der Vetsera Denkschrift*, 95–96, in Markus and Unterreiner, 265.
42. Ibid., 98, in Markus and Unterreiner, 266.
43. Ibid., 100–102, in Markus and Unterreiner, 267.
44. Ibid., 100–101, in Markus and Unterreiner, 267.
45. Barkeley, 262; Judtmann, 170.
46. *Der Polizeibericht*, 27.
47. Slatin, *Abschrift*; Lónyay, 190–91.
48. Gorup, in *Wiener Montagspost*, September 12, 1927.
49. *Der Polizeibericht*, 28.
50. Slatin, *Abschrift*; Lónyay, 186–87; Bibl, 112.
51. *Der Vetsera Denkschrift*, 106, in Markus and Unterreiner, 268–69; Countess Zoë Wassilko-Serecki, Protocol of September 5, 1955, quoted in Judtmann, 344.
52. Slatin, *Abschrift*.
53. *Der Vetsera Denkschrift*, 107–9, in Markus and Unterreiner, 269.
54. *Der Polizeibericht*, 33–34; Lónyay, 185.
55. Lónyay, 193.
56. *Der Vetsera Denkschrift*, 110–11, in Markus and Unterreiner, 270; Slatin, *Abschrift*; Larisch, *My Past*, 349–50; Markus, 13; Barkeley, 260; Baltazzi-Scharschmid and Swistun, 208.
57. Lónyay, 185; Slatin, *Abschrift*.
58. Slatin, *Abschrift*.
59. Ibid.; Lónyay, 185; Loehr, 54–55; *Der Vetsera Denkschrift*, 111, in Markus and Unterreiner, 270.

60. *Der Vetsera Denkschrift*, 113–14, in Markus and Unterreiner, 270–71.
61. Larisch, *My Past*, 349–40, 351.
62. Lónyay, 186.
63. Larisch, *My Past*, 351–52.
64. Lónyay, 191; Larisch, *My Past*, 351; Slatin, *Abschrift.*
65. Lónyay, 191.
66. *Der Vetsera Denkschrift*, 114, in Markus and Unterreiner, 271; Baltazzi-Scharschmid and Swistun, 209; Barkeley, 261; Lónyay, 191; Larisch, *My Past*, 352.
67. *Der Vetsera Denkschrift*, 118, in Markus and Unterreiner, 272
68. Judtmann, 169–70; Lónyay, 192; Larisch, *My Past*, 352.
69. *Le Temps*, February 7, 1889; *Le Temps*, February 14, 1889; de Weindel, 196; Judtmann, 199.

CHAPTER 12

1. Marie Valerie, diary entry of January 29, 1889, in Schad and Schad, 171.
2. *Wiener Zeitung*, February 2, 1889; Judtmann, 185; Unterreiner, *Crown Prince Rudolf*, 25.
3. Friedrich, *Der Kriminalfall Mayerling*, 277.
4. *Wiener Zeitung*, February 2, 1889.
5. Barta, 48; Judtmann, 262.
6. *Neue Freie Presse*, December 25, 1927; Empress Friedrich to Queen Victoria, letter of April 20, 1889, in Ponsonby, 371.
7. Püchel, *Reichspost*, January 31, 1926.
8. Judtmann, 181.
9. Ibid., 260; Countess Zoë Wassilko-Serecki, Protocol of September 5, 1955, quoted in Judtmann, 344.
10. Monts, 105.
11. Robert, Baron Doblhoff, statement of 1951, quoted in Friedrich, *Der Kriminfall Mayerling*, 272; Judtmann, 267; Monts, 105.
12. *Le Gaulois*, February 4, 1889.
13. Ibid., 98.
14. Margutti, 74.
15. Marie Valerie, diary entry of January 29, 1889, in Schad and Schad, 170.
16. Ibid., diary entry of February 5, 1889, in Schad and Schad, 173–75.
17. Mitis, 166.
18. *Le Temps*, February 3, 1889.
19. *Wiener Zeitung*, February 1, 1889.
20. *Le Matin*, February 2, 1889.
21. *Wiener Tagblatt*, February 1, 1889.
22. *Le Figaro*, February 2, 1889.
23. Lónyay, 180; Ernst, 190–91; Judtmann, 233.
24. Mitis, 154.
25. Judtmann, 234; Listowel, 236–37.

26. Cantacuzène, 88.
27. Reuss, dispatch of February 5, 1889, in Hollaender, in Hantsch and Novotny, 140–41.
28. Judtmann, 283; Mitis, 153.
29. Morton, *Nervous*, 256–57; Judtmann, 281–82; *Le Figaro*, February 3, 1889; *Le Matin*, February 5 and February 6, 1889; *Le Temps*, February 5, 1889.
30. *Le Gaulois*, February 5, 1889; *Le Temps*, February 6, 1889.
31. Morton, *Nervous*, 258; Markus, 131.
32. Marie Valerie, diary entry of January 29, 1889, in Schad and Schad, 169–70.
33. Ibid., diary entry of February 4, 1889, in Schad and Schad, 173.
34. Ibid., diary entry of January 29, 1889, in Schad and Schad, 171.
35. *Revue Artistique Littéraire et Industrielle*,1, December 1, 1896.
36. Corti, *Empress Elisabeth*, 400–401.
37. Marie Valerie, diary entry of February 7, 1889, in Schad and Schad, 175.
38. Thiele, *Crown Prince Rudolf*, 87; Morton, *Nervous*, 261–62.
39. Franz Josef to Katharina Schratt, letter of February 5, 1889, in Haslip, *Emperor and the Actress*, 109.
40. Corti, *Empress Elisabeth*, 401; *New York Times*, February 6, 1889.
41. Kugler, 3.
42. Thiele, *Crown Prince Rudolf*, 97; Judtmann, 282.
43. *New York Times*, February 6, 1889; Morton, *Nervous*, 262.
44. Barkeley, 253–54.
45. *New York Times*, February 6, 1889.
46. Unterreiner, *Crown Prince Rudolf*, 26.
47. Corti, *Empress Elisabeth*, 401.
48. Unterreiner, *Crown Prince Rudolf*, 26; Morton, *Nervous*, 264.
49. Barkeley, 256–57.
50. Bibl, 80.
51. Franz Josef to Katharina Schratt, March 7, 1889, in Bourgoing, 135.
52. Unterreiner, *Emperor Franz Joseph*, 55.
53. Marek, 288.
54. Empress Friedrich to Queen Victoria, letter of April 20, 1889, in Ponsonby, 371.
55. Bibl, 79.
56. Franz Josef to Katharina Schratt, letter of February 5, 1889, in Haslip, *Emperor and the Actress*, 109
57. *Le Gaulois*, February 7, 1889.
58. Judtmann, 369n68.

CHAPTER 13

1. *Le Temps*, February 7, 1889.
2. *New York Times*, February 3, 1889.

3. *Der Polizeibericht*, 39–39.
4. *Le Figaro*, February 3, 1889.
5. *Le Temps*, February 5, 1889.
6. *Le Matin*, February 5, 1889.
7. Paget, *Embassies*, 2:470.
8. Louise of Belgium, 114.
9. Prince Philipp of Coburg to Queen Victoria, letter of February 10, 1889, in Hollaender, in Hantsch and Novotny, 148.
10. *Revue Artistique Littéraire et Industrielle* 1, December 1, 1896.
11. Judtmann, 369n68.
12. Prince of Wales to Queen Victoria, letter of February 12, 1889, cited in Van der Kiste, 106
13. Bibl, 114; Slatin, *Abschrift*.
14. Hoyos Memorandum, HHS, Box 21; also in Mitis, 281.
15. Loschek, in *Neues Wiener Tagblatt*, April 24, 1932.
16. Judtmann, 321.
17. Ibid., 325–26.
18. Ibid., 333–34.
19. Countess Zoë Wassilko-Serecki, Protocol of September 5, 1955, quoted in Judtmann, 343–44.
20. Judtmann, 315–16.
21. *Wiener Tagblatt*, March 9, 1926.
22. *Neues Wiener Tagblatt*, November 28, 1937.
23. Judtmann, 338–39.
24. Judtmann, 55; Listowel, 235–36.
25. Loschek, in *Neues Wiener Tagblatt*, April 24, 1932; Listowel, 254.
26. Antonia Konhäuser statement, quoted in Friedrich, *Der Kriminfall Mayerling*, 263.
27. Krauss to Taaffe, report of February 2 (misdated March 2), 1889, in Lónyay, 209.
28. Judtmann, 358n5.
29. *Der Polizeibereicht*, 48–49.
30. Sokop, 223–24.
31. Larisch, *My Past*, 358.
32. Judtmann, 72; Larisch, *My Royal Relatives*, 222.
33. Ffoulkes, 316.
34. Stephanie, 259–60.
35. Ascherson, 214.
36. *Le Figaro*, February 9, 1889.
37. Reuss, dispatch of February 9, 1889, in Hollaender , in Hantsch and Novotny, 141–42.
38. Quoted in Friedrich, *Der Kriminalfall Mayerling*, 401.
39. http://levantineheritage.com/testi47.htm.
40. Sokop, 237–38.

41. http://levantineheritage.com/testi47.htm.
42. Barkeley, 263; Judtmann, 174.
43. Judtmann, 175–76.
44. Ibid., 172–73; Bibl, 127.
45. Barkeley, 264; Lónyay, 212; Judtmann, 196.
46. Judtmann, 197; Marek, 285.
47. Friedrich, *Der Kriminalfall Mayerling*, 54; Judtmann, 72.
48. Lónyay, 212–13.
49. Judtmann, 174.
50. Markus, 35.
51. Judtmann, 177–78; Friedrich, *Der Kriminalfall Mayerling*, 224, 226.
52. Holler, 364.
53. Friedrich, *Der Kriminalfall Mayerling*, 237–39.
54. Ibid., 226.
55. Holler, 364.
56. Ibid., 140, 164–69.
57. Friedrich, *Der Kriminalfall Mayerling*, 442.
58. Markus, 56.
59. Professor Klaus Jarosch, University of Linz, report of September 11, 1991, in Markus, 72–73; Barta, 41; Markus and Unterreiner, 38–39.
60. Markus, v.
61. Professor Dr. Johann Szilvássy, Report of November 20, 1991, in Markus, 73; Barta, 41; Markus and Unterreiner, 39–40.
62. Markus, 76; *Neue Kronen Zeitung*, December 22, 1992; *Neue Kronen Zeitung*, December 24, 1992.
63. Friedrich, *Der Kriminalfall Mayerling*, 316.
64. Markus and Unterreiner, 45.
65. Markus, 141.

CHAPTER 14

1. Fugger, 184.
2. See Wolfson, 173–76.
3. See Lardé.
4. Markus, 65.
5. *Le Figaro*, February 3, 1889.
6. *Le Temps*, February 4, 1889.
7. *New York Times*, February 6, 1889; *Le Gaulois*, February 7, 1889.
8. *Neue Freie Press*, February 1, 1889; *New York Times*, February 1, 1889; Mitis, 165; Freisler, 10; Fugger, 202; Judtmann, 192.
9. *New York Times*, February 2, 1889.
10. Ibid., February 3, 1889.
11. *Le Matin*, February 4, 1889.
12. *Le Gaulois*, February 5, 1889.

13. *Le Temps*, February 5, 1889, and February 7, 1889; also *Daily News*, February 6, 1889.
14. See Friedrich, *Der Kriminalfall Mayerling*, 195, for a list of all of those present at Mayerling from January 28 to 30, 1889.
15. Stephanie, 24.
16. Margutti, 97.
17. Ibid., 99–100.
18. Ibid., 101–102.
19. Ketterl, 76–77.
20. Friedrich, *Der Kriminalfall Mayerling*, 209
21. *Le Figaro*, February 2, 1889.
22. *Le Matin*, February 2, 1889.
23. *Le Gaulois*, February 3 and February 4, 1889; *Le Temps*, February 3 and February 9, 1889; *Journal des Débats*, February 4, 1889.
24. *Der Polizeibericht*, 54–55; de Fontenoy, *Within Royal Palaces*, 527; Vivian, 48–49; Marek, 254; Listowel, 253.
25. *The Times*, December 1, 1955.
26. Judtmann, 244; Barkeley, 271.
27. Reuss, dispatch of February 9, 1889, in Hollaender, Hantsch and Novotny, 141–42.
28. *Le Temps*, February 15, 1889.
29. Reuss, dispatch of February 9, 1889, in Hollaender, Hantsch and Novotny, 141.
30. Ibid., 142.
31. Judtmann, 198; Thiele, *Crown Prince Rudolf*, 101; Sinclair, 140; de Weindel, 191; Corti, *Empress Elisabeth*, 398; Ronay, 55.
32. *Corriere della Sera*, July 3, 1907; see also *Le Matin*, January 6 and January 7, 1910.
33. Judtmann, 252–53.
34. *Corriere della Sera*, July 3, 1907; *Le Matin*, January 6 and January 7, 1910; Judtmann, 255.
35. Louisa of Tuscany, 241; Larisch, 344; Mauritz Löffler statement, quoted in Friedrich, *Der Kriminalfall Mayerling*, 252–58.
36. Cited in Friedrich, *Das Mayerling Sammelsurium*, 93; Judtmann, 277, 365–66n53.
37. Barta, 37–38.
38. *Society Recollections*, 235.
39. *New York Times*, January 30, 1910.
40. Louise of Belgium, 100.
41. Louisa of Tuscany, 239–42.
42. *Recollections of a Royal Governess*, 160–61; Vivian, 64.
43. *Neues Wiener Journal*, December 8, 1928; *Neues Wiener Tagblatt*, June 22, 1935

44. Loehr, 174; Mauritz Löffler statement, 1943, quoted in Friedrich, *Der Kriminalfall Mayerling*, 252–58; Karl Albrecht statement, 1963, quoted in ibid., 273–74.
45. Wölfing, 51–53.
46. Ibid., 51.
47. Louise of Belgium, 131.
48. Friedrich, *Der Kriminalfall Mayerling*, 214.
49. Ibid., 273–74.
50. Friedrich, *Der Kriminalfall Mayerling*, 214.
51. Graves, 219–20; *Society Recollections*, 235; Barta, 37–38; *Petit Parisien*, April 16 1933; Friedrich, *Der Kriminalfall Mayerling*, 252–58, 267–271; Vivian, 62–64.
52. Friedrich, *Der Kriminalfall Mayerling*, 252–58; *Society Recollections*, 234–35; Vivian, 65.
53. Friedrich, *Der Kriminalfall Mayerling*, 414.
54. Hamann, *Der Weg nach Mayerling*, 7.

CHAPTER 15

1. Mahaffy, 182–83; Judtmann, 25; Listowel, 84.
2. Listowel, 84.
3. Szeps, *My Life and History*, 61.
4. Judtmann, 25, 27–29; Lónyay, 159; Listowel, 216.
5. Palmer, 263.
6. Stephanie, 259, 256.
7. Judtmann, 25.
8. Richter, 241.
9. Polzer-Hoditz, 434–35.
10. Markus, 63–64; Brook-Shepherd, 320; *The Times*, December 20, 1983; *The Times*, January 2, 1989.
11. Listowel, 84, 216; Mahaffy, 182–83; Judtmann, 25–29; Lónyay, 159.
12. Judtmann, 55–56; Mitis, 185; Lónyay, 149.
13. Larisch, *My Past*, 277–82.
14. Ibid., 323, 377.
15. Judtmann, 27. Rudolf's first biographer, Baron Oskar von Mitis, questioned whether the crown prince would actually have handed a box supposedly containing compromising papers to Larisch, given her reputation for blackmail, but by this time she was so deeply enmeshed in his liaison with Mary that he might not have had another viable option. See Mitis, 182.
16. Larisch, *My Past*, 366.
17. Cassels, *Clash*, 87, 135–38.
18. Mitis, 81; Louisa of Tuscany, 231; de Weindel, 138–39; de Fontenoy, *Secret Memoirs*, 2:82–83; Listowel, 179; Cassels, *Clash*, 138.

19. Judtmann, 27; Lónyay, 159; Listowel, 216.
20. Polzer-Hoditz, in *Neues Wiener Tagblatt*, June 22, 1935, Judtmann, 273; *Neues Wiener Journal*, December 8, 1928.
21. Polzer-Hoditz, 434.
22. Judtmann, 271, 273.
23. Larisch, *My Past*, 366–69.
24. Ibid., 317.
25. Listowel, 252; Polzer-Hoditz, 429–31; de Fontenoy, *Secret Memoirs*, 2:60, 2:82–83; Louisa of Tuscany, 230–33.
26. *Die Stunde*, September 28, 1923.
27. *Der Standard*, January 2, 1993.
28. Judtmann, 56; Mitis, 186.
29. Listowel, 3, 230.
30. Judtmann, 28–29.
31. Marek, 267.
32. Listowel, 1.
33. Ibid., 236–39.
34. Ibid., 238, 247.
35. Ibid., 218.
36. Szeps, *My Life and History*, 100.
37. Mitis, 145; Bismarck, 2:280.
38. Salvendy, 148; Wolfson, 98.
39. *New York Times*, February 2, 1889.
40. Graves, 221.
41. Grant, 17–19, 31.
42. Ibid., 184.
43. Ibid., 75.
44. Ibid., 185.
45. Ibid., 261, 280–82.
46. Ibid., 264–65.
47. Ibid., 270–74.
48. Wolfson, 91.
49. Ibid., 130.
50. Grant, 194–95, 227.
51. Judtmann, 188.
52. Wolfson, 65.
53. *Neue Kronen Zeitung*, March 11, 1983.
54. Ibid., November 20, 1983; *The Times*, December 20, 1983.
55. Szeps, *My Life and History*, 37–38.
56. Listowel, 159; Szeps, *My Life and History*, 110–11; Watson, 91.
57. Feigl, 7–65; *Neue Kronen Zeitung*, March 11, 1983.
58. Markus, 63.
59. *Neue Kronen Zeitung*, March 11, 1983.

60. Brook-Shepherd, 321.
61. *The Times*, January 2, 1989; Brook-Shepherd, 321; Hamann, *Der Weg nach Mayerling*, 142.
62. Brook-Shepherd, 321.

CHAPTER 16

1. Haslip, *Lonely Empress*, 404.
2. Eisenmenger, 31.
3. Lónyay, 2.
4. Mitis, 168.
5. Taylor, *Habsburg Monarchy*, 47; Haslip, *Mexico*, 23; Woods, 185.
6. Larisch, *My Past*, 159, 162–63; Vivian, 117; Radziwill, *Austrian Court*, 58, 88; Radziwill, *Secrets*, 111–12, 114–15; de Weindel, 145–46; de Fontenoy, *Secret Memoirs*, 2:114; Lónyay, 35; Marek, 57.
7. Stephanie, 23.
8. Chapman-Huston, 166–67, 176–77; King, 255; Channon, 111; Tschudi, 145.
9. King, 253–55; Chapman-Huston, 166–67, 176–77; Channon, 111.
10. Hamann, *Reluctant Empress*, 21, 272; Corti, *Empress Elisabeth*, 3.
11. Mitis, 176.
12. Information from Dr. Stefanie Platt to the authors.
13. Barkeley, 21–22; Listowel, 25.
14. Barta, 6; Thiele, *Crown Prince Rudolf*, 18.
15. Corti, *Empress Elisabeth*, 288.
16. Ibid.; Franzel, 78; Listowel, 62.
17. Haslip, *Lonely Empress*, 326.
18. Rudolf, notebook entry, December 1873, in HHS, Box 12; also in Mitis, 26–27.
19. Information from Dr. Stefanie Platt to authors.
20. Ibid.
21. Rudolf to Szeps, letter of August 21, 1888, in Szeps, *Politische Briefe*, 163–64.
22. Information from Dr. Stefanie Platt to authors.
23. Salvendy, 173.
24. Ibid., 91.
25. Stephanie, 264.
26. Ibid., 256.
27. Information from Dr. Stefanie Platt to authors.
28. Wölfing, 51, 64.
29. Grant, 214.
30. Ibid., 213.
31. *Der Polizeibericht*, 46.
32. Polzer-Hoditz, 434.
33. Paget, *Embassies*, 2:475–76.

34. Larisch, *My Past*, 260.
35. Louise of Belgium, 104.
36. Larisch, *My Past*, 256–60.
37. Baltazzi-Scharschmid and Swistun, 171; Morton, *Nervous*, 81.
38. Haslip, *Emperor and the Actress*, 73–74.
39. Ibid., 91–95.

CHAPTER 17

1. Markus, 29; Hoyos Addendum, HHS, Box 21; also in Mitis, 281.
2. Holler, 364; Harding, 298; Markus, 61–62; *Wiener Morgenpost*, October 10, 1927; Haslip, *Emperor and the Actress*, 95.
3. Judtmann, 346.
4. Stephanie, 43.
5. Paleologue, 164.
6. Countess Zoë Wassilko-Serecki, Protocol of September 5, 1955, quoted in Judtmann, 342–44.
7. *Der Polizeibericht*, 62.
8. Haslip, *Emperor and the Actress*, 94–95.
9. Morton, *Nervous*, 222–23.
10. Judtmann, 151.
11. *Der Spiegel* 32, March 8, 1960,; Friedrich, *Der Kriminalfall Mayerling*, 46.
12. Hollaender, Hantsch and Novotny, 160n62.
13. *Martyrdom of an Empress*, 206–7; Vivian, 37–40, 56; de Weindel, 195; *Recollections of a Royal Governess,* 158; Marek, 255; Burg, 173, 226.
14. Louise of Belgium, 111.
15. Louisa of Tuscany, 241–42.
16. Judtmann, 55–56; Mitis, 185; Lónyay, 149.
17. Slatin, *Abschrift.*
18. *Berliner Tagblatt*, February 13, 1889; *Der Polizeibericht*, 21; *Martyrdom of an Empress*, 212; de Weindel, 185; Redlich, 433; Crankshaw, 299; Haslip, *Emperor and the Actress*, 97; *Recollections of a Royal Governess*, 159; Ketterl, 75–76; Pöldinger and Wagner, 176; Thiele, *Elisabeth*, 677.
19. Vivian, 54; Loehr, 173
20. Louise of Belgium, 112.
21. Margutti, 94–95.
22. Szeps, *My Life and History*, 119.
23. Baron Robert Doblhoff, statement of 1952, in Friedrich, *Der Kriminalfall Mayerling*, 268–70.
24. Lambsdorff, 178, Mitis, 156–57.
25. Reuss, dispatch of February 5, 1889, in Hollaender, Hantsch and Novotny, 141.
26. Margutti, 95.
27. Lambsdorff, 178, Mitis, 156–57.
28. Stephanie, 38.

29. Sophie von Planker-Klaps, in *Neues Wiener Journal*, January 27, 1929.
30. Margutti, 98.
31. Morton, *Nervous*, 221.
32. Larisch, *My Past*, 277–82.
33. Ibid., 257–60.
34. *Der Vetsera Denkschrift*, 66, in Markus and Unterreiner, 256.
35. Fugger, 206; see also Judtmann, 109; Vivian, 60.
36. Larisch, *My Past*, 264–65, 287–88.
37. Corti and Sokol, 118.
38. Larisch, *My Past*, 295.
39. Szeps, *My Life and History*, 120.
40. *Der Polizeibericht*, 47.
41. Information from Dr. Stefanie Platt to authors.

CHAPTER 18

1. Larisch, *My Past*, 258.
2. Mitis, 181; Judtmann, 57.
3. Judtmann, 27.
4. Rudolf Püchel, in *Reichspost*, January 31, 1926.
5. Larisch, *My Past*, 308.
6. Judtmann, 129.
7. *Der Vetsera Denkschrift*, 35, in Markus and Unterreiner, 277–78.
8. Listowel, 187; cited in Salvendy, 166.
9. Larisch, *My Past*, 250.
10. *Der Vetsera Denkschrift*, 50, in Markus and Unterreiner, 251.
11. Hoyos Addendum, HHS, Box 21; also in Mitis, 283.
12. Judtmann, 55, 111; Mitis, 185–86; Lónyay, 159–60.
13. *Le Temps*, January 31, 1889.

CHAPTER 19

1. Judtmann, 151.
2. Bibl, 67–69; *Der Vetsera Denkschrift*, 92–93, in Markus and Unterreiner, 264.
3. *Der Vetsera Denkschrift*, 52, in Markus and Unterreiner, 251.
4. Ibid.
5. Ibid., 145–46, in Markus and Unterreiner, 281.
6. Ibid., 147–48, in Markus and Unterreiner, 281.
7. Judtmann, 151.
8. Hoyos Memorandum, HHS, Box 21; also in Mitis, 276–77.
9. Loschek, in *Neues Wiener Tagblatt*, April 24, 1932; Antonia Konhäuser statement, in Friedrich, *Das Kriminfall Mayerling*, 263; Baltazzi-Scharschmid and Swistun, 222.
10. Loschek, in *Neues Wiener Tagblatt*, April 24, 1932.

11. *Der Vetsera Denkschrift*, 153, in Markus and Unterreiner, 264.
12. Loschek, in *Neues Wiener Tagblatt*, April 24, 1932.
13. Professor Dr. Klaus Jarosch, Report of September 11, 1991; Professor Christian Reiter, undated report; and Professor Dr. Johann Szilvássy, report of November 20, 1991, in Barta, 41.
14. Ibid.
15. See Krauss notes on January 31, 1889, meeting with Taaffe, in *Der Polizeibericht*, 26–27.
16. Judtmann, 261.
17. Corti, *Empress Elisabeth*, 398; *Neues Wiener Journal*, February 18, 1937; Bibl, 69; Hamann, *Reluctant Empress*, 342; *Le Temps*, June 20, 1923.
18. Fugger, 194–95.
19. Stephanie, 248.
20. Marie Valerie, diary entry of January 29, 1889, in Schad and Schad, 170.
21. Count Corti, manuscript copy of Marie Valerie's diary entry of January 30, 1889, per Ida von Ferenczy, quoted in Judtmann, 145–46; Corti, *Empress Elisabeth*, 397.
22. Paleologue, 164.
23. Marie Valerie, diary entry of March 14, 1889, in Schad and Schad, 196; Corti, *Empress Elisabeth*, 398; *Neues Wiener Journal*, February 18, 1937; Bibl, 69; Hamann, *Reluctant Empress*, 342.
24. Judtmann, 143.
25. Information from Dr. Stefanie Platt to authors.

EPILOGUE

1. Stephanie, 166.
2. Stephanie to Louise, letter of March 7, 1889, cited in Salvendy, 104.
3. Cited in Hamann, *Reluctant Empress*, 342.
4. *Society Recollections*, 236.
5. Schiel, 229.
6. Margutti, 86.
7. Listowel, 250–51.
8. *Recollections of a Royal Governess*, 310.
9. Markus, 135; *Society Recollections*, 232.
10. Margutti, 75.
11. Nostitz-Rieneck, 2:130.
12. Margutti, 85–86.
13. Ibid., 291–92; Barkeley, 249.
14. Kiszling, 19.
15. Ascherson, 215.
16. Schiel, 520–21.
17. Judtmann, 18.
18. Weissensteiner, 142.
19. Friedrich, *Der Kriminalfall Mayerling*, 490.

20. Beéche, 202–3; Ascherson, 206–11.
21. Cassels, *Clash*, 210.
22. Larisch, *My Past*, 212.
23. Ffoulkes, 314, 323.
24. Sokop, 407.
25. Rumbold, *Final Recollections*, 374; Rumbold, *Francis Joseph*, 349.
26. Cited in Friedrich, *Der Kriminalfall Mayerling*, 97.
27. Ibid., 104.
28. Quoted in Friedrich, *Der Kriminalfall Mayerling*, 647.
29. Listowel, 2.
30. Ibid., 254; Friedrich, *Der Kriminalfall Mayerling*, 82.
31. Franz Josef to Katharina Schratt, letter of June 7, 1890, in Namier, 72.
32. Friedrich, *Der Kriminalfall Mayerling*, 47.
33. Judtmann, 31.
34. Sulzberger, 381.
35. Greene, 22.
36. Judtmann, 82.
37. Listowel, 192.
38. Judtmann, 308; Haslinger and Trumler, 126.
39. Schiel, 319; de Fontenoy, *Within Royal Palaces*, 540.
40. Corti, *Empress Elisabeth*, 415.
41. Marie Valerie, diary entry of January 30, 1890, in Schad and Schad, 212.
42. www.Karmel-Mayerling.org; *Neue Kronen Zeitung*, June 27, 2007.
43. Judtmann, 119–21, 311; Haslinger and Trumler, 126.

BIBLIOGRAPHY

It is tempting to think that Mayerling documents and files remain to be found: the missing Taaffe papers, secret reports, unsuspected letters—anything that might shed new light on what happened at Rudolf's hunting lodge. But after 125 years of extensive searches, it is unlikely that such materials—if they still exist—will ever surface, at least not in the foreseeable future. The historian who tackles the Mayerling story thus faces a seemingly insurmountable obstacle, forced to comb through the accumulated information in surviving reports and obscure memoirs seeking a bit of previously ignored evidence or an unrecognized hint that assumes significance when the tragedy is reassessed.

There is no shortage of books on Mayerling: The first, *Die volle Wahrheit über den Tod des Kronprinzen Rudolf von Öesterreich* (The Whole Truth About the Death of Crown Prince Rudolf of Austria) by Ernst von der Planitz, was published in Berlin in May 1889—just three months after Rudolf's death. Austrian officials promptly banned it, perhaps hoping to quell any unwanted discussion, perhaps because the book suggested that Mary Vetsera had ultimately fallen victim to an insane crown prince.

In 1928 Baron Oskar von Mitis produced his seminal biography, *Das Leben des Kronprinzen Rudolf* (published in an abridged English translation in 1930 under the title *The Life of Crown Prince Rudolph of Habsburg*). As the former director of the Haus, Hof-und Staatsarchiv, Mitis benefited from privileged access to a wealth of previously unpublished letters and diaries covering Rudolf's life. Of necessity he dealt with Mayerling, though one gets the sense that, as a former Habsburg courtier, he found the discussion painful bordering on the traitorous. While attempting a modicum of explanation about events at the lodge, he was overly conscious of offending both the prevailing favorable sentiment surrounding the former dynasty that arose in the 1920s, as well as the crown prince's remaining family. Certain unwelcome topics, like Rudolf's drug use and extramarital affairs, were skipped over completely, while Mitis judiciously edited out certain passages in the Hoyos statements that he deemed too intimate for public consumption.

BIBLIOGRAPHY

A few years after Stephanie's death, her nephew Carl Lónyay, drawing on her private papers, published *Rudolf: The Tragedy of Mayerling*. This offered some original documentation on events at the lodge, reproducing police reports that Stephanie had secreted in her personal archives. The tone, though, was unfortunate. If Carl Lónyay despised the Habsburgs, he positively loathed his late aunt by marriage. His hysterical descriptions of her as an unsympathetic shrew fell little short of blatant and unreasoned misogyny—establishing a highly questionable condemnatory strain that runs through many of the works on Rudolf's life and death.

Other documents about the Mayerling tragedy have come to light by accident. After Hitler's Third Reich absorbed Austria in 1938, the Nazis appointed SS officer Josef Fitzthum as deputy chief of the Vienna police. Fitzthum apparently scoured the official archives and stole certain documents, taking them back to Berlin in the last days of World War II. After the fall of the Third Reich, the new German government appointed a certain municipal councilor named Baierle to confiscate former Nazi possessions, among them Fitzthum's belongings. Rather than turn the Viennese files over to authorities, Baierle apparently kept the dusty dossiers stashed away in his own apartment. Sorting through Baierle's papers after his death in 1955, officials discovered former Viennese Chief of Police Krauss's 1889 files on Mayerling. After some intense negotiations over rightful ownership, the dossier was returned to Vienna, but not before being published as *Der Polizeibericht: Mayerling: Authentische Darstellung des soeben aufgefundenen originalaktes des K. K. Polizeipräsidiums Wien No. 1 Reservat 1889*. This discovery filled in some gaps, although Prime Minister Taaffe had forced Krauss to end his investigation a few days after the tragedy. Two years later the historian Albert Hollaender discovered a cache of English and German ambassadorial reports about Mayerling that British officials had seized from Berlin after World War II and taken to London. Published in *Festschrift für Heinrich Benedikt*, a book of historical essays, these documents not only added layers of context to the story but also revealed the origin of many of the conspiracy theories surrounding the tragedy.

Other important works on the Mayerling story include Viktor Bibl's 1938 book, *Kronprinz Rudolf: die Tragödie eines sinkenden Reiches*, which benefited from access to the remaining participants, including the crown prince's only daughter, Elisabeth; and Richard Barkeley's 1958 work *The Road to Mayerling: The Life and Death of Crown Prince Rudolph of Austria*, which, though overly fawning to the point of credulity where Rudolf was concerned, contained some interesting archival materials. Then, in 1968, came Fritz Judtmann's seminal work on the tragedy, *Mayerling ohne Mythos* (published in 1971 in English translation as *Mayerling: The Facts Behind the Legend*). This, more than any other book, set itself the task of ferreting out truth from fiction, pulling together the available scattered information, and examining the contradictions about the tragedy. Reproducing a number of important statements previously hidden in forgotten files, Judtmann offered a sober analysis of events at the lodge that stripped away many of the previous conspiratorial claims. While groundbreaking, the book suffered from a certain reticence. The rather genteel treatment of

Mary and her mother likely stemmed from Judtmann's friendship with Helene Vetsera's modern descendants, while he selectively edited a few official documents to remove some of Rudolf's more inflammatory statements. Though outdated in several respects, Judtmann's remains the crucial work on Mayerling and is essential reading for anyone attempting to understand the tragedy.

That same year Heinrich Baltazzi-Scharschmid—Helene Vetsera's nephew—coauthored *Die Familien Baltazzi-Vetsera im Kaiserlichen Wien* with the historian Hermann Swistun. While presenting important materials from the family's private collection, the book took a rather too credulous approach to the Mayerling story, presenting Helene Vetsera's version of events without question and ignoring contradictory evidence, especially any that portrayed Mary and her liaison with the crown prince in a less than flattering light. More details about Mary's life emerged in Swistun's 1983 book, *Mary Vetsera: Gefährtin für den Tod*, though the tone was still tempered by considerations for her modern-day relations. A slew of minor titles heralded the hundredth anniversary of the tragedy in 1989: Gerd Holler's *Mayerling: Neue Dokumente zur Tragödie 100 Jahre danach*; Clemens Loehr's *Mayerling: Eine Wahre Legende*; and Clemens Gruber's *Die Schicksalstage von Mayerling*. But not until the historian Georg Markus's 1993 work, *Kriminalfall Mayerling: Leben und Sterben der Mary Vetsera* (published in English translation as *Crime at Mayerling: The Life and Death of Mary Vetsera*), did the story take a new turn in examining the 1991 theft of her corpse. Markus's slim volume detailing this extraordinary development seems to have been rushed into print to capitalize on the attendant publicity. As a result Markus missed the results of some of the later forensic tests on Mary's remains and the denouement of the case.

Markus returned to the subject in 2014 when, with the historian Katrin Unterreiner, he published *Das Original Mayerling-Protokoll der Helene Vetsera: "Gerechtigkeit für Mary,"* which included not only a biographical essay on the young baroness but also reprinted her mother's original *Denkschrift*. The most notable of recent titles was Lars Friedrich's 2009 work, *Das Mayerling Sammelsurium*. Setting himself the goal of picking up and expanding Judtmann's book, Friedrich studiously analyzed the various theories advanced about Mayerling and gathered all known statements by those claiming knowledge of events at the lodge. Additionally Friedrich has published his original manuscript, *Der Kriminalfall Mayerling*, online, along with recent discoveries, making his work an important resource for anyone interested in researching the story.

The collected writings and papers of Crown Prince Rudolf are held in the twenty-two boxes of Nachlass Kronprinz-Rudolf-Selekt, deposited as part of the Archiv des Kaiserlichen Hauses (Archive of the Imperial House) in the Haus-, Hof-, und Staatsarchiv in Vienna. Relevant citations to these materials are listed using the abbreviation HHS followed by the box number. In addition, through the generosity of Paul Slatin, we have been fortunate to utilize his grandfather Dr. Heinrich Slatin's unpublished manuscript of May 21, 1929, detailing his experiences with the Mayerling tragedy (cited in the notes as Slatin, *Abschrift*).

BIBLIOGRAPHY

BOOKS

Aronson, Theo. *The Coburgs of Belgium*. London: Cassell & Company Ltd., 1968.

Ascherson, Neal. *The King Incorporated: Leopold II in the Age of Trusts*. London: George Allen & Unwin, 1963.

Bagger, Eugene. *The Emperor Francis Joseph of Austria*. New York: G. P. Putnam's Sons, 1927.

Baltazzi-Scharschmid, Heinrich, and Hermann Swistun. *Die Familien Baltazzi-Vetsera im Kaiserlichen Wien*. Vienna: Böhlau, 1980.

Barkeley, Richard. *The Road to Mayerling: The Life and Death of Crown Prince Rudolph of Austria*. London: Macmillan, 1958.

Barta, Ilsebill. *Kronprinz Rudolf: Lebensspuren*. Vienna: Schloss Schönbrunn Kultur- und Betriebsges, 2008.

Beéche, Arturo E. *The Coburgs of Europe: The Rise and Fall of Queen Victoria and Prince Albert's European Family*. East Richmond Heights, CA: Eurohistory, 2013.

Belgium, Princess Louise of (Princess Louise of Coburg). *My Own Affairs*. London: Cassell, 1921.

Beller, Steven. *Francis Joseph*. London: Longman, 1996.

Bibl, Viktor. *Kronprinz Rudolf: Die Tragödie eines sinkenden Reiches*. Leipzig: Gladius Verlag, 1938.

Bismarck, Otto von. *Reflections and Reminiscences*. New York: Harper, 1899.

Bourgoing, Jean de. *Briefe Kaiser Franz Josefs an Frau Katharina Schratt*. Vienna: Oldenbourg, 1949.

Brook-Shepherd, Gordon. *The Last Empress: The Life and Times of Zita of Austria-Hungary*. London: HarperCollins, 1991.

Burg, Katrina von. *Elisabeth of Austria: A Life Misunderstood*. Swansea, Wales: Windsor Publications, 1995.

Cantacuzène, Julia, Princess. *My Life Here and There*. Boston: Scribner's, 1923.

Cassels, Lavender. *Clash of Generations: A Habsburg Family Drama in the Nineteenth Century*. London: John Murray, 1973.

———. *The Archduke and the Assassin: Sarajevo, June 28, 1914*. New York: Stein and Day, 1984.

Channon, Henry. *The Ludwigs of Bavaria*. London: Methuen, 1933.

Chapman-Huston, Desmond. *Bavarian Fantasy: The Story of Ludwig II*. London: John Murray, 1955.

Chlumecky, Leopold von. *Erzherzog Franz Ferdinands Wirken und Wollen*. Berlin: Verlag für Kulturpolitik, 1928.

Cone, Polly, ed. *The Imperial Style: Fashions of the Hapsburg Era*. New York: Rizzoli, 1980.

Cornwallis-West, Mrs. George. *The Reminiscences of Lady Randolph Churchill*. New York: Century, 1908.

Corti, Egon Caesar, Conte. *Elisabeth, Empress of Austria*. New Haven, CT: Yale University Press, 1936.

———, and Hans Sokol. *Der Alte Kaiser*. Vienna: Styria Verlag, 1955.

Crankshaw, Edward. *The Fall of the House of Habsburg*. New York: Viking, 1963.

Defrance, Oliver, and Joseph van Loon. *La Fortune de Dora: Une petite fille de Leopold II chez les nazis*. La Rochelle, France: Racine, 2013.
Der Polizeibericht: Mayerling: Authentische Darstellung des soeben aufgefundenen Originalaktes des K. K. Polizeipräsidiums Wien No. 1 Reservat 1889. Vienna: Wilhelm Frick Verlag, 1955.
Eisenmenger, Victor. *Archduke Franz Ferdinand*. London: Selwyn & Blount, 1928.
Ernst, Otto. *Franz Josef, As Revealed by His Letters*. London: Methuen, 1927.
Feigl, Erich. *Kaiserin Zita, Von Österreich nach Österreich*. Vienna: Amalthea, 1986.
Ffoulkes, Maude. *My Own Past*. London: Cassell and Company, 1915.
Fontenoy, Marquise de (pseudonym of Marguerite Cunliffe-Owen). *Within Royal Palaces*. Philadelphia: Hubbard Publishing, 1892.
———. *Secret Memoirs of William II and Francis Joseph*. 2 vols. London: Hutchinson, 1900.
Franzel, Emil. *Crown Prince Rudolph and the Mayerling Tragedy: Fact and Fiction*. Munich: Verlag Herold, 1974.
Friedrich, Lars. *Das Mayerling Sammelsurium*. Books on Demand, 2009.
Freisler, Camilla. *Letters from Mayerling*. Heiligenkreuz, Austria: Heiligenkreuzer Verlag, 1973.
Fugger, Nora, Princess. *The Glory of the Habsburgs: The Memoirs of Princess Fugger*. London: George G. Harrap & Co., 1932.
Grant, Hamil, ed. *The Last Days of Archduke Rudolph*. New York: Dodd, Mead and Company, 1916.
Graves, Armgaard Karl. *The Secrets of the Hohenzollerns*. New York: A. L. Burt, 1915.
Greene, Graham. *The Third Man*. London: Penguin, 1996.
Gribble, Francis. *The Life of the Emperor Francis Joseph*. London: Eveleigh Nash, 1914.
Gruber, Clemens. *Die Schicksalstage von Mayerling*. Vienna: Verlag Mlakar, 1989.
Hamilton, Lord Frederic. *The Vanished Pomps of Yesterday*. New York: George H. Doran, 1921.
Hamann, Brigitte, ed. *Majestät, ich warne Sie. . . . Geheime und private Schriften*. Munich: Piper Verlag, 1979.
———. *The Reluctant Empress*. New York: Alfred A. Knopf, 1986.
———. *Rudolf, Der Weg nach Mayerling*. Vienna: Amalthea, 1988.
———. *Rudolf: Kronprinz und Rebell*. Vienna: Piper, 2005.
———, and Elisabeth Hassmann. *Elisabeth: Stages in a Life*. Vienna: Christian Brandstätter Verlag, 1998.
Hanslick, Eduard. *Aus meinem Leben*. Berlin: Verein für Deutsche Literatur, 1894.
Haslinger, Ingrid, and Gerhard Trumler. *So lebten Die Habsburger*. Vienna: Christian Brandstätter Verlag, 2007.
Haslip, Joan. *The Lonely Empress*. London: Weidenfeld & Nicolson, 1965.
———. *The Crown of Mexico*. New York: Holt, Rinehart and Winston, 1971.
———. *The Emperor and the Actress: The Love Story of Emperor Franz Josef & Katharina Schratt*. London: Weidenfeld & Nicolson, 1982.

Hollaender, Albert. "Streiflichter auf die Kronprinzentragödie von Mayerling." In *Festschrift für Heinrich Benedikt*, edited by Hugo Hantsch and Alexander Novotny, 129–166. Vienna: Verlag Notring der wissenschaftlichen Verbände Österreichs, 1955.

Holler, Gerd. *Mayerling: Die Lösung des Rätsels: Der Tod des Kronprinzen Rudolf und der Baroness Vetsera aus medizinischer Sicht*. Vienna: Verlag Fritz Molden, 1980.

Hough, Richard, ed. *Advice to My Granddaughter: Letters from Queen Victoria to Princess Victoria of Hesse*. New York: Simon & Schuster, 1975.

Jászi, Oscar. *The Dissolution of the Habsburg Monarchy*. Chicago: University of Chicago Press, 1929.

Judtmann, Fritz. *Mayerling: The Facts Behind the Legend*. London: George G. Harrap & Co., 1971.

Ketterl, Eugen. *The Emperor Francis Joseph I*. Boston: Stratford, n.d.

King, Greg. *The Mad King: The Life of Ludwig II of Bavaria*. Secaucus, NJ: Carol Publishing, 1995.

———, and Sue Woolmans. *The Assassination of the Archduke: Sarajevo 1914 and the Romance That Changed the World*. New York: St. Martin's Press, 2013.

Kiszling, Rudolf. *Erzherzog Franz Ferdinand von Österreich-Este*. Cologne: Hermann Böhlaus, 1956.

Kugler, Georg, ed. *Kunsthistoriches Museum Wien*. Vienna: Kunsthistoriches Museum Verlag, 1999.

Kürnberg, Joachim von. *A Woman of Vienna: A Romantic Biography of Katharina Schratt*. London: Cassell and Company, 1955.

Lambsdorff, Vladimir. *Dnevnik (1886–1890)*. Moscow: Gosudarstvennoye Izdatelstvo, 1926.

Lansdale, Maria Horner. *Vienna and the Viennese*. Philadelphia: Henry T. Coates & Co., 1902.

Lardé, Enrique. *The Crown Prince Rudolf: His Mysterious Life After Mayerling*. Pittsburgh: Dorrance, 1994.

Larisch, Countess Marie von. *My Past*. London: Eveleigh Nash, 1913.

———. *My Royal Relatives*. London: John Long, 1936.

Lee, Sidney. *King Edward VII: A Biography*. 2 Vols. New York: Macmillan, 1927.

Leehner, R. *The Newest Plan and Guide of Vienna*. Vienna: Oldenbourg, 1911.

Levetus, A. S. *Imperial Vienna*. London: John Lane, 1905.

Listowel, Judith. *A Habsburg Tragedy: Crown Prince Rudolf*. New York: Dorset Press, 1978.

Loehr, Clemens. *Mayerling: Eine Wahre Legende*. Frankfurt-am-Main: Ullstein, 1989.

Lónyay, Carl. *Rudolph: The Tragedy of Mayerling*. New York: Charles Scribner's Sons, 1949.

Mahaffy, R. P. *Francis Joseph: His Life and Times*. London: Duckworth, 1908.

Marek, George. *The Eagles Die: Franz Josef, Elisabeth, and Their Austria*. New York: Harper & Row, 1974.

Margutti, Albert, Baron von. *The Emperor Francis Joseph and His Times*. London: Hutchinson, 1921.

Markus, Georg. *Crime at Mayerling: The Life and Death of Mary Vetsera: With New Expert Opinions Following the Desecration of Her Grave*. Riverside, CA: Ariadne, 1995.

———, and Katrin Unterreiner. *Das Original Mayerling-Protokoll der Helene Vetsera: "Gerechtigkeit für Mary."* Vienna: Amalthea, 2014.

The Martyrdom of an Empress. New York: Harper & Brothers, 1899.

Monts, Anton, Graf von. *Erinnerungen und Gedanken des Botschafters Anton Graf Monts*. Berlin: Verlag für Kulturpolitik, 1932.

Morton, Frederic. *A Nervous Splendor: Vienna, 1888–1889*. Boston: Little, Brown, 1979.

———.*Thunder at Twilight: Vienna, 1913–1914*. New York: Scribner's, 1989.

Motley, John Lothrop. *The Correspondence of John Lothrop Motley*. 2 Vols. London: John Murray, 1889.

Namier, Sir Lewis. *Vanished Supremacies*. London: Hamish Hamilton, 1958.

Nemec, Vilem, and Jana Nemec-Jirak. *Twenty-Five Years in Africa: The Beginning*. London: Tate Publishing, 2011.

Nikitsch-Boulles, Paul. *Vor dem Sturm: Erinnerungen an Erzherzog Thronfolger Franz Ferdinand*. Berlin: Verlag für Kulturpolitik, 1925.

Nostitz-Rieneck, Georg von, ed. *Briefe Kaiser Franz Josephs an Kaiserin Elisabeth, 1859–1898*. Vienna: Herold Verlag, 1966.

Oskar, Baron von Mitis. *The Life of Crown Prince Rudolph of Habsburg*. London: Skeffington, 1930.

Paget, Walburga, Lady. *Scenes and Memories*. New York: Charles Scribner's Sons, 1912.

———. *Embassies of Other Days*. 2 Volumes. London: Hutchinson, 1923.

———. *The Linings of My Life*. London: Hurst & Blackett, 1928.

Paleologue, Maurice. *The Tragic Empress: Intimate Conversations with the Empress Eugénie, 1901–1911*. London: Thornton Butterworth, 1922.

Palmer, Alan. *Twilight of the Habsburgs: The Life and Times of Emperor Francis Joseph*. New York: Atlantic Monthly Press, 1994.

Paoli, Xavier. *My Royal Clients*. London: Hodder and Stoughton, 1911.

Planitz, Ernst Edler von. *Die volle Wahrheit über den Tod des Kronprinzen Rudolf von Öesterreich*. Berlin: Verlag H. Piehler, 1889.

Pöldinger, W., and W. Wagner, eds. *Aggression, Selbstaggression, Familie und Gesellschaft: Das Mayerling-Symposium*. Vienna: Springer-Verlag, 1989.

Polzer, Wilhelm. *Die Tragödie des Kronprinzen Rudolf*. Graz: Verlag Oskar Karinger, 1954.

Polzer-Hoditz, Count Arthur. *The Emperor Karl*. Boston: Houghton Mifflin Company, 1931.

Ponsonby, Sir Frederick, ed. *The Letters of the Empress Frederick*. London: Macmillan, 1928.

Praschl-Bichler, Gabriele. *Kinder Jahre Kaiser Karls*. Vienna: Amalthea, 2014.

Radziwill, Princess Catherine. *My Recollections*. New York: James Pott Company, 1904.

———.*The Austrian Court from Within*. New York: Frederick A. Stokes, 1917.

———. *Secrets of Dethroned Royalty*. New York: John Lane, 1920.
Rappoport, Angelo. *Leopold the Second, King of the Belgians*. London: Hutchinson, 1910.
Recollections of a Royal Governess. New York: D. Appleton and Company, 1916.
Redlich, Joseph. *Emperor Francis Joseph of Austria*. New York: Macmillan, 1929.
Richter, Werner. *Kronprinz von Österreich*. Zurich: Eugen Retsch, 1941.
Rudolf, Crown Prince of Austria-Hungary. *Travels in the East*. London: Richard Bentley and Son, 1984.
———. *Notes on Sport and Ornithology*. London: Gurney & Jackson, 1889.
Rumbold, Sir Horace. *The Austrian Court in the Nineteenth Century*. London: Methuen, 1908.
———. *Final Recollections of a Diplomatist*. London: Edward Arnold, 1905.
———. *Francis Joseph and His Times*. New York: Appleton, 1909.
———. *Recollections of a Diplomatist*. London: Edward Arnold, 1902.
Ryan, Nellie. *My Years at the Austrian Court*. London: John Lane, 1915.
Salvendy, John T. *Royal Rebel: A Psychological Portrait of Crown Prince Rudolf of Austria-Hungary*. Lanham, MD: University Press of America, 1988.
Schad, Martha, and Horst Schad, eds. *Marie Valerie: Das Tagebuch der Lieblingstochter von Kaiserin Elisabeth von Österreich*. Munich: Langen Müller, 1998.
Schiel, Irmgard. *Stephanie: Kronprinzessin im Schatten der Tragödie von Mayerling*. Munich: Wilhelm Heyne Verlag, 1978.
Sinclair, Andrew. *Death by Fame*. New York: St. Martin's Press, 1999.
Society Recollections in Paris and Vienna. London: John Long, 1907.
Sokop, Brigitte. *Jene Gräfin Larisch*. Vienna: Böhlau Verlag, 1985.
Stephanie, Princess of Belgium, Archduchess of Austria-Hungary. *I Was to Be Empress*. London: Nicholson & Watson, 1937.
Strong, George V. *Seedtime for Fascism: The Disintegration of Austrian Political Culture, 1867–1918*. Armonk, NY: M. E. Sharpe, 1998.
Sulzberger, C. L. *The Fall of Eagles*. New York: Crown, 1977.
Swistun, Hermann. *Mary Vetsera: Gefährtin für den Tod*. Vienna: Böhlau Verlag, 1983.
Szeps, Bertha. *My Life and History*. London: Cassell, 1938.
Szeps, Julius, ed. *Politische Briefe an einen Freund, 1882–1889*. Vienna: Rikola, 1922.
Taylor, A. J. P. *The Habsburg Monarchy, 1809–1918: A History of the Austrian Empire and Austria-Hungary*. London: Hamish Hamilton, 1948.
Taylor, Edmund. *The Fall of the Dynasties*. Garden City, NY: Doubleday, 1962.
Thiele, Johannes. *Elisabeth: Das Buch ihres Lebens*. Munich: Paul List Verlag, 1996.
———. *Crown Prince Rudolf: Myth and Truth*. Vienna: Christian Brandstätter Verlag, 2008.
Tschudi, Clara. *Ludwig the Second, King of Bavaria*. New York: Dutton, 1908.
Tuchman, Barbara W. *The Guns of August*. New York: Macmillan, 1962.
Tuscany, Princess Louisa of (Archduchess of Tuscany and Crown Princess of Saxony). *My Own Story*. Toronto: Musson, 1911.
Unterreiner, Katrin. *Emperor Franz Joseph: Myth and Truth*. Vienna: Christian Brandstätter Verlag, 2006.

———. *Crown Prince Rudolf: The Imperial Apartments of the Vienna Hofburg.* Vienna: Schloss Schönnbrunn Kultur und BestriebsgesnbH, 2008.
Vacaresco, Helene. *Kings and Queens I Have Known.* New York: Harper & Brothers, 1904.
Van der Kiste, John. *Windsor and Habsburg: The British and Austrian Reigning Houses, 1848–1922.* Stroud, Gloucestershire, UK: Alan Sutton, 1987.
Vivian, Herbert, ed. *Francis Joseph and His Court.* New York: John Lane, 1917.
Waddington, Mary King. *My First Years as a Frenchwoman, 1876–1879.* New York: Charles Scribner's Sons, 1914.
Watson, David. *Georges Clemenceau: A Political Biography.* London: Methuen, 1974.
de Weindel, Henri. *The Real Francis Joseph.* New York: Appleton, 1909.
Weissensteiner, Friedrich. *Elisabeth: Die rote Erzherzogin.* Vienna: Piper Verlag, 1982.
Wilhelm II. *The Kaiser's Memoirs.* New York: Harper, 1923.
Wölfing, Leopold (Archduke Leopold of Tuscany). *My Life Story: From Archduke to Grocer.* New York: E. P. Dutton & Co., 1932.
Wolfson, Victor. *The Mayerling Murder.* Englewood Cliffs, NJ: Prentice-Hall, 1969.
Woods, Frederick Adams. *Mental and Moral Heredity in Royalty.* New York: Henry Holt, 1906.
Zweig, Stefan. *The World of Yesterday.* London: Pushkin, 2011.

NEWSPAPERS

Dates are referenced within the specific notes.
Berliner Börsencourier, Berlin.
Berliner Tagblatt, Berlin.
Corriere della Sera, Milan.
Daily News, London.
L'Éclair, Paris.
Le Figaro, Paris.
Le Gaulois, Paris.
Le Journal, Paris.
Journal des Débats, Paris.
Kurier, Vienna.
Le Matin, Paris.
Neue Freie Presse, Vienna.
Neue Illustrierte Wochenschau, Vienna.
Neue Kronen Zeitung, Vienna.
Neues Wiener Journal, Vienna.
Neues Wiener Tagblatt, Vienna.
New York Times, New York.
Petit Parisien, Paris.
Reichspost, Vienna.
Revue Artistique Littéraire et Industrielle, Brussels.
Der Spiegel, Berlin.

Der Standard, Vienna.
Die Stunde, Vienna.
Le Temps, Paris.
The Times, London.
Wiener Morgenpost, Vienna.
Wiener Montagspost, Vienna.
Wiener Tagblatt, Vienna.
Wiener Zeitung, Vienna.

PERIODICALS

Binion, Rudolph. "From Mayerling to Sarajevo." *Journal of Modern History* 47, no. 2 (June 1975): 280–316.
"Glimpses." *Royalty Digest* 1, no. 1 (July 1991): 20.
Ronay, Gabriel. "Death in the Vienna Woods." *History Today* 58, no. 9 (September 2008): 52–60.

WEBSITES

Karmel Mayerling, at www.Karmel-Mayerling.org.
Der Kriminalfall Mayerling ohne Mythos: Ein neuer Tatsachenbericht zum Tode von Kronprinz Erzherzog Rudolf von Österreich und Baroness Marie Alexandrine von Vetsera am 30. Januar 1889 in Mayerling (cited as *Der Kriminalfall Mayerling*), online manuscript by Lars Friedrich, at https://mayerlingarchiv.files.wordpress.com/2015/11/das-unredigierte-mayerling-manuskript-stand-03-11-2015.pdf.
Levantine Heritage: The Story of a Community, at http://levantineheritage.com/testi47.htm.
"Sensational Find at the Austrian National Library Reveals Passion of One of History's Great Affairs," press release from Österreischische Nationalbibliothek, August 2, 2015, at Österreischische Nationalbibliothek, Vienna. http://artdaily.com/news/80422/-Sensational-find—at-the-Austrian-National-Library-reveals-passion-of-one-of-history-s-great-affairs#.Vbzsg3hLrwx.

INDEX

25th Infantry Division, 46
36th Imperial and Royal Infantry Regiment, 35

Abazzia, 101
Abdul Aziz I, Sultan, 59
Ajdukiewicz, Tadeusz, 174
Albert, Prince (Queen Victoria's consort), 175
Albert Edward, Prince of Wales, 29, 39, 56, 58, 75, 79–80, 90, 145, 171, 210
Albrecht, Archduke, xiv, 88, 92, 102, 199, 204–5, 220
Albrecht, Karl, 195
Albrecht, Thomas, 195
Alexander, Prince of Battenberg, 102
Alexander, Tsar, 200
Alexandra, Princess of Bavaria, 217
Alleen, Maureen, 75
anarchists, 263
Andrássy, Count Gyula, 22
Anet, Claude, 265
Anonymous author, *The Last Days of Archduke Rudolf,* 207–8
antisemitism, 88
Apponyi, Count Ludwig, 187–88
archdukes
  palaces given to, 34
  service in the army, 35
aristocracy
  Austrian, 6, 36, 89, 101
  British, 75
  Hungarian, 57
  parties and balls, 67
  pedigree of, 62
Armas, Justo (pseudonym), 186
Army High Command conferences, 102, 220
Army Reform Bill (1889), 201, 203, 233, 242, 246
ashtray with inscription "revolver not poison," 146
assassinations, 15, 263–64, 270
Auchenthaler, Dr. Franz, xv, 50, 151–52, 153, 155, 254
Auersperg, Princess Aglaia von, 189
Auersperg, Prince Karl von, 189
Ausgleich, 15, 199
Austria, 13
Austro-Hungarian Empire, 15

Bachrach, Adolf, 126
Bad Homburg, 75
Bad Ischl, 85
Baden (village), 113, 127
Balkans, 32–33
Baltazzi, Alexander, xv, 116–17, 119–20, 195–96, 227, 231, 254, 270
  arranges for Mary's burial, 149–53
  horsemanship, 57–58
  plan to marry Mary, 238–39
Baltazzi, Aristide, xv, 57–58, 270
Baltazzi, Elizabeth (married Albert Nugent), xv, 176

INDEX

Baltazzi, Eveline (married Georg von Stockau), xv, 149
Baltazzi, Hector, xv, 57–58, 226–27, 270
Baltazzi, Heinrich, xv, 57, 73, 177, 195–96, 222, 267, 270
Baltazzi, Marie Virginie (married Otto von Stockau), xv
Baltazzi, Theodor, 59
Baltazzi brothers, 57–58, 76, 176–77, 226, 269
Baltazzi family, 59–62, 72, 73, 75, 163, 178, 182
Baltazzi-Scharschmid, Heinrich, 196
baron (*freiherr*), title of, 60
Bauer, Georg, 182
Bavaria, 42, 158, 216–17
Bayer, Edward, 135
Belgium, 42–45
Bernhardt, Sarah, 82
Bismarck, Otto von, 15, 160, 189, 208–9
  hostility to Rudolf, 205–6
Bohemians, 13, 32
Bombelles, Heinrich von, 34
Bombelles, Vice Admiral Count Karl von, xv, 34, 108, 128, 135
Bosnia, 16
Boyer, Charles, 265
Bragança, Dom Duarte de, 77
Braganza, Duke Miguel of, xiv, 76–77, 97, 140, 190, 195, 224, 225, 238
Braganza, House of, 77
Bratfisch, Josef, xvi, 79, 80, 81, 83, 103, 112–13, 115, 127, 173, 174, 224, 250–51, 256, 269
  asked to wait to return Mary to Vienna, 122
  heard to say "the Crown Prince is dead," 124
  Rudolf's favorite driver, 53
Britain, 26, 206
  aristocracy, 75
  travel to, 34
Brook-Shepherd, Gordon, 210
Brucks, Otto, 267–68
Brussels, travels to, 43
Burgtheater, 79–80
Buska, Johanna, 41
Bylandt-Rheydt, Count Hendrik von, 270

Cairo, 66
Capuchin Crypt, 163–65, 263, 270
Carmelite nuns, 272–73
Caspar, Marie ("Mitzi"), xvi, 53, 78, 102, 109, 121, 147, 174, 221, 230, 240, 257, 258
  introduced to Rudolf, becomes favorite mistress, 48
  later life, 269
  money of Rudolf's bequeathed to, 147
  Rudolf speaks of suicide and a suicide pact to, 97
Catholicism, 30–31, 42, 43, 145, 170, 211
  refuses suicide burials, 150
Chambige, Henri, 243
Charles V, Emperor, 13
Charlotte, Empress of Mexico (Princess of Belgium), 16, 42, 45
Chotek, Count Bohuslav, 42
Chotek, Countess Sophie, 264
Christmas celebrations (1888), 98
Clemenceau, Georges, 209–11
coffeehouses, 4
Congo Free State, 43
Corriere della Sera, 191
Corti, Egon Caesar Conte, 137–38, 257
Croats, 16
Czechs, 16, 32
Czernin, Count Ottokar von, 211

Darrieux, Danielle, 265
Dediè, Father Malachias, 153
Dual Monarchy, 15, 22
Dubray, Gabriel, 61, 65, 69, 75, 243
duels, 189, 266

education of elite children, 61
Eliot, T. S., 268
Elisabeth, Archduchess (Rudolf's daughter "Erszi"), xiii, 145–46, 175, 262–63
  birth, 46
  called the Red Archduchess, 266
  guardianship of, 261–63
  later life, 265–66
  Rudolf tries to see before leaving for Mayerling, 113
Elisabeth, Empress, xiii, 19–24, 98, 119, 175, 187, 268, 272–73
  assassination of, 263
  attitude toward Marie Larisch, 174–75

INDEX

attitude toward Stephanie, 44–45, 47, 49, 261
avoidance of imperial duties, 21–23
equestrian circle of, 57, 58–59
films about, 271
infected by venereal disease, by Franz Josef, 21–22
lineage, and mental illness, 216–17
mourning for father's death, 101
and Rudolf
attitude toward Rudolf, 36
informed of Rudolf's death, 129–31
as parent, 20, 25–28, 218
Rudolf's final letter to, 137–38, 257
upset at Rudolf's mental derangement, 158, 162–63
worries about Rudolf, 94, 221
tomb of, 270
travels of, 9, 22–23, 27, 34–35, 263
Elisabeth, Princess of Thurn und Taxis, 77
Elisabeth, Queen of Romania, 220
England, relations with, 206
Esterházy, Prince Nikolaus, 58
Esterházy, Prince Paul, 58
Eugen, Archduke, 63
Eugénie, Empress of France, 138, 229–30
Eulalia, Infanta, 42

Feigl, Erich, 210
Ferdinand I, Emperor, 14, 216
Ferdinand IV, Grand Duke of Tuscany, xiv, 145, 190, 192, 193–94
Ferenczy, Ida von, xvi, 23, 129, 131, 137–38, 147, 257
Festetics, Countess Marie, 36, 58–59, 71–72, 73, 219, 234
Festetics, Vilmos, 58
Ffoulkes, Maude, 267
Flatzelsteiner, Helmut, 181–82
France, relations with Austria, 206, 209–11
Franz Ferdinand, Archduke, 88, 97, 165, 216
assassination of, 270
denied useful role in government, 264
as heir, 109, 263–64
morganatic marriage to Sophie Chotek, 264
Franz I, Emperor, 18
Franz Josef I, Emperor, xiii, 8–9, 13–24, 56, 60, 80, 88, 119, 175, 266, 267, 268–69, 272–73
anger at Marie Larisch, 174
attitude toward Stephanie after Rudolf's death, 261–62
falsely rumored to visit Mayerling, 191
fifty-eighth birthday, 85
at German embassy soiree, 108–9, 239
guardian of "Erszi," 261–63
illegitimate children of, 24
lineage, 216
long life, death in 1916, 263, 264
marriage to Elisabeth, 18–24
and Mayerling tragedy
actions after Rudolf's death, 143–46, 150, 159–66, 185, 188
informed of Rudolf's death, 126, 129
reaction to Rudolf's death, 157–58, 258
viewing Rudolf's corpse, 194
mistress of (Katharina von Schratt), 24
opinion of Leopold II, 43
personal life and interests
lack of interests, 17
lonely work routine of, 23–24
personality, 17
political role
abdication rumor, 208
assassination attempt, 15
as divine ruler, 15
early rule, 14–16
heir of, 25–26
learns of Hungarian conspiracy, supposedly, 204
political views, 90
and Rudolf
attitude toward Rudolf, 36, 88–92
conversations with Rudolf, 106, 231, 236
disregards Rudolf's ideas, 87, 92
has Rudolf introduced to sex, 39
insists on Rudolf marrying, 42
not aware of the Rudolf-Mary affair, 226–27
as parent to Rudolf, 218
titles, 16
tomb of, 270
Franz Karl, Archduke, 14, 18

INDEX

Franz Salvator, Archduke, 94, 165
French Revolution, 32
Freud, Sigmund, 5
Freudenau racecourse, 68–69
Friedrich, Empress of Germany (daughter of Queen Victoria), 156
Friedrich III, Kaiser, 6, 92, 96, 220
Friedrich August, Crown Prince of Saxony, 194
Friedrich Wilhelm, Crown Prince (later Friedrich III), 90, 92
Fritsche, Lieutenant Viktor von, xvi, 97, 207, 234
Fugger, Prince, 68
Fugger, Princess Nora, 64, 148, 185, 239

Galimberti, Monsignor Luigi, 7, 160, 189–90, 191, 194, 229, 235
Ganglbauer, Cardinal Prince Cölestin, 7, 163
German Confederation, 15
German Embassy, soiree at (January 27, 1889), 6–11, 108–9, 239, 241
German Empire, Habsburg Empire alliance with, 206–7
German language, 201
German National Party, 88
Gieslingen, Baron Artur Giesl von, 97, 142, 144, 207
Gilded Age (America), 64
Gisela, Archduchess, xiii, 25, 27, 37, 94, 162–65, 210, 218
  notes alarming change in Rudolf, 91
Glaser (chorus girl), 225
Gödöllö, palace of, 22, 57
Gondrecourt, Major General Count Leopold, xvi, 28
gonorrhea, 21–22, 51, 96, 152, 220, 235
Gorup (inspector), 150, 153
Grant, Julia Dent, 4, 7
Graves, Dr. Armgaard Karl, 206–7
Greene, Graham, 271
Gross, Jenny, 73
Grünböck, Abbot Heinrich, 137, 150–51, 257

Habrda (police superintendant), 150, 151, 153
Habsburg empire, 13–15
  court balls, 67
  decay of, 13–14
  end of, in World War I, 211
  growth through marriage, 13
  Hungary in, 199
  male heirs to, 25, 52
  Spanish etiquette of court, 20, 25, 128
Habsburg family
  Family Statute of 1839, 42
  genetic flaws in, 8, 216
  protocol of, 17
  rule of, 4–5, 32–33
  sentimentality about, 271–73
Hamann, Brigitte, 21
Hamilton, Lord Frederic, 5
Haslip, Joan, 24
Heiligenkreuz monastery, 137–38
  burial of Mary's body at, 149–54
  Mary's grave at, 175, 177–83, 272
Heine, Heinrich, 98
Helene of Bavaria (sister of Empress Elizabeth), 18, 217
Hertz, Cornelius, 210
Herzegovina, 16
Hirsch, Baron Maurice, 147, 257
Hofburg imperial palace, 5–6
  Augustiner Bastion, 53, 80, 112
  indoor plumbing installed by Stephanie, 46–47
  Rudolf's bachelor apartments in, 80–81, 272
  Schweizerhof Wing, 34, 46
  Stephanie's apartments in, 261
  Vetsera Staircase in, 81, 272
Hofkapelle, 161
Hofmann, Professor Eduard, 155
Hohenlohe, Prince Constantine von, 127, 128, 142, 171
Hohnel, Ludwig Ritter von, 188
Holler, Gerd, 181
Holy Roman Empire, 13
Hornsteiner (gamekeeper), 121
horse racing, 68–69, 75
horse society, 57–58
horsemanship, 34
Hotze, Major Friedrich, 35
Hoyos-Sprintzenstein, Count Josef ("Josl"), xvi, 81, 137, 169, 170–71, 176, 188, 246, 254, 256, 268–69
  finds the two corpses, 124–29, 135
  at German embassy soiree, 9–10

at Mayerling, 107, 118–19, 121–22, 250–52
memo on tragedy at Mayerling, 269
Hungarian language, 138, 201, 258
Hungarians, 13, 22
nationalism of, 14, 201
Hungary, 13
Apostolic King of, 199
aristocratic estates in, 57
conspiracy to separate from Empire, 199–205, 231, 233, 235–37, 245, 246–47, 258–59
independence movement, 233, 242, 246
Rudolf's love of, 33, 138
Husarentempel at Mödling, 97

Ireland, travel to, 34–35
Italian provinces, loss of, 15

Jahoda, Agnes, xvi, 65, 69, 76, 103–5, 140, 174, 238
Jarosch, Dr. Klaus, 181–82
Jesuits, 88
asked to speak to Rudolf about his dissolute life, his outrage, 49–50
Jews, 30, 60, 62, 88
Johann Salvator, Archduke of Tuscany (later known as Johann Orth), xiv, 97, 103, 202
renounces titles, and disappears, 203
Judtmann, Fritz, 171–72, 203

Kaisergruft, 163
Kálnoky, Count Gustav, 89, 160
Karl I, Emperor, xiv, 63, 193, 200–201, 211, 264
Karl Ludwig, Archduke, 39–40, 77, 145, 146, 165, 216
Karl Theodor, Duke in Bavaria, 52, 77
Karolina Augusta of Bavaria, 18
Károly, Countess Lajos, 57
Károlyi, Count István ("Pista"), xvii, 201, 203, 233, 242
telegrams to Rudolf, 242, 246, 249, 252
Kégl, István, 137, 243
Kerzl, Dr. Josef, 50
Ketterl, Eugen, 188
Khevenhüller-Metsch, Franz Karl, Prince, 93–94
Kinsky, Count Eugen, 126
Kinsky, Count Karl, 57
Kirschner, Ferdinand, 155
Klein, Alois, 180, 254
Klimt, Gustav, 5
Königgrätz, battle of, 15
Kossuth, Lajos, 14
Krauss, Baron Franz von, xvii, 121, 134–35, 157, 172, 173, 205
Mary's disapearance reported to, 116–18, 119–20
Mitzi reports Rudolf's suicide threat to, 97
Kubasek, Rudolf, 146
Kundrath, Hans, 155

Larisch, Count Georg von, 72, 267
Larisch, Heinrich Georg (illeg.), 73, 267
Larisch, Countess Marie, xiv, 71–81, 96, 104, 105, 120, 134, 135, 141, 146–47, 176, 239, 241–44
delivers Mary for Mayerling, 107, 111–13, 115–18
exiled from Viennese court, 174, 267
facilitated Rudolf-Mary affair, 173–75, 222–23, 225
given a locked box by Rudolf, 201–3, 237
later life, 267
memoirs, 267–68
notes alarming change in Rudolf, 221
Larisch, Marie Henriette (illeg.), 73
Latour von Thurmberg, Colonel Josef, xvi, 28–33, 44, 56, 106, 234, 236
correspondence with Rudolf, 39, 42, 45, 87, 93, 96
opinion of Rudolf, 35, 48, 90, 226
Le Figaro, 134, 140, 169, 175, 186, 188
Le Gaulois, 187
Le Matin, 187, 189
Le Temps, 186, 187, 189, 190
Leiningen-Westerburg, Count Reinhard von, 114, 188
Leo XIII, Pope, 159–61, 234–35, 263
Leopold, Archduke of Tuscany, 193–95, 224
Leopold, Prince of Bavaria, 37, 102, 165
Leopold II, king of Belgium, 42, 43–45, 143, 145, 162, 165, 170, 235
Leopold Salvator, Archduke (later Leopold Wölfing), xiv, 195

Libényi, János, 15, 144
liberalism, 29, 31, 87, 90
Liechtenstein, Prince Heinrich von, 121
Listowel, Judith, 204–5
Litvak, Anatole, 265
locked box, Rudolf's, 237
  with code RIUO, 201–3
Lombardy, 14, 15
Lónyay, Count Elemér, 195, 262, 264, 265–66
Loschek, Johann, xvi, 121, 122, 127, 135–36, 137, 169, 171, 173, 174, 187, 191, 192, 252–56, 257
  finds the two corpses, 123–27
  gunshots heard, 254–56
  memoirs, 269
Louise, Archduchess of Tuscany, xiv, 192–95, 232
Louise, Princess of Coburg (Princess of Belgium), xiv, 7–8, 9, 49, 53, 56, 82–83, 103, 107, 131, 192, 195, 225, 232, 234, 261, 262
  appearance, 78
  introduces Stephanie to Rudolf, 42
  later life, 266–67
  marries Philipp of Coburg, 41–42
Ludovika, Princess of Bavaria, 18, 217
Ludwig, Duke in Bavaria, 71, 217
Ludwig I, king of Bavaria, 217
Ludwig II, king of Bavaria, 31, 217
Ludwig Viktor, Archduke, 165, 170, 216

madams and prostitutes, 48
Madeira, 22
Magyars, 14, 16. *See also* Hungary
Mahler, Gustav, 5
Margutti, Baron Albert von, 16–17, 50, 187–88
Maria Antonia, daughter of Ferdinand IV, 41
Maria Josépha of Braganza, 76
Maria Theresa, Archduchess (wife of Karl Ludwig), 39–40, 190, 216, 261
Maria Theresa, Empress, 13
Maria Theresa of Braganza, 77
Marie, Archduchess (sister of Ferdinand I), 216
Marie Antoinette, Queen of France, 13
Marie Henriette, Queen of Belgium, 41, 42, 44–45, 143, 145, 162, 165
Marie of Bavaria (sister of Empress Elizabeth), 217
Marie Valerie, Archduchess, xiii, 26, 45, 94–95, 98, 136, 146, 147, 158, 162–63, 166, 189, 210, 218, 257, 272–73
  attitude toward Stephanie, 49
  diary of, 137–38
  dinner to celebrate her engagement, 119
  informed of Rudolf's death, 129–30
  mother's pet, 37
  notes alarming change in Rudolf, 91, 221
Markus, Georg, 182
marriage
  incestuous, in Habsburg lineage, 216
  Rudolf's cynical view of, 23, 42
Marschall, Bishop Dr. Gottfried, 234
Mathilda, princess of Saxony, 42
Mathilde of Bavaria (sister of Empress Elizabeth), 217
Mattacic, Count Géza, 266–67
Max, Duke in Bavaria, 18, 217
Maximilian, Archduke, Emperor of Mexico, 15, 16, 42, 90
Maximilian I Josef, King of Bavaria, 14, 216
Maximilian II, King of Bavaria, 71
Mayer, Dr. Laurenz, 142, 193, 202
Mayerling hunting lodge
  description of, 114–15
  imperial jurisdiction of, 149
  Rudolf goes to (January 28), 106–7, 111–15, 242
  Rudolf planned to go in February, 103
  transformed into a convent for Carmelite nuns, 272–73
Mayerling tragedy
  books and memoirs about, 137–38, 192–95, 196, 206
  facts of the case
    the bullets and the gun, 136, 190
    discovery of bodies, 125–26
    gunshots heard, 123, 254–56
    informing Vienna about, 126–31
    Mary naked, 135
    Rudolf decides to go to Mayerling on Tuesday (January 29), 241–42
    sight of corpses, 125–26, 135–36, 141
    after the tragedy, 135–42

films about, 268
investigation of
investigation called off, reporting ceased, 166, 171, 185
official concealment of facts, 171–73, 185
rumors about what happened, 159, 169–71, 185–90
Taaffe papers on, 171–73
motives for, 215
Habsburg descendants' desire to find other motivation than murder-suicide, 211
"secret" of, alluded to by Otto, 186
speculation of cause, 133–34
quotes about
"anything was better than the truth," 170
"death alone can save my good name," 257
"I am not worthy to be his son," 258
"I have killed," 257
reporting of
foreign accounts of, 179
news of, in Vienna, 133–34
newspapers on, 175
stories and theories about
abortion story, 181
arrest-for-treason story, 204
assassin story, 190–91
castration story, 190
Champagne bottle strike story, 191–96, 204
conspiracy theories, 181, 183, 271
cover-up story, 131
French assassination story, 209–11
German assassination story, 205–8
gossip and rumors about, 185–90
heart attack story, 130–31, 133
Hungarian plot story, 199–205
killed-by-wronged-husband story, 187–88
love affair story, 187
Mary shot at raucous party at Mayerling story, 192
mental derangement story, 156, 157–60
as murder-suicide, 145, 190, 196–97
official stories about, changing, 185
poisoning story, 126, 128, 130, 134, 144
political motivation story, 199–212
raucous party story, 191–96
Rudolf-didn't-die-but-disappeared story, 185–86
shot-in-duel story, 188–89
struck by a bottle or stick story, 191
suicide letters claimed to be forgeries, 208
theories and stories about, because of official concealment of facts, 271
vengeful gamekeeper story, 186–87
tourist sites relating to, 271–73
what actually happened, 123–32, 185–97
a plausible version of events, 249–59
Meissner, Florian, 121, 174, 206, 230
Mendel, Henriette (Baroness Wallersee), 71
Menger, Karl, 89
Mexico, 15–16
Middleton, Captain George ("Bay"), 35, 58, 187
military
archdukes serving in, 35
language used in (German), 201
venereal disease in, 51
Miller, Emil, 181
Miller, Theresia, 181
Miramar, Trieste, 261
Mitis, Baron Oskar von, 158, 216, 217
Modena, 15
monarchy, 32
Montenuovo, Prince Alfred, 173
Montez, Lola, 217
Monts, Count Anton, 73, 128
Moravians, 16
morphine, 51, 91–92, 102
Morton, Frederic, 67, 78
Muslims, 16

Naples, 15
Napoleon III, 16
nationalism, 13, 32
nationalities, autonomy to, 86
Nazis, 266
Neue Freie Presse, 143, 186
Neues Wiener Tagblatt, 87, 88, 143
Neuhammer, Karl, 80
New York Times, 186, 192, 206

newspapers
  confiscation of, 143, 157, 186
  reporting the Mayerling tragedy, 169, 185–90
  special printings to eliminate unpleasant news, 18
Nicholas, Tsarevich (future Nicholas II), 145
Nicholas I, Tsar, 14
Nigra, Count Constantine, 191, 229
Nopcsa, Baron Ferenc, 128
Nugent, Baron Albert, 75
Nugent, Lady Elizabeth, 56, 75

Orsini und Rosenberg, Count Maximilian, 142
Orth, Johann (pseudonym), 203
Otto, Archduke (b. 1912), 271
Otto, Archduke (Rudolf's cousin), 63, 76, 97, 186, 203, 210, 216, 237
Otto, Prince of Bavaria, 217
Otto-Kreckwitz, Friedrich Karl von, 267
Otto-Kreckwitz, Karl Ernst von, 267

Paar, Count Eduard, 129, 134, 253, 263
Paget, Sir Augustus, 7, 105–6, 128
Paget, Lady Walburga, 7, 10, 60, 65, 68, 95, 105–6, 128, 170, 225
Palmer, Eduard, 79, 103
Paris, 4, 65
Parma, 15
Paul I of Russia, 200
Petznek, Leopold, 265, 266
Philipp, Prince of Coburg, xiv, 7, 48, 76, 82, 103, 123, 165, 170, 171, 195, 246, 256
  coarse-natured, and Rudolf's good friend, 41–42
  in duel, 266
  finds the two corpses, 125–26
  later life, 266–67
  at Mayerling, 107, 118–19, 125
  testimony of, 156
Philippe, Count of Flanders, 170
Pick, Anna, 44, 114, 188
Pius, Duke, 217
Pius X, Pope, 263
Planker-Klaps, Sophie von, 106, 113, 130
Poles, 16
Poliakowitz, Nikolaus, 155
Polzer-Hoditz, Count Artur, 146, 193, 200–201, 202, 225
Portugal, 42
Potocki, Count Artur, 53, 261–62
Pötschner, Dr. Peter, 232
Prague, 45–46
Prussia, 6, 15, 205
Püchel, Rudolf, 106, 111, 156, 242

radicalism, 5
Radziwill, Princess Catherine, 36, 64, 66
Raffé, Rolf, 268
Rampolla, Mariano, 159, 160–61, 263
Rathaus (Vienna City Hall), 6
reactionaries, 32, 86
Reiter, Dr. Christian, 254
Ressegtier, Count Roger de, 193
Reuss, Prince Heinrich VII, 6, 7, 107–8, 126, 127, 160, 175, 189–90, 206, 235
Revolutions of 1848, 14
Riefenstahl, Leni, 268
Ringtheater fire, 63
Robert, Duke of Parma, 193
Roll Commando sharpshooters, 204
Rónay, Jácinth János von, 33
Roosevelt, Theodore, 16
Rothschild, Baron Albert, 127
Rothschild, Nathaniel, 127
royal families of Europe, 3–4
  fall of, after World War I, 270
  heirs of, lack of meaningful work for, 89–90
Rudolf, Count (founder of Habsburg dynasty), 25
Rudolf, Crown Prince, xiii, 7–10
  ancestry, 216–18
  birth and upbringing, 25–27
    character as child, 27
    education and tutoring, 27–33
    parents' failure to nurture, 218
    religious upbringing and doubts, 30, 46
  the body
    autopsy report, 50, 155–57, 158
    body returned to Vienna, 141–42
    casket for, 141
    path of bullet, 190

skull and brain, 156–57
view of corpse, 135–36, 141, 144–46, 191, 192–94
family relations
conversations with Franz Josef, 106
fear of, among family, 93–95, 98, 102
pain of memory of, 263
farewell letters, 242, 246, 256–59
no final letter for Franz Josef, 144, 166, 258
Franz Josef quoted
"died like a *Schneider*" (coward), 144
"you are not worthy to be my successor," 236
funeral and burial
Catholic funeral, 158–66, 259
lying in state, 157, 161–64
tomb of, 263, 270
German press campaign against, 93, 96, 206, 220
habits of abuse
Champagne, Cognac, and morphine regime, 92, 102, 220
drug use, 52, 91–92, 102
drunkenness, 92
health
erectile dysfunction (impotence) due to drugs and drinking, 53, 220
medical records, 50–51
physical decline, 94
sleeping 4 to 5 hours a night, 221
venereal disease contracted, 50–52, 91, 96, 220, 221, 271
"honor" important to, 258
intelligent mind of, 37, 90, 216
interests
horses, 34, 69
indifference to music and art, 30
lust for killing, 219
obsession with death, 95–96, 218–19, 244
life style
bachelor apartment in Hofburg, 155
contents of his rooms, 146–47
introduced to women and alcohol, 34
lack of meaningful work, 89–91
nervous and careless life of, 53
pleasure-seeking life, 48
reaches majority, annual stipend awarded, 33–34
reckless behavior, 221
self-destructive way of life, 271
shooting accident, terrifies Franz Josef, 93
thirtieth birthday reflections, 85
visiting seedy nightspots, 53
"a wasted life, a needless death" (the late Archduke Otto), 271
and Mayerling tragedy
goes to Mayerling, 111–15
at Mayerling, 118–19, 121–26
pursued by Mary Vetsera, 71–83
suicide of, after killing Mary, 145, 256–59
mental state
anxiety and depression of, 31, 91, 93–94, 96, 101–2, 218
Bipolar I disorder, possible, 219, 221, 258–59
change noticed in, 102
emotional breakdown at 1889 Christmas, 98
mental derangement supposed, 158–60, 215–16
moody appearance, 36
not insane, but manic, 259
psychological damage in childhood, 37
military positions
colonel, 35
inspector general of infantry, 89, 92, 220
stationed in Prague, 45–46
murder-suicide by, shame of, 145
at the opera, 80
personal traits
appearance, 8
speaking voice, 36
political role
belief he could have transformed Habsburg empire, 270–71
and Bismark (mutual dislike), 205–6
conspiracy against Franz Josef, 200–205
"enlightened prince," 90
excluded from political influence by Franz Josef, 88–91
Hungarian plot, 222, 247
memoranda on military matters, given to Franz Josef, 87, 92

Rudolf, Crown Prince (*continued*)
political impotence, empty life, 219–20
political views (liberal), 31–33, 85–90
shadowing of and spying on, by government, 87–88, 199
prayers for his unhappy soul, 273
at Queen Victoria's Golden Jubilee, 55–57
at the races, 69
sex life, 39–54
consorting with prostitutes, 53
illegitimate children produced, 41, 221, 230
"nothing I could teach him" (Prince of Wales), 39
seduced by Helene von Vetsera, 59
sexual behavior, 221
sexual partners of, frequent changes of, 39–40
suicidal thoughts and talk, 96–97, 109, 221, 240, 244, 250, 257
wills
the first, 54, 86
the second, of 1887, 54, 138, 261
writings by
anonymous articles for liberal newspapers, 87–88, 93
memoranda to Franz Josef, 87, 92
on nonpolitical topics (e.g., on his travels), 89
See also Mayerling tragedy; *next entries*
Rudolf-Mary affair, 103–5
blackmail potential, 232–33
facilitators of, 173–75, 222–23, 267
Franz Josef learns of, 231–33
Franz Josef orders it ended, 249–50
Helen Vetsera's attempts to end, 224–27
Krauss investigates, 119–21
length of, publicly admitted and actual, 103–4
Mary reveals she's pregnant (January 13), 245
romantic myth of, 223–24, 242, 251–52, 253
Rudolf promises Franz Josef to end, 241, 245, 249–50
Rudolf's attempts to end, 223–26, 229–31, 237, 240, 241–43, 245–47, 249–50, 252–53
scandal of, 134, 224, 232–33, 239
Rudolf-Stephanie marriage
marriage proposal, 43–44
marriage strains, 47–48, 49–53, 96, 235
Rudolf's annulment request, 234–36
Rumanians, 16
Russians, 102
Rustimo (African boy kept as pet), 21

Salisbury, Lord, 171
Salm family, 272
Sarajevo
assassination at, 264
travels to, 91
Sáromberke estate, 200
Sarrell, Eliza, 59
Sarto, Cardinal Giuseppe, 263
Saxe-Coburg and Gotha dynasty, 41, 42
Saxony, 42, 145
Schloss Ellischau, 171–72
Schloss Laxenburg, 45, 261
Schloss Oroszvár, 262, 265
Schloss Orth, 102–3
Schloss Schwarzau, 63
Schönborn-Buchheim, Archbishop Count, 242
Schönbrunn palace, 83
Schönerer, Georg von, 88
Schratt, Katharina von, xvi, 24, 56, 74–75, 129, 163, 166, 226–27, 231, 270
Schuldes, Julius, 269
Schuselka, Franz, 5
Schwarz-Gelb, 93, 208
Semitic influences, 60
Serbia, 145
Serbs, 16
Seven Weeks' War, 15, 22
Sicily, 15
silver boxes presented to Rudolf's ex-lovers, 40
Sixtus, Prince of Bourbon-Parma, 211
Skedl, Artur, 172
Slatin, Dr. Heinrich, xvi, 136–37, 150, 151, 152–53, 189, 254
Slavs, 13, 16, 32–33
Slovenians, 16
smart set, 62
Social Democratic Party, 265

society
newspaper accounts of, 67
social season in Vienna, 101
tiers of, 62
Sophie, Archduchess (died young), 25
Sophie, Archduchess (Princess of Bavaria, and grandmother of Rudolf), xiii, 14–15, 18–21, 25, 218–19
and Rudolf's upbringing, 26–28
Sophie of Bavaria (sister of Empress Elizabeth), 217
South Slavs, 16, 32–33
Soviet troops, 265–66
Mary's grave desecrated by, 180
Spain, 42
Spindler, Heinrich Ritter von, 207
Stephanie, Crown Princess (Princess of Belgium), xiii, 7–10, 74–75, 101–2, 119, 200, 220, 229, 239, 257, 267, 272
appearance, 8, 78
blamed for Rudolf's death, 162–63, 175, 261–62, 272
confrontations with Mary Vetsera, 82–83, 108
critics of, 47, 49
health
infected by Rudolf's venereal disease, 51–52, 96
infertility from gonorrhea infection, 234, 235
later life, 264–66
married life
early contentment, 45–47
marriage proposal, 42–45
marriage strains, 49–53, 96
quarrels with Rudolf, 97, 108
ring of iron given to, 82
Rudolf's last letter to, 147–48
memoirs, 265
and Queen Victoria's Golden Jubilee (did not go), 55–56
remarries, stripped of titles, 262
rivalry with Mary, 77–80, 82–83, 108
after Rudolf's death, 145–46, 261–62
takes a lover (Artur Potocki), 53
worries about Rudolf, 94, 220–21
See also Rudolf-Stephanie marriage
Stockau, Count Georg von, 149–53, 254
Stockau, Marie von, 56
Stockau, Count Otto von, 56
Stockhausen, Countess Juliana von, 265
Stubel, Ludmilla "Milli," 203
Stubel, Marie, 203
suicide
Catholic burial refused in case of, 150, 158
insanity excuses, 160
suicide pacts, 82, 97, 131, 221, 243, 251
using a hand-held mirror to adjust aim, 95, 137, 243
Vienna's fascination with, 95–97, 221, 244, 251
syphilis, 50, 220, 269
Szeps, Bertha, 234
Szeps, Moritz, xvi, 87–89, 93, 101–2, 108–9, 159, 206, 209–10, 220, 234, 239, 269
Szilvássy, Dr. Johann, 182
Szögyény-Marich, Count Ladislaus von, xvii, 89, 138–39, 146–47, 233, 234, 236, 242
Rudolf's letter to, 258–59

Taaffe, Count Eduard von, xvii, 7, 96, 131, 171, 172, 177, 187
confiscates newspapers, 143, 157
disliked Rudolf, 133–34
Mary's disapearance reported to, 120–21
prime minister, crushes liberalism, 86–87
supposedly welcomed Rudolf's death, 204–5
takes control of the Mayerling tragedy investigation, 149–50
Taaffe, Heinrich, 171–72
Taaffe, Rudolf, 172–73, 204
telegrams to Rudolf, from Károly, 242, 246, 249, 252
Teleki von Szék, Count Samuel, 200, 203
Tisza, Kálmán von, xvii, 199, 201, 233, 246
Tobias, Gabriele, 61
Tobias, Hermine, xvi, 61, 74, 75, 80–81, 103, 243–44
Toselli, Enrico, 194
Turks, 4
Tuscany, 15

Vanderbilt, Alva, 64
Venice, 14, 15

Vetsera, Baron Albin von, xiv, 60–61, 66, 232
Vetsera, Franz von ("Feri"), xv, 61, 140, 270
Vetsera, Georg, 60
Vetsera, Helene von (born Baltazzi), xv, 58–68, 107–8, 111, 243, 244, 253
attempts to end the Rudolf-Mary affair, 225–27
blackmailing propensity of, 223, 233
designs grave for Mary and reburies her, 176–77
facilitated Rudolf-Mary affair, 173, 222–24, 238
at German embassy soiree, 10–11
later life, 269–70
learns Mary is dead, 131
learns of Mary's possible pregnancy, 238–39
letters from Mary to, 139–40, 252, 270
outraged at government's burial of Mary, 151–54
pamphlet on the affair, 178–79, 267
poor reputation of, 57, 270
prostitutes her daughter Mary for social climbing, 73–77
reports Mary missing, 115–17, 119–21
searches Mary's room, 105
told by government to leave Vienna, 134, 149–50
Vetsera, Ilona, 63
Vetsera, Johanna von ("Hanna"), xv, 10, 60, 64, 76, 108, 115, 140, 179, 244, 246, 270
letter from Mary to, 252
Vetsera, Ladislaus von, xv, 60, 63, 177
Vetsera, Marie Alexandrine von ("Mary"), xv, 9–11, 103–5
affair with Rudolf
delivered to Hofburg then to Mayerling, 107, 111–15, 241
pursuit of Rudolf, 69, 71–83
secret visits to Rudolf, 80–81, 103
appearance, 64, 243
burial
bones of, removed and reburied, 180–83
coffin for, 153
corpse secretly removed from Mayerling and obscurely buried, 151–54
genetic testing of bones, not done, 182
grave at Heiligenkreuz, 175–83, 272
obituary, falsified in newspapers, 154
facts of the case
the corpse, 135–36, 141, 151–53
ice-skating ensemble worn at Mayerling, 111–12, 243
nakedness of the corpse, 253
path of the bullet through the head, 254
father uncertain (possibly Franz Josef), 232
final letters from, 252
foreign press stories, 169–70
fortune-teller prediction of death, 104–5, 238, 244–45
gifts to Rudolf, 103
cigarette case purchased for Rudolf, 105, 229
hopes and thoughts
collapse of her world, 238–40
decides to join Rudolf in death, 251–53
devastated by Rudolf's rejection, 251
not an intellectual, 78
suicidal thoughts, not likely, 243–45
was exaltedly looking to the future, 245
made a will (January 18), 244
and Mayerling tragedy
delivered to Hofburg then to Mayerling, 111–15, 208, 242–43
disappearance of, officially commanded, after death, 148–49
"disappearance" of, while going to Mayerling, 112–13, 115–18, 120–21
at Mayerling, 121–22, 125–26, 175
presence at Mayerling, concealed, 186, 189
personality, 65
histrionic declarations, not taken seriously, 244
moral character lacking, 223
naive wishful thinking, 250
photographs of, 243
pregnancy, possible, 229–30, 238–39, 245
at Queen Victoria's Golden Jubilee, 55–57, 65
sex life
love affairs, 66–69
marriage plans of Helene, 238–39
marriageability, 64–65
upbringing, 61–65

venereal disease of, 152
what actually happened
murdered by Rudolf ("I have killed"), 257
murdered by Rudolf while awake (not while sleeping), 253–57
suicide not likely, 152, 243–45
See also Mayerling tragedy; Rudolf-Mary affair
Vetsera family, 150, 178, 182, 238
Vetsera Palace, 272
Victoria, Queen, 26, 42, 90, 126, 175
family life of, 29
Golden Jubilee, 55–57
informed of the Rudolf case, 156, 170, 171, 215
opinion of Rudolf, 49, 56
Rudolf visits, 34
Vienna, 3–7, 18
aristocratic, 36, 101
Ringstrasse, 4
Vienna Woods, 113

Wagemut, Karl, 193
Wagner, Otto, 5
Wagner, Richard, 83, 217
Wassilko-Serecki, Countess Zoë von, 172, 230
Weber, Franz (driver), 111, 112–13, 120
Welden, Baroness Karolina von, 25–26
Werlmann, Karl von, 200
Werner (fictitious gamekeeper), 187
Widerhofer, Dr. Hermann, xvi, 50, 91, 127, 135, 143–44, 155, 157, 171, 191, 193–94, 236, 254
Wiener Tagblatt, 88, 93, 157
Wiener Zeitung, 159
Wilhelm I, Kaiser, 90
Wilhelm II, Kaiser, 6, 90, 92–93, 108
Windisch-Grätz, Prince Ernst von, 263, 266
Windisch-Grätz, Prince Franz Josef von, 263, 266
Windisch-Grätz, Prince Otto Weriand von, 262, 265, 266
Windisch-Grätz, Prince Rudolf von, 263, 266
Windisch-Grätz, Princess Stephanie von, 263, 266
Winterhalter, Franz Xaver, 23
Wittelsbach dynasty, 19, 37, 158
mental flaws in, 216–17
Wodicka, Franz, 106–7, 124
Wolf, Frau Johanna, 48, 174
Wolf, Friedrich, 191–92
Wölfing, Leopold (pseudonym), 195
Wolfson, Victor, 208–9
World War I, 211, 270
World War II, 264, 265–66, 270

Zita, Empress (Princess of Bourbon-Parma), xiv, 63, 193, 201, 209–11, 264
Zwerger, Alois, 124, 151